# INDIA

SIR THOMAS HUNGERFORD HOLDICH
K. C. M. G., K. C. I. E., C. B., R. E.

GYAN

*Published by*

Gyan Publishing House
5, Ansari Road
Daryaganj, New Delhi-110002
Phone: 011-47034999, 9811692060
E-mail: books@gyanbooks.com

*Distribution Network*
gyanbooks.com
India, USA, Canada, UK, Australia, France



ISBN: 978-81-212-8808-8 (PB)
First Published, 1904

2nd Impression 2023

*Printed at:* Gyan Press, Delhi.



**INDIA**
Author: Thomas Hungerford Holdich

# INDIA

# INDIA, SOUTHERN SECTION

# INDIA

BY

COLONEL

SIR THOMAS HUNGERFORD HOLDICH

K.C.M.G., K.C.I.E., C.B., R.E.

LATE DEPUTY SUPERINTENDENT, SURVEY OF INDIA

*With Maps and Diagrams*

THE·REGIONS OF·THE·WORLD

LONDON

HENRY FROWDE

OXFORD UNIVERSITY PRESS WAREHOUSE

AMEN CORNER, E.C.

1904

# PREFACE

WHEN, at the request of Mr. Mackinder, I undertook to write this little book, I was carefully warned against statistics and details. Indian statistics have, indeed, been dealt with so ably, and have been presented to the public in such attractive form by the late Sir W. W. Hunter in his "Imperial Gazetteer of India," that for more exact statistical details and figures than those contained in this brief volume the reader is referred to that great authority.

I have, accordingly, relied chiefly on descriptive methods of treating the infinite variety of the geographical configuration and the geographical distributions of India; and where my opportunities for personal observation have failed, I have had free recourse to the works of such well-known authorities as Sir W. W. Hunter, Sir John Strachey, Sir Alfred Lyall, Sir Lepel Griffin, Sir George Birdwood, General Woodthorpe, Sir James Scott, Professor Ball, Mr. Oldham (of the Indian Geological Survey), and others, all of whom write of Indian subjects with the refreshing vigour of intimate personal acquaintance.

The maps have the authority of the Survey of India to support them. The spelling of place names is the spelling authorised by the Indian Government, which, partly arbitrary and partly systematic, has been found to answer fairly well. The system (where any system at all has been adopted) is closely allied to that of the Royal Geographical Society.

T. H. H.

# CONTENTS

# LIST OF ILLUSTRATIONS

## *MAPS*



## *MAPS AND DIAGRAMS*

# INDIA

## CHAPTER I

### EARLY INDIA

STATISTICS.—British India and Burma together occupy 905,000 square miles of the Continent of Asia, and the native states and dependencies of India absorb 611,000 more. This is exclusive of Baluchistan (130,000 square miles), which is, in fact, as much a dependency of British India as any native state within the frontier. The total population of this area amounted to 287 millions of souls by the census of 1891, showing a net increase of 27½ millions during the preceding decade. In 1901 the total had increased to 231,000,000. This equals about 15 per cent. of the entire population of the world.

The commerce of India, represented by exports and imports, amounted in 1899 to £124,850,000 and £95,499,000 respectively, the increase during the last sixty-five years of the century being fifteen-fold.

The revenue of India in 1900 was £29,500,000 sterling, nearly three-fourths of which are derived from land.

IN no country in the world has geographical position relatively to surrounding continents and seas shaped the history and the destinies of a people more surely than in India. A land of promise, where Nature offers her gifts with lavish hand, and where the soil is peculiarly favourable to the reproduction of mankind, yet forming a sort of geographical *cul-de-sac* with a few notable gateways leading thereto from the north, and no exit, except by sea, to the east, south, or west; India has been from time immemorial peopled by immigrants who have multiplied within her borders with such prodigious vitality that no recent wave of conquest sweeping through her historic gates has made any permanent impression, whilst each in turn has added something to her perplexing ethnography.

No single name existed amongst the early settlers

which would include all the various races of the country which is now known as India. One tribe, or clan, alone which passed into the peninsula from the north was sufficiently powerful to impress its name upon the north-western districts of the country, and its designation, Bhárata, is the earliest appellation which can be recognised as being more than locally applicable to any part of those districts. The nations of the West, equally with those of the East, first knew India as the land of the Indus. To all tides of immigration, from whatever landward direction they were derived, the Indus was the first great barrier encountered as they passed through the narrow channels open to them in the mountains of the north-west, and spread into the plains of the Punjab or of Sind. The great river of the West, with its network of waterways and islands, was to them as the open sea, and thus the same Sanscrit word which they applied to the ocean itself served to designate the mighty barrier which was set between them and the plains of the South. So that Sindhus became gradually the recognised name for the districts watered by the Indus, and a variation in its form (Sindhavas) indicated the inhabitants of the valley. Other variations followed from the dialectic peculiarities of foreign nations. To the ancient Persians it was Hendu; to the Greeks Indikos; and finally Virgil calls the country India. In the far East the Chinese made use of the name Shin-ta and Hien Tau, but it is to the modern Persian that we owe the term Hindustan; and the Imperial title, "Kaisar-i-Hind" of to-day confers on the King of England the titular sovereignty of a country which literally only embraces the Punjab and a part of the Gangetic basin, but is universally accepted as representing all India.

The shape of India should be described as rhomboidal rather than triangular, with an acute apex pointing southward into the ocean. The length of the north-eastern side of the rhomboid, from the head of the Bay of Bengal to the extreme north-west of Kashmir along the mountain mass of the Himalaya, is about 1400 miles. From Kashmir to Karachi, its north-western side is about 1200 miles;

on the south-west, from Karachi to Cape Comorin, 1750 miles of coast-line face the Arabian Sea; and from Cape Comorin to the mouths of the Ganges are 1300 miles of seaboard washed by the Bay of Bengal. If we take about 300 miles of the north-eastern face of the rhomboid extending upwards from the mouth of the Ganges, and base thereon an acute-angled triangle reaching 550 miles to the north-east, it will include the province of Assam; and if again, on the south-eastern face of the latter, we extend another long attenuated triangle for some 1200 miles southward and eastward till it narrows to a point about two degrees north of Cape Comorin, we shall roughly represent the extent of the Burmese provinces under British rule.

It is a notable fact that one of the greatest of Greek geographers, Strabo, defines the shape of India as rhomboidal, and he gives the following distances for the length of the sides respectively. From the sources of the Indus to the mouth of the Ganges, 16,000 stadia. From the mouth of the Ganges to Cape Comorin, 16,000. From Cape Comorin to the mouth of the Indus, 19,000. From the mouth of the Indus to its source in the mountains, 13,000. The Greek stadium was undoubtedly an elastic quantity, but the generally accepted length of it is 606¾ feet, or about .115 of a mile. These measurements preserve the general proportion of the sides of the figure fairly well, but they are all about 200 miles in excess of the actual lengths. It is a remarkable testimony to the accuracy of Greek research.

Geographically, if not politically, the island of Ceylon must be regarded as a part of India. The latitude of its southern extremity is only six degrees north of the equator. The extreme north latitude of the north-western corner of Kashmir is thirty-seven degrees north, and the altitude of the land surface of India varies from flats a few inches above sea-level to peaks 28,000 feet above it. Thus every conceivable variety of climate, every condition of physical existence from the equatorial to the arctic, is to be found in India—and occasionally found in close juxtaposition.

The total area of the Indian Empire approaches $1\frac{3}{4}$ million of square miles, and its total population is about 280 millions of souls, considerably "more than double Gibbon's estimate of 120 millions for all the races and nations which obeyed Imperial Rome."[1]

The physiography of the country (regarded as a whole)

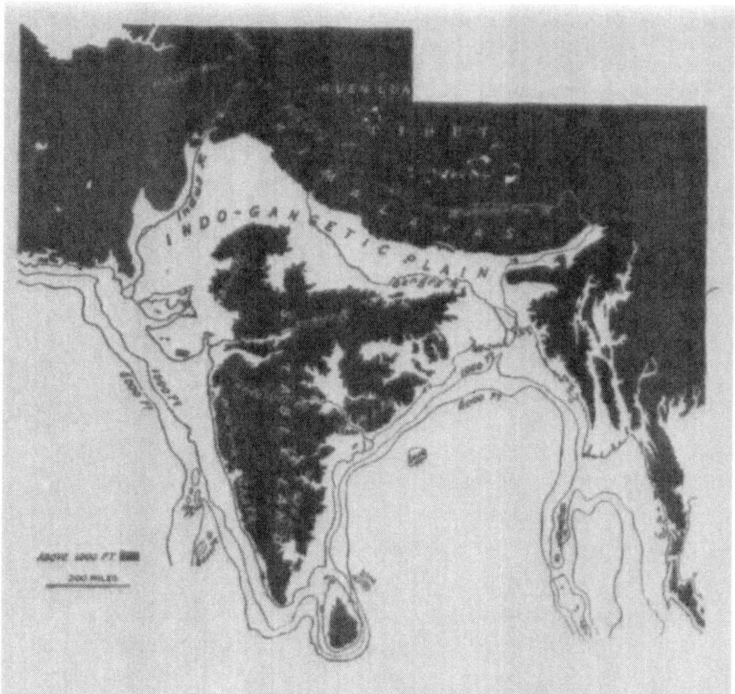


FIG. 1.—The Indo-Gangetic Plain.

is not very complicated. To the north-east and north-west are vast elevations of land surface, from the foot of which the peninsula of India stretches away southwards in gradually ascending grades. Thus we have on the two northern sides of the rhomboid, to the north-east and to the north-west, elevated regions of plateau and table-land buttressed by mountain systems which form

[1] Hunter's "Imperial Gazetteer," vol. vi.

the staircases between the plains and the plateau. On the north-east the huge upheaval of Tibet, rising to 16,000 feet above sea-level, shuts off the rest of Asia with an impassable barrier of sterile and stony uplands, bordered Indiawards by a vast mountain region which comprises many complicated minor systems whose central peaks are the highest in the world. These are the Himalayas. From the eastern extremity of the central Tibetan upheaval, mountain ranges curving southwards determine the initial direction of the rivers of China, Siam, Burma, and Assam, and round off the north-eastern borderland of India with a series of walls as impassable as the solid block of the Tibetan plateau. On the extreme north, abutting on the north-west of Kashmir, the Pamirs (well called the Roof of the World) flank the depression north of the Tibetan plateau westward, and mark the geographical centre from which spring the Kuen Lun, hedging in Tibet to the north ; the Himalayas dividing Tibet from India ; the Thian-shan, which are but the south-western links in the central orographical axis of Asia which reaches north-east for 4600 miles to the Behring Straits ; and the Hindu Kush, with its subsidiary ranges, forming the north-western barrier of India. It is this north-western barrier which is geographically of such importance to India, and which demands the most careful consideration. Mountainous, difficult, rugged, and often dangerous, it yet, by reason of its inferior altitude, does not offer an obstacle of such impassability as is presented by the Pamirs of the north and the Himalayas of the north-east. It is across the north-west barrier that the flood of immigration or invasion has almost invariably advanced.

Next in order to the region of mountains is the region of depression which lies at its south-eastern foot, curving northward across the breadth of the peninsula from the Bay of Bengal to the Arabian Sea, and including all the most fertile and densely populated districts of Hindustan. This is the great silt-formed land of India, the land of great rivers which flow through the

Himalayas and the western mountains, bringing the soil of Tibet, of Afghanistan and Baluchistan to nourish the swarming populations of Bengal, the North-West Provinces, the Punjab, and Sind. In this area of depression (never rising more than a few hundred feet above sea-level, and often only a few inches above) we must include Assam, the valley of the Brahmaputra, only noting here in anticipation of further detail, that all the three great river systems of India—the Indus, the Ganges, and the Brahmaputra—derive a part of their water-supply from sources which lie in the highlands beyond the Himalayas and the western mountains, and part from the countless valleys which lie hidden within the mountain folds.

To the south of the area of depression succeeds the region of southern table-land, or peninsular area, which includes the Central Provinces, Bombay, Madras, Mysore, and several other minor states and provinces. This three-sided tract of territory, known to the ancients as the Dakshin (Deccan) or "south land," supports a population of about two-thirds the strength of the population of the depression, and is buttressed by the Vindhya mountains on the north, and by the Eastern and Western Ghâts of the Bengal and Arabian sea coasts respectively; the two latter running to an angle near Cape Comorin.

Sweeping round the island of Ceylon and the Coromandel coast to the head of the Bay of Bengal, and then extending an arm southwards embracing the Andaman and Nicobar Islands, and stretching very nearly to Sumatra, is the 100 fathom line of sea bottom, bounding a shoreward width of about fifty miles, with a fairly uniform contour at another fifty mile interval, which represents the 500 fathom limit. Opposite the mouth of the Ganges these intervals are very much extended by deltaic influence. Inland from the coast-line of Madras for a width of 50 to 100 miles, and reaching to the Gangetic delta, is a belt of shore formation of low elevation fringing the foot of the Eastern Ghâts. The width of low foreshore on the western coast of India is very much less than this of the east, whilst the 100 fathom line reaches farther out to sea, and the 500 fathom line is far enough seaward to include the Laccadive Islands. Such, in brief outline, is the orographical configuration of the continent of India—and the story of its evolution may be learnt from the rocks of which it is composed.

Measured by the vast ages of geological existence, the peninsular area of India (the region of southern table-land) is by far the oldest. On the north-western borders of this area, stretching across the plains of Rajputana, are the remnants of a very ancient range of mountains called the Aravalli. To the south of these mountains the peninsula of India, as we know it now, has been a land area since the close of the palæozoic era. Across the extra peninsula regions to the north-west of the Aravalli hills the sea has repeatedly flowed even to the commencement of tertiary ages; and between the two regions thus separated by the Aravallis there exists most striking differences both in structure and in conformation. The present shape of the peninsula—itself but a remnant of a far more widely extended continent—has only been assumed since the occurrence of the vast series of earth movements which resulted in the creation of the region of depression—the alluvial basins of the Indus and of the Ganges. Over the substratum of granite and gneiss which forms the "bed-rock" of peninsular geologic structure, and eastward from the Aravallis, stretch the wide red sandstone deposits which are known as the Vindhyan system, and which (even when buried beneath the Deccan trap) preserve a generally horizontal position. Geologists maintain that these wide-spread unfossiliferous beds are but the detritus washed down from the peaks and valleys of the inconceivably ancient mountain range which is now represented by the comparatively low and degraded Aravallis. Almost coeval with the Aravallis (and possibly at one period connected with them) is the much broken and ragged formation known as the "Eastern Ghâts" overlooking the Bay of Bengal. So ancient is this eastern buttress of the peninsular table-land that since the close of the palæozoic era the waters of the bay have never washed westward, and the coast of Madras was the eastern coast-line of that pre-Indian continent of which India is now the much-diminished representative. But whilst the Aravallis were clearly the north-western limit of this prehistoric continent, it is not quite so clear what formed the boundary on the north-east. There was no Gangetic basin in those days, and it was probable that the Rajmahal hills and the hills of Assam continued the land area to the Himalayas east of Sikkim; for it is certain that the Eastern Himalayas are vastly older than the western, and that the Burmese mountains are comparatively young. Next followed a long period of repose and of the silent process of alluvial deposit by river action, during which the wide central beds called Gondwana were formed. Here we must note the existence of ice-worn boulders and the evidence of former glaciers in Rajputana; and at this point we are faced with the almost indisputable fact that the India of the Aravallis and of the Rajmahal hills was but an extension from South Africa. The evidence which has been collected to prove this ancient connection seems to be conclusive. Plants of Indian and African coal measures are identical, and not only plants, but the fauna of that period claim a similar affinity. Near the coast of South Africa a series of beds occur which is similar in all respects to an existing Rajmahal series; whilst the distribution of marine fossils proves that to the north-west and to the south-east respectively of a land barrier which must have included the Maldives, Laccadives and Madagascar, were two distinct seas. This land connection must have existed at the commencement of cretaceous

PROBABLE LAND AREA AT CLOSE OF JURASSIC TIMES

FIG. 2.

times. There are no marine sedimentary beds in the Eastern Himalayas analogous to those of Burma, of the North-West Himalayas and of the mountains west of the Indus. These wide highlands, together with the great plateau of Tibet, were then under sea, subject (so far as we can tell) to no great earth movements in very early ages, but undergoing quiet and placid intervals of subsidence and upheaval, of alternate existence as open lacustrine land surface or sea bottom. At the close of the jurassic period not only were the North-Western Himalaya non-existent, but the very rocks of which the ranges to the west of the Indus are formed were still uncreated. Only the Aravalli peaks stood lonely and silent overlooking a vast north-western sea. Not till the close of the cretaceous period was India shaken by a series of eruptive cataclysms into something of its present shape. A succession of volcanic eruptions, exceeding in force and grandeur anything that the world has ever seen (except indeed it be in South America), covered 200,000 square miles of India with lava and tuffs to a depth of thousands of feet. India must have been for a time one vast volcanic furnace. This was but the prelude to the mountain building. Then, at the commencement of the tertiary period, set in that long succession of earth movements which, culminating in intensity about the pliocene period, are still in perceptible activity. The sea was driven back; rocks were crushed and forced upwards until marine limestones were upheaved to 20,000 feet above sea-level. Then were the sea-formed rocks of the trans-Indus hills ranged and folded and set in order. It was the period of the creation of our Indian frontier.[1]

Geologists have decided that the fossils of Burma and of the western frontier alike place the formation of these regions in the eocene, or latter part of the tertiary era. But the great bulk of the North-Western Himalayas must have been a formidable mountain barrier in times previous to the eocene period, and, moreover, even in those early times, the river systems of the Himalayas must

[1] Oldham, "Evolution of Indian Geography," vol. iii. (*Journal*, R.G.S.).

have been traced very much as they are at present. At the foot of the Himalayas there existed for geologic ages a long series of river deposits which have been compressed and upheaved in very recent times to form what is known as the Siwalik range, an entirely subsidiary and secondary range of hills which flanks the Himalayas on its southern face, forming an elevated longitudinal valley between itself and the foothills of the main system. In the neighbourhood of those rivers which issue from Himalayan valleys and cross the elevated valley and the bordering Siwalik hills there have been found beds of conglomerate which prove by their composition that rivers large and rapid, having their sources in the Himalayas or beyond, must have passed that way from time immemorial very near to their present channels ; and the evidence of the rocks connects the origin of these rivers with the pliocene period. Thus it seems probable that the North-West Himalayas existed as mountains of very considerable altitude in pliocene times. Another result of this succession of earth movements was the formation of that great Indo-Gangetic depression which forms one of the natural geographical divisions of India. The break in the connection between the Rajmahal and the Assam hills which gave an opening for the eastward flow of the Ganges is comparatively recent. Originally the whole southern flank of the Himalayan system was drained by the Indus, and the diversion of the Jumna eastward into the Gangetic basin may be almost historic. Probably there was an interval, during which the Jumna either joined the Indus, or found a way south-west through some of the dry river channels still existing across the Rajputana desert. The present division of the two drainage systems, or water parting, is now marked in the Himalayas by a ridge on which stands the church at Simla. It is further probable that the same earth movements caused the submergence which separated India from Africa. By the end of the eocene period the west coast of India was formed, and the only existing evidence of that old-world connection is now to be seen in the islands of the Laccadive and Maldive groups. The Western Gháts, facing the Arabian Sea, are of quite recent formation, exhibiting some of the hydrographic phenomena which are common to mountains belonging to similar periods, with rivers cutting their way back from narrow and steep-sided valleys, and still changing their features

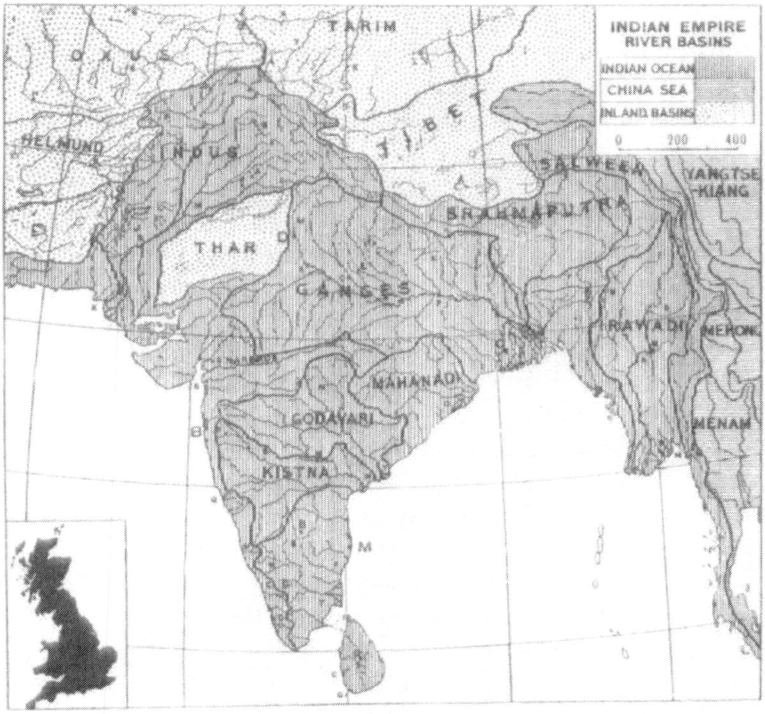


FIG. 3.

from day to day. From the Western Gháts all the peninsular rivers of India run eastwards, with the exception of the Narbada and Tapti. From the edge of the Tapti basin to the extreme south, the Western Gháts form the main water parting of the Indian continent.

If from the story of the rocks we turn to the uncertain records of early Indian tradition, we find nothing to enlighten us as regards the physical conformation of the country, and little to illustrate the geographical distribution of the races of men who first occupied the peninsula. Indian tradition indeed (such traditions as we find embodied in their great epics, the Ramayána and Mahabhárata) tell obscurely of ancient conflicts between northern races, aliens to the aboriginal non-Aryan peoples who occupied the southern plains, and there are dim visions of moving populations from High Asia ever sweeping into India from the north-west; sufficient indication that through all historic ages the land routes to India have been as they now are. The first authentic sea trade with the Indian coasts was that maintained by the fleets of Solomon and Hiram, whose ship captains "not only brought Indian apes, peacocks, and sandalwood to Palestine; they also brought their Sanscrit names."[1] Our earliest exact knowledge of India is derived from the Greeks. The profound philosophy of the Brahmanical school which, in weaning men from the pomps and vanities of an evanescent world, weaned them also from trivial contemplation of the world itself, absolutely forbid such authentic records of the actual facts of human existence as might have been expected from a highly advanced Aryan community, and it is to the West that we must look for our first historical knowledge of the East. Hekataios of Miletus (549–486 B.C.) first distinguishes India as a geographical entity, but it is Herodotus (450 B.C.) to whom we owe the earliest definition of the political divisions of the countries bordering India, although his eastern horizon was limited by the Indus. Herodotus has never yet received a full measure of acknowledgment for the general geographical accuracy of those compilations which define the position of the tribal communities of the remote Persian satrapies of his time. The same processes of geographical survey which have lately unravelled the hazy tangle of subsequent Arab geography, have proved that from the days of Herodotus to modern times a very large proportion of the tribes of Eastern Persia and of the wild districts intervening between Persia and Western India are to be found in the relative positions

[1] Hunter, p. 163.

indicated by him under names that are sometimes identical, sometimes closely connected, with the original Greek. It is indeed hardly too much to say that five centuries before our era the political geography of the Khorasán and Makrán was better known to the ancient Greeks than it was to English geographers of fifty years

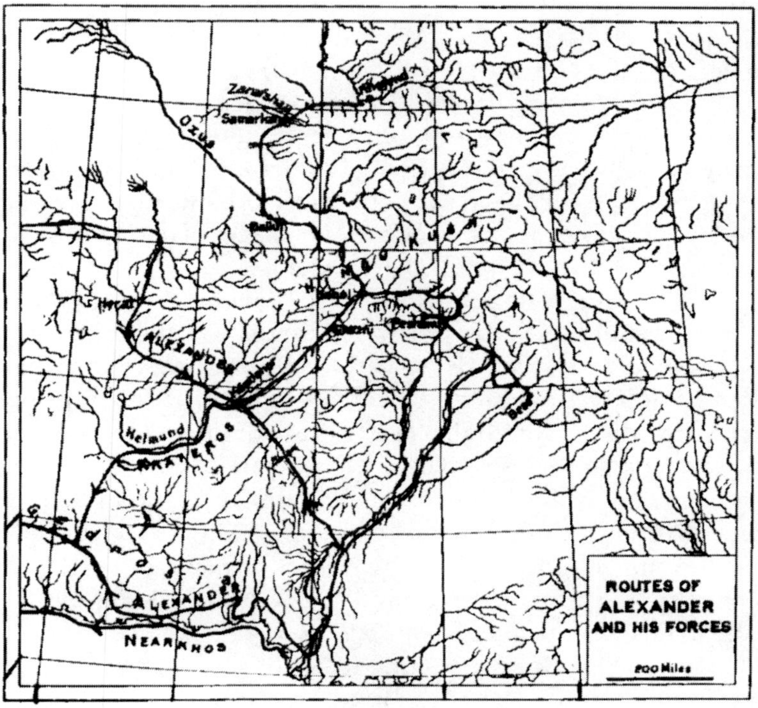


FIG. 4.

ago. It was, however, the first scientifically conducted military expedition of the world—the invasion of India by Alexander the Great about 327 B.C.—that furnished for centuries all the data available for the construction of a map, or plan, which should indicate with the roughest degree of accuracy the physiography of India. Mountain ranges thenceforward began to shape themselves correctly, relatively to the valleys of the great rivers. The Helmund, the Indus, the Kabul, and two or three of the rivers of the Punjab assumed their right positions, and were traced to their correct conclusions. Although Alexander believed that the Indus was identical with the Nile whilst he was yet engaged in military operations on its upper reaches, the subsequent exploration of that river to its mouth, and, above all, the admirably conducted voyage of his chief sea captain, Nearkhos, from the Indus to the head of the Persian Gulf, furnished the world with geographical records of sufficient accuracy to enable modern geographers not only to trace step by step the progress of the army and of the fleet back to Persia, but even to estimate the nature of those changes in riverain and coast topography which have taken place during the last twenty-two centuries. Alexander never penetrated into the southern peninsula area. He turned at the Beás (Hyphasis), a river of the Punjab, and thenceforward set his face westwards towards Persia, where he died. But he left behind him a troublesome heritage of Indian frontier which eventually fell to the administration of one of his generals, Seleukos Nikator, the founder of the Syrian monarchy. Then for the first time, a little light was thrown into the dark corners of peninsular geography by the ambassador Megasthenes, who was deputed to the court of the great king Chandra Gupta (the Sandrakottos of the Greeks) at Palimbothra (the modern Patna) on the Ganges. The Greek settlements in the Punjab and Kabul valleys were ceded to the Indian monarch about twenty-five years after Alexander's departure from India, but the Greek language is said to have held its own in those regions for more than seven hundred years subsequently—until, indeed, the Muhammadan conquests stamped it out of existence. Nevertheless the Greek adaptation of place names is even now to be found recognisable under modern dialectic forms about the regions where the Indus issues from the mountains. Until the time of Megasthenes but two classes of Indians were known to the Greeks—the mountaineers of the Caucasus, and the fish-eaters of Makrán—sufficient indication of the very meagre extent of their geographical knowledge. The time of Megasthenes was the era of early rivalry between the two great religious cults of India, Brahmanism and Buddhism, and the first indications of the great system of caste, the division of the peoples into social sects, was given to the Western world by this observant ambassador, who from the point of view maintained by a resident of "court and camp and capital," placed European knowledge of Indian social geography on a definite and fairly accurate footing.

So far we are only able to recognise with distinctness two great migrations across the western mountains into India, the early settlements of the Vedic tribes who gave the "race type" to Indian civilisation, and the short advent of the Greeks, who left the impress of their culture on Indian art for centuries after they had themselves disappeared. But along with the recognisable Aryan advance there had been since the dawn of tradition a movement of the Turanian peoples of High Asia in the same direction and along the same lines. These Scythic movements finally culminated in the displacement of the Greek and the establishment of Turanian sovereignty in Northern India about the commencement of the Christian era, and from this date we almost lose sight of all such collateral information as may serve to establish points for maintaining a geographical conception of India. Until the rise of the Muhammadan power in the East we are dependent on the indefinite and often perplexing records of Chinese pilgrims who, in search of religious light, journeyed through the wildest and worst passes of the Himalayas after visiting the mediæval Buddhist centres of High Asia (cities which once flourished where now are nothing but rolling waves of sand) to offer their devotions at the shrines of Gandhara, or to circle round the stûpas of Sanchi or Benares. Recent geographical surveys carried across the Hindu Kush to Afghanistan and to the Chinese borders of Asiatic Russia, together with the marvellous results of researches made by Sven Hedin and other travellers in the deserts of Western China, have resulted in clearing up many of the geographical difficulties which lay in the way of a satisfactory translation of these Chinese records. The weary route pursued by the Buddhist devotees can now be traced almost step by step, but they end chiefly in the northern plains of the Punjab, and add little or nothing to our early geographical knowledge of peninsular India. Possessing a knowledge of trans-Himalayan regions, we can follow the pilgrims ; but the record of the pilgrims hardly enlightens us on any more important point than the impracticable nature of the Northern Himalayan routes. It is true that the great Greek geographer Ptolemy had, long before the downfall of Greek ascendency, not only collected a great store of information consisting of place names covering a vast area of the known world, but had evolved the first practicable scheme for the construction of a map by the co-ordination of these places in latitude and longitude. Many maps of India illustrating the Ptolemaic scheme have been made and published within comparatively modern times, and they are of great interest and value as indications of the theoretical knowledge which had been derived and collated from Greek adventure and exploration, which under one form or another had doubtless penetrated to the far East long before the days of Alexander. But little practical advantage is to be gained by the purely academic study of Indian geography in such early times, and it is to the hitherto but partially illustrated movements of Arab invaders, and of explorers from Western Asia, that we should now turn if we wish to appreciate the influence on the destinies of India which has been exercised by the geographical configuration of her western borderland. Practical geographical exploration into India ceased for a time with one great military invasion—that of Alexander ; it reopened with another—that of the Arab general, Muhammad Kasim, about ten centuries later.

From the very beginning of civilisation, and the consequent demand for luxuries in Egypt, trade with India and the East has been the desire of Western nations. The command of it has raised them to pre-eminence ; the decline of it has marked the ebb of their greatness. And from the very beginning that trade has been in Semitic hands. When Israel was yet a consolidated nationality, the trade routes from India by the Persian Gulf and Euphrates, or by the Red Sea, and the time-worn track still followed by the pilgrims of Mecca, were well-known commercial channels. Egypt, Assyria, Babylon, Persia, Macedonia, and Rome made supreme and successful efforts to secure the command of them. Ptolemy Philadelphus was only deterred by fear of inundations from constructing the Suez Canal two centuries and a half before our era; and by the first century A.D. Hippalus had discovered how to make use of the monsoon winds to cross the Arabian Sea; whilst Egyptian craft carried merchandise along the coast-lines, where scattered remnants of the ancient trade (chiefly débris of glass utensils and ornaments) are to be found to this present day. With the decline of Rome in the sixth century A.D. the Saracen Arabs took the field, and Bagdad and Basra claimed preeminence as commercial centres. The Kalifs were greater than Solomon—more magnificent in their dispensations, more splendid in the display of their wealth.

But whilst the sea routes undoubtedly formed the chief commercial connection between East and West for more centuries than we can count, the land routes also were constantly traversed, and they shared with the Red Sea and the Persian Gulf the position of main arteries of commercial intercourse in the hands of the Arabs, until Turk and Moghul finally blocked the way about the beginning of the fifteenth century A.D. Of these land routes much has been written and said about those which connected Northern India with the Oxus, and then striking into the great trans-Asian line of the silk trade from China, reached Europe either by way of the Caspian or Black Sea. All High Asia is traversed by a network of ancient Arab routes, and many are the indications of the past wealth and magnificence of the mediæval cities of the Oxus basin that were traced by the Russo-Afghan Boundary Commission in 1883–85. But not much has been said about the direct land route between Western India and Bagdad which passed through Makrán and traversed the length of Central Persia, the possession of which, far more than the desire to punish a band of Karak (Karachi) pirates, was the probable objective of the Arab advance into Sind in the eighth century of our era.

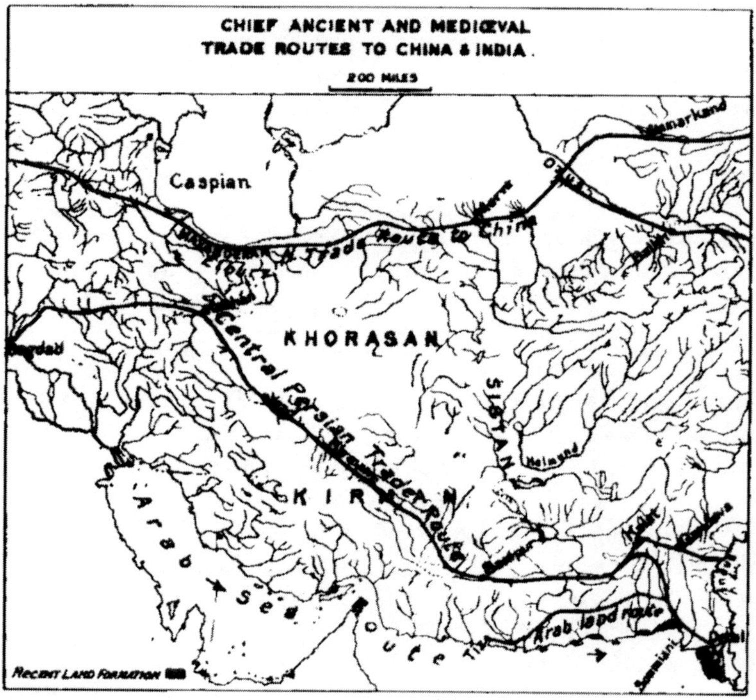


FIG. 5.

The Muhammadan conquest of Sind, and the establishment of Mussulman dynasties in India, was almost coincident with the general disappearance of Buddhism from the land of its birth, although Buddhist provinces still maintained a failing struggle for existence on the western borders in the days when the great traveller, Ibn Haukel, constructed the first intelligible map of the Baluchistan districts between India and Eastern Persia (A.D. 943–976).

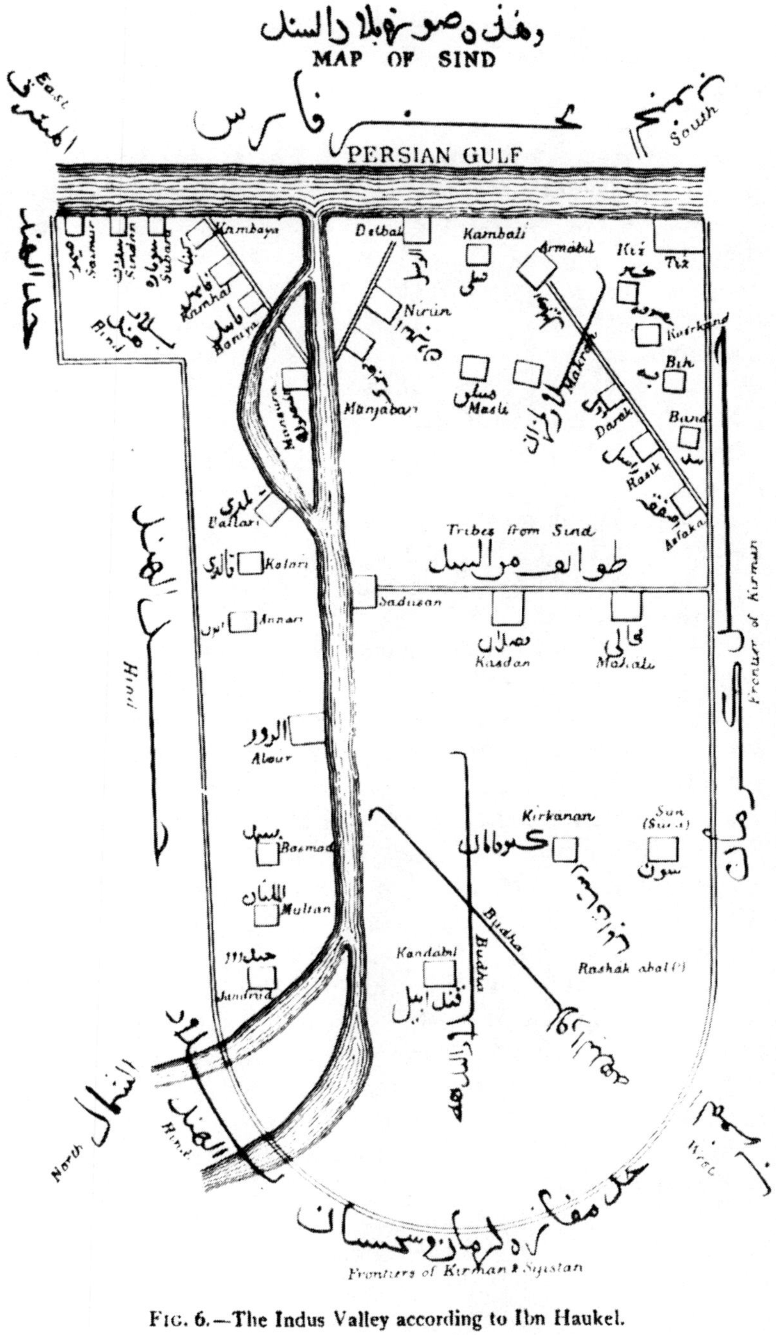


FIG. 6.—The Indus Valley according to Ibn Haukel.

From the scattered records of this period of Muhammadan occupation we gain a new conception of the geographical position of India relatively to the West, which has been strengthened by recent surveys and explorations in the intermediate countries. The Muhammadan advance is the one prominent instance of the successful invasion of India by a land force which did not pass through the narrow portals of the north-western mountains. It exhibits the facility with which India may be approached from the Persian border, provided only that the invader has command of the sea; for it must be remembered that this first advance of the Muhammadan on India was supported by a naval contingent; and it opens up an entirely new vista of mediæval geography, enabling us to collate the evidence of a series of Arab writers (some of whom were actual explorers who wrote of what they themselves had seen) intelligently and readily.

Thus, with ever-shifting local expansion and contraction, the general political boundaries of the Indian frontier and the land and sea connection between Northern India and Europe remained almost unchanged for four or five centuries. During this time a continued stream of commerce poured to and fro through the now desert wastes of Makrán, and across the great table-land of Persia to Bagdad and the farther west, until at length the Crusaders first broke the power of the Saracen, and then the Turk and Moghul swarmed into Western Asia and for a time shouldered both Crusader and Indian commerce into the sea.

This indeed (about the middle of the fifteenth century) was the commencement of the great international race of the western powers for command of the Eastern Ocean. For century after century a full knowledge of the commercial geography of the farther east had been the heritage of the Arab. Arabia was first mistress of the seas, and to Arabia we owe not only the early lines of our first ocean sailing ships, but many of our modern nautical terms as well. The complete history of the extraordinary diffusion of Arab influence—Himyaritic, Sabæan, or Muhammadan

—throughout the world, and its enduring effect in shaping the early beginnings of modern civilisation has yet to be written.

Previously to the capture of Constantinople by the Turks in 1453 the eastern trade by the Black Sea route (which had formed the chief wealth of the Byzantine Empire) had been largely developed by Venetian merchants who settled at Constantinople after its capture by the Crusaders in 1204. For fifty years Venice retained possession of the Black Sea trade, and was queen of the Mediterranean Sea. The Genoese supplanted the Venetians about the middle of the thirteenth century, and held their own until the advent of the Turk; but both Venetian and Genoese influence is still perceptible in the Persian and Makrán coast districts (Venetian gold coins were the only recognised gold currency of Makrán until quite recently), and it certainly appears probable that the Perso-Makrán route was at least as important in its time as that of the Black Sea or any of the more northern highways. For a time the truculent Turk only barely held his own against the Arab navigator, and both were still sea powers to be reckoned with, when the discovery of the Cape route to India by Vasco da Gama in 1497 opened an entirely new chapter in the history of Indian commercial geography.

The subsequent story of Portuguese ascendency, the marvellous rapidity of its development until it culminated in the absolute command of oriental trade from Japan to the Cape of Good Hope, lasting through the whole of the sixteenth century; and its equally rapid decline and final disappearance before the persistent advance of the Dutch, belongs to the pages of history rather than of geography, and is only of purely geographical interest by reason of the glimpses which it affords us of the distribution of political power in India whilst it lasted.

When the Portuguese first arrived in India, Delhi and the whole of Bengal were under the sway of the Afghan. The Deccan was divided into the five Muhammadan kingdoms of Ahmadnagar, Bijapur, Elichpur, Golconda, and Bídar, whilst the most powerful monarch in all India was the Hindu rajah of Vijayanagar, who reigned paramount over the southern provinces.

In 1683 Portuguese power was at dead low tide, the Mahrattas advanced to the very gates of Goa—the Portuguese capital—and the "further history of the Portuguese in India is a miserable chronicle of pride, poverty, and sounding titles."[1]

All that remains to them now are Goa, Daman, and Diu on the west coast, with an area of about 2350 square miles and less than half a million population.

During the seventeenth century the Dutch were the foremost power on the high seas. In 1651 they founded a colony at the Cape of Good Hope, and in 1658 they had wrested the last stronghold from the Portuguese in Ceylon. Just one century later Clive broke their power finally at Chinsurah, and at the present time there is not a Dutch settlement on the mainland of India. In the census of 1881 but seventy-nine Dutchmen were enumerated throughout the country.

Next followed the French and English; and modern history recounts the further process of building up the Indian Empire until it finally took shape as we now find it, and as we shall now attempt to describe it. The India of to-day is not the India of the ancients; it is not the India of mediæval Arab history; it is not the India of Portuguese and Dutch ascendency which was limited to a narrow fringe of country washed by the sea and represented by scattered commercial "factories." India must be accepted as the whole area of Southern Asia over which British political influence now extends, whether strictly within the limits of the red line of "British" India or beyond it. As a geographical expression it cannot be dissociated from the frontier which binds it, or from the wide border mountain lands of the west and north-west, wherein are to be found the gates of it. No geographical description of the peninsula of India would be complete

[1] Hunter, "Imperial Gazetteer," vol. vi.

without reference to the strange wild hinterland which has exercised such a profound influence on its destinies through all past ages.

A comprehensive and up-to-date compilation of existing records of Early Indian geography is very much wanted. M'Crindle's excellent series of translations from classical authors (especially his "Periplus of the Erythræan Sea" and his "Ancient India as described by Megasthenes and Arrian") are most useful books for reference. In Elliott's "History of India" (first chapter) exists a valuable comparison of all existing evidence derived from the accounts of the mediæval Arab geographers. From that source has been taken the illustration of Ibn Haukel's map of Sind and Makrán. The works of Yule, Smith, and Cunningham are, of course, standard references for all time, but there has been a great deal of recent geographical evidence lately collected by members of the Indian Survey department which has yet to be published. For geological history I am chiefly indebted to the paper by R. D. Oldham, which is to be found in the third volume of the *Geographical Journal* for 1894—perhaps the best contribution to the history of Indian geological evolution that can be found in a small compass. Another useful authority on the subject of the ancient geographical conformation of the Indus delta is Major-General M. R. Haig, whose "Indus Delta Country" explains many doubtful points besetting the histories of Alexander and Nearkhos. Maps of Early India which thoroughly illustrate the geography of the country in mediæval times when India first began to attract the attention of western commercial enterprise are not to be found. The Ptolemaic conceptions of India are interesting, but hardly instructive. Smith's Ancient Atlas is still our best authority, but it requires considerable revision to bring it up to modern requirements.

# CHAPTER II

## THE GEOGRAPHY OF THE FRONTIER: BALUCHISTAN

STATISTICS.—Baluchistan is a state feudatory to India, lying between 25° and 32° N. lat., and between 61° and 70° E. long. It is about 550 miles in length, with an average breadth of 450 miles. Area about 130,000 square miles, population about 500,000.

The province of Baluchistan includes: (1) Independent Baluchistan; (2) Quetta and the Bolan administered by the British Government; (3) British Baluchistan.

The chief towns are Kalát, Quetta, Kozdar, Bela, Kalatak, Bagh, Gandáva, and Dádar. The leading chief is the Khan of Kalát, Mir Mahmud Khan, who succeeded his father in 1893.

The treaty of 1876, effected between Sir R. Sandeman and the chiefs of Baluchistan, renewed the treaty of 1854, which established an alliance offensive and defensive; and it recognised the status of the Sirdars or minor chiefs, making the British Government arbitrator in disputes between them and the Khan. British troops were then located in the Khan's territory; Quetta was built, telegraphs and railways were commenced, and a subsidy of Rs.100,000 per annum granted to the Khan.

British Baluchistan was incorporated with British India by a resolution of November 1, 1887, and divided into two districts: (1) Quetta-Peshin; (2) Tal-Chotiáli, and the political agents of these districts became Deputy-Commissioners with a regular staff.

The Khan's revenue includes Rs.100,000 per annum subsidy from the Indian Government; Rs.25.000 quit-rent from the Quetta district, and a share in the agricultural produce of Independent Baluchistan, which in a good year may equal Rs.500,000.

The agricultural produce of the country generally is small, but is largely increasing in Peshin and Zhob. The rainfall is scanty. Baluchistan is largely a grazing country—chiefly sheep and camels.

The chief exports are wool, hides, madder, dried fruit, tobacco, and dates.

The value of the trade is roughly as follows:—

| | | Imports. | Exports. |
|---|---|---|---|
| In 1899 | Las Bela | Rx.60,800 | Rx.26,500 |
| ,, | Kalát | Rx.70,000 | Rx.50,500 |

Rx. = 10 Rupees.

FOR purposes of description it will be convenient to recognise the accepted definition supplied by the map or atlas sheet, and to adhere to the geographical boundaries shown therein. Thus, by the Indian peninsula we mean that continent which is bounded by the Bay of Bengal and the Indian Ocean on the east and west respectively, and which lies south of the Himalaya mountains, including both the region of depression and the southern table-land within the limits of the red line which denotes British India. This red line includes the Punjab on the north-west, the boundaries of which are generally those which we inherited by right of conquest from the Sikhs, but which have been considerably modified by our occupation of various posts on the main lines of routes connecting India with trans-frontier countries. To the north of the Punjab we exclude Kashmir (which is a "native" state), but we include the hill districts of Kumaon (which are part of the North-West Provinces), and thence carry the boundary of British India eastwards, south of Nipál, Bhutan, and other independent hill states, till we touch the extreme north-east corner of the province of Assam. Here the Indian frontier, as generally recognised, takes an abrupt bend to the south, and thenceforward runs with a south-westerly trend to the Bay of Bengal, parting British India from British Burma. For all political and administrative purposes Burma has become an integral part of the Indian empire, but it is geographically dissociated from the peninsula of India, and it will be convenient to regard it as distinct. There is not really more actual distinction in topographical or ethnographical characteristics between Burma and Southern India than there is between Southern India and the North-West, but Burma and South India are divided by a great natural barrier of mountain and sea such as nowhere divides the provinces of the Indian peninsula, and Burma may well remain apart for purposes of geographical consideration.

But the political and commercial interests of the India of the future, no less than the history of the India of the past, are so intimately associated with these trans-frontier countries which extend along her northern border, from the Arabian Sea to the Bay of Bengal, that this borderland is not to be separated from any general consideration of Indian geography. National interest, indeed, from day to day centres more and more on the northern borders of India, and is drawn farther and farther from the historical India of Clive and Hastings—the India of England's beginnings in the race for Empire ; so that it may be well to commence with a general geographical description of those border countries across which lie the routes to India from the west and north-west.

All the great highroads of the past, the overland trade routes of the days ere Vasco da Gama rounded the Cape, found their entrance to India within comparatively narrow limits. From the Arabian sea-coast at Karachi to the Kabul River is a direct distance, roughly, of 700 miles. This represents about one-fifth of the total length of the northern frontiers of India, if we exclude Burma ; and it is remarkable that England, who herself boasts a frontier impregnable to the march of hostile armies, should have acquired empire over a region so vast and, at the same time, so difficult of land approach as India. There is no historical record, no tradition even worthy of attention, which points to the violation of the frontier of India at any point beyond these 700 miles of rugged and difficult hills extending between Karachi and the Kabul River basin. Between these limits every tide of foreign immigration, every horde of Mongols or Turks, every Asiatic contribution to the mixed nationalities of the Indian empire has found its way at one time or another ; insomuch that there is hardly a living soul in the plains of the peninsula (apart from the purely aboriginal tribes, and the comparatively few whose progenitors arrived by sea) who cannot claim descent from one or other of the former great nationalities of Asia who passed into India by these north-western gates. Greeks, Assyrians, Medes, Chaldeans and Persians, Skyths, Turks, Tartars and Mongols all came that way ; and some of them have continued to pass long since Arabs,

Portuguese, Dutch, and English formed a straighter line of advance over the open seas.

Leaving for the present the fascinating subject of ethnographical developments in India, we will note very briefly the geographical substratum on which the modern trans-frontier states of India are founded before proceeding to topographical definitions.

In not very remote times all the outlying kingdoms and provinces of the north-western trans-frontier of India were Persian territory, and were included under the one provincial designation Khorasán. Khorasán is the name which, to this day, is applied by Afghan and Pathan to the modern kingdom of Afghanistan and to all the border mountain lands which lie between Afghanistan and India. Khorasán still possesses a narrow geographical existence, but it has shrunk into the limits of a small province on the extreme east of Persia, of which Mashad is the capital. The Khorasán of Persian empire, which has contributed an indestructible Persian element to the population of these border countries, included not only a great section of Eastern Persia and nearly all of Baluchistan, Afghanistan, and Kashmir (as we know them now), but the Indus provinces of the Punjab and Sind as well. As late as the thirteenth century Persian garrisons held the Peshawur valley, where they were found by the Conqueror Chenghis Khan. This ancient Persian element has almost disappeared from the population of the Punjab and Sind, but it is to be readily found throughout the rest of ancient Khorasán. In Baluchistan it is represented by the lowest class of agriculturists. The ancient lords of the soil are now little better than the household slaves of the mixed community of conquering races who have flooded the country since the days of the Arab occupation. Throughout Northern Afghanistan the same original Persian stock exists—as the tiller of the soil in the western districts, but in the east in much more dominant form. The Tajak population of the turbulent districts to the north of Kabul, the people who occupy the plains that wind along the foot of the Paghmán mountains south of Charikar and west of Kafiristan, and who were amongst our most formidable opponents during the Afghan war of 1879, are of Persian extraction, largely admixed (as their name denotes) with Arab blood. Persian-speaking communities (such as the Kizzilbashes of Kabul) are scattered still throughout Northern Afghanistan, and Persian is spoken by the educated classes amongst the conquering races of Afghans and Ghilzais, whose domestic tongue is Pushtu.

On to this Persian element, which exists in fading evidence of the vast extent embraced by the ancient Persian empire, are grafted all those other foreign races who have taken their turn and played their parts in the troubled history of the Indian trans-frontier. The province of Khorasán only shrunk to its present dimensions in comparatively recent times. In the middle of the eighteenth century the great bandit king of Persia (Nadir Shah) still held all Baluchistan, Afghanistan, Sind, the Punjab, and Kashmir under his undivided authority. The Khorasán province was still intact. It was only after his death that the Durani empire was carved out of Khorasán by the Afghan adventurer Ahmad Shah; and it was not till the beginning of the present century, when the Durani empire (which extended as far east as Lahore) fell to pieces in its turn from want of capacity amongst its rulers and of the stability which is only born of developed internal resources, that Baluchistan shaped itself into a federation of powerful independent tribes recognising the supremacy of the Kambarani Khan of Kalát; and that Afghanistan was moulded into the semblance of an independent kingdom by the strong hand of Dost Mahomed, the Barakzai Afghan.

The boundaries of Baluchistan and Afghanistan alike have been constant themes of irritation and discussion between the government of India and her border neighbours (Russian, Persian, Afghan, and Baluch) for the last half century, and it is only quite recently (within the last few years) that territorial limits have been definitely set to them. It is within those limits that we shall describe

# INDIA, N.W. SECTION.

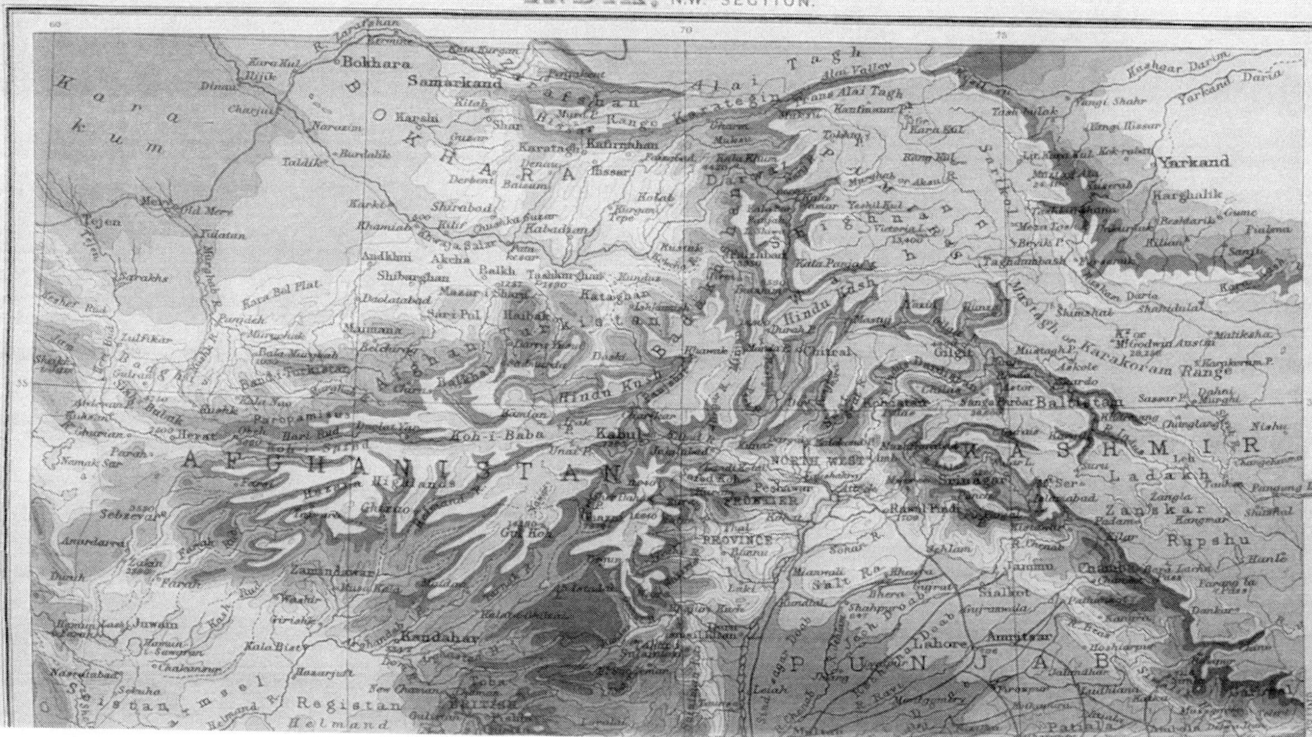

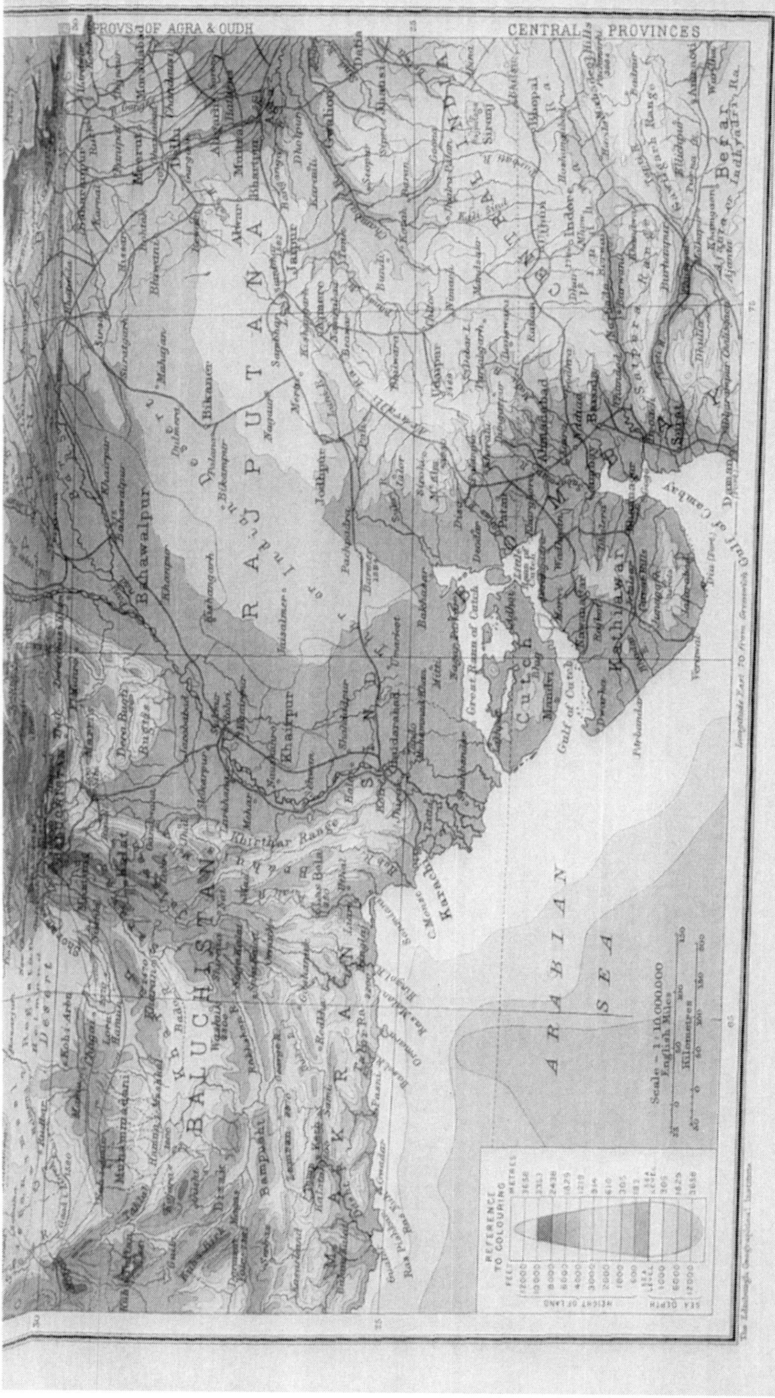
PROVS. OF AGRA & OUDH
CENTRAL PROVINCES
BALUCHISTAN
RAJPUTANA
Bahawalpur
Bikaner
Jodhpur
Jaipur
Ajmere
Indore
Bhopal
Gwalior
Kathiawar
Cutch
Great Rann of Cutch
Gulf of Cutch
Gulf of Cambay
Karachi
Khairpur
Bugtis
Kirthar Range
ARABIAN SEA
Satpura Range
Berar
Ahmadabad
Surat
Daman
REFERENCE TO COLOURING
FEET
METRES
HEIGHT OF LAND
SEA DEPTH
Scale 1:10,000,000
English Miles
Kilometres
Longitude East 70 from Greenwich

the geographical characteristics of these countries and note the chief highways to India which intersect them.

Baluchistan is bounded on the south by the Arabian Sea, and on the west by the frontier Persian provinces of Kirmán and Khorasán. The boundary is definitely fixed by international commission, and it is not necessary to follow it in much detail. It leaves the Arabian sea-coast near the little fishing-port of Gwatar (not Gwadar, which is some fifty miles to the east of it), between the Chil and the Dasht rivers, and runs north-east through the hilly wilderness of western Makrán to the Mashkhel River. Leaving the small and comparatively insignificant (but much discussed) province of Kohuk to Persia, it starts again from the Mashkhel (very close to its junction with the Rakshán, one of the chief rivers of Southern Baluchistan), and runs north-west, first touching the Hamun, or swamp, which receives the Mashkhel - Rakshán drainage, and then, following a well-defined line of strong natural features to the north-west, it joins the Afghan and Persian boundaries on the historical peak of Malik Siah Koh. The trijunction of the three kingdoms might be called the apotheosis of desolation ; it overlooks a vast extent of sandy waste and rugged hills from a height of 5000 or 6000 feet above sea-level. To the north are the wide flats of Southern Seistán—plains that once were green with the irrigated crops which won for Seistán the title of the "granary of Asia," but which are now a barren and deserted wilderness. Not thirty miles to the east is the salt-white swamp of Gaod-i-Zirreh, about which there is

FIG. 7.—The North-West Borderland.

more to be said in connection with the hydrography of Baluchistan. Far away to the south, on a clear day, may be discerned a faint smoke-cloud arising from the great volcano, the Koh-i-Taftán (" or burning mountain "), snow-capped at 13,500 feet above sea-level ; whilst west as well as south are the broken uplands of Sarhad, the happy

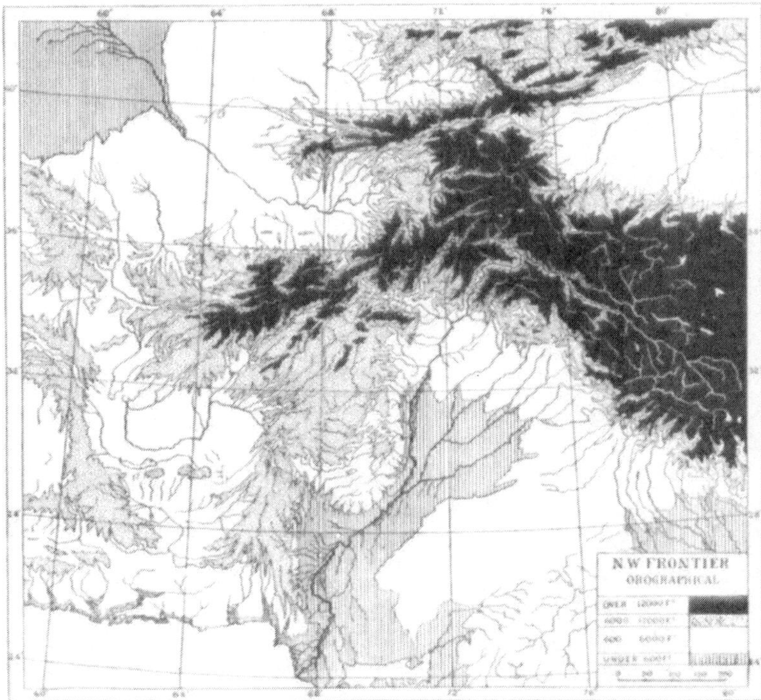


FIG. 8.

hunting-ground of bands of Kurdish robbers—a country where "law is not, and God is forgotten." Nor is the northern frontier of Baluchistan carried through districts of much more promise than its western border. From the Malik Siah Koh to the borders of the Quetta district the boundary intersects the great desert of the Helmund, passing about fifty miles to the south of the river, and partly defining the southern watershed of its basin.

It is only quite recently that this water parting between the Helmund and the great Mashkhel swamp (which, besides the drainage contributed by the two important rivers Mashkhel and Rakshán, receives the periodic torrents which flow from this water parting) has been defined, and it is only lately that this desert has been

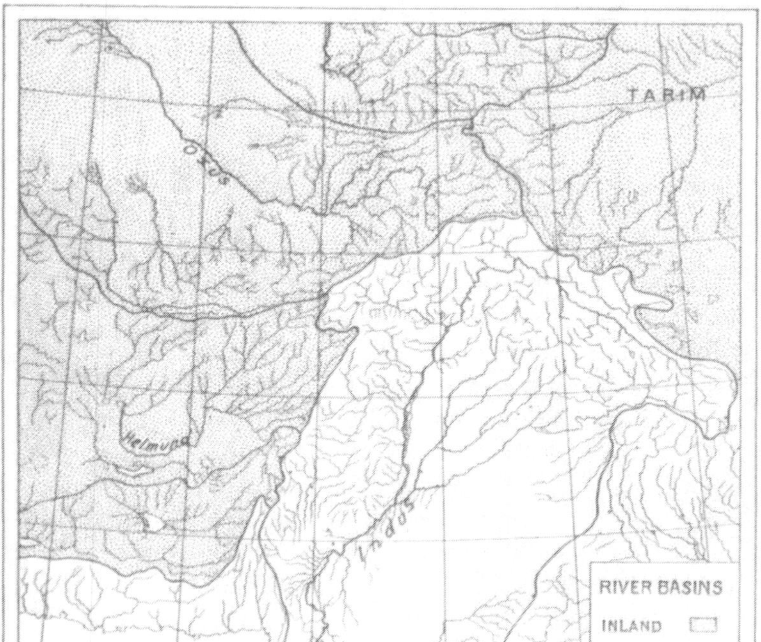


FIG. 9.

traversed and the caravan route established which now connects Seistán with Quetta. From a point about forty miles W.S.W. of Quetta the dividing line between Afghanistan and Baluchistan strikes northward, and traces an uneven course to the western edge of the cultivation surrounding the little station of New Chaman, which represents the terminus of the Sind-Peshin railway in the direction of Kandahar. New Chaman is not more than seven or eight miles in a direct line from the northern mouth of that tunnel which pierces the Khojak range and carries the railway in a fairly direct course about half-way between Quetta and Kandahar. At New Chaman British India is practically in touch with Afghanistan. It is true that Baluchistan intervenes for more than 200 miles between New Chaman and the frontier of Sind near Jacobabad, but it is the Baluchistan of British occupation, one half of the distance lying within the hill districts ceded or rented to the British Government by Kalát, and the other in that Kachi (or low land) which forms such a marked geographical feature at this point of our frontier, dovetailing in between the hills of Kalát and those belonging to the great independent tribes of Marri and Bugti. From New Chaman the general run of the Afghan-Baluch boundary is to the north-east. It is an irregular and much-indented line defining many local agricultural interests (for this part of Baluchistan is not the desert of the west and south), but following well-marked natural features where possible, until it touches the Gomal River at Domandi.

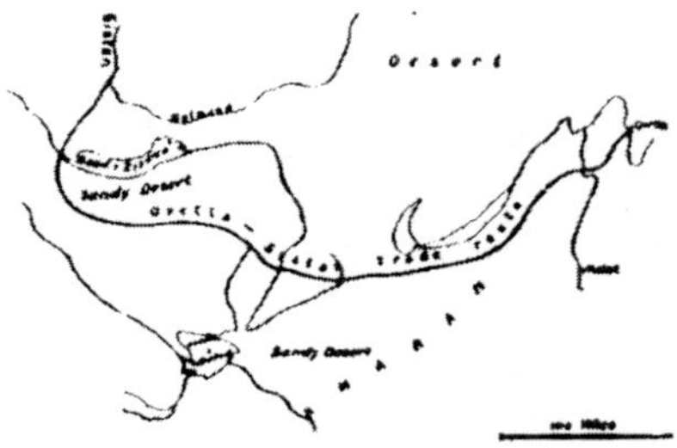

FIG. 10.—The Route from Quetta to Siestán.

The Gomal now represents the northern limit of Baluchistan. Its eastern boundary from the mouth of the river Hab (some twenty miles west of Karachi) to the debouchment of the Gomal River into the plains of the Derajat near Dera Ismail Khan, requires little definition. For administrative purposes it follows the line of the old pre-British frontiers of Sind, and may be said, roughly, to divide the hills from the plains; excepting for a certain space where, leaving the Kalát Hills, it intersects the plains of Kach Gandava, and passing a little north of Jacobabad strikes the lowest slopes of the Bugti Mountains. For nearly 600 miles from the sea to the Gomal the frontier of India was thus defined by a well-marked line of topographical features, which, if imperfect as a military barrier, possessed at least the merit of great simplicity and easy recognition.

Just so far as the shelving slopes of the clay and conglomerate foot hills that buttressed the central limestone ridges of the Sulimáni and Kirthar mountains were productive and available for the sowing of crops when stones and superincumbent débris was cleared therefrom, so far did the old landowners of Sind and the Punjab claim full advantage of the soil, caring nothing for the rugged intricacies of the hills in front of them, nor troubling themselves about the development of a few square yards of cultivation here and there along the narrow edges of the torrent-swept water-courses which drained their cramped valleys.

Every now and then there would be a descent of the Baluch clansmen into Sind, or of the Pathans of the Sulimáni hills into the nearest plains; and a general lifting of cattle and goods ensued which called for reprisal and vengeance. The plains of India have ever furnished the hills of the frontier with a vicarious subsistence of this nature, but the ruggedness and intricacy of that borderland was far too effective, and the savage energy of the Rind descendants of early Arab occupation, or of the Pathan clans of the Sulimánis, was too well appreciated for any great show of reprisal, or for the conduct of a hill warfare such as might lead to permanent conquest. The Arab and Dravidian tribes of the Baluch frontier (Rinds and Brahuis) were never conquered and reduced to dependence any more than were the Pathans of the north, before our time. Through their fastnesses generations of immigrants, invaders, and a few conquerors have passed from the highlands of Persia and Afghanistan to the plains of the Indus Valley, and in more recent years the process has been reversed by a reflex wave of migration; but the independence of these mountaineers has never been seriously compromised, not even by the assertion of a right of way through their hills, and the balance of mutual understanding between highlanders and plains-people has been more generally adjusted by weight of silver than of gun-metal.

Some explanation seems necessary of the political boundaries of Baluchistan as they usually appear in our frontier maps, where a central section of the country enclosed within a narrow red line indicates British

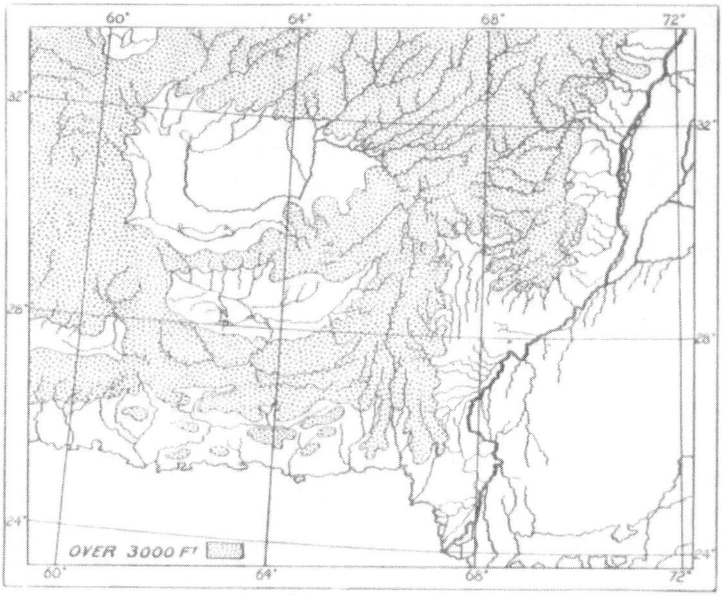


FIG. 11.—The Trans-Indus Inland Basins.

Baluchistan dividing the independent Pathan tribes of Northern Baluchistan from the equally independent Baluch tribes of the south. Within the limits of British Baluchistan are the districts of Quetta and Bolan, held and administered by the Indian Government on behalf of Mir Mahmud Khan, the ruler of Kalát, in lieu of an annual subsidy of 25,000 rupees—which has lately been increased since Nushki has been included within the red line. A further sum of 30,000 rupees is paid to the Khan as compensation for duties levied in the Bolan.

Besides Quetta and Bolan there are the assigned districts of Peshin, Shorarud, Kach, Kawas, Harnai, Sibi, and Tal-Chotiali which formerly belonged to Afghanistan, but which have been placed directly under British rule since the conclusion of the first phase of the Afghan War of 1878–79, and which, together with Quetta and Bolan, constitute the province of British Baluchistan. Within

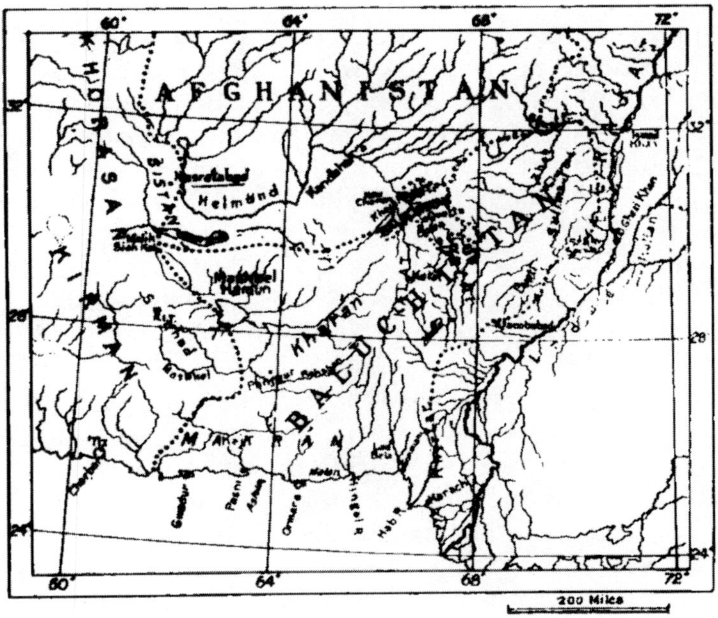


FIG. 12.—The Boundaries of Baluchistan.

this province the form of settled administration is that of the regulation provinces of the Indian peninsula. Beyond it, the Khan of Kalát heads a powerful confederacy of Baluch chiefs who administer the Government of Independent Baluchistan on their own ancient feudal system, recognising, firstly, the suzerainty of the Khan of Kalát, and, ultimately, the position of the Governor-General's Agent at Quetta as arbitrator in all disputes which may arise between them. Amongst the Pathan tribes of Northern Baluchistan the Khan of Kalát possesses no authority. Their position is analogous in most respects to that of the Pathan tribes still farther north. Certain of these tribes immediately south of the Gomal (including the Sheranis) have recently been transferred for purposes of administration to the newly-formed north-western agency.

Baluchistan is now represented by a long, narrow province running approximately parallel to the Indus for about 750 miles from the Arabian Sea, with an average width of 200 miles, excepting where a triangular horn of desert reaches out from the Kalát highlands westwards to Seistán. With the exception of this Muhammadáni and Kharán desert, of the delta of the Purâli River of Las Bela, and of the Kachhi, or desert, which stretches from Jacobabad to the mouth of the Bolan pass, the whole country is mountainous.

From the Gomal River to Jacobabad there stretches one continuous chain of mountain peaks, which, although now distinguished by many local names, may well be known under their ancient designation of Sulimáni. They are, and they have ever been, through the ages of an immense past, the original habitat of the Pakhtun or Pashtu speaking mountaineers whom we now call Pathans. The Sulimáni system is not a water parting; it is not a central divide that throws off the beginning of a great system of drainage east and west. The slopes of the Sulimáni hills, both east and west, drain equally to the Indus, and it is the drainage of the western slopes that, turning suddenly and bursting through the main chain of central limestone ridges, forms those terrific gorges and rock-bound mountain gates which are our only means of access to the traversable valleys of the western plateau. The main Sulimáni ridge, which is the dominating feature of the Indus frontier south of the Gomal, lies back from the foot of the hills some thirty miles—which thirty miles of gradual descent from the plateau to the plains is packed close with narrow, rugged, sun-scorched, treeless ridges, composed chiefly of recent clays and conglomerates, which preserve an approximate parallelism in their strike, likening the whole system to a gigantic gridiron. Narrow little "subsequent" valleys between these sharp-backed ridges contribute an intermittent flow of brackish water to the main arteries, and these again, as before described, break transversely across the general strike of the minor ridges ere they debouch into the Indus plain.

And if we transfer the general view of a system of steep, narrow, parallel ridges, alternating with equally-constricted valleys, and give an altitude to the hills such as will carry their peaks 8000 feet above sea-level ; clothe them with a scanty vegetation of grass, wild olive, and juniper ; widen out certain intermediate valleys, and fill them with occasional bunches of tamarisk jungle and coarse grass, admitting narrow bands of cultivation bordering streams that are occasionally perennial, we shall gain a fair general conception of the Baluchistan of the highlands lying west of the Sulimáni and extending to the newly-defined frontier of Afghanistan.

The dominating mountain of the Sulimáni range is usually called the Takht-i-Sulimán. This is (as usual with our Indian frontier nomenclature) an inaccurate designation, unrecognised by the people of the country ; the Takht-i-Sulimán being a famous ziarat, or shrine, which is situated some distance below the summit at the southern extremity of the mountain. The mountain itself is better known locally as the Kaisargarh, the name of the highest northern peak (11,300 feet above sea-level), which forms a magnificently dominant feature in the landscape, whether viewed from the far-away Indus plains, or from the shadowed sides of the precipitous hills which encompass it. For many years the Kaisargarh (which is some forty miles south of the Gomal River) was reckoned the highest peak of the Indian border south of the Himalayas. It is, however, surpassed by more than one of the gigantic mountains which overlook the valleys of Peshin and Quetta ; but for grandeur of outline enhanced by isolation, and for the traditional interest which hangs around its limestone crags, the Kaisargarh stands unrivalled amongst frontier landmarks.

Traversing this northern section of Baluchistan from the head of the Peshin Valley to the Gomal River is the valley of the Zhob. The gradual (and surprising) development of this valley since its first introduction to the domain of practical Indian geography and politics; the extraordinary resources possessed by its scarred and broken slopes, which presented not many years ago an aspect of barren, wind-swept desolation, tempered only by a few uneven patches of rice cultivation—all this is matter of modern history. Its future, as offering a line of direct railway communication between Lahore and Quetta, is matter of present discussion. We must leave the Zhob and its ancient Kakur (Pathan) inhabitants to turn to the central uplands of Peshin and Quetta, which divide Northern Baluchistan from Kalát and the south.

A glance at the map will show that the Sind-Peshin Railway cuts Baluchistan into two divisions, and that it occupies a peculiarly well-balanced and central position with regard to the two sections of the province which it divides. The Kachhi, or flat, alluvial plain of Kach Gandava (which may justly be termed desert in all that central part of it occupied by the railway, and which is annually subject to flooding by the spill waters of the Indus) carries the line almost to the heart of the province ere it touches the hills at the debouchment of the Bolan and the Nari streams. Here the railway divides. One branch follows the line of Harnai and Nari drainage upwards from the plains to the valley of Peshin; and the other, only lately diverted from the lower part of the old Bolan route to the valley of Mashkaf, reunites with the Bolan line at Mach, and finds more direct access to Quetta without touching the Peshin. Both lines will be lasting monuments of skilful engineering, but probably the Mashkaf development of the Bolan route will prove of the greatest practical value in the long run.

The Harnai and the Bolan together introduce a special system of hydrography for central Baluchistan. The valley of Peshin and the plain of Quetta form a central elevation which parts the long lines of lateral drainage to the north (represented by the Zhob) from the yet longer lines of lateral drainage on the south, the direction of

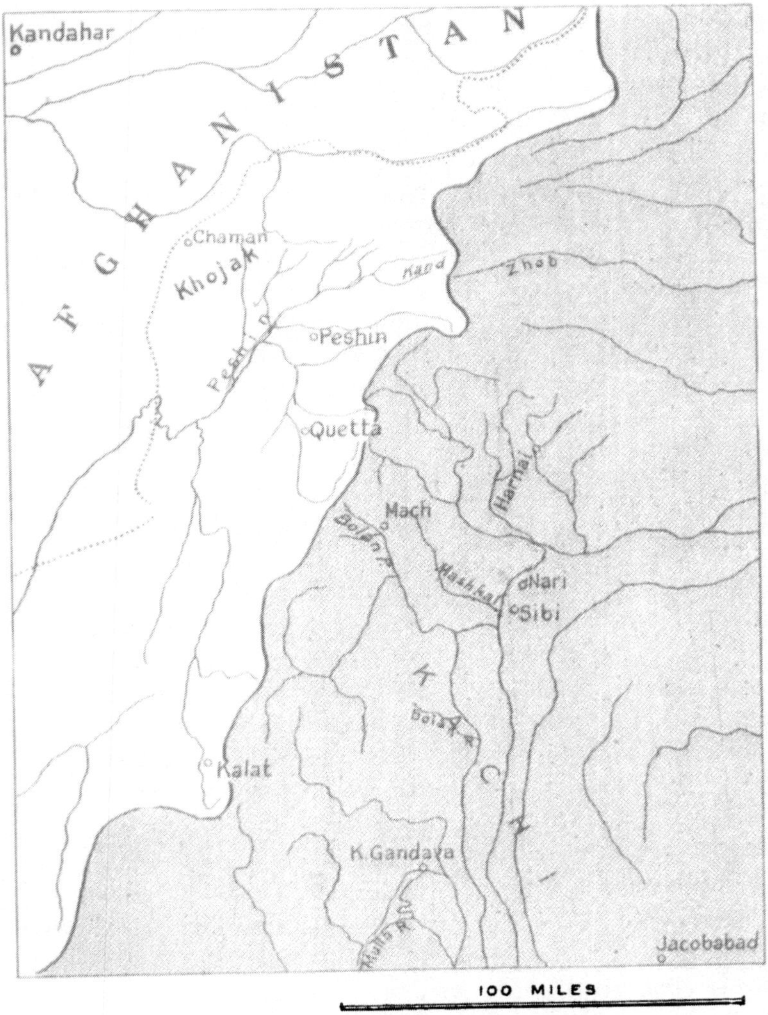


FIG. 13.—The Frontier Hydrography Radiating from Quetta.

which is determined by the mountain system which governs the districts of Kalát and Kharán. The Bolan and the Harnai rivers both carry their tributaries straight across Baluchistan eastward to the Indus from the high plains surrounding Quetta. The catchment area of these rivers is comparatively small, but the shape of them, and especially the absence of surface soil in the rocky regions of their upper sources, leads to a sudden gathering of flood waters in their channels when the heavy storms of spring break over the Quetta Mountains such as is rare even in this flood-riddled country. The Bolan line of railway was washed out of existence by one such terrific flood before the Mashkaf alternative was adopted.

Of the popular station of modern Quetta occupying the central highland of Baluchistan little need be said. From its geographical position it must always have been a point of strategical importance as well as a considerable commercial centre. It is surrounded by gigantic mountain peaks, running to 11,400 feet of elevation, the highest that Baluchistan can boast, and only eclipsed by the weird and isolated snow-capped volcano, the Koh-i-Taftán of the Persian border. The double-peaked Takatu on the north, balanced by Chiltan (Chahiltan) on the south-west, and the square-headed giant Murdar on the south-east (to all of which Quetta looks up from an altitude of about 5800 feet above sea), form an entourage of mountains such as few cities in the world can boast. Beyond them again, to the east, the ramparts of Kalifat close up the landscape, blazing scarlet when winter sunset lights up the world of hills and snows with level shafts; nor is it necessary to move far to gain a view of the silver cone of Kand, which parts the head waters of Peshin from those of Zhob. Looking towards Kandahar the level barrier of the Khojak is always visible whenever the yellow dusty haze of summer gives place to the clear definitions of winter atmosphere. Irrigation has developed the plain of Quetta and the valley of Peshin into a green oasis amongst these mountains in spring and summer. Nothing but a wide vista of crops—green fields broken by the dark outlines of orchard trees and hamlets—is then to be seen from the top of the Miri, that most ancient débris of mud volcano which dominates Quetta as its fortress and protection. Such is the result of British interference with frontier misgovernment for less than the space of one quarter of a century.

Leaving Quetta and turning to the southern districts

FIG. 14.—The Plain of Quetta.

of Baluchistan (which may be dealt with in three divisions, *i.e.* the hill state of Kalát, the desert of Kharán, and the sea bordering the district of Makrán), we at once encounter a topographical system analogous to that which we left on the north. Those great evolutionary processes of Nature which moulded the eastern edge of the great Baluch-Afghan plateau into a succession of gigantic wrinkles (each wrinkle represented by a long narrow mountain ridge or upfold) like the sand ripples of a receding tide, were applied to the same general purpose and effect along a line which extends from the Kaisargarh Mountain near the Gomal through Southern Baluchistan to the Persian border; and thence, with certain modifications (here and there following the course of the Persian Gulf littoral), to Western Persia and the Caucasus. What may have been the nature of the primeval agency which cracked these wrinkles transversely across their axis, or permitted all the main arteries of drainage to maintain a course almost at right angles to the strike of them, may be still open to question. It is enough to note that the general conformation of the mountains in Southern Baluchistan is similar to that in the northern section of the province. Long narrow valleys lead from Quetta first southwards, rising for about ninety miles to Kalát, and then, falling and bending with graceful curve from their meridional direction to a westerly trend, they run parallel to the coast of the Arabian Sea through Makrán to the Persian border. From the close packed mountain regions south of Kalát a section of this border conformation continues its course due southward, culminating in the Kirthar range, and thus determines the shape of the Indus Valley. Between these southerly and westerly extensions space is gained for a triangle of comparatively low country which lies in the fork between them. This little triangular space is the frontier state of Las Bela, which consists chiefly of the delta of the Puráli River (the ancient Arabis) draining into the Arabian Sea at Sonmiáni, not far north of Karachi.

The state of Kalát lies at a general elevation which is higher by more than 1000 feet than Quetta. The fortress of Kalát may be said to define the geographical "hub"—the great central watershed—of Southern Baluchistan, from which, to north and south, the hydrographical system of the country spreads outwards. Southwards we pass by gentle gradients through the long narrow valleys (which extend perchance for hundreds of miles, bounded on either hand by level-topped mountain ridges without an apparent break in their flat brown sides), either to Las Bela and the sandy flats of the Purâli delta, or to the palm-fringed valleys of Makrán and Mashkhel. If we move directly west we shall be landed in the wide spaces of the Kharán desert with Seistán on the western horizon. The desert of Kharán, and the yet wider wastes which are peopled by nomadic Baluch tribes between Kharán and the Helmund, have upon closer acquaintance proved to be infinitely less hostile to traffic than was supposed some years ago. A great central space of the desert is occupied by mountains, rough, jagged, and sun-scorched in appearance, but which, nevertheless, give rise to a fringe of fresh-water springs at the foot of their shelving slopes, about the clefts and edges of which vegetation is occasionally abundant. A trade route between Seistán and Quetta, passing through this desert space and touching these mountains, was not unknown to the mediæval Arab occupants of Baluchistan, and it has lately been re-opened to frontier trade. A marked geographical feature of the Kharán desert is the great swamp, or lagoon, which, under the name of the Mashkhel Hamun, absorbs the drainage of an enormous area of Southern Afghanistan and Eastern Persia of which the hydrography is unconnected with the sea. The sea-board sill or fringe of Persia and Baluchistan which contributes water to the Gulf or to the Arabian Sea is exceedingly narrow—perhaps less, on an average, than 200 miles in width. There is, in fact, no river of any importance draining into the sea between the Indus and the Euphrates.

The coast province of Makrán has played so important a part in the early histories of Indian occupation, and is still so intimately associated with frontier political problems, that a short reference to the peculiarities of its geographical conformation becomes necessary. Like the rest of the Indian frontier, the marked parallelism in strike in its principal mountain ranges is the prominent feature of their conformation. There are districts in Makrán (as there are in the basin of the Zhob north of Quetta) where many square miles of area are tight packed with an outcrop of innumerable little ridges, knife edged, and jagged, yearly diminishing in height under the influence of denudation, so that the intervening valleys are gradually filling and the ridges gradually lowering, until a line of sharp edges, presented by the thin strata of indurated clay protruding from the ground at an angle

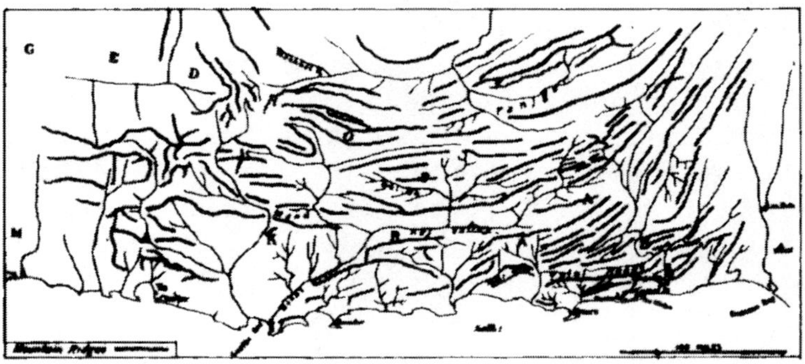

FIG. 15.—The Orography of Makrán.

indicating the general dip of the formation, is frequently the only sign left of a buried barrier of miles in length. And this natural action of levelling down, the progress of which can be so readily discerned on the smaller scale, is a dominant feature throughout the larger Makrán mountain system ; so much so, that Makrán might almost be called the land of disintegrating hills. The result to the traveller who crosses its stony wastes is inconceivably disagreeable. Excepting along the lateral valleys which intersect this Makrán wilderness from end to end he either encounters little but stone-covered flats where boulders lie thick as the pebbles on a sea-shore, or else he stumbles across the sharp edges of a protruding slate stratification, equally aggressive and more dangerous. The coast-line of Makrán is separated from the hills by a narrow sill of sandy littoral, broken, however, near the Hinglaz River by the square-headed buttresses of Malán, the feet of which are washed by the Arabian Sea. Here indeed is some variation in the usually rigid conformation of ridge and valley. Amongst the gigantic cliffs of Malán which overlook the deep-set valley of the Hingol River are narrow little gorges and ravines, each carrying its tribute of fresh water (so rare elsewhere in the country) to the blue depths of the main stream, and abounding in a freshness of green vegetation which is to be found nowhere amongst the hills of lesser altitude. The scenery is impressive and grand, as is usually the case where the rivers of the frontier burst through the barrier of frontier mountains ; and the rare beauty of this exception to the sterility of Makrán landscape has been recognised through past ages by a people who are ever ready to devote all things beautiful in Nature to the direct service of the gods. Near Hinglaz, hidden away in one of these green byways of the mountains, is a shrine (the shrine of Bibi Nani) which is celebrated from the Euphrates to the Ganges. Here Hindoo and Muhammadan pilgrims alike resort, each claiming the divine protection of the presiding goddess or of the departed saint, according to the tenets of their faith ; and neither recognising that the object of their veneration is probably the same goddess who was known to the Chaldeans under the same old world name (Nana) a thousand years before the time of Abraham. Nothing testifies so strongly to the unchangeable nature of the geographical link formed by Makrán between east and west than does this remarkable ziarat hidden away in the deep folds of the Malán Mountains.

A curious feature in coast formation is presented by the headlands of Ormara, Pasni, and Gwadur, which, with the enchanted island of Astola, lying between Pasni and Ormara, apparently indicate the former existence of a now submerged mountain chain in which these headlands were dominating incidents. The nature of recent changes that have occurred on the Arabian sea-coast will, however, be referred to hereafter. Meanwhile it should be noted that these headlands represent a series of great natural breakwaters which give to Makrán her only seaports, and it is from the harbours afforded by them that all routes northward into the interior of Southern Baluchistan diverge. It is at the remote stations of the Indo-Persian telegraph system which are established at these points on the coast that the only European occupation of Makrán at present exists. The port of Gwadur is exceptional. Gwadur is a dependency of Muscat, and is not subject to Baluch authority.[1]

The appearance of arid, sun-dried desolation that marks the coast scenery of Makrán when viewed from the sea, largely disappears inland. There is a scanty vegetation, consisting chiefly of coarse grass and tamarisk, wherever there is water to support it. Near Sonmiáni Bay, on the southern littoral of the Las Bela State, there are still the mangrove swamps which attracted the attention of the historians of Nearkhos 300 years B.C., and which now flourish in the neighbourhood of Karachi. Many of the spices which were so prominent in the ancient coast trade of the Arabian Sea may yet be found between the Hingol River and Karachi; the palms of Gwadur have now extended to the inland valleys, but the Gwadur myrtle has disappeared for ever. Passing inland from any of the coast ports, as the track winds through the intricacies of the closely massed system of inferior and barren ridges which intervene between the coast and the lateral palm-filled valleys of the interior, there are signs of a far more general occupation of the country in mediæval times than exists at present. There are the remains of terraced fields on the hill-sides with partially destroyed revetments, whilst here and there a few clumps of palms amongst the prevailing growth of tamarisk and scrub betoken a former period of careful cultivation. But taken as a whole, the words of the old Arab traveller and geographer, Ibn Haukel, who describes Makrán as "a vast country, mostly desert," may be accepted as a fair indication of the physical characteristics of that country even to this day.

[1] Written in 1899. There is a change in the telegraph system impending.

An exception to the general rule of arid desolation is found in the long valleys of the interior—the valleys of Kej, of Bolida, of Panjgúr and others of minor importance, where the wealth of cultivated crops overshadowed by a thick growth of feathery date-palms affords a scene of luxuriant beauty which is all the more impressive from the rugged nature of its setting of desolate hills. The dates of Panjgúr are celebrated, and, with wool, which is also of an exceptionally fine quality, and dried fish, form the chief exports of Makrán. Date groves of an inferior sort are also to be found in the salt swamps adjoining the Mashkhel Hamun ; but inferior as is the quality of the fruit grown there, its bare existence is quite sufficient to render these groves the object of constant raids. They have been the scene of much bloody border strife which continued almost without intermission until the question of boundary rights was settled by the Perso-Baluch Boundary Commission of 1895–96.

This very cursory description of the nature of the Baluch and Makrán mountain wilderness, that country of which the inhabitants are wont to say that "when God made the world He left the rubbish in Baluchistan," but which yet possesses many points of great physical beauty, would be incomplete without some account of the ancient highways of Southern Asia which pass through it India-wards, and which have assisted to shape the ethnographical, if not the material, development of the peninsula. For the sake of preserving continuity when associated with the routes of Afghanistan we will commence with the Southern Coast.

During many centuries of mediæval history eastern trade by land and sea with India was in Arab hands. For centuries previous to the Christian era it is probable that Arabs traded down the coasts of the Red Sea and Persian Gulf, and found their way to the Indus by hugging the coast-line of the Arabian Sea. Thence creeping round the Indian Continent they reached Ceylon and the East Indian islands. But in order to avoid the full force of the monsoon at certain seasons, they established an important post at Tiz, the ruins of which are to be found close to the telegraph post of Charbar, some 100 miles to the west of Gwadur, in Persian territory. From Tiz they established a somewhat circuitous overland route which is rendered obligatory, partly by the great barrier of the Malán mountains blocking the coast, and partly by the deep indentations, or arms of the sea, extending far inland from the present fishing village of Sonmiáni which lies at the head of the bay of that name. It was a well-known and well-formed highroad with regular stages and large flourishing towns at intervals which then connected Tiz with the Indus Valley. The stages were, however, long (as stages ridden by Arabs on camels usually are), and the full length of the journey from Tiz to the ancient city of Debal in the Indus delta was completed in far less time than we should now be able to traverse it by similar methods. This route passed by Turbat (near the ancient Kej) and then followed the Kej Valley to a point near its head. Passing by Las Bela and Uthal (formerly known under other names) it turned the barrier of the Sind frontier hills not very far from Karachi and debouched into the Indus delta.

When the Arab conqueror, Muhammad Kasim, invaded India and conquered all Sind about the year A.D. 720, he found no difficulty in traversing Makrán with his Syrian Arabs, Makrán being then an Arab dependency; and probably far more developed in the matter of internal resources than it has ever been since. No practicable military road to India from the west lies along the coast of Makrán, in spite of the fact that it denotes the line of telegraph communication between India and Europe; and yet it is near the coast that we find most, and clearest, evidences of successive migrations from Mesopotamia, Media, and Persia towards India. The Parsis of Bombay, last existing representatives of Zoroastrian supremacy in Persia, have here left evidence of their final exodus from Persia eastwards. Before them were Dravidian irruptions innumerable in prehistoric times, the traces of which can be found written in the face of the hills and valleys of

Southern Makrán in unmistakable characters ; and it was, as we know with historical certainty, along the coast-line that Alexander endeavoured to retreat when he lead his army out of India back to Persia. He failed, and he lost two-thirds of his broken force. He failed because he attempted to support his fleet with his army, and turned northwards, inland, too late. All the great immigrations of western tribes and armies through Makrán which have influenced Indian history and Indian ethnography must, however, eventually have broken through the Sind barrier at one point only—a point which is within striking distance of Karachi. It is a remarkable fact that we may examine the Sind ranges northward for 230 miles before we find again any really practicable break in them. There is no section of the western frontier of India so securely guarded against any approach from the west as that 200 miles of impassable barrier formed by the straight-backed Khirtar Mountains. At the end of it, 200 miles from the sea, we find the Mulla Pass, a long and circuitous defile which connects Kalát with the Indus plains at Gandava.

There are some historical authorities who think that the Mulla route may once have served a military purpose when Alexander despatched his general, Krateros, in command of the heavy division to make his way to Persia by some other line than that of the Makrán coast, although we know that the Mulla was only developed into a recognised trade route in later days, when Gandava became a great trade centre under the rule of the Arabs in Sind. We know that Krateros passed by Quetta and Kandahar to the Helmund, so that it appears to be equally possible that the one great open highroad to Quetta which has been recognised through all modern histories as affording the most direct access to Kandahar — the Bolan — was the route which he selected. Kalát, as already suggested, was ever a dominating position on those trade routes which connected Seistán with India by way of the Kharán desert, or by tracks passing through the deserts south of the Helmund.

Between Kalát and the Gandava plains the Mulla

route is the natural connection, in spite of its physical disadvantages, and it undoubtedly once possessed more importance than it does at present; but the most obvious, because the most direct and the easiest, connection between Southern Afghanistan and the plains of Sind passing through Baluchistan is the one which, in two branches, is now occupied by the line of the Sind-Peshin Railway, connecting Jacobabad with Quetta.

Greatest of all the mediæval cities of the Indus Valley was Multan. There were other great cities which have left nothing but a shadowy outline of their greatness on the spaces where they once stood; but Multan, which still lives, was ever the greatest trade centre of Western India. Its magnificent buildings and fabulous wealth; its mosques and its far-famed idol (which seems to have survived the introduction of the mosques); its spacious streets and gardens; its "sarais," and all the many seductions which gladden the heart of the weary traveller, placed Multan without a rival as the capital of Western India and the objective of every great caravan road which followed the Indus. There must have been a direct highway from Kalát and Quetta to Multan, a road to link Southern Afghanistan with India, very much straighter than that which followed the Bolán or Nari rivers into the plains.

Such a route is found in the Sakki Sarwar, which takes its name from a ziarat, or shrine, at the foot of the hills opposite Dera Ghazi Khan, and which is the route probably followed by Nadir Shah in the eighteenth century when he withdrew his victorious army from Delhi. A modification of the old route now connects Dera Ghazi Khan with Quetta and Peshin, and it is the only highroad crossing the border which is of any great importance between the Bolán and the Gomal.

North of the Sakki Sarwar, between that pass and the Gomal, the Sulimáni Hills (long supposed to be impenetrable from India) are practically riddled with intersecting tracks and passes of various degrees of difficulty, not one of which is, however, important, except as affording access to the border hills in case of military or political necessity.

Beyond the Sulimánis, on their western slopes, there extends a system of flanking lateral valleys (of which the Zhob is the longest) which connectedly form a line of military communication parallel to that range and (with reference to India) in rear of it. These valleys, with their olive-covered slopes and grassy declivities, are all under British occupation, dominated from a central position at Fort Sandeman; and thus the great band of Sulimáni Mountains, their rugged peaks and gorges, the rocky line of summits intersected by goat tracks, are held as securely as if they were occupied by military posts. Their ever-restless Pathan inhabitants find themselves with no back door of escape from certain punishment if, from their own position of independence, they venture to interfere with that of their neighbours. It is this (and the same principle holds good for all the Baluch frontier) rather than any wide distinction between the warlike characteristics of one tribe of Pathans and another, or between Baluch and Afghan, that renders our southern frontier safe from periodic eruptions such as have lately convulsed the north. Doubtless the conditions which govern Baluch existence, the system of tribal confederation approaching the feudalism of the middle ages, and the influence of the chief rather than that of the Mullah (which is a marked characteristic amongst Baluchis as compared with Pathans), has much to say to the apparent readiness with which they have accepted British control, with all the advantages of mutual inter-tribal toleration and goodwill.

But the Baluch is by heredity and by instinct quite as much a fighting man as the Pathan, and in many respects he is composed of far finer material. He is more chivalrous and less fanatical. He is of better physique and more temperate habits. What grander specimen of the border chieftain could be found in the record of any frontier highland history than was presented in the person of Azad Khan, the late ruler of Kharán, who at ninety years of age was as bold a rider, as swift and capable a leader of his unruly band of raiders, as powerful an athlete as any man of thirty who followed him? Nor is the marked difference of action pursued in the conduct of military tactics by Baluch and Pathan respectively altogether conducive to our recognition of the latter as the superior fighting man. It is characteristic of the two races that the Pathan should trust to the accuracy of a long-range rifle and his capacity for concealing himself behind the most elementary cover; and that the Baluch, finding himself outmastered in the open field, should die at the head of his men in one final effort to close with his enemy. There is no lack of chivalrous courage about the Baluch chief, and no cringing to the voice of any fanatical priesthood. His ancestry and his traditions are his pride, and his own right hand is his defence.

The complicated question of the ethnography of Baluchistan and its relation not only to the tribal distribution of the western frontier, but to a very large section of the Dravidian population of Southern India, is one which claims more exhaustive treatment than it can receive here. The geography of Herodotus, from which we learn the names of the tribes and people occupying the seventeenth Satrapy of the Persian empire (which includes a great part of modern Baluchistan), enumerates many peoples which can be identified to this day; and Arrian's history of Alexander's retreat further leads us to the conclusion that there was no vast difference between the distribution of tribes of Dravidian or Persian origin who occupy Baluchistan now and that of 2500 years ago. The governing race of Baluchistan was, until quite recent historical times, that of the Bolédi, a race which is mentioned by Ptolemy, and whose real name (according to Bellew) "seems to have been Bola, probably deriving from the Assyrian (Asura of the Mahabharat), Bael, Bal, or Bel." However that may be, it seems possible that they gave their name to Baluchistan. It was only during the eighteenth century that the Bolédi were dispossessed by the Gichki, a dynasty of Rajput extraction. The Dravidian peoples encountered by Alexander are still to be found where he found them, and we can trace a Dravidian ancestry for the Brahui (or Bar Rohi, *i.e.* the hill men), who hold all that impenetrable mass of hill frontier country which extends along the Sind border from Kalát to the sea. The date of the first Dravidian occupation of the Baluch frontier is lost in the mists of antiquity. It was certainly anterior to the great irruption of Aryan races from Central Asia about 2000 years B.C. Vast successive waves of Turanian immigration swept in from the west—from the plains of Mesopotamia and the highlands of Persia—and they must have included pre-Semitic races from ancient Chaldæa. Strange monuments of evident Turanian origin are to be found amongst the Makrán Hills; curious evidences of relationship to peoples who were buried in the valley of the Euphrates. Some of these human tides may have flowed through Southern Baluchistan, and creeping along by the coast-line down the western borders of the Indian continent may have spread into the jungles of the Central Provinces. Others, such as the Brahuis who still talk a language allied to that of the Dravidian tribes of Southern India, found themselves driven southward into a compact mass of hills on the Sind border with no convenient outlet to the east, and taking possession of this wilderness, have been able easily to hold their own against all comers through successive ages ever since. Thus the Dravidian and Persian ethnographical stock of Baluchistan is the earliest for whose existence we can in any way account, although there are indications of a yet earlier prehistoric occupation to be found in Arrian's account of those Makrán fish-eating savages who were encountered by the Greeks near the mouth of the Hingol River.

Grafted on to the early Persian, Dravidian, and Ethiopian stock, we find representatives of a vast number of other races all more or less historically modern. Chief amongst them, claiming precedence of all others, and rejoicing in the distinction of being "assal" (true) Baluch, are those tribes of Arabic origin who are best represented by the great confederation of Rinds.

The Arabs not only held possession of all the Indus Valley for centuries after its conquest by Muhammad Kasim, but they had colonised Southern Baluchistan, and turned Makrán into an Arab dependency, long ere that conquest was effected. Muhammad Kasim in his advance on India was largely dependent on the assistance afforded by the Arab governor of Baluchistan for the facility with which he traversed the country. Having once reached Sind there is historical evidence to show that the original Arab conquerors (who were recruited chiefly from Syria) never returned to their own country. They took "wives of the people," and as a natural consequence the Arab tongue ceased to be spoken in the course of a few generations. Hardly a word of Arabic (excepting in technical geographical expressions) is to be found in the vocabulary of the Baluch frontier now, and little or nothing remains of that remarkable and most successful invasion of India, except the Semitic features of a vast majority of the Rinds, and a tenacious clinging to traditions and genealogies which represent every Baluch chief of importance as a member of the prophet's own tribe.

Roughly speaking, the Rinds (Arabs), Naoshirwánis, *i.e.* the people of Kharán (Persians), and Brahuis (Dravidians), divide Southern Baluchistan between them. Northern Baluchistan, from Peshin to the Gomal, is in the hands of an ancient Pushtu-speaking people, represented by many tribes and tribal sections, of whom it is sufficient to say that they were mostly there in the days of Herodotus, before Alexander entered India. They are Pathans whose origin is lost in antiquity, and it is only in deference to political convenience that they are included within the borders of official Baluchistan.

Geographical information dealing with the general configuration of Baluchistan has been acquired within the last twenty years through the agency of the Survey of India. Previous to the commencement of systematic geographical surveys in that country there was little or nothing known which proved to be of any great use in the compilation of existing maps. Consequently the author is indebted chiefly to his own notes for the information contained in this chapter, so far as it deals with modern topography. In collecting data for such reference to the ethnography, archæology, and ancient history of the Baluch borderland as are herein to be found, the researches of members of the Survey parties employed in mapping the country were directed to points of interest indicated by the very few ancient and modern writers who have dealt with Baluchistan. Bellew is perhaps the principal authority, although his attention was directed chiefly to the neighbouring state of Afghanistan. Pottinger was one of the first to differentiate between the many Baluch tribes in modern times, and to give some shape to the ethnographical status of the country. There are ancient references to Baluchistan to be found in the work of Herodotus, who enumerates the tribes of the great satrapies of the Persian Empire. Arrian's history of the Greek retreat from India has also added much to our knowledge of ancient geography of Makrán. G. P. Tate's pamphlet, "Kalát," the Census reports of the Indian Government, and Thornton's "Life of Sandeman" may also be studied with advantage. The best maps are of course the sheets of the Indian Survey, which include the topography of the whole country—some of it on a fairly large scale. But they are difficult to get in England.

# CHAPTER III

## THE GEOGRAPHY OF THE FRONTIER: AFGHANISTAN

STATISTICS.—The independent kingdom of Afghanistan is about 500 miles in breadth and 600 in length from Herat to the Khaibar. Its area is about 215,500 square miles, and population about four millions.

It is bounded on the west by Persia; on the north by Central Asian states under Russian influence; on the east by the Independent tribes of the British frontier (touching British India at those points where we hold the passes into the country passing through tribal territory); and on the south by Baluchistan (touching India at the northern limits of British Baluchistan).

The government of the country is that of an hereditary monarchy, and its political status practically that of an independent state, subject only to British influence. The present Amir is Habibulla Khan, son of Abdur Rahman Khan, who succeeded his father in the year 1900.

There are five provinces in Afghanistan, viz. Kabul, Herat, Kandahar, Turkestan, and Badakshan, each under a provincial governor who distributes justice through the sirdars and chiefs on a feudal system which admits of many irregularities, but which is not unsuited to the temper of the people. The population is mixed, consisting chiefly of Duranis (or pure Afghans), Ghilzais, Tajaks, Hazaras, Aimák tribes and Usbegs.

The exact value of the revenue of the country is unknown, but a subsidy of Rx.180,000 paid yearly by the Indian Government is expended almost entirely on the army.

The army includes between 50,000 and 60,000 regular troops, besides twice that number of "kasidars," or irregulars, who are mostly mountaineers.

The cavalry (numbering about 8000) and artillery are well equipped, and form an efficient body of troops. There are at present more mountain guns in Afghanistan than in India, and it is probable that a rifle could be placed in the hands of every capable fighting man in the country. The Kabul workshops, under European supervision, turn out ammunition sufficient for the needs of the country besides guns and rifles. The Hazara corps of sappers and miners is also a most excellent factor of the regular service. The infantry is usually badly turned out, and the officers are uneducated and untrustworthy leaders in the field. The traditional Afghan army has more frequently bought its victories than won them by hard fighting.

The trade between Northern Afghanistan (Kabul) and India was registered at Rx.294,600 exports from India, and Rx.217,230 imports in 1899. The exports consist chiefly of cotton goods, indigo, sugar, and tea. The imports include horses, fruit, grain, drugs, wool, silk, cattle, hides, and tobacco. The heavy transit duties prohibit trade altogether between India and the countries north of the Oxus.

The trade between Kandahar and India amounted to Rx.263,880 exports from India, and Rx.329,920 imports into India in 1898–99. Three-fourths of the exports from India consisted of cotton piece goods. Three-eighths of the imports consist of raw wool, the remainder being chiefly fruit.

FROM the Gomal River which debouches on to the Indus Valley plains (here called the Deraját) near Dera Ismail Khan to the Malik-Siah Koh Mountain, the frontier landmark of Southern Seistán, the boundary of Afghanistan marches with that of Baluchistan already described.

From the Malik Siah Koh to the Helmund swamps northward it was determined by the Seistán arbitration of 1872. This part of it consists of a direct (but undemarcated) line dividing Seistán, and trending north-east till it touches the Helmund River just above the head of the irrigation system which waters the plains about Nasratabad. Nasratabad (the fortress of which place is called Husainabad, and frequently gives its name locally to the whole town) is the modern capital of Seistán. So far, the boundary of Afghanistan runs for about eighty miles through the flat alluvial districts formed by the Helmund delta, all of which were once irrigated and trained into one vast area of cultivation. The Afghan side of the line is now bare of crops, a wilderness no longer fertilised by the ancient irrigation which once distributed the Helmund waters from the great "bund" (or dam) of Kamal Khan by a central canal running westward past the ancient city of Taraki. On the Persian side the natural wealth of this whilom "granary of Asia" is fairly well sustained. From the point where the boundary meets it, the Helmund River itself becomes the boundary as far as the final swamps into which its waters are merged,[1] and from these swamps northward for about 200 miles there is no demarcated boundary.

The elevated plateau of the Perso-Afghan border consists of open undulating plains of sandy formation, varied by wide gravel-covered flats intersected at intervals by short ridges and isolated peaks, the last south-westerly

[1] Recent changes in the river's course have necessitated re-demarcation, and a commission is at present engaged on this duty.

offshoots of the mountains which dominate the province of Herat south of the Hari Rud. This formation is usually called "desert" in official publications, but the word is hardly applicable. Water is indeed scarce, and in the immediate neighbourhood of the central watershed which forms the natural boundary between Persia and Afghanistan, it is unobtainable. But there is a fairly constant vegetation of scrub—chiefly wormwood—and the profusion of low-

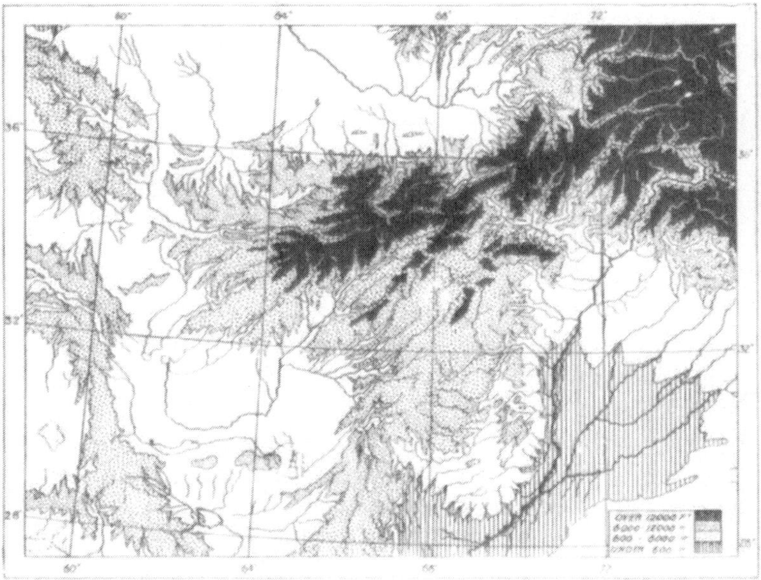

FIG. 16.—The Extension of the Hindu Kush from the Himalayas.

growing plants and flowers which appear after the spring rains in this wind-swept region entirely belie the appellation of desert. The native term for these wide, but not barren, sandy spaces (which are a marked feature throughout Afghanistan and Baluchistan) is "dasht," and that word will be adopted in future to denote an elevated plain, or talus, extending from the foot-hills of high mountains, sometimes sandy and affording freedom to lateral movement, and sometimes stone-covered and traversable with difficulty. The "dasht" is never entirely devoid of vegetation. Occasionally it is carpeted with grass and flowers, knee-deep and compact, something like an American prairie. The "dasht" is indeed to the nomadic peoples of these border countries what the prairie is, or was, to the Red Indian—his home, his world, the support of his flocks and herds, his happy hunting-ground. Absolutely barren desert is rare in Southern Asia. Where it occurs it is

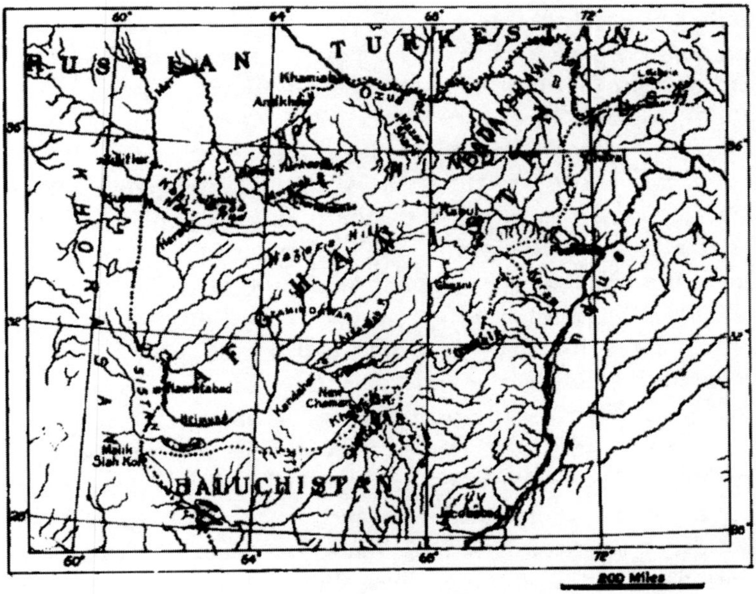


FIG. 17.—Boundaries of Afghanistan.

usually in connection with "kavirs" or swamps where salt strata underlying the soil effectually destroys all vegetable growth for many miles around a central depression.

A short space of demarcated boundary occurs near Hashtádun before touching the banks of the Hari Rud (the river of Herat), not far from the old town of Kuhsán. Thenceforward it is marked by the course of the stream to the now historical Russian post of Zulfikar, from which point to the Oxus River near Khamiáb it was demarcated and defined by pillars erected during the progress of the

Anglo-Russian Boundary Commission of 1884–86. From Zulfikar it cuts across two great affluents of the Murghab River (the Kushk and Kashán streams), touching a point on the Kushk River about sixty miles north of Herat, but separated from that city by the Koh-i-Baba Mountains. Thence it runs north-east through "Chol" and flat Turkoman "dasht" to the cultivation that borders the Oxus at Khamiáb. The "Chol" is but a vast procession of low hills cut out by the drainage action of ages from loess formations which, composed partly of washed-down detritus from the mountains and partly of blown sand from the great north-western deserts of Kara Kum, form a wide ramp stretching from the Band-i-Turkestan Mountains far northward into the plains of the Oxus. The Band-i-Turkestan are the northern offshoots of the great central mass of mountains which separate the Oxus plains from the highlands of Afghanistan. For the winter half of the year the Chol country is a barren and desolate region, especially beloved of marmots and rats. From off the face of it every vestige of vegetation has been swept by the fierce blasts of the autumn winds, until it presents the appearance of a desolate sea of rigid sand waves. In spring and summer it becomes glad with the brilliant hues of acres of tulips, poppies, and purple-headed thistles amidst knee-deep grass—a land of beauty, which the wild ass and the antelope share between them. There is little space in the narrow intersecting valleys of the Chol for cultivation, but it is probable that under the more settled conditions that have prevailed in that country during the last fifteen years, that little has been greatly developed. Passing about twenty miles to the west of the modern city of Andkui (the probable site of the ancient Antiokhia, built by Antiokhus, son of Seleukus), through the flat, but not entirely arid, Turkoman dasht to the saxsal covered sand dunes of the Oxus River and the cultivation of Khamiáb, the Afghan boundary at length touches the banks of the river. From this point to Lake Victoria (the great central lake of the Pamirs), for 650 miles, the Oxus defines it, and lifts it through every variety of plain and mountain scenery for 12,400 feet to the great reservoirs of the "roof of the world." The Oxus level at Khamiáb is about 1000 feet above sea ; at Lake Victoria it is 13,400 feet. Although the Oxus is not actually beyond the pale of Indian polity, it is so far removed from the Indian frontier that a consideration of the physical characteristics of the river itself would carry us too far afield. One noticeable feature may, however, claim a passing reference. Within historical periods this great central Asian waterway has shifted its course. A short distance south of Khamiáb the ancient bed may be traced through the shifting sands which surround Tash Kuduk, but whether it ever debouched into the Caspian Sea is still a matter of dispute amongst geographers. The Caspian has itself so changed its outline as to leave the nature of the connection uncertain. It is, however, probable that the gradual evolution of an elevated ridge, or anticlinal, which appears to be in process of formation through the plains of Afghan Turkestan parallel to the Oxus has affected the hydrography of the country. Rivers flowing northward from the mountains intervening between the Oxus plains and the Afghan highlands no longer reach the Oxus. They are lost in the great swamps and marshes which surround Akcha, or in the cultivated districts of Mazar-i-Sharif.

All the great plain lying between the Oxus and the central Afghan mountain system of Hindu Kush and its continuation westwards to the Band-i-Turkestan, is known as Afghan Turkestan. Beyond it on the north-east lies Badakshan, and beyond Badakshan, the Pamir region. The northern Turkestan province of Afghanistan is so far removed from the rest of the kingdom by the central mass of intervening mountains that it will be convenient to note some of its most prominent characteristics before following the Afghan boundary farther.

The western portion of Afghan Turkestan, which lies on the northern slopes of the Koh-i-Baba (intervening between Kushk and Herat), and of the Tirband-i-Turkestan, is a broken mass of rolling downs and Chol country easily traversable in any direction, grass-covered in summer and bare and wind-swept in winter. Through this western portion northward runs the Kushk River, the Murgháb, and its affluent, the Chaharshamba, all of which streams afford good and easy highways after leaving the mountains. Along the line of the Kushk River, southward from the Russo-Afghan boundary, extends the recognised highroad to Herat. Eastwards of this line of approach to Western Afghanistan no other line occurs until we reach the

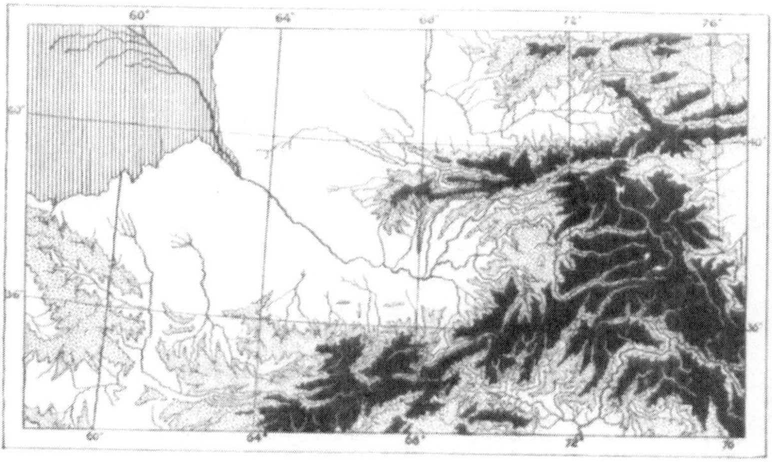

FIG. 18.—The Oxus Basin.

eastern limits of the Afghan Turkestan province at Mazar-i-Sharif. Between the Kushk and Mazar no practicable route exists across the wild elevated plateau held by the Mongol races of Afghanistan. From Mazar-i-Sharif to Kabul there is indeed a highroad, a sort of road which is sufficiently practicable for commercial purposes, although it crosses the backbone of the Hindu Kush, but which could be rendered quite impracticable for military purposes at many points on its devious course.

Between the Kushk River and Mazar-i-Sharif, and facing the Russian boundary, are the following Afghan towns: Bala Murghab, Maimana, Andkhui, Akcha, and

Balkh. All of them are situated on those lines of drainage which should (but which do not) reach the Oxus, and all command a certain amount of cultivated space, and boast local bazaars and markets. None of them are of political importance except Mazar-i-Sharif, which is not only the headquarters of the Governor of Afghan Turkestan, but is a very sacred Muhammadan centre.

Balkh, the "mother of cities" (said to have been founded by Nimrod), has figured in ancient history as the central

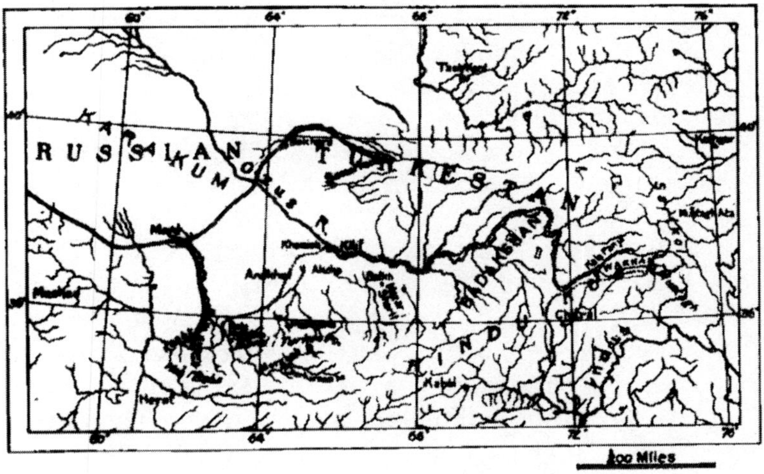


FIG. 19.—The Russian Position North of Afghanistan.

focus of Asiatic trade, dominating the vast extent of the lower Oxus plain once cultivated and teeming with a civilised population. This can never be again. Its glories have been overshadowed by the sacred shrines of Mazar-i-Sharif since the ruthless hands of such world's destroyers as Chenghiz Khan and his Mongol successors swept the walls of Balkh from their foundations and destroyed its inhabitants at recurrent intervals. It is also possible that the gradual evolutions of Nature, tending towards the elevation of the Balkh plain, may have had much to do with the decline of its fertility. Irrigation has become impossible where irrigation once existed.

Both Balkh and Mazar-i-Sharif possess considerable strategical importance from the fact that they dominate all communication between Kunduz (or Badakshan) and Kabul, as well as those lines of approach which lead southward from the ferries and crossings of the Oxus at Kilif.

From the eastern end of Lake Victoria (where now stands the pillar which denotes the introduction of scientific methods of geographical analysis into High Asia, and the junction of Indian and Russian surveys) an irregular line of pillar demarcation extending eastwards for about 90 miles brings the Russo-Afghan boundary to a trijunction with China amidst a scene of such mountain grandeur as the world can but seldom present. Here the three empires professedly meet. In order to render the geographical relations of India with Russia and China clear it will be as well to give a slight sketch of the central lines of these stupendous mountain formations which distinguish the "world's roof."

Between the vast elevated plateau of the Pamirs on one hand and the comparatively low level of the plains of Chinese Turkestan on the other, there exists an imposing mountain barrier (which we now call Sarikol), which assumes a meridional form where it bounds the eastern limits of the Pamirs. This barrier has been known in history either as the Taurus of classic literature, or as the Bolor Mountains of mediæval writers. It is divided into two distinct and approximately parallel chains, the westernmost of which is the true watershed between the Oxus and the Pacific, and the eastern, now known in our maps as the "Kashgar" range (through which the drainage of the western watershed forces its exit to the plains), is capped and pinnacled by the highest mountain-peaks of Asia north of the Himalayas. This eastern range, which is really subsidiary to the true watershed, far out-tops and dwarfs the western. It is here that the Muztagh Ata of Sven Hedin, 23,000 feet above sea-level, rears its white dome and pinnacles to the sky; and there are several other peaks but very little inferior to Muztagh Ata in altitude.

At its southern extremity (after circling round the head of the Tagdumbash Pamir, which diverts it from its meridional strike) the Sarikol system unites with the giant chain of Muztagh on the east, separating China from the sphere of Indian influence, and merges into the Hindu Kush range on the west. The axis of the Hindu Kush now becomes the Afghan boundary, which, striking off in a westerly direction, and separating the head waters of the Oxus from those of the Indus, follows an uneven trend for about 100 miles to a point where it overlooks Kala Panja on the Upper Oxus. Thence the main range changes its general direction to south-west, and for 300 miles more follows a much indented and most irregular course to the neighbourhood of Bamián, where it terminates in the Koh-i-Baba mountain system. Thus the Hindu Kush mountain chain (so called from the fact that a Hindu force was lost in the attempt to cross into Turkestan by a pass north of Kabul, now known as the Hindu Kush, or "dead Hindu"—also known as the Kaoshan), has a total length of about 400 miles, and throughout this distance forms the main watershed between the Oxus and the Indus. It is riddled with passes, the altitude of which varies between 12,500 and 19,000 feet, but it is a remarkable fact that this gigantic watershed, cradled amongst the highest mountains of the world, claims but one single peak of special prominence. The Sad Istragh (overlooking the Panja River) is, as far as we know, the highest on the watershed. Its summit is 24,170 feet above sea-level. But this is comparatively insignificant when compared to the magnificent array of snow-capped sentinels which guard the upper reaches of the Indus tributaries on the great spurs which are thrown off southwards. Although not much higher than Sad Istragh (Tirach Mir, overlooking Chitral is 25,400, and Rakapushi, between Hunza and Gilgit, 25,500 feet), they form by their comparative isolation and relative altitude to surrounding peaks and ridges, as well as by the grandeur of their outlines, a group of such magnificence as is only to be found again around Everest on the north-east frontier of India. The main axis

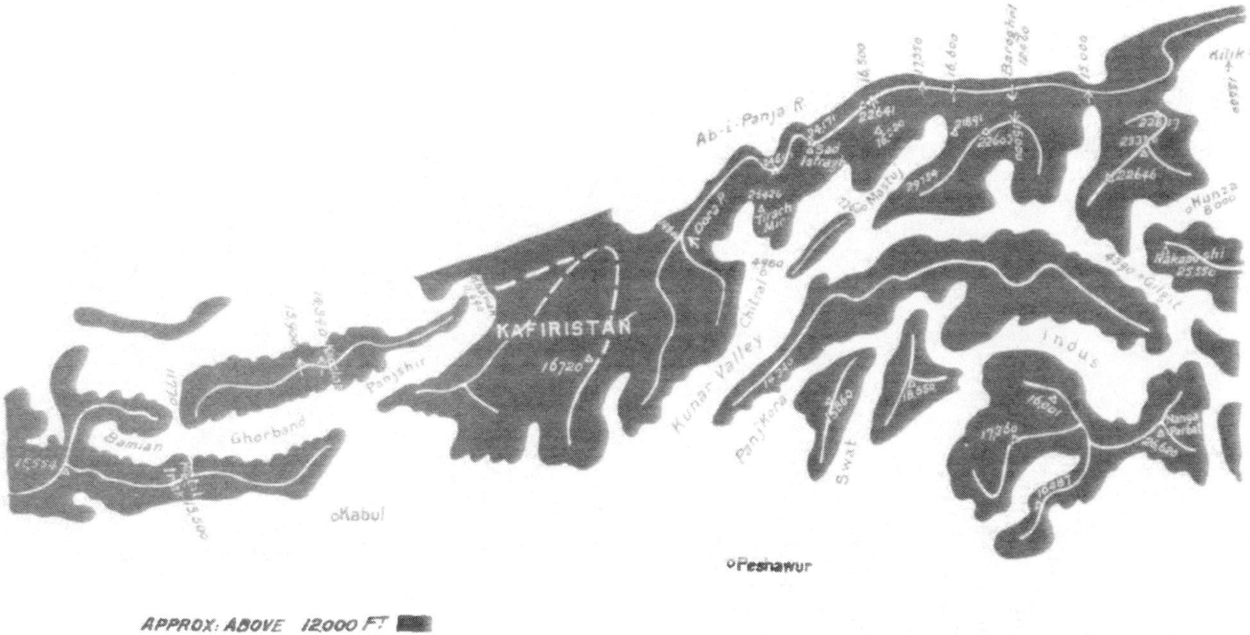


FIG. 20.—The Orography of the Hindu Kush.

of the Hindu Kush presents the aspect of a flattish-backed watershed (often falling to less than 17,000 feet above sea-level) with a surface scored by glaciers and indented by lakes, which have been found wherever its highest ridges have been explored. There is no continuous central line of water parting such as is common to its spurs, and in this particular it is not so perfect a natural boundary as would be offered by a more definite mountain backbone.

From the point where the Sarikol dividing barrier between Russia and China touches the Hindu Kush at its junction with the great Muztagh barrier between India and China, it becomes the southern boundary of Afghanistan, which territory lies between it on the south and the upper tributaries of the Oxus (or Panja) River on the north. Afghanistan thus stretches out a long arm to the north-east from Badakshan, touching China at its farthest eastern extremity, and preserving a narrow "buffer" between Russia and India. This long arm is the Afghan province of Wakhan, and it is worthy of note that at the point where the Hindu Kush overlooks Kala Panja on the Oxus, the northern spurs which comprise the full width of Afghanistan intervening between Russia and India are something less than ten miles in length, from summit to base.

Before leaving the Pamir regions (to which we shall not again revert) to trace the Afghan boundary southwards a few words may be added about the source of the Oxus. Many and various are the initial sources which have been assigned by different authorities to this historic river; but (as often happens) the clearer light derived from detailed survey proves them all to be more or less incorrect. First in the historical list was Lake Victoria (Wood's Lake), which lies near the head of the Great Pamir drainage. Next perhaps in importance is Lake Chakmaktin, the lake of the Little Pamir, whence flows the Aksu or Murghab River by a long and devious course to the main stream of the Oxus. This is undoubtedly the longest, if not the chief, tributary. Then we heard of the

Southern Wakhan tributary as claiming precedence from the fact of its draining the highest mountain basin and originating in the most stupendous glaciers. But it was found that Lake Victoria is not in itself a source, any more than is Lake Chakmaktin. Both lakes are but incidents in the course of glacier-fed streams[1] which derive their

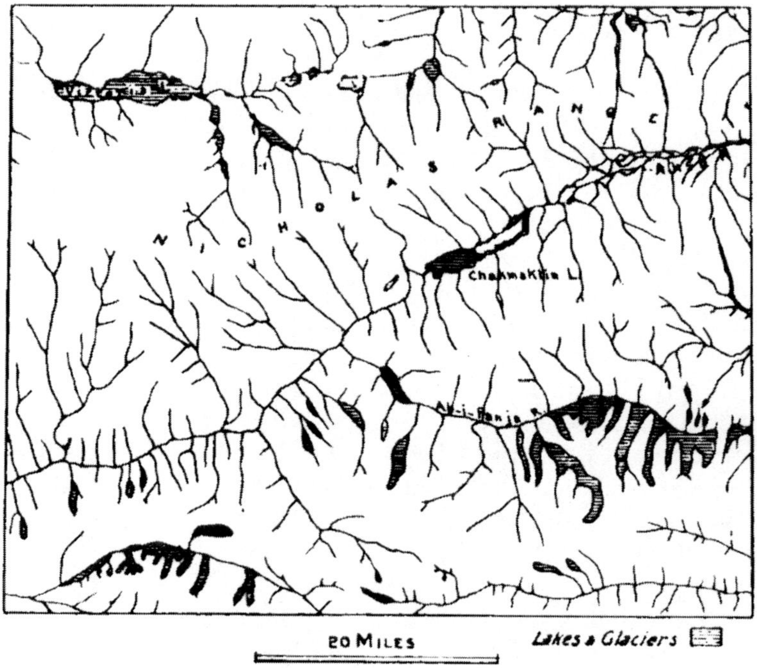


FIG. 21.—The Sources of the Oxus.

sources from above these lakes, and in the case of Lake Victoria, at least, form a subsidiary chain of lakes draining from higher altitudes. Chakmaktin was originally reported to possess a double outlet, east and west, and the report finally was proved to be nearer the truth than its subsequent contradiction. The main glacier torrent which passes through Chakmaktin actually divides in the swamps to the west of the lake, and part of it passes to the east to

[1] Themselves but the remains of ancient glaciers.

the Aksu, and part to the west down the Ab-i-Panja. Thus the glacier, or the great bed of glaciers and snowfields which feeds the Aksu, feed also this northern affluent of the Wakhan; and the same gigantic but indefinite snow-capped watershed of the Nicolas range which forms the glacial sources of the Aksu and Wakhan on the one side, forms those of Lake Victoria on the other. So that the glaciers of the Nicolas range in about East longitude 74, become the sources of the main affluents of the Oxus, excepting the southern head of the Wakhan. Whether the glaciers of Nicolas or those at the head of the southern affluent of the Wakhan are the mightiest, is another question. It is one which, at any rate, cannot be decided by a comparative estimate of the capacity of the various channels through which the glacial streams work their way to the great river.

From about the longitude of Kala Panja, where Afghan territory narrows to about ten miles of width, the boundary bends south-west, and still following the axis of the Hindu Kush, runs for nearly another hundred miles to the Dorah Pass, leading from Ishkashim in Badakshan to Chitrál. It is in this section of its length that the highest peaks are found, and even beyond this section, southwards from the Dorah, where a long spur defines the boundary for another fifty or sixty miles. Parting the Chitrál River from an important affluent called the Arnawai or Bashgol, in Eastern Afghanistan, we have as magnificent a natural barrier on the north-west frontier of Kashmir as can be found in the width of the Himalaya. It is true that between the trijunction of the three boundaries of Russia, China, and India, to the junction of the Bashgol River of Kafiristan with the river of Chitrál, two principal passes cross the Hindu Kush, besides several of minor importance. These two are the Baroghél (12,500 feet) and the Dorah (14,800 feet), and one of them (the Baroghél) presents no great obstacle for some six months of the year when not under deep snow; but the difficulties to passage presented by the routes in which these passes are incident is not to be measured by the altitude of the passes themselves, or by their own inherent ruggedness. The great barrier of the Hindu Kush, from the point where it springs from the Himalayan system to the east buttress of that spur which hangs over the deep channel of the Chitrál torrent, will never be broken in menace to India, unless the breaking of it is rendered possible by the construction of roads where none at present exist.

Near the junction of the Bashgol and Chitrál rivers the boundary of Afghanistan crosses the united streams and follows a subsidiary, but prominent, spur from the river banks to the water parting that hedges in the Chitrál

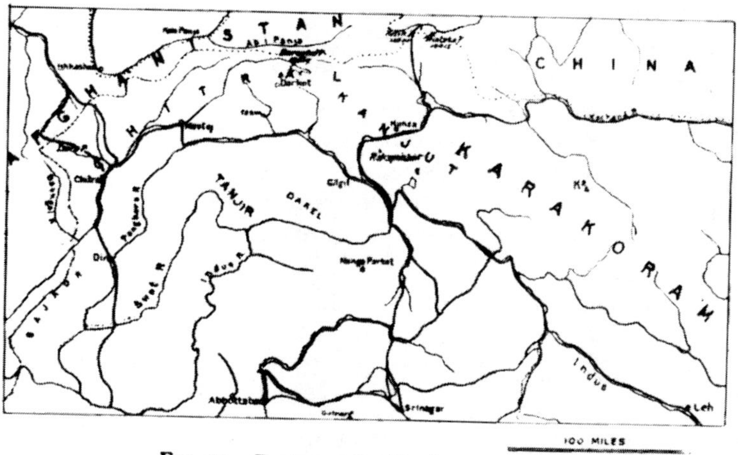


FIG. 22.—Routes on the Northern Frontier.

Valley on the east, and separates it from the territories of Dir and Bajaor. Once again it finds expression in a fine natural landmark, which, extending south-west towards the Kabul Valley, presents all the requirements of a good frontier line. Across this line there are passes in plenty, and one or two of them are of historical importance, for they are links in the chain of ancient communication between Kabul and India. Former invaders of India who based their operations on Kabul (and there have been many of them, from the Greek Alexander to the Turk Babar) preferred this line to the Khaibar, and invariably prefaced the advance on Delhi by the preliminary subjugation of Bajaor and Swat, which lay on the flank of their advance. The passes connecting the Kunar Valley with Bajaor have, however, never been crossed by a British force. Leaving the watershed at a prominent point overlooking the ancient town of Kunar, the boundary follows an irregular and undemarcated line through Mohmand territory, and across the Kabul River, till it touches the Khaibar route near our advanced post at Lundi Kotal. Here, then, Afghanistan and British India actually touch. From Lundi Kotal the boundary next rises to the summit of the Safed Koh range (overlooking the Afridi Tirah), and

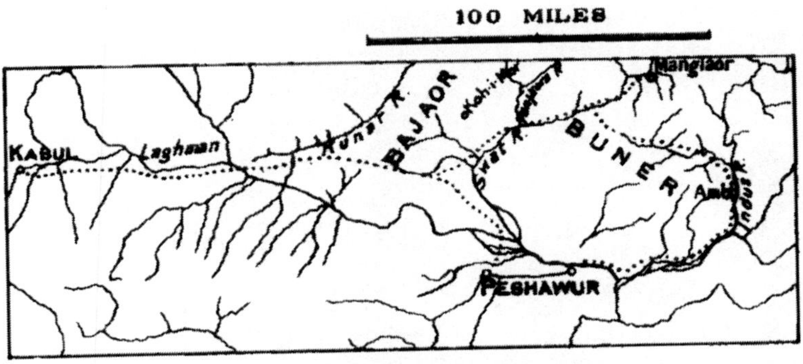


FIG. 23.—Mediæval Routes from Peshawur to Kabul.

passes along the watershed of this grand array of mountain-peaks till it drops to mark another junction between Afghanistan and British India at the Peiwar Kotal, on the Kuram route to Kabul. Cutting across the head of the Kuram, it defines the southern watershed of the river for some distance before reaching out across its Kaitu affluent to the well-defined frontier peak of Laram. Across the head of the Tochi River, and round the western border of Waziristan to Domandi on the Gomal, where Afghanistan ends and Baluchistan begins, we need hardly follow it in detail.

The principal feature to be noted about this boundary from the Pamirs to the Gomal is that it is the boundary of Afghanistan, and not that of India. Between it and the Indian frontier (the old frontier of Sikh supremacy, which we inherited with the conquest of the Punjab) is a subsidiary buffer of independent tribes occupying an intermediate province which may be divided into several sections. On the extreme north are those outlying districts tributary to Kashmir (Chitrál, Gilgit, &c.) in which we have lately taken much political interest. South of these, and between them and the Kabul River, is Bajaor and the Mohmand country. The Khaibar route falls between the Mohmands and the Afridis. We hold it as far as Lundi Kotal now, but it was lately in the hands of the Afridis, who occupy the Tirah country on the southern slopes of the Safed Koh, and, together with a number of less important tribes of various origin and troublesome names, spread between the Khaibar and the Kuram. Almost immediately south of the Kuram, and covering the head of the Tochi, we have the Waziris of Waziristan, who continue the occupation of this intermediate province to the Gomal River. Beyond these again are the Pathan inhabitants of the Sulimáni Mountains, which we have already referred to in connection with Baluchistan. This long narrow frontier buffer is a province of rugged tracts and impassable mountains from one end to the other; and from Chitrál to the division between Pathan and Baluch in Peshin, near Quetta, it is the habitat of Pathan tribes, who, whatever their origin (whether Afghan, Indian, or Skythic), all talk a common language, although they claim no sort of international cohesion or affinity. The ancient name for a large part of this border district was Roh (a name of Sanscrit origin, which, like Koh, means a mountain), and it will be convenient to recognise it under this name and to denote its inhabitants as Rohilla, the name under which they were known in mediæval ages. The Rohillas of Rohilkand are but an offshoot of the more ancient Pathans of Roh. Through this province of Roh pass all the most important lines of communication between India and Afghanistan, and it will be best to note them in order from north to south.

Every military expedition of consequence which has been directed against India, with Peshawur as the first objective and Lahore and Delhi as the ultimate aim of invasion, has been, so far as history can tell us, directed either from Kabul or Ghazni ; and it may be safely assumed that no comprehensive scheme for the conquest of India by land invasion could possibly overlook the lessons contained in the past records and leave this line unoccupied or unguarded. The position of Kabul in the geography of Afghanistan assures its continuance as a great centre of Asiatic trade quite as

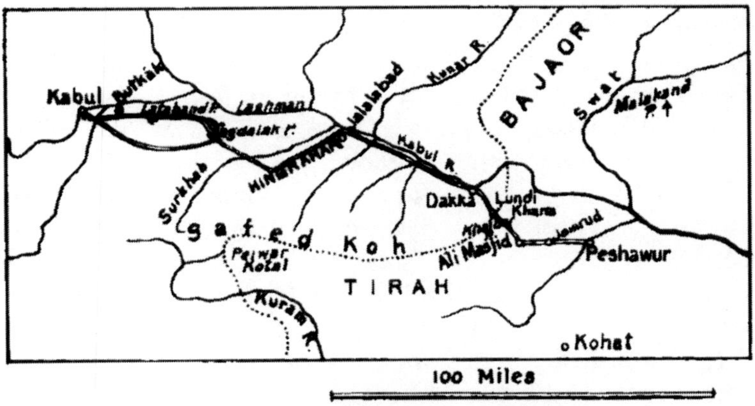


FIG. 24.—The Khaibar Route to Kabul.

much as it defines a point of strategic value ; so that of all the many routes which cross our frontier and lead from High Asia to the plains of the Indian continent that which connects Kabul with the ancient Afghan city of Peshawur (now our chief military outpost on the north-west) is by far the most important. A natural inference to draw from a look at the map of Afghanistan would be that the Kabul River valley would itself offer the best possible line along which to direct a great trade or military road between Kabul and Peshawur, but the Kabul River valley forms a remarkable exception to a general rule. Of the 170 miles of military road which separates the two cities, about 50 only follow the Kabul stream, and within the limits of those 50 the actual banks of the river are seldom approached. Travelling from Peshawur westwards, the course of the river is left far to the north. It is here that it forms a curve, or loop, extending into the mountain districts occupied by the Mohmands, all of which is hidden amidst the declivities of such a series of rugged and impassable defiles that nothing short of an engineering process of great complexity and difficulty could carve out a practicable route for wheels along its banks. Passing into the Khaibar, a few miles west of the little frontier fortress of Jamrud, the traveller is conducted over an excellent road passing under the shadow of the hill fortress of Ali Masjid, until, crossing a small subsidiary watershed at Lundi Kotal (3600 feet), it touches the limits of our frontier near Lundi Khana. So far we hold a narrow line passing through independent territory, steeply enclosed (for the most part) by lofty mountains inhabited by Afridi and Afghan Pathans who overlook and dominate the road; the former of whom have hitherto enjoyed the undivided responsibility of keeping it open for traffic both in the trade interests of Afghanistan and the military interests of India. At Lundi Khana (or very close thereto) the territories of the Amir and those of British India actually meet; and dropping down from the pass (or Kotal) to Dakka, the route passes into Afghanistan. The road is a good and sound highway, and so continues to Kabul; for it is to the interests of the Amir that the old line of communication of the Afghan war of 1878–79 should be maintained in fair order, and the Amir is ever ready to recognise the paramount importance of trade interests to his impoverished country. From Dakka to Jalalabad the road traverses the comparatively open plains which lie at the foot of the northern slopes of the great lateral range of Safed Koh, and here and there touches the banks of the Kabul River, but from a little beyond Jalalabad, at which point the Kabul and the Kunar (the river of Chitrál) unite, the road again diverges, leaving the Kabul River to water the Laghman plains to the north, and follows the banks of an affluent called the Surkhab, through the district of Ningrahar, to the historic pass of Pezwán. From Pezwán to the edge of the Kabul plain at Butkák, the road becomes involved among the intricacies of a mass of hills formed by the lower spurs thrown off from the western abutment of the Safed Koh. Through these hills there is more than one road to Kabul. It is near this point that the terrible defile of Jagdalak (so fatal to us in 1843) occurs, but an alternative route now traverses the plains above the defile leading directly to the Lataband Pass and to Butkák. The road between Lataband and Butkák runs parallel to the rivers at no great distance south of it, for here a stupendous gorge encloses the torrent in its course from the elevated plain of Kabul (7000 feet) to the plain of Laghman (3000 feet). From the edge of the cliffs above this gorge it is barely possible to watch the rush of the waters below. Between this gorge at Butkák and the open plains of Laghman the river falls some 4000 feet, passing through a succession of defiles that have hitherto effectually barred the way to road-making. The route just described is that known to us so familiarly as the Khaibar, a name which was originally adopted from a comparatively insignificant pass near Dakka, and is now applied to the whole road from Kabul to its debouchment opposite Jamrud into the plains of India. This was not, however, the route which was adopted for commercial or for military purposes formerly. The valley of Ningrahar was left to the south, and the Kabul River itself shaped the line through the Laghman (or Lamgan) plains more directly to a point at the eastern limits of those plains, where it passed by easy gradients into the Kunar Valley, and so, over the low watershed on its eastern banks, into Bajaor and Swat. The Khaibar route, or rather the Khaibar combination of routes, has always been, and must ever be, the most important of all lines of approach to the north-west frontier of India. It has figured in history from the remotest ages as the golden gateway to the wealth of the plains. Through it have passed not only those military invasions which have changed the destinies and dynasties of India, but it is through this channel that many tides of humanity have surged from age to age, which, rising in the recesses of Tartary and Mongolia, have swept southwards to repeople the land of the sun. Military invasions have passed into India by other routes; and the southern borderland, as well as the northern, has witnessed many irruptive human tides, but none have possessed such influence in shaping out the destinies of this great continent in the past, and none are so likely to prove of paramount importance in the future.

Next to the Khaibar, and separated from it by the Safed Koh range and its subsidiary spurs and offshoots (enclosed amongst which are the Afridis of Tirah, the Orakzais, Turis, and many other Pathan Rohilla tribes), is the Kuram Pass. Here again we traverse the full width of that independent frontier province which we call Roh, and meet the Afghan on his own border at the Peiwar Kotal. Just as Peshawur forms the base or starting point in India for the Khaibar route to Kabul, so does Kohat stand as the base for the Kuram line of route to the same goal.

FIG. 25.—Peshawur to Kohat.

Between Peshawur and Kohat there is a connecting highroad which is the first link in a long line of communication passing down the frontier beyond Kohat, parallel to the line of the Pathan hills, and linking up all the frontier stations between Kohat and the Sind border. It connects Bannu (or Edwardesabad), Dera Ismail Khan, and Dera Ghazi Khan with the north. The frontier province traversed by this road bordering the Indus, and lying between that river and the hills, is usually termed the Derajat. Between Peshawur and Kohat, however, this most important military road does not run parallel to the Indian frontier as defined by the old Sikh boundary (which is still the boundary of British India), because of an extension of the hill formation eastwards towards the Indus, which crosses the line of connection almost at right angles midway between the two places. Round the base of this extension the British India frontier line was drawn in conformity with its general frontier elsewhere at the base of the hills (*i.e.* the farthest limit of cultivable soil) when laid down by our Sikh predecessors in the Punjab. Across this salient extension of the frontier mountains the road from Peshawur to Kohat is carried, and thus a considerable section of it lies within the limits of independent territory, and we are ourselves dependent on the goodwill of the Jowaki occupants of these hills for the maintenance of our right of way. This is, however, no more or less than happens in the case of every route to Afghanistan which crosses the independent hills.

From Kohat (which lies under the southern slopes of this Jowaki hill extension) the highway to Kuram runs first upwards through the lower Miranzai valley, and then, crossing a flat water-parting, drops with a continuance of its south-westerly trend to the base of the Kuram Valley, following the course of the upper Miranzai. This Miranzai route from Kohat to Kuram lies altogether under the shadow of the Orakzai and Afridi hills, and is dominated through a great part of its length by the Samána range—a range which defines the shape of the valley on the north, and thus renders the occupation of it a necessary corollary to our retention of Kuram. The Kuram Valley itself offers no such topographical difficulties to advance as does the Khaibar. It is an open and well-populated valley, full of the ancient sites of towns, showing it to have been a valuable asset to Afghanistan in times past; and it is not until the head of it is approached near the Peiwar Pass that it thrusts itself into the deep gorges of a mountain valley.

Before this happens, however, the road leaves the river and passes under the upper ridges of the Safed Koh (from the heights of which one may look down on the Khaibar route northward and that of Kuram to the south) and continues at a high level till it dips again into the valley of the Logar leading northward to Kabul. In this interval it surmounts the Peiwar Pass (9200 feet) and the

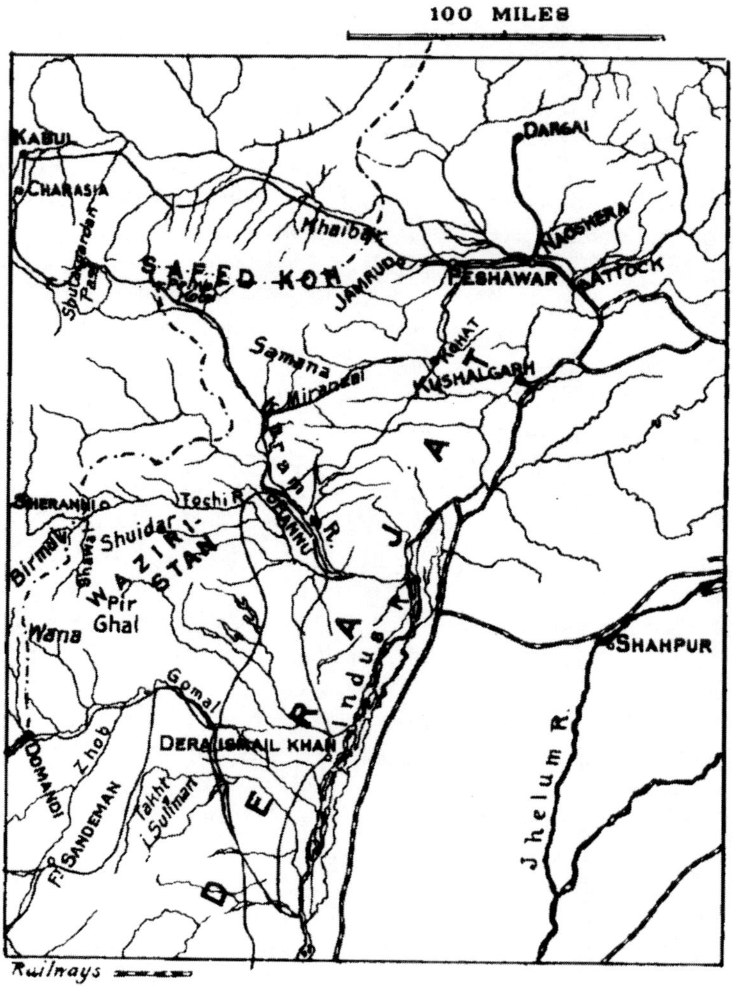


FIG. 26.—The Frontier Railways.

Shutargardan (11,900 feet); both of them passes over southern spurs of the Safed Koh, which range culminates above the Peiwar in a gigantic peak 15,600 feet above sea-level. Along the reaches of the Logar, and through the gap in the encircling hills of Kabul, which occurs near Charasia, we need follow it no farther. It turns the western extremity of the Safed Koh, and passes over the high level of the Afghan plateau, never dropping again to a level much below 7000 feet above sea-level.

At the point where it debouches on to the Logar plains, it is about equidistant from Kabul and from Ghazni, and between neither of these important centres of Afghan political authority is there any great physical obstacle to be encountered. The great altitude of the Shutargardan Pass alone renders it a barrier to Afghan trade with India.

The next gateway of importance between Afghanistan and India is afforded by the Tochi Valley, which is based on the frontier station of Bannu or Edwardesabad. The Tochi River is an affluent of the Kuram, which it joins not very far from their united junction with the Indus. It takes its rise in the western slopes of the Waziristan mountains, and the Pathan people who occupy this mountain district (called Waziris or Wazirs) intervene as an independent barrier between Afghanistan and India in continuation of the Roh province which has been intersected by our occupation of the Kuram Valley.

Formerly, no doubt, the Tochi formed the shortest connecting link between the capital of Afghanistan, once centred at Ghazni, and those plains of India from whence the material financial support of the unstable kingdom of Afghanistan has ever been derived. It was down this pass (according to all local tradition) that Mahmud of Ghazni used occasionally to sweep when Multan and Sind rather than Peshawur and the Punjab were his immediate objective, followed by hordes of irregular horsemen (undeserving the name of cavalry), and vast companies of Pathan freebooters who played the jackal to his leading, during a series of raids which lasted through the opening decades of the eleventh century. It is not, and it never has been, a great trade route, and it is, in part at least, still one of those unravelled knots in frontier geography which require further investigation before its exact position in the scale of importance amongst north-western gateways can be determined.

Up to the lately demarcated frontier of Afghanistan the Tochi is a fairly wide and well-cultivated valley, with a gradual but not excessive gradient, rising towards the comparatively narrow band of stiff and rugged mountain ridges (reaching to 12,000 feet in altitude) which intervene between the cultivated tracts of Sherannia and the uneven plateau which lies eastward and southward of Ghazni. Its importance to us is chiefly strategical, for it dominates the ever-restless confederation of Waziri clans to the south, who will never cease from troubling until they find themselves permanently outflanked. Between Ghazni and our advanced posts in Kuram and on the Tochi the direct distance does not differ largely from that between Kabul and our advanced post on the Khaibar; one hundred and twenty miles would cover either of them. The actual distance of intervening route would, of course, largely exceed this direct measurement.

South of the Waziri Switzerland, and dividing it from the northern buttresses of the great Sulimáni system of Baluchistan, is the Gomal River, affording yet another great open highway to the Afghan plateau. The Gomal route is the oldest of all trade routes. Down it there yearly pours a succession of Khafilas led and followed by thousands of well-armed Pathan traders (called Povindahs) from the plains of Afghanistan to India. The Povindahs mostly belong to the Ghilzai tribes, and are not therefore true Afghans. Leaving their women and children encamped within British territory on our border, and their arms in the keeping of our frontier political officials, the Povindah makes his way southwards with his camel-loads of fruit and silk, bales of camel and goat hair or sheepskin goods, carpets and other merchandise from Kabul and Bokhara, and conveys himself through the length and breadth of the Indian peninsula. He may be met with in the extreme south of Madras, or on the westernmost edge of the western coast, but the Ghilzai Povindah does not leave the shores of India. He returns yearly to the cool summits of the Afghan hills and the open grassy plains, where his countless flocks of sheep and camels are scattered for the summer grazing. He leaves it to the Pathan Kakur of the Baluch highlands to travel seawards to Australia or South Africa as camel driver or contractor, and there to make himself objectionable in out-of-the-way settlements by his truculent behaviour. The point at which the Afghan frontier crosses the Gomal is called Domandi, and it is north of this, on the upper tributaries of a comparatively small affluent which here joins the Gomal, that those plains of Wana are situated which have lately attracted attention in political and military annals.

Wana commands the western slopes of Waziristan, and overlooks the upper course of the Gomal, which is here still confined in the narrow waterways of a mountain region, whilst from its northern watershed one may look down the valleys of Birmul and Shawál formed by the head affluents of the Tochi River. The Tochi thus encircles the main peaks of the Waziristan mountains, which tower above these valleys to a height of 11,500 feet above sea-level.

It is impossible to enter into any detailed description of such immense variety of scenery as is to be found on the Pathan frontier in immediate connection with those main routes which we have already indicated as forming the chief highways into Northern India ; but amongst the minor valleys Birmul perhaps takes precedence by right of its natural beauty. Here are stretches of park-like scenery where grass-covered slopes are dotted with clumps of deodar and pine and intersected with rivulets hidden in banks of fern ; soft green glades open out to view from every turn in the folds of the hills, and above them the silent watch-towers of Pirghal and Shuidar, the western guardians of Waziristan, look down from their snow-clad heights across the Afghan uplands to the hills beyond Ghazni. Not even the rugged limestone cliffs of the Kaisargarh, chief amongst the Sulimáni peaks, backed by the forest of chilghôsa pine which clings to its crest, and split to its foundations by waterways which intersect its terrific spurs and buttresses, can rival the softer beauty of those western slopes of the Waziri mountains. But such scenery as the heights of Kaisargarh or the valley of Birmul may present is unusual on the Indian frontier south of Peshawur. The official who passes an uneasy life amongst the Pathan tribes of the frontier has not much to say about the beauties of Nature as a general rule. Natural landscape beauty, indeed, may here be measured to a certain extent by altitude. The low ranges of sun-scorched, blackened ridge-and-furrow formation which form the approaches to the higher altitudes of the Afghan upland, and which are almost as regularly laid out by the hand of Nature in some parts of the frontier as are the parallels and approaches of the attack under the superintendence of the engineer who is besieging a fortress —these are by no means "things of beauty," and it is this class of formation and this form of barren desolation that is most familiar to the frontier officer. It is true that the strata of clays and silts which overlie the salt formations found in certain sections of the lower hills of the frontier are distinguished by shades and tints of colour that are as varied as the coloured sands on the southern coast of England. But shades of delicate purple and grey will not make up for the absence of the living green of vegetation ; and the fantastic outlines assumed by disintegrating masses of conglomerate schist is frequently impressive only from its weird and outrageous defiance of all the rules of Ruskin in relation to lines of landscape beauty. But with higher altitudes a cooler climate and snow-fed soil is found, and as soon as vegetation grasps a root-hold there is the beginning of fine scenery. The upper pine-covered slopes of the Safed Koh are as picturesque as those of the Swiss Alps ; they are capped and crowned by peaks whose wind-swept altitudes are frozen beyond the possibility of vegetation, and are usually covered with snow wherever snow can lie. In Waziristan, hidden away in the high recesses of its great mountains, are many valleys of great natural beauty, where we find the spreading poplar and the ilex in all the robust growth of an indigenous flora. Waziristan is, indeed, a miniature frontier Switzerland. South of the Gomal, and beyond the striking scenery of such mountain masses as Kaisargarh, we find in the uplands, above the line of the barren border ridges, softer spaces of rounded outline, where the long sweeping spurs of subsidiary hills are covered with forests of the wild olive tree, which here attains to an enormous size, and forms as distinctive a landscape feature between Fort Sandeman and the western slopes of the Sulimánis as in Southern Italy. Farther south again, in the hills that circle about the head of the Peshin Valley, at still higher altitudes (8000 feet or thereabouts), are forests of juniper. Here the ragged growth of twisted and knotted trees presents a fresh characteristic of weird scenery such as is probably not to be matched in all India. Ziarat, the hill station of Quetta, which lies on the slopes of Kalifat (the highest mountain of Baluchistan), is surrounded with juniper forest.

On the grandeur of those approaches to the heights of Baluchistan and Afghanistan which are carved out of the hills by water-channels forming gigantic rifts (such as the well-known Chappar rift on the Harnai line of railway) there is no space to dilate. Familiarity with them can only breed a growing wonder at the tenacity of those primeval waterways which, through an immeasurable past, have ever retained their original course.

Passing on to the elevated plateau or uplands of Afghanistan (averaging 6000 feet towards the north, and falling to 4000 feet above sea-level as it approaches the boundary of Baluchistan on the south-west—the "hinterland" of the Indian frontier lying within that boundary), we have to add a few general notes on its geographical conformation, its ethnography, and its possibilities of economic and strategic development.

Afghanistan is a political expression denoting the territory ruled over by the Amir of Kabul. It is not (necessarily) the land of the Afghan, for the Afghan extends his occupation over districts which are beyond the Amir's control. Neither do the Afghans occupy Afghanistan exclusively. The Afghan represents the ruling race amongst a mixed agglomeration of tribes of varied Asiatic nationalities who divide the country between them. The Afghan speaks of his own country as Khorasán, and he distinguishes himself as Durani—or Ben-i-Israel—leaving the name "Afghan" to be applied to him by foreigners, *i.e.* by the majority of the inhabitants of Afghanistan. The plateau of Afghanistan is rough and uneven, and it is scored with mountain ranges. These, again, are intersected by valleys, elevated and narrow in the Kohistán (the hill districts) of the north, but which widen out into broad areas towards Kandahar and Herat on the south and west, forming the wide "dasht" so familiar to the records of our Afghan campaigns. Chief amongst these ranges are the Hindu Kush, itself but the northern section of that great trans-continental watershed, which extends from the Himalayas of the Pamirs across Afghanistan and Persia to the Caspian.

From its Himalayan origin to the Dorah Pass (connecting Badakshan with the Chitrál river basin) the Hindu Kush range has been sufficiently described as the boundary of Afghanistan. From the Dorah, westward and southward, till lost in the hills of the Koh-i-Baba, south-west of Kabul, it is the northern bulwark of the Kabul province. From its geographical axis great snow-fed tributaries descend through the unmapped maze of Kafiristan and the more open valleys that lie west of Kafiristan, to the Kabul river, forming almost without exception the only practicable lines of approach through the otherwise impassable mountains of Kohistan and Kafiristan.

Somewhere amongst the snow-bound fastnesses of the higher peaks of Kafiristan the Hindu Kush loses its flat-backed formation, and develops into a double system of parallel ranges, forming two long narrow lateral valleys which, draining from opposite directions to a junction, eventually find an outlet through the southernmost ridge to the broken plains of the Koh Daman (the "skirts of the mountains") north of Kabul. These two valleys are the Panjshir and the Ghorband respectively, whose waters unite at Charikar to form the chief head tributary of the Kabul River.

Thus Charikar becomes practically the guardian fortress of all passes which cross from Turkestan into the valleys of the Panjshir or Ghorband, and these passes are many and important. The Khawák, at the head of the Panjshir (11,600 feet), is now a well-known and much-

FIG. 27.—Routes from Kabul over the Hindu Kush.

traversed trade route with Turkestan. It is said to be kept free from snow during the winter months by a systematic process of clearing; posts of workmen being established at intervals for this express purpose; and thus it is maintained open to Khafila traffic all the year round. Not less energy has been shown by the late Amir in opening up another great trade route crossing the main watershed of the Hindu Kush at Chahardar (13,900 feet), and dropping southwards into the Ghorband Valley. This was the route followed by the Russo-Afghan Boundary Commission party on its return from Turkestan to Kabul in 1886, and it has since been developed into a highroad; but the Chahardar Pass is too elevated to be always practicable in the winter months. Curiously enough it was neither of these two passes, but one intermediate, called the Kaoshán, or Hindu Kush (14,300 feet) (the name of which was subsequently transferred to the whole mountain range), which has been the recognised gateway through all ages from High Asia into Kabul and India. It was well known to the Greeks, and Alexander made use of it, assisted no doubt by Kyrenian emigrants who were already colonising Andarab in Badakshan. Long before the time of the Greek it was the pass utilised by the inrushing hordes of Aryans, Skyths, Goths, Turks, and Mongols, who have overwhelmed Kabul from time immemorial, and who finally peopled India. It is, indeed, the highway of history from High Asia to India. Even those mighty bands of emigrants, who started from the north of China to discover a more congenial home in the south, appear to have passed westwards to this entrance, finding no way across the Hindu Kush and its great offshoots farther east.

But the great altitude of the Kaoshán renders it liable to interruption for many months in the year, and the natural difficulties of other passes of less altitude having been overcome by artificial means, this historical pass will in future rank low in the scale of practicable gateways to the plains of Kabul. Another historical crossing of the main watershed between Turkestan and Afghanistan occurs west of Kabul, where the Kotal-i-Irak (13,500 feet) leads into the valley of Bamián, so celebrated for its rock-cut figures and other Buddhist relics; but west of this we may search in vain for any open way southwards from the Oxus basin till we reach Herat; for the Koh-i-Baba, the Band-i-Baián, and other ranges north of Herat, merging into each other, form one continuous chain of elevated water parting, which, with the intricate system of subsidiary spurs thrown off northwards, present an effectual barrier to approach from the north. Thus, noting that the northern approaches to Afghanistan are entirely concentrated on two important lines—*i.e.* those of Kabul and of Herat—we may leave that part of Afghanistan which forms the Oxus basin and turn to its southern provinces which form the basin of Helmund.

The three great cities of Kabul, Kandahar, and Herat, each of which is the capital of a province and under a distinct local government, form the points of a triangle, of which the sides Kabul-Kandahar and Herat-

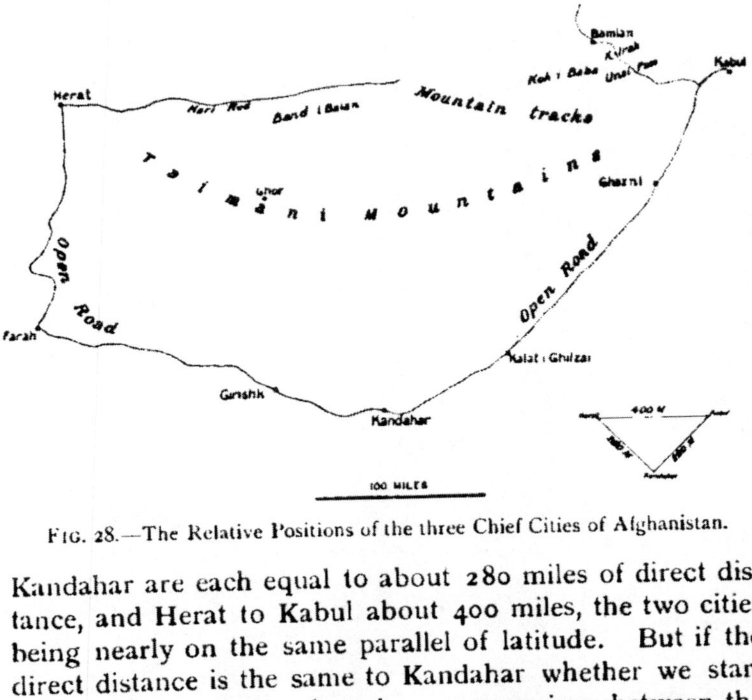


FIG. 28.—The Relative Positions of the three Chief Cities of Afghanistan.

Kandahar are each equal to about 280 miles of direct distance, and Herat to Kabul about 400 miles, the two cities being nearly on the same parallel of latitude. But if the direct distance is the same to Kandahar whether we start from Kabul or Herat, there is no comparison between the two routes in regard to the facility with which that distance may be traversed. From Herat to Kandahar there is indeed no direct route across the intervening wilderness of Taimani hills occupied by the Hazara Mongols of the Chahar Aimák. As far as the ancient capital of Ghor there was, indeed, once in the days of long ago, a trade route which was well known and much frequented; but it has passed into the stage of forgotten highways, and Ghor itself is now to be numbered only amongst the dead cities of Asia. It is hardly recognisable in the few broken ruins which lie amidst the desolate hills of this forsaken region. The Khafila route from Herat now passes southwards parallel to the Persian border to Farah, and thence reaches Kandahar by way of Girishk—a circuitous route of not less than 360 miles in length—a route which

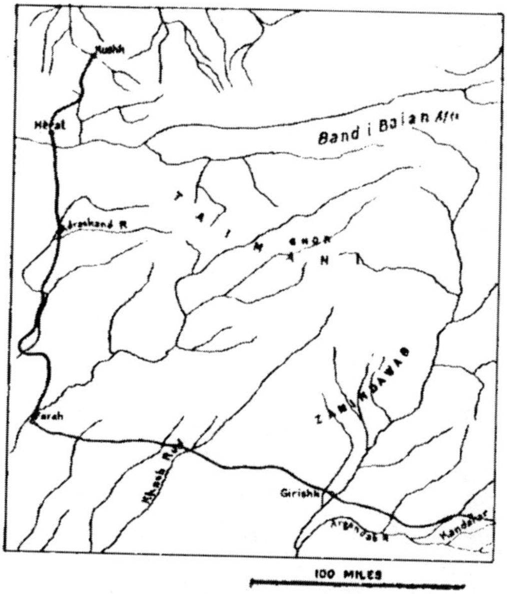


FIG. 29.—The Route from Herat to Kandahar.

traverses wide spaces of sandy and waterless "dasht," and is flanked throughout by a region containing the fiercest and most fanatical tribes of the Afghan community. Nevertheless it taps all the best developed and most civilised centres of western Afghan trade. From Kabul to Kandahar, on the other hand, is a straight highroad hardly to be matched for excellence by any of the best roads in Europe of equal length. It passes through Ghazni—once also a capital of Afghanistan—a famous city of palaces and of fabulous wealth, the centre of all authority in the days of the great Mahmud, and the military base of innumerable incursions Indiawards. Nothing now is left of the glories of the past Ghazni but one or two minars standing erect in a wilderness of desolation, silent witnesses to the mutability of Afghan greatness. But the connecting road between Kabul on the one hand and Kandahar on the other (to which latter place it is linked by the rock fortress of Kalat-i-Ghilzai) is indestructible from its geographical situation. It follows the main lines of central drainage, and the main strike of the hills which flank it on the north.

Whilst Kabul, then, dominates all routes converging on India on the extreme north-west of the Punjab, it also dominates (more or less) those which gather in by Kandahar and thence are directed towards the southern extremity of our western borderland. This, doubtless, is the reason why Kabul rather than Kandahar or Herat has held the keys of India's destiny so surely and so often during the countless ages of India's chequered history.

The three ruling Afghan cities, Kabul, Herat, and Kandahar, differing largely in the conditions of their population and environment, are all much of the same construction. Each of them occupies approximately a square mile of enclosure, and is protected by an outside wall covering a citadel which overlooks and commands the city. The leading feature in each is a bazaar with four streets radiating from a central "Charsu" or market-place, covered in, and roofed for protection from sun and rain. The markets themselves are hardly to be distinguished from most well-known Indian bazaars, and present the same apparently incongruous admixture of retail trade and manufacture; the same busy, jostling activity in the street, and the same indolence in the flanking lines of open-fronted shops that we see in all Indian markets. Piles of magnificent fruit, including melons, apples, grapes, pomegranates, peaches, walnuts, and apricots are a distinguishing feature in many of them. Work in copper, brass, and iron, earthenware and pottery shops, eating houses and tea shops; silk goods from Bokhara, "numnahs" and carpets from Central Asia and Turkestan, "pushmina" and woollen materials of local manufacture, sheepskin rugs and coats ("postins"), with the usual establishment of butchers, bakers, tailors, and bootmakers are to be found in all. There is a fair trade also in Russian and English goods. In the year 1886 English piece goods predominated in the Kabul market, where also Russian crockery ware was much in favour; but the facilities afforded to Russian trade by railway development have acted largely in favour of Russia since then. On the other hand, a cosmopolitan taste for many of the luxuries of civilisation (including soap) has lately been introduced by the energy of the firm which is represented by an English manager at Kabul; and the late Amir's own determined support of the economic developments of his capital has introduced so many modern improvements that a strong line of distinction must now be drawn between Kabul and her sister cities. In estimating the mutual value of the trade relations that exist between Afghanistan and India it must be remembered that the tide of trade sets almost entirely southward. Never since Afghanistan was a part of the Durani empire of Ahmad Shah has there been the opportunity that is afforded by long periods of peace for the development of the internal resources of the country sufficient to render it self-supporting. A large agricultural population has no doubt been able to subsist on the produce of irrigated cultivation, for the soil of Afghanistan is fruitful and the climate kind, and the only requirement for good harvest is a fair supply of water and labour. But the periods of peace have been too short to admit of any large development of cultivation beyond the limits absolutely necessary for bare subsistence, so that the demands of the army, and the necessities of a hungry and turbulent nobility, have hitherto been met by periodic raids on India and appeals to the force of arms.

Even now, after twenty years of fairly settled Government under the Amir Abdur Rahman, Afghanistan is but in her cradle of national economic development. She still looks to India for material support, and it is probable that her army could not be held together without liberal yearly contributions from India. Doubtless every year of peace makes greatly for the increase of her internal wealth and national growth, but the views of the Kabul Government, under Abdur Rahman, on the subject of revenue, taxes, and trade imports, have not been conducive to commercial development. The trade of Afghanistan, such as it is, sets southward rather than northward for the reason that the Central Asian States and districts north of Afghanistan produce much the same marketable commodities that Afghanistan itself produces, and that they trade through Afghan territory to India. The heavy duties levied by the Amir's officials at frontier posts have forced a good deal of this Central Asian trade westward lately, so that carpets of Turkestan, for instance, find their way to the Quetta market through the ports of the Persian Gulf rather than through Kandahar and Chaman. Doubtless there is much unnecessary loss to the country through similar extortion on the northern routes ; but in spite of commercial stagnation, the great fact still remains that the late Amir set himself to work with energy at the mastery of some, at least, of the first principles of national development. He has made roads, built bridges, erected buildings, and encouraged irrigation, and he was, to the day of his death, busy in connecting the uttermost parts of his kingdom by passable roads through districts which have been hitherto regarded as impracticable. The question then arises whether Afghanistan can ever be rendered self-supporting and independent of India ; whether her army (which we cannot regard with indifference so long as it constitutes a fighting factor between British India and Russia) can be paid and fed by the country it is raised to serve ; whether Afghanistan could, to put it shortly, be rendered a financial success. Under a strong Government, and favoured by peace, there is little doubt that it might be so, although it is not in many directions that her capabilities for production could be largely extended. In the northern districts of Afghanistan, in the basin of the Oxus, in Badakshan and Turkestan, limited space for extended cultivation of the soil may probably be found, although it cannot be on any very large scale. The rich valley of Herat leaves no space for further irrigation projects. The margin of the Oxus is already cultivated to

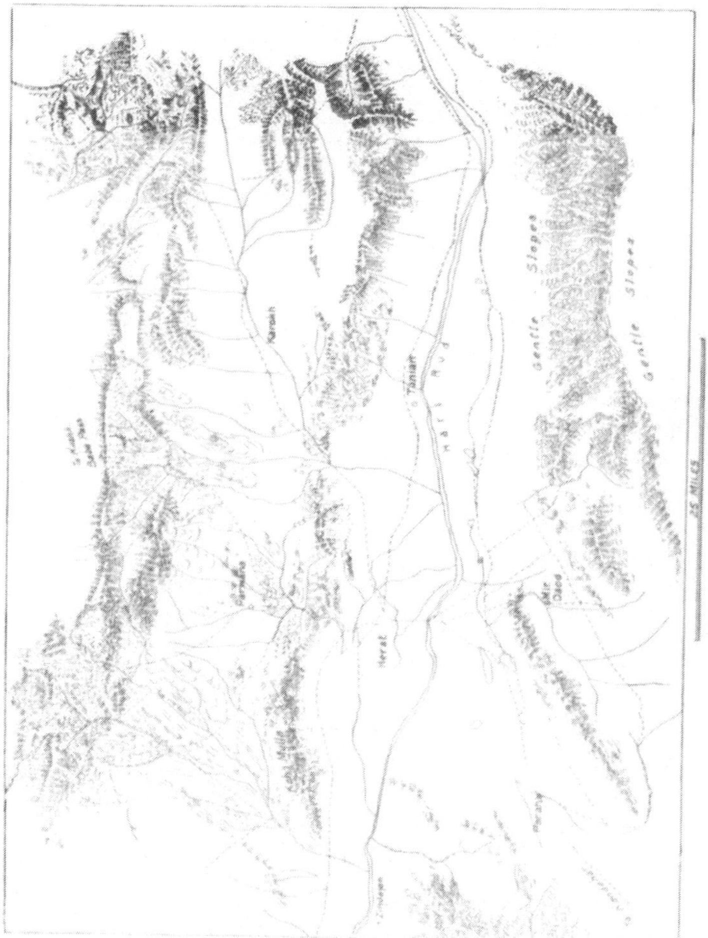

FIG. 30.—The Valley of the Hari Rud.

the very edge of the sand wastes that will eventually overwhelm it. The waters of these northern streams which are lost in the Oxus plains are already utilised to their fullest extent. The Pamirs offer no field for anything but the produce of intermittent grazing. The ancient kingdom of Bactria (Badakshan) may possibly possess, in its magnificent valleys and temperate climate, soil as yet unredeemed from the wilderness which may prove to be as fruitful as that of Kashmir, but it is not probable that there is much of it.

The basin of the Kabul River is already famous for its fruit. It would be difficult indeed to rival the rich cultivation of Koh Daman north of Kabul ; of the plains of Chardeh to the west ; or of the open valleys of the Logar to the south, where the eye may rest on miles of uninterrupted fields of wheat, broken only by patches of mulberry, walnuts, or apricot trees. But it would be difficult also to suggest to those most practical native engineers who have covered the country with a network of irrigation channels any method of improvement either in their system of utilising the water available, or in the development of the original supply. They run their rivers dry already. As for that portion of Kafiristan which falls within the Kabul basin, there are indeed hopes that here, at least, there may be fresh field for development. The oak forests and pines that clothe the mountain sides are of magnificent growth—there is no such wealth of forest anywhere else in Afghanistan. Here, too, are the "wild vine and the ivy," the pomegranate, and the fig-tree, all in a condition of primeval undevelopment. If the area for crop-growing is circumscribed by the steep mountain slopes, there is at least ample room for investigation beyond its present limits, and for the development of much material wealth amongst the hills themselves.

Of the third great basin of Afghanistan—that of the Helmund—it is difficult to speak with certainty. The upper valleys that contribute to that river are unsurveyed in detail ; but we know enough about the wilderness of the Hazara Hills to be fairly certain that in those bleak, storm-swept and desolate altitudes there is little or no chance of agricultural development on any large scale. And this general view of the Hazara Hills extends itself to the Taimani plateau on its west, which drains, not into the Helmund, but into the great basin, or Hamun, which receives the Helmund. The Taimani country has indeed been fairly well explored, and it has been found to be worth but little to the agriculturist. Nearly all the wealth of Southern Afghanistan is concentrated about Kandahar. The valleys of the Argandáb and Arghasán, and the teeming Zamindáwar district contain all the best of Western Afghan soil, but in all of them there is little room for enlarging the borders of the cultivated land, so that we may say that (so far as our geographical researches can tell us) Afghanistan is already cultivated to nearly its fullest extent. We must look then rather to the possible mineral wealth of Afghanistan, and to its resources in silk, camel-hair clothing, and wool, and to the further development of its trade in horses, and possibly, too, in timber, for those financial returns which will enable the country to support itself and its own defences. A certain amount of mineral wealth is known at present to be concentrated in the mines of lapis-lazuli in Badakshan ; of copper in several places ; of tin in the Panshir Valley ; and of lead in Ghorband. Coal is to be found in Afghan Turkestan, and gold was once worked from quartz veins near Kandahar ; but this is not a very promising field in which to look for contributions to the Kabul treasury, and it is on the development of the commerce of the country with India that Afghanistan must chiefly depend for future financial advancement and final stability.

Instead of long strings of slow moving camels, which even now may be counted by the score toiling along the road adjoining the line of the Quetta-Chaman railway—still adhering with obstinate persistency to the old-world tracks over the Khojak rather than give way to the pushing and impertinent railway that has already thrust itself to the edge of Afghanistan with its railhead pointing to Kandahar—an extension of that same railway to Kandahar is the first development needed. On the northern routes Kabul and Peshawur must also be connected by rail, and finally a far more direct and efficient linking up of the lateral routes between Peshawur and Quetta must be considered once again. With the impetus to the natural trade of the country which would be given by the removal of ridiculous imposts, and the introduction of facilities for transport, there is no reason why the Afghanistan of the future should not pay its own way, and even if it could never become the financial success that Egypt has been in our hands, at least it may cease to be a drain on the heavily-taxed resources of India.

The ethnography of Afghanistan is a subject which cannot be altogether disregarded in dealing with the

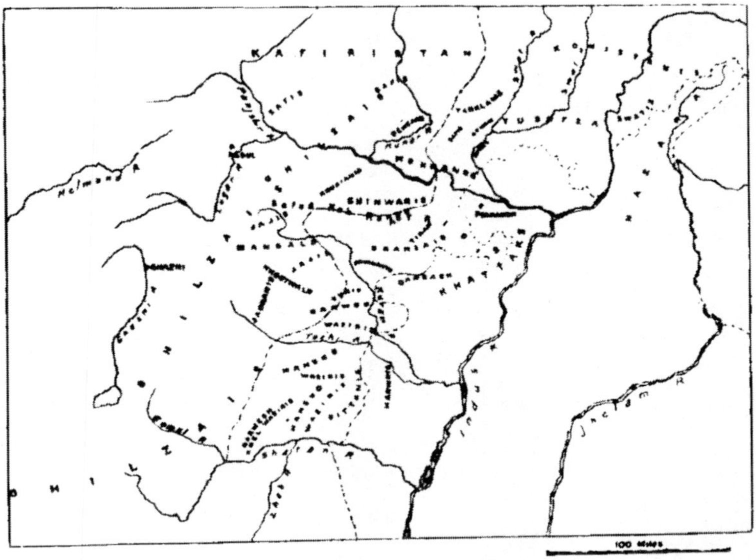


FIG. 31.—Northern Frontier—Tribal Distribution.

origin of our Indian population. It is one of the very deepest interest, demanding a far wider knowledge of the ancient conditions of Central Asian occupation, and a more scholarly application of that knowledge than has ever yet been given to it.

We have seen that the population of Baluchistan may be regarded in very general terms as ancient Persian overlaid by Arabic immigration. That of Afghanistan may similarly be reduced to an ancient Persian (or Tajak) stock overlaid by Afghan, Turk, and Mongolian invaders. The Tajak shows himself chiefly in the Kohistani districts north of Kabul and bordering Kafiristan, where he becomes dominant and aggressive in proportion as he is newly converted to the tenets of the Muhammadan faith. In the west of Afghanistan, though still prevalent, he is less predominant, being there subordinate to the Afghan. He is the tiller of the soil, the "ghulám" or slave of the community. The blue-coated agriculturist, who with round felt hat and triangular spade cultivates the poppy beds about Herat, is a Tajak. The Tajak is indeed by ancestry closely allied to the normal Persian villager of the Khorasán, and he talks more or less the same language. His master, the Afghan, who calls himself Durani, claims descent from the "lost tribes," rejoices in the name of "Ben-i-Israel," and firmly believes himself to be of the seed of Abraham, of the chosen people of Jehovah. His traditions, his family names, his Semitic features, his civil code of unwritten law are all more or less Israelitish, and it is difficult to tell, if his traditions are false, how he came by all these evidences of their truth. On the other hand his language is Pushtu, an ancient tongue of Sanscrit origin showing no trace of Hebrew influence. And because his language is Pushtu, he claims a certain affinity in language and laws with the Pushtu tribes of the frontier, and acknowledges himself to be a Pathan—which means only that he talks the Pushtu language. The Afghan has gradually migrated and spread from his original seat in Southern Afghanistan to the north—to the Kabul Valley. As "Mohmand" and "Yusufzai" he has possessed himself of large tracts of country in Swat and those contiguous districts which are beyond the limits of what we now recognise as Afghanistan, so that there is direct affinity of race as well as language and traditions between the Afghans of Afghanistan and the Mohmands and Swatis of our independent border provinces. The Amir of Kabul is the priestly head of them all, and the defender of their faith. There is no real recognition of the Sultan of Turkey as their religious head.

The Turkish element in the Afghan population is represented by Turkomans and Usbegs in the Oxus regions, and Ghilzais in Central Afghanistan. The Turkoman, once the terror of the peaceful country side throughout the Persian border and the open desert regions of the Oxus Valley, is gradually, under civilising influences, developing agricultural proclivities, and he now lives in peaceful relations with his neighbours, contenting himself with the stirring records of raids and robberies of no very ancient date. In common with the Usbeg (who has long since lost the fierce fighting qualities that he possessed in the days of Babar, the outcast prince of a Central Asian Khanate, who founded the Turk dynasty of India) the Turkoman talks Turki, a comparatively pure and very ancient language which is the basis of the bastard tongue of Constantinople; differing in this particular, as in many physical characteristics, from those Turkish races south of the Hindu Kush and Koh-i-Baba who have enrolled themselves amongst Pathans and talk Pushtu. These southern tribes are called Ghilzai (or Khilje), and were introduced into Afghanistan within historic times. They form a very powerful confederation of tribes, second only to the Durani in power and influence, and it is from the Ghilzai that the Durani dynasties of Kabul have ever experienced the most dangerous opposition. Those "povindahs," or Khafila leaders, who annually spread through India, and who are noted for their strength and magnificent physique, are mostly Ghilzais of the Nasir and Sulimáni clans.

The Mongol tribes of Afghanistan are represented by the Hazára people, whose origin in their present habitat (which is along the skirts of the northern slopes of the Hindu Kush west of Kafiristan, and that great central tract of elevated country which stretches between Kabul and Herat, and reaches south-westward toward the Helmund lagoons), is traced to the invasions of Chenghiz Khan early in the thirteenth century. They are of the Shiah sect of Muhammadan, differing in appearance but little from the cognate Ghurkha of Nipal, although they are generally of finer physique. The Hazára talks Persian, and, like the Persian-speaking communities throughout Afghanistan, he holds a social position below that of the Pathan, who is his master whenever they meet. The Hazára is, however, built of excellent material. In the field of manual labour he is unrivalled amongst Eastern workmen—patient, hard-working, and cheerful, and easily amenable to discipline. The Amir has formed a most efficient corps of sappers and miners from this recruiting ground, and there is no doubt that Hazáras would make most excellent soldiers in any capacity.

It is not to be supposed that this very superficial sketch of the ethnography of Afghanistan embodies more than an outline of that strange conglomeration of mixed nationalities that is included within the boundary recently demarcated. There are remnants of Chaldæan, Turk, and Mongolian races innumerable engrafted in the Aryan stock, of which the ancient Aria, or Herat, is represented to be the original home; and in the wilderness of inaccessible mountains which we call Kafiristan there is solid proof of existing remnants of Pelasgic origin. Within these hills are probably gathered together representatives of whole colonies of ancient peoples who, unable to hold their own against the restless and ever-moving waves of Central Asian immigration and the ferocious progress of Islam, have retired farther and farther into the inaccessible mountains, their progressive movements having been spread over ages, until at last they are hidden in the remotest valleys that lie under the shadow of the highest peaks of the Hindu Kush—as strange an agglomeration of tribal survivals as can be found in the whole world. Speaking a great variety of dialects (if not actually diverse languages), acknowledging no common affinity or confederation, the people of one valley being frequently unable to converse with those of the next, they are all lumped together by the orthodox Muhammadan under the term Kafir, or infidel. Amongst them no doubt are survivals of the Greek dominion in this part of Asia which was the result of Alexander's conquest of the Persian empire, and the evidence seems strong that we may include amongst the Bashgol Kafirs those yet more ancient people of Pelasgic origin who, as Nyceans, claimed Alexander's protection during his advance through Swat. The Kafirs occupied a great part of Swat and the lower Kunar Valley as late as the sixteenth century, and thence retired into the Kashmund mountains north-west of Jalalabad within historic times. The area of their occupation can almost be traced by the entire absence of Buddhist remains within the limits of a district which is almost surrounded by such relics of the past. In the sixth century B.C. colonies of captive Greeks had been transferred from Kyrene and Milesia by Darius Hystaspes and Xerxes to Central Asia ; and their descendants may yet be found (according to Bellew) in the Logar Valley, south of Kabul, in certain districts of Kunduz in Afghan Turkestan, and on the slopes of the Hindu Kush near the historic pass of Kaoshán. There is at least no difficulty in accounting for the very marked influence of Greek art in the sculptures of the Buddhist monasteries and temples of the Peshawur Valley. Not only did Greek dynasties hold Baktria (which included most of Afghan Turkestan and Badakshan up to the Pamirs) for two hundred years after Alexander's invasion until they were turned out by the Jata Skyths about 126 B.C., but it seems exceedingly probable that the roads and passes of Badakshan and the Kabul basin were better known to the Macedonians in the year 335 B.C. (before Alexander's advent) than they are to the English Intelligence Department in the year 1900.

Quite recently a new province or political agency has been carved out of the borderland districts on the extreme north-west of India which presents many points of analogy with Baluchistan on the south. Like Baluchistan it includes territories within the pale of settled administration by the Indian Government, and independent territories beyond the Indian frontier which are under tribal control. The trans-Indus provinces of the Punjab (or Derajat) with the Peshawur Valley form the section of the Punjab which has thus been cut off; whilst north of it and west of it are added the unreclaimed mountain tracts between Chitrál on the extreme north, and the Vihowa River (a river which descends from the uplands west of the Sulimáni Mountains to the Indus plain about half-way between Dera Ismael Khan and Dera Ghazi Khan) on the south. The western limit of this provincial political authority is the eastern boundary of Afghanistan. Practically this is the Pathan section of the trans-frontier, embracing the Afghan Pathan communities of Bajaor, Swat, and the Mohmand country; and the non-Afghan Pathans (Afridis, Jowakis, Orakzais, Dawaris, Waziris, Sheranis, &c.) of the ancient hill province of Roh. There are indeed Pathan tribes on both sides the border, for the Kuttaks and Bungashes of the Kohat district are a Pushtu-speaking people who have submitted to British rule since the conquest of the Punjab. But with the general resemblance between the politico-geographical construction of the province and of its administration by an agent to the Governor-General supported by a political staff, as well as the adoption of the principle of tribal levies for the safeguarding of the important routes which traverse the border, the analogy with Baluchistan ends. The simple feudal system under which the hereditary Baluch chief governs his estates is wanting in the independent Pathan hills. The Pathan is nothing if he is not a republican, and it is the voice of his priest (modified by the dictates of his village "punchayet," or municipal council) which alone stirs him to action or teaches him obedience. Thus the process of direct dealing between the British agent and the Pathan people is rendered infinitely difficult, for there is nothing of the chivalrous courtesy and diplomatic tact of the high-bred Baluch chief about the wily and fanatical person of the north country Mullah, although indeed the tribal councils may occasionally exhibit most unexpected appreciation of the qualities of justice and common-sense. Geographically it is the most important of all the border provinces of India, for it is traversed by four of the most important routes leading into India from the west, *i.e.* the Khaibar, the Kuram, the Tochi, and the Gomal. The province is officially known as the North-West Frontier province.

As in the case of Baluchistan, it is the Indian Survey records which have furnished most of the material for this chapter combined with the author's unpublished notes. The Afghan War of 1839-42 originated much literature on the subject of Afghanistan, but it has (with the exception of Broadfoot's remarkable exploration between the Indian frontier and Ghazni) been superseded by more recent surveys and explorations carried out in connection with the Afghan War of 1878-80, the Russo-Afghan Boundary Commission of 1883-86, and subsequent geographical researches on the Indian frontier by the native employees of the Indian Survey Department. It is only within recent years that the border line of mountains has been mapped, and the progress of the mapping has led to better information on the kindred subjects of ethnography and history than existed before. The most important contributor to our knowledge of Afghan ethnography is Dr. H. W. Bellew, C.S.I., whose paper in the *Asiatic Quarterly Review* of 1891 gives a fairly concise epitome of his views on the subject. For notes on the geology of the country I am indebted to Major C. L. Griesbach, C.S.I. (once head of the Indian Geological Department), who enjoyed unusual opportunities for its examination. Since the close of the Russo-Afghan Boundary Commission, Sir G. Robertson's "Kaffiristan" gives the best account we possess of an outlying province of Afghanistan. For any account of Badakshan and the outlying districts reaching to the Pamirs, we must refer to the records of the Pamir Boundary Commission and the report of the Forsyth Mission to Yarkand. The best map of Afghanistan is the Indian Survey compilation on the scale of 16 miles = 1 inch; obtainable at Calcutta.

# CHAPTER IV

## KASHMIR AND THE HIMALAYAS

THE state of Kashmir was at our disposal at the close of the first Sikh war. It was then under the administration of one Goláb Sing, who had risen to prominence in the service of the great Sikh leader, Ranjit Sing. To Goláb Sing and his heirs the state of Kashmir was assigned in 1846 for a money consideration amounting to about one million sterling, and on the understanding that he would remain neutral when the second Sikh war (which was then imminent) should commence. Goláb Sing was true to his engagement. He deserted his Sikh masters and paid for Kashmir with money looted from the Lahore treasury. Thus Kashmir became an independent state, after the fashion in which native states within the limits of British India are independent. Its geographical position to the north of the Punjab and its world-famed climate and scenery, as well as its influence on the conditions of life in the plains of the Punjab as the cradle of some of its great rivers—all these have rendered Kashmir prominent amongst the native states of India, and have made that country the final objective of almost every conqueror who has invaded the peninsula. In later years Kashmir has acquired a new interest and fresh importance, firstly, as a possible sphere for European colonisation; and, secondly, as the guardian state of those entrances to India from the north which are directly connected with the eastern passes over the Hindu Kush.

Originally defined as lying between the Indus and the Ravi, Kashmir now stretches out an arm so as to include a part of the Gilgit basin; and the political influence of the British resident at Srinagar reaches beyond Gilgit to

Chitrál. The unexplored mountain wildernesses of Tangir and Darél (lying west of Gilgit and bordering the plains of Swat) are still absolutely independent. We know little about them. The same may be said of those districts of the Indus basin which include Bunér and the hills south of that valley. Over a great part of Swat and Bajaor, together with a portion of the Mohmand districts, we have lately extended a certain amount of political control with the object of preserving our right of way from the plains of Peshawur to Chitrál; but it is an influence which has to be supported by force of arms, although it aims only at securing the good-will of the local chiefs in Swat, Bajaor, and Dir. Chitrál and Gilgit are important to us in so far as they serve as outposts from which we may keep watch over certain northern gateways of the Trans-Himalaya, and to afford us opportunity of influencing the border tribes in their neighbourhood. Otherwise the vast wilderness of snow-clad mountains which encloses them, intersected by narrow valleys buried beneath overhanging masses of cliff and crag (too narrow to do more than support a scanty and hardy population of mountaineers), is too difficult of access, and too remote from civilised centres, to be a source of anything but periodical embarrassment.

Until we made a road to Gilgit the mountain tracks to that place were well-nigh impassable; beyond Chitrál and Gilgit these tracks still retain their primitive simplicity —a simplicity which only occasionally admits of the passing to and fro of those mountaineers who habitually use them. For throughout all this region the rigours of an eight-months' winter binds the land in an iron grip, and when these passes are spoken of as "practicable," the term is understood to be strictly limited to four months of the year, intervening between 1st June and 31st October. During these four months, indeed, the mountain floods are loosened, and every ridge and fold in the hills despatches its rivulet of snow-fed water to swell the torrents in the river beds. In June the winter covering of snow is withdrawn from the slopes about the passes, and a new carpet, bright with every conceivable hue of summer flower, is spread abroad. The little lakelets nestling amongst surrounding crags on the broad back of the Hindu Kush are unbound, and the glory of the budding summer replaces the dreary silences of winter. It is then, and then only, that travellers may make their way to the northern borders of Kashmir, and cross the dividing line between Kashmir and Afghanistan.

The northern boundary of the dependencies of Kashmir (including Chitrál, Gilgit, and the Kanjut province) is the boundary of that arm of Afghanistan which reaches out to the extreme north-east to interpose as a buffer between India and Russia. It extends along the water-parting of the Hindu Kush until it reaches the Dorah Pass, where a subsidiary range or offshoot carries it southward, dividing the Bashgol valley of Kafiristan from the valley of Chitrál. Not far from the point already indicated as the geographical tri-junction, from which springs the Hindu Kush, the Mustagh, and the third great watershed which reaches meridionally northward to serve (provisionally) as the boundary between Russia and China (now called the Sarikol), we have a vast agglomeration of snow-fields and glacial lakes at an average height of 18,000 feet above sea-level. Amongst them lies the hidden water-parting of the Hindu Kush, and from them emanate all those river systems which offer opportunities of approach to India from the north. Here the Chitrál River rises, and, sweeping southwards in two large tributaries through a mass of glacial hills, sometimes over a comparatively wide and shingly bed, sometimes narrowed to a torrent between precipitous cliffs, waters Chitrál, the Kunar Valley, and Jalalabad. The Chitrál River and the Kunar are one and the same. A third name for the same river is Kashkar. This river, with its various heads, forms the principal line of approach to India from the north; the Panjkora and the Swat Rivers take their rise farther south, amidst the unexplored mountain gorges of Darél, and only offer a difficult route towards the Peshawur Valley, along their cliff-bound banks south of Gilgit.

Striking more to the eastward from this same mountain tri-junction, the Gilgit River takes its way to the Indus, receiving the tributary of Hunza *en route*. Thus, should any one enter India from the north, it must be by some pass crossing the Hindu Kush watershed between the Mustagh range (which bounds the Eastern Pamirs on the south) and the Dorah Pass of the Hindu Kush, leading either to Gilgit or Chitrál. Westwards from the Dorah, the nature of that section of the Hindu Kush which bisects Kafiristan forbids all idea of a cross passage, unless, indeed, a highroad to Badakshan is made artificially through the head of the Kafiristan mountains. No such approach from the north has ever yet been found or made use of historically. Only small parties of hardy Buddhist pilgrims in search of religious instruction, and full of the spirit of self-sacrifice which distinguishes the devotee, have passed from the great plains of China over the Hindu Kush to Chitrál, Gilgit, Darél, and Swat (all of which were once centres of the Buddhist faith) in the early centuries of our era. Avoiding the Kunar Valley between Chitrál and Jalalabad, which was then and for centuries later occupied by Kafirs, these searchers for spiritual knowledge appear to have struck into those hidden tracks that border the Indus, the Panjkora, and the Swat Rivers, and to have made their way with infinite pain and difficulty to the great monasteries and stupas of the Peshawur plains. No military force of any consequence ever has, or ever could, follow their footsteps.

The northern hinterland of Kashmir (which includes Dardistan) is distinguished even amongst the vast altitudes of the Himalayas for the magnificence of its snowy peaks and the wide expanse of snow-field and glacier which spread like a polar sea around them. The valleys are comparatively low; the valley of the Indus near Gilgit being but 4600 feet above sea-level—low enough to admit of a narrow belt of cultivation and to encourage the growth of the fruit-trees of the plains. It is from altitudes such as this that one looks up to the heights of Nanga Parbat (26,600 feet) or to Rakapushi (which may be called the Himalayan Matterhorn), shimmering amongst the clouds at an elevation of 25,500 feet. Tirach Mir, north of Chitrál, is another gigantic, square-headed mass, the summit of which is also above the 25,000 foot line; and there are countless other peaks, subordinate indeed to these, but still towering many thousands of feet above

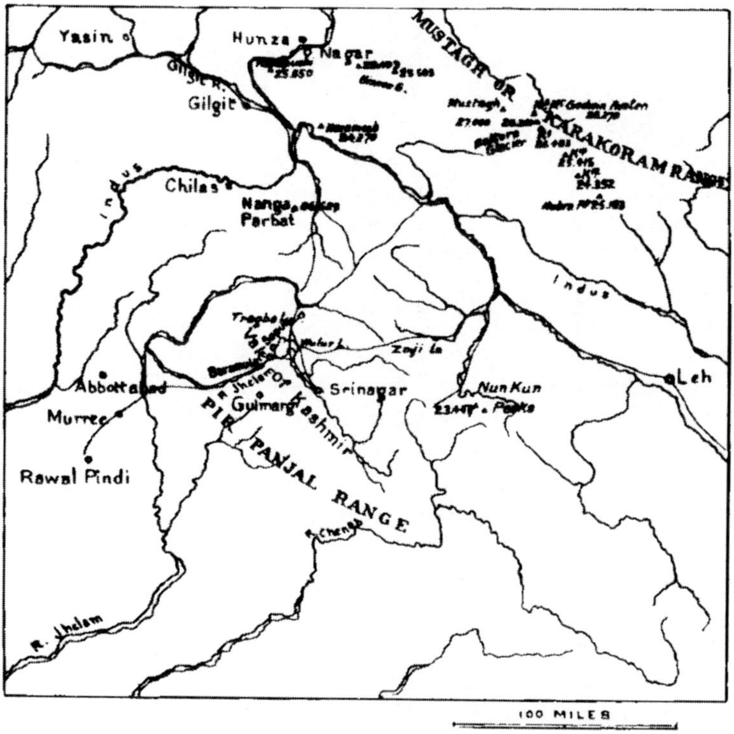


FIG. 32.—Routes in Kashmir.

the highest of the European Alps. The main water-parting of the Hindu Kush is comparatively low, falling to 12,500 feet between Gilgit and the Pamirs. It is the lofty peaks of its great southern spurs which group themselves together into such a combination of magnificent altitude—only rivalled by the highest mountain group in the world. From the intersecting mountain chains of the Pamirs, dividing the Little from the Great Pamir, at altitudes not exceeding 18,000 feet, this grand array of Kashmir peaks may easily be seen overtopping the broad back of the Hindu Kush itself; and it is thus that opportunity has been afforded for carrying the triangulation of the Indian surveys northwards into the Pamir region.

Apart from this northern wilderness, which combines the fresh beauty of many a sunny valley with the stern grandeur of ice-bound peaks, Kashmir is a land of such surpassing beauty as almost to justify the rhapsodies which have been poured out in its praise by the most imaginative of oriental poets. It is one of the few countries in the world which never seems to disappoint the expectations that have been formed of it. There is not a fruit or a vegetable that will grow in a temperate climate that cannot be grown in Kashmir. Wine of really excellent quality is produced there. Silk can be cultivated. The growth of tea, chinchona, and hops have all proved a success, whilst the natural products of the country are varied and abundant. The manufactures of Kashmir are famous—its shawl-weaving and its silver-work, its silk embroideries and its carpets. The great valley which stretches from the Wulur Lake to Srinagar is full of that interest which always attaches itself to the architectural evidences of an ancient faith.

It is difficult to write of Kashmir scenery in adequate terms. From the top of the Tragbál Pass, at 11,000 feet of elevation, north of the Wulur Lake, looking across the Happy Valley on a clear October day, one is in presence of the full majesty of a complete range of snow-capped mountains extending from east to west, and shutting off the valley from farther intervening hills that stretch to the plains of India. This is the Pir Panjál range. At either end of the Pir Panjál a farther vista of silver peaks embraces a mountain panorama, which gradually increases in altitude to the unbroken snow-fields of Haramosh and the far-off solitudes of Nanga Parbat. All around is snow; all around is the eternal silence of vast altitudes—the mystery of unapproachable ice-bound pinnacles and glaciers. And amidst it all lies the valley of the Wulur Lake, golden with the lights of autumn crops, edged with purple and russet where the lower spurs of the mountains bind the yellow plain. In the midst of the valley is the lake, reflecting each feature of the surrounding hills as in a mirror, but broken with dark blotches of chenar-covered islands and floating gardens. Small wonder that the gods of the woods and the mountains still hold their own in the superstitious veneration of the Muhammadan inhabitants, who have not learned yet to forget the teachings of their ancient Hindu faith, and still cherish some faint survival of the yet more ancient symbols of Turanian demonology!

The capital of Kashmir, Srinagar, consists of a collection of rickety wood-built structures erected on the banks of the Jehlam, exceedingly picturesque to the eye, but otherwise foul with the abominations of centuries. It is here that the shawl and carpet-weaving is maintained, and here is the centre of European occupation. Srinagar is readily accessible from the plains of India. A good tonga road from Murree (the hill-station of the Punjab) already runs some hundred miles to Baramulla on the Jehlam, at the entrance of the Kashmir valley, and a further extension to Srinagar will shortly be completed.[1]

Our practical interest in Kashmir lies in its possible capability for supporting a purely European colony such as might eventually prove a source of strength to the Empire in India. There is little doubt indeed about its adaptability to European life—in a measure and to an extent greater than is to be found elsewhere in India. Eurasian (or half-caste) colonies exist all over India, chiefly on the skirts of the larger towns and stations, and they are dependent almost entirely on the European community for employment and means of subsistence. But there are no pure European colonies in India yet. There are a few European settlers in the Nilgiris and the hill-stations of the Himalayas, but they do not form colonies. Their sons and daughters are usually educated in England, and do not in their turn look to India as the land

[1] 1899.

of their adoption. In Kashmir alone are there signs of possible colonisation. Already on the banks of the Dal Lake there is springing up a small English town with English houses and gardens which bears signs of permanency.

The greater portion of the cultivable area of the Kashmir state is concentrated in the valley of the Jehlam, where the river winds with sluggish current and tortuous windings to the Wulur Lake, and passes thence by the narrow outlet at Sopur to a rapid and broken descent to the plains of India. Thus the valley offers to the geologist an important Himalayan example of the formation of a wide and highly fertile plain by the local elevation of a stream bed above a narrowing outlet, which has led to a vast deposit of alluvium and to the flattening of the river gradient. Within the limits of this plain are gathered the chief centres of local industry, together with innumerable villages of the Kashmir peasantry, whose lives, passed amid scenes of surpassing natural beauty, have been chequered and degraded in the past by oppression and misrule, and their numbers thinned by pestilence, famine, and earthquake. Under the rule of the present Maharaja, Sir Pratab Sing, many useful reforms have been inaugurated, including a land assessment and the formation of a permanent residence for a British political officer at Srinagar. The political influence which centres at Srinagar reaches to Kashgar, to Leh (the capital of Ladak), to Gilgit and to Chitrál. With the establishment of the Residency, there has been a great increase of English visitors and of new settlements. Gulmarg, in one of the glades on the northern slopes of the Pir Panjál, is already a popular resort, although the erection of permanent buildings has not yet been sanctioned by the state. The improvement in communications and the introduction of telegraphs have developed the internal traffic of the country, and conduced to a general increase in trade and in land revenue. The change in the condition of the people, who were in 1887 in a position of absolute serfdom without rights or power to represent their grievances, is perhaps the most notable result of the influence of British representation in the councils of the durbar. The character of the Kashmiri had been moulded by bad administration into a timid and passive endurance of degrading oppression, and yet these people represent an intellectual nationality probably older than any to be found in Northern India, still holding to the land of their ancestors in spite of the despotism of Pathan, Moghul, Sikh, and Dogra, which has been successively imposed upon them. Of the 820,000 souls who inhabit the Kashmir valley (including 120,000 in Srinagar alone), 93 per cent. are Muhammadan, and the rest chiefly Hindus. There is but little crime amongst them. They are a law-abiding race, as they were under their ancient Hindu kings, and now they enjoy at last a certain measure of prosperity and contentment under the new land settlement regulations.

The state of Kashmir occupies a square mountainous block of territory, about 300 miles in length by 300 in breadth at the north-western extremity of the Himalayas, and is divided into two almost equal parts by the Indus diagonally crossing from north-west to south-east. Geographically the mountain area south of the Indus only is Himalayan, and the northern features belong to the Trans-Himalayan system—a somewhat arbitrary distinction which is rendered necessary for purposes of definition. Measured by the process of Himalayan evolution it will be remembered that the north-western section of the entire mass is very much more recent than the eastern, which is separated by geological ages from the comparatively recent formations found east of the Brahmaputra, throughout the Tibetan plateau, and on the north-western borders of India. Geological evidence, therefore, supports the popular view of Himalayan geography, which places the true Himalaya (the "Abode of Snow," from the Sanscrit *hima*, "frost," and *álaya*, "a house") within the gigantic arms of the Indus and the Brahmaputra, and regards the entire system as the southern *revêtement* or buttress of the Tibetan plateau, analogous to the Kuen Lun mountains which border that plateau on the north. Accepting this definition, the Himalayas extend along the northern frontier of India for about 1500 miles, with a varying breadth of 150 to 200 miles. Throughout this length they are dominated by one conspicuous main chain, which, under the name of Zaskar (in Kashmir), includes all the most prominent snow-clad peaks from Haramosh (16,900 feet), on the north-west, to Kanchanjanga (28,176 feet) and Everest (29,002 feet), on the south-east.

Some authorities maintain that this central range extends beyond the Indus to the north-west, and includes

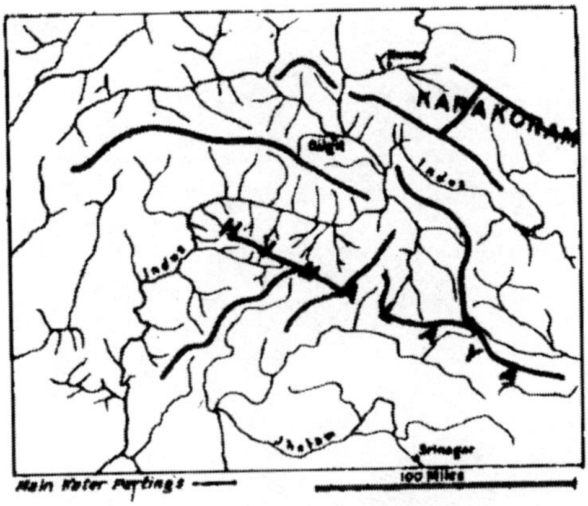


FIG. 33.—The Bend of the Indus.

Nanga Parbat and other high peaks overlooking the Gilgit basin from the south. This theory involves the assumption that the Indus River (maintaining its course through prehistoric ages whilst the mountain system was in gradual process of evolution) splits the main chain apart at the point where it changes from a north-westerly to a south-westerly direction near the junction of the Gilgit River—a phenomenon which is undoubtedly repeated by the Sutlej River and the Gandak in the Central Himalayas. This, however, is certainly not true of the Brahmaputra on the extreme east, which river has clearly been diverted from an original primeval course towards China by the recent formation of the close parallel folds of the mountains extending from the eastern limits of the Tibetan plateau southwards into Burma. There is no true basis, either geographical or geological, for the analagous statement that the Himalayan system reaches east of the Brahmaputra.

To the south of the main chain several minor chains, or folds, preserving an approximate parallelism to it, are recognisable (especially in the north-western regions of the Himalayas), with intervals filled in by irregular spurs and subsidiary ridges. North of it we find (according

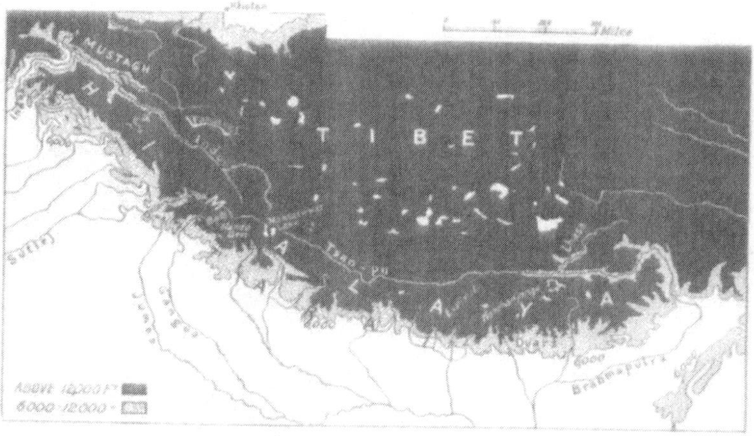


FIG. 34.—The Tibetan Plateau.

to some authorities)[1] a secondary wall of mountains, flanked by the long trough of the upper Indus and Brahmaputra (here called the Tsan-pu) which receive the drainage of the northern Himalayan slopes. There is certainly not sufficient geographical evidence at present to maintain the theory of a secondary continuous wall or chain in this position; and we must for the present remain satisfied with the known fact that the main central axis of upheaval, forming the true watershed of India, crosses the plateau of Tibet from west to east to the south of the central lake region. Within the limits of the

[1] See "Hunter's Gazetteer," vol. vi., "India."

Kashmir northern dependencies we are perhaps justified in assuming that the northern rim of the Indus basin, the Karakoram mountain range, which includes Mount Godwin-Austen (28,278 feet) and other mighty peaks, indicates the central crystalline axis of upheaval of the great mass of elevated plateau and mountain. But these magnificent Trans-Himalayan chains subside into the plateau about the longitude of the Pangong Lake (79° E.L.), and are apparently only recognisable farther by geological indications. It is about the point of their subsidence that the most direct and easiest access is found from Leh

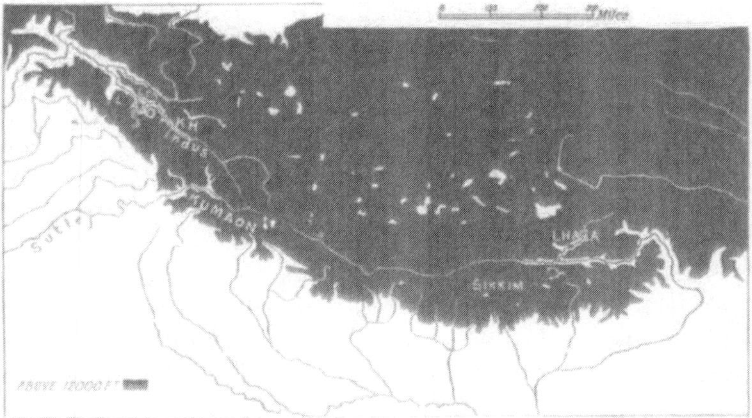


FIG. 35.—The Sources of the Indus, Ganges, and Brahmaputra.

(the capital of Ladak) eastward into Tibet, and from prehistoric days this has been the main line of communication between Kashmir and Lhasa. It is more or less along this line (about 200–300 miles from the Kashmir border) that through all ages those gold mines have been worked which were famous in the days of Herodotus. Tibetan gold has found its way to Kashmir on the west, Kashgar on the north, Pekin on the east, and, finally, to India on the south by many routes and passes, those of the Kumaon (or Sutlej River) group being now most traversed. The Ladak group, the Kumaon group, and the Sikkim group form the three best-known and most practicable groups of passes traversing the Himalayas in the north-west, centre, and south-east respectively.

In such an extent of mountain and valley as is represented by the Himalayas, we may expect to find every conceivable climate and every variety of vegetation, from the tropical growths of the low-lying valleys where the heat is at times as great as anything known in the plains of India, to the scanty, snow-bound vegetation of the highest altitudes which permit of vegetable growth at all. The Himalayas have consequently been more misrepresented by travellers than any other portion of the infinitely varied continent of India. The lower ranges, which at some points slope up steeply from the plains, are elsewhere divided from the plains by subsidiary ranges of recent formation, enclosing valleys, called Dún; at elevations of 2000 to 3000 feet between themselves and their foothills. These outer ranges, facing south and south-west, are covered with luxuriant vegetation, varying with the varying altitude, tropical in character towards Assam and the eastern branches of the Himalayas, but allied to the vegetation of temperate zones in the north-west. Here the various pines (chiefly the *pinus excelsa* and *pinus longifolia*) flourish alongside the Himalayan oak and rhododendron, which latter grow to the size of shade trees. In some parts firs predominate over pines ; in others there are no firs and only pines, deodar (the cedar of Lebanon), oak forests, and rhododendrons. The dividing line between different classes of flora are often strongly marked. For instance, eight miles from Simla, along the great Tibet road, at Mashobra, we find pines replaced by firs, and the silver oak giving place to the green oak, whilst trees of new species exist which are unknown in Simla. Altitude, doubtless, has much influence on the differentiation of vegetable growth, even as instanced in some particular species. At altitudes of 7000 or 8000 feet, the rhododendron grows to the size of trees, and the brilliant scarlet and pink blossoms of it are the glory of Simla in the late spring. On the spur or offshoot of the snowy mountains which enclose the reputed head of the Ganges at Gangotri, scarlet rhododendrons cover scores of square miles, massed together in a dense forest reaching as far as the eye can overlook the successive billows of the hills. As summer comes on the petals fall, and the hillsides are hidden under scarlet leaves, until little is left but a magnificent blaze of vivid colour, set against a background of white snow and deep-blue sky. But as one ascends gradually to higher altitudes beneath the snow-line, the colour changes from scarlet to purple, then to lilac, and finally, amidst the snow, the rhododendron trees diminish to the more compact form known in England, and the colour of the flower is often pure white.

It has frequently been observed that in the north-west Himalayan region the southern spurs of the ranges are barren and scarred with landslips, and, as a rule, devoid of forest growth, whilst the northern slopes facing the snows support a vigorous vegetation. The subsoil is the same on either side, yet the difference in the character of the southern and northern slopes of the mountains is so marked as to be conspicuous even on the smallest spurs aud eminences. This is largely due to the effects of the sun in hot weather, and to the fact that the southern slopes are more inhabited and cultivated than the northern. The winter snow lies longer and is more easily retained on the north slopes, and thus the forest trees retain the moisture and have a better chance of existence than is possible on the south, where the scorched and sun-dried vegetation is not only subject to the effects of jungle fires, but to destruction by herds of goats and flocks of sheep. It is probable, also, that the hillside cultivators themselves set fire to the grass in order to improve the quality of the grazing.

The south-eastern Himalayas bordering Assam exhibit in their lower valleys all the luxuriance and beauty of tropical vegetation. Forests of bamboo cover the steep hillsides, and in the narrow gullies and clefts of the mountains the tree fern expands its splendid crown. The rainfall is much more abundant and more evenly distributed throughout the year in these southerly districts, consequently the forests are denser, and the variety of trees infinitely greater.

In the south-east of the Himalayas the highest group of mountains in the world is to be found gathering around Mount Everest (29,000 feet). Mount Everest (or Gauri-sankar) is itself only one peak amidst a number of surrounding satellites so little inferior to it in height that when its altitude was first observed trigonometrically, it was by no means selected as either the highest or the most conspicuous. It is, consequently, very difficult to obtain a clear view of this mountain monarch of the world, and though the whole group may be observed from several points accessible to travellers not far from Darjiling, it is doubtful whether the actual peak can be seen. On the borders of Sikkim, not far to the east of Mount Everest, is another gigantic peak, Kanchanjanga (28,180 feet), but little inferior in altitude, and far surpassing Everest in the majestic grandeur of its appearance. As it faces the hill-station of Darjiling at a distance of fifty miles, and is particularly well placed for observation (there being no intervening ranges of great altitude), it may be doubted whether a more impressive experience of the silent and unapproachable grandeur that surrounds the "everlasting hills" can be obtained in the whole wide world. If Everest is monarch of the world, Kanchanjanga is at least prince of the Himalayas. And the impressiveness that attends vast altitudes is in no way diminished by the wealth of forest vegetation which envelops the lower spurs and buttresses of the snow peaks. It may happen indeed that, under stress of winter cold, even these forests may for a time be buried in snow. Then the delicate tracery formed by the forests of snow-weighted bamboo form a fleeting shroud of intricate lace drawn across the depths from hill to hill, in delicate contrast with the stern grandeur of the snow clad peaks above.

From the foot of the lower spurs of the Himálayas throughout the south-eastern districts, and extending more or less along the line of junction with the plains as far to the north as the district of Kumaon, there is a broad belt of forest country usually known as Tarai. Southwards it consists usually of a dense jungle of grass and immense forest trees, and is impassable to all but elephants, rhinoceros, and buffaloes. Such are the Bhután Duars north of the Brahmaputra River. Towards the north-west the character of the vegetation alters with the changing climate, but the Tarai jungle is still a marked feature dividing the hills from the plains, notorious for its deadly climate during certain seasons of the year, and famous as a game preserve. The Tarai ends on the north-west where the subsidiary range called Siwaliks begins, the formation of high level valleys between the Siwaliks and the Himalaya offering a varied geographical feature, partaking of many of the characteristics of Tarai both in climate and vegetation.

The physical conformation of the Himalayas as a whole is not so complicated as a first view of the intricate maze of mountain ranges on the map would seem to indicate. The general high level upheaval above the earth's surface which crosses Asia from the Pamirs to the Burmese and Chinese frontier is all mountainous, but not all mountainous in the same degree. That apparent water-parting, which extends with more or less regularity from Kashmir to Eastern Assam and Burma, which is set back from the plains at about one hundred miles distance, and is distinguished as the "snowy range," divides this vast elevated region laterally into two systems with different characteristics. Northward of it, and beyond it, lies the true source of all the chief rivers in India (the central snowy range being no true divide or watershed), and in this northern section it would seem that in the course of countless ages the influence of glacial action had changed the relative altitude of hill and plain, the mountain crests becoming lower and the valleys more elevated and consequently more extensive. Thus we find wide plateaux in Tibet intersected by rugged lines of mountains which have no analogy whatever to the southern subsidiary ranges of the Himalayas. The grassy highland valleys of the Pamirs and the vast sterile stony steppes of Tibet are equally removed from the comparatively narrow and low level lines of southern Himalayan watercourse and watershed, where rushing torrents are crushed in between steep cliffs and grassy slopes, or find their way to the plains amidst a wilderness of magnificent mountain forest. There is no comparison whatsoever between the dreary, wind-swept solitudes, 15,000 to 16,000 feet in elevation, which stretch from Kashmir to the Chinese frontier north of the Indus and Brahmaputra, and the lovely, but often heat-ridden valleys of the Himalaya, which enclose the upper tributaries of the Sutlej and the Ganges.

There is a point about half-way between Kashmir and Eastern Assam, situated at the back of the great central

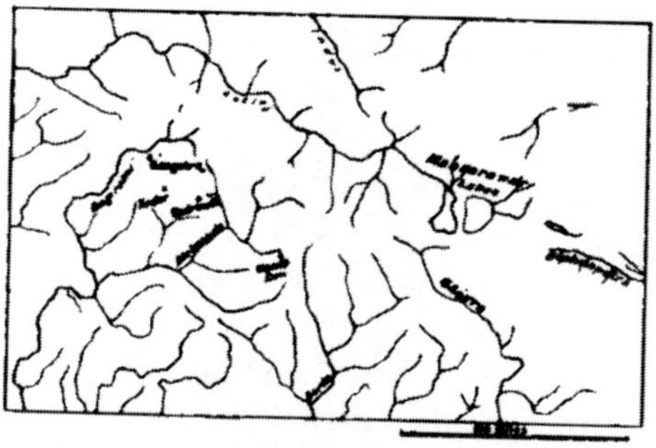

FIG. 36.—The Sources of the Indus, Sutlej, Ghágra, and Brahmaputra.

snow barrier to which I have alluded, which forms one of the world's great hydrographic centres. It is approximately marked by the Manasarawar Lake, or collection of lakes, to the south-east of Kashmir. Here rises the Indus, which takes a straight course north-westward through Kashmir for some 500 miles (dividing the Mustagh and Karakoram mountains of the Trans-Himalayan region from the Himalayas) ere it takes its great bend south-west, not very far from Gilgit, and thenceforward runs fairly straight for another 1000 miles to the Arabian Sea. Here, too, rises the Brahmaputra, which, under the name of the Tsanpo (Great River), travels eastward for 800 miles through Tibet, passing south of Lhasa, till it, too, takes a great bend to the south and south-west through unknown hills, and in its farther course of 600 miles carries the drainage of Assam to the Bay of Bengal. Enclosed between these two mighty river arms the Himalayas may be said to lie. Not very far from the same hydrographical centre are the sources of the Sutlej, which, winding through the mountains past Simla, waters the eastern Punjab and is lost in the Indus, and of the Sarda or Ghágra, which is so much the largest tributary of the Ganges as to render it doubtful whether it is not the main stream. The Ganges is traditionally supposed to rise at Gangotri, where the Gaimukh (or cow's mouth) is pointed out as the glacial origin of the river. But the stream which issues from the ice cave at Gangotri is the Bhágirathi, a comparatively small affluent of the Ganges compared to the Alaknanda which drains from the Badrinath and Nandadevi group of snowy peaks ; or to the far larger Ghágra which rises beyond Nepal, and joins the Ganges some 500 miles from its mouth.

Interlaced between the upper tributaries of these four great rivers is the gigantic system of mountains which form the true Himalayas, culminating in a vast and continuous chain of snow-covered mountains stretching from the bend of the Indus to the bend of the Brahmaputra, crowned with the highest peaks that the world has to show, across which lie the direct passes into Tibet. Tibet can be entered from Eastern Kashmir by way of Leh and the Pangong Lake, but even here the practicable passes which might lead to Lhasa are jealously guarded, and such is the present exclusiveness of Tibetan officialdom, that there is no way into Tibet between Leh and Darjiling that is open to the European.

The line of perpetual snow on this culminating chain of peaks is reckoned at 16,000 feet above sea-level, consequently there is always a "snowy range" visible from every hill-station on the outer spurs of the Himalaya. Beyond this chain either in Tibet, or in the far north-west of Kashmir, on the Mustagh and the Karakoram which divide Kashmir from that part of Chinese territory which is called the "New Dominion,"[1] or even on the Hindu Kush, the line of perpetual snow is very much higher. From the hills encircling Kabul it is not unusual in the late summer and early autumn to look northward without seeing snow at all. This is due to the comparatively dry atmosphere of the Trans-Himalayan districts which precludes the formation of snow in spite of the intense severity of the cold. These regions are beyond monsoon influences, as will be explained hereafter, and it is only the southern slopes of the Himalayas, which face the moisture-laden currents of the south-west monsoon, that retain the snow to comparatively low altitudes.

Within the Himalayan region we have a subdivision into districts which are directly under British administration, and districts which are under their own local rulers called "native states," just as we have them in the plains of the Indian peninsula. By far the greater part of the Himalayas are, however, under independent government. In Assam, on the extreme south-east, we only hold the skirts of the hills south of Bhután which is entirely beyond our political control. We hold two military posts, one at Buxa and the other at Dewangiri, which were acquired by us at the close of the Bhután campaign in 1865, both of which are on the lower spurs of the Himalayas and separated from the Brahmaputra by about fifty miles of densely forest-clad plains called the Duars. Assam itself consists of the long, narrow, sub-Himalayan plains bordering the Brahmaputra, and of the irregular and broken plateaux held by Khasias, Nagas, &c., which extend southwards for one hundred miles from the river. With Bhután we endeavoured to establish political relations in 1863, but the attempt ended in failure, and a desultory and unsatisfactory campaign followed, which sufficiently proved the impossibility of moving a large armed force through the uncertain tracks and byways which lead from the plains to the capital of Bhután at Punakha. Since then Bhután has been left alone. West of Bhután lies the small state of Sikkim, on the southern edge of

[1] Chinese Turkestan or Kashgaria.

which is the hill-station of Darjiling, and its northern border is within 150 miles of Lhasa, the capital of Tibet. Recent boundary disputes with the Tibetan authorities led to an expedition into Sikkim, which has resulted in the rectification of the frontier, but to no better understanding as regards European visitors to Tibet. Over the state of Sikkim we now exercise paramount political control.

For about 450 miles to the west of Sikkim, with an average breadth of about 100 miles, stretches the native state of Nepal, by far the most important of all the native states of the Himalayas. Nepal is absolutely independent, and has been so since 1815–16, when the Nepalese were defeated after an arduous and difficult hill campaign, and lost their richest districts of Kumaon and Garhwal. Since then they have maintained a policy of "absolute but friendly isolation," treating the British resident at the capital (Khatmandu) as an honoured prisoner, but closing their gates to Europeans. The result of this policy has certainly been that no disputes with Nepal have arisen for eighty years, and at the same time no exploration of the country has been possible. We do not even now know for a certainty which is the best route to Khatmandu. A considerable fringe of the Tarai jungle at the foot of the Himalayas is included within the Nepalese boundary. Here is, perhaps, the finest game preserve in India ; and here also a new interest has lately been added by the discovery of the birthplace of Gautama (the founder of Buddhism), and the sites of his early experiences. Although Nepal is as much an unexplored wilderness to us as many parts of Africa, the good feeling which has ever subsisted between the two Governments is a distinct source of strength to our position in India. For the goodwill of the Governments extends to the people. Between English and Gurkhas (who are either true Nepalese, or are very closely allied to them) there has ever been a spirit of mutual respect and reliance.

The districts of Kumaon and Garhwal (now entirely British) lie to the west of Nepal, and on the north of the North-West Provinces in which they are included.

In the Kumaon mountains is the pretty but rather confined hill-station of Naini Tal, situated on the banks of a lake surrounded by steep-sided hills, not always secure from the danger of landslips ; and within its area of 12,000 square miles are to be found some of the grandest scenes that Himalayan mountains can present. Sir John Strachey writes with a special reference to Kumaon when he says that, "to the traveller who remembers the wild magnificence of the peaks and glaciers of the Himalaya, and the general sublimity of its aspect, Zermatt and Chamouni seem insignificant. The mere

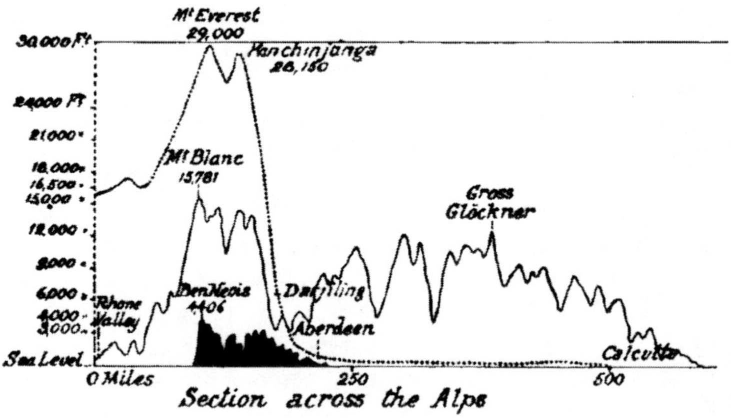


FIG. 37.—Comparative Elevations, British, Alpine, Himalayan.

fact that the ranges of the Himalaya are often twice as high as those of the Alps gives no idea of their respective magnitude. The whole of the Bernese Alps might, it has been said, be cast into a single Himalayan valley. You might almost as reasonably, when the Scotch or Welsh hills are white with snow, compare them with Mont Blanc and Monte Rosa, as compare anything in the Alps with Nanda Devi and Trisul. If, preserving the form of its great obelisk, you could pile the Matterhorn on the Jungfrau you would not reach the highest summits of the Himalaya, and would have a mountain less wonderful than the astonishing peak of Dunagiri."

But comparisons of this sort fail to impress the mind with an idea of the real grandeur of the Himalayas. To watch the early dawn breaking over a line of towering snow peaks in the clear mornings of early October, and from the shadowy hillside to count the pinnacles one by one as the first rays of the sun awaken them from the blue stillness of sleep to the brilliant glow of early life ; to see the shadows chased away out of the rifts of crag and gully till the flat depths of mountain mystery

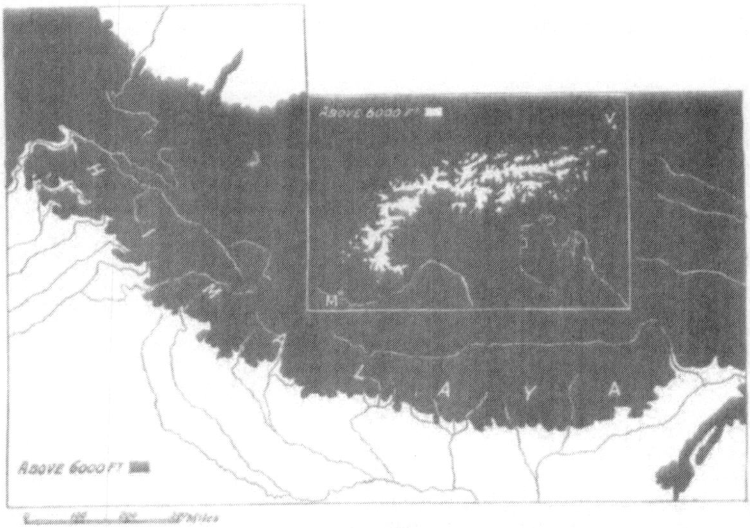


FIG. 38.—The Alps and the Himalayas on the same Scale.

are broken into countless shapes with the chequered beauty of light and shade, and the great majesty of the everlasting hills slowly resumes its daily form—this is the way to secure a lasting impression of the Himalayas.

Beyond Kumaon to the north-west, stretching across the Jumna to the borders of Kashmir, are a variety of small native states, both Sikh and Rajput, all under British control, some of them of little or no political importance, others (such as Patiala) a source of strength to the Empire for the loyal support that they bring to the Government in times of stress and difficulty. Others again are distinguished no less for loyalty than for the enormous antiquity of their ruling dynasties (these are the Rajput states), but all of them are developing rapidly and changing the old order under the gradually increasing influence of that European civilisation which is ever expanding around the hill-stations of Northern India.

In the absence of settled colonies of Englishmen these Himalayan hill-stations, centres of European life and interest, exercise a most important function in the gradual process of social development. But for them the conditions of modern European life in India would be

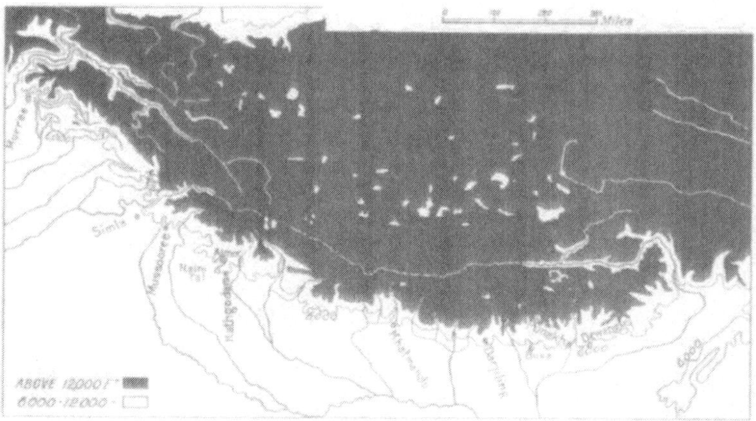


FIG. 39.—High Stations of the Himalayas.

almost intolerable. It is the increasing facility with which the overworked official, with damaged health and tired brain, enervated by daily official routine in the stifling atmosphere of the civil law courts, or worn out by those bodily derangements which are inseparable from the experience of duties performed in the heat of an Indian summer, can speed to the hills and recoup his strength in a pure atmosphere and a comparatively cool climate, that keeps the great machinery of government in working order, and prevents the dislocation that would inevitably follow on a constant change of administration. But for the hill-stations of India an Indian career would imply a continuous series of rapid journeys from India to Europe and back again. Life would be but an everlasting oscillation for most men and for nearly all women. The hill-stations are India's salvation. It would not be too much to say that they alone make the permanent occupation of India a possibility; and if they are thus beneficial to the European community they as certainly exercise a good effect on the social relations between Englishmen and Indians. It is only in the hills that schools can be maintained for the education of that large and growing class who fill the subordinate posts in all departments of the State, through whom we are more directly in touch with native feeling than is possible with any other branch of Anglo-Indian society. It there is contact at all between the ruling class and the people ruled, it is to be found in this social borderland, where Europeans and natives work side by side with the same ends in view and receive their promotion on equal terms. Amongst the higher social functionaries efforts are constantly made to bring together the best educated representatives of the native community and the official classes of India, but the results are not satisfactory. No lasting friendships spring out of this formal intercourse. The average English official remains as utterly ignorant of the inner life and domestic habits of the Muhammadan or Hindu gentleman as he is of those of the Esquimaux. Our hill-stations are at least cosmopolitan, and it is in them, if anywhere, that all classes meet together and interchange social amenities. Nor is it possible to doubt that the vitality and energy recouped in the atmosphere of the mountains is reflected in the daily official business life of the plains. In short, vigorous administration in all branches of civil and military service in India depends largely on those resources of renewed vitality that is found in the hill-stations. They deserve, therefore, more than the passing reference which is all that is possible in a work of this nature.

Simla ranks first in importance by reason of its selection as the summer residence of the Viceroy, and the seat of the supreme Government as well as that of the Punjab administration. By the last census returns Simla was credited with 30,000 inhabitants, of whom 4000 are Europeans, and there can be little doubt that the advent of the railway, which is even now in progress, will much increase this total. Situated on the sloping spurs of a lofty hill called Jakko, there is naturally a great range of elevation between the highest and the lowest residences of the town —the highest being over 8000 feet (on the summit of the hill) and the lowest about 6500. During the early summer months and in the late autumn the climate is delightful. The early summer occasionally brings with it much of the dust-laden atmosphere which then pervades the plains, and the burnt and barren hill-sides are oppressively dull in tint and tone, losing all the beauty of colour-perspective ; but under clear autumnal skies the crisp freshness of the air and the beauty of the endless panorama of snowy hills, or blue plains spreading away from the glorious tints of an autumn foreground, are unequalled even in Switzerland.

Simla is now rapidly developing as a winter residence. Snow occasionally lies deep, but the cold is never very severe, and many English residents prefer their comfortable homes in the hills to the long and often expensive journeys entailed by a return to the plains. The disadvantage of the Himalayan climate is the periodic return of the rainy season for a month or two, when the cloud-drifts envelop hill and gully, and the moisture-laden atmosphere penetrates into every crevice and corner of the house, raising a fungus growth which is most detrimental to household property. The rainfall varies in the different hill-stations, but it may be taken at an average of about 80 inches in the Himalayas, decreasing towards the north-west where (as at Murree) the full force of the south-west monsoon is not experienced, and increasing towards the south-east. The actual rainfall does not, however, represent the measure of discomfort which is induced by an atmosphere overcharged with damp. The shape and position of the minor hill ranges has far more to say to the amount of the cloud envelope which is so depressing and so detrimental in its effects. One part of a station may, indeed, even in the worst seasons, be almost entirely free from the grey mist which wraps up all the rest of it in unbroken fog.

Next to Simla perhaps Mussoorie takes rank in importance as a hill-station. It is infinitely more accessible from the plains, a ride of seven miles being all that intervenes between Rajpur, at the foot of the hills, and the town above, whilst fifty-eight miles of driving road have to be traversed in order to reach Simla from Kalka. Kalka is, however, connected with the great railway systems of the plains, whilst Rajpur is still some forty-eight miles from the railway terminus at Saharanpur.[1] Eventually both stations will (like Darjiling on the south-east) possess their own railway facilities.

The distinguishing feature of Mussoorie, which is a station of the North-West Provinces but not the seat of the provincial Government, is its direct connection with the elevated valley of Dehra Dun, which lies between the foot of the Himalaya and the sibsidiary Siwalik range, immediately below the station. The Dun is one of the gardens of India, approaching Kashmir in its fertility and possible agricultural resources. It is already the centre of a considerable group of tea estates, although tea cultivation has hardly proved the success in these northern latitudes that it has on the outer slopes below Darjiling, in Assam, or in Ceylon. A very large colony of Eurasians and a few Europeans have settled in Dehra Dun, which possesses an equable climate, ready access to a hill-station, and some of the most beautiful scenery to be found in Northern India. The large forest reserves in the valley have also tended towards the development and preservation of game, whilst the resources of the Dun streams in fishing have ever been celebrated. Herds of elephants still roam through the jungles of the Eastern Dun, and tigers are occasionally plentiful.

Naini Tal, in the Kumaon district, is a very popular

[1] The railway terminus is now (1903) at Dehra Dun, a few miles only from Rajpur, and the line to Simla is advancing rapidly.

hill-station, and the seat of the local Government of the North-West Provinces. It is easily accessible from its satellite station at the foot of the hills, Kathgodam, which is a railway terminus. But Naini Tal is a cramped little place, shut in round the lake which gives it its name, and incapable of expansion in its own immediate vicinity. The shaly nature of the surface rocks on some sections of the hill-sides has given Naini Tal an unenviable notoriety as the scene of some disastrous landslips. Naini Tal leads to the military cantonments of Ranikhet and Almorah, and outside its own little circle of hills there is possibility of developing further sites suitable to European occupation.

Darjiling is the hill-station *par excellence* of Calcutta and Bengal, and enjoys the advantage of direct railway communication with the plains. Of its great natural beauty I have already spoken. But its rainfall is excessive, and its climate lacks the bracing qualities of that of the north-west.

Murree is on the extreme north-west. It is the station of the Punjab, and, with a series of minor stations called "gullies" (from "galli," a neck or spur), proves a most delightful resort for the over-worked and over-heated Punjab official. It is connected with Rawal Pindi by about fifty miles of good carriage road. The characteristics of Murree scenery (particularly of the "gullies") are those of Kashmir, of which country it forms, as it were, the commercial base. Much of the trade of Kashmir (in which fruit is a predominant feature) passes down the highroad leading through Murree to the plains; countless loads of apples being yearly exported to the Punjab; and it is through Murree that Srinagar is supplied with European goods, and its yearly stream of European visitors.

There are many other minor Himalayan stations, some of them purely military, others (as for instance the settlements in that most charming of sub-Himalayan valleys, Kulu) purely agricultural, each possessing its own special local advantages in climate and position, to which it is not possible to refer in detail. Of most of them it may be said that they are but partially fitted to the full requirements of European colonisation, although they are the "staff of life" to the Indian official. To this general statement two possible exceptions may be made. Kashmir possesses already a resident population of Europeans, and there indeed permanent settlements may eventually develop under more enlightened administration than exists at present; and in Kulu, again, a tea-growing and fruit-cultivating community exists, which is almost analogous to a colony. But the Kulu Valley is too restricted in size to serve as an experiment of any value from which to form conclusive deductions.

Kashmir has been a fruitful source of literature from time immemorial, but not much has been written illustrative of its physical configuration. Again, the Indian Survey reports are chiefly responsible for the opinions expressed in this chapter. Godwin-Austen, Tanner, Montgomerie, and others have all contributed to an accurate knowledge of the construction of the Kashmir mountain systems on both sides the Indus. A. Durand and Knight have written charming books on the scenery and the ethnographical characteristics of the remoter districts of Gilgit and the trans-Indus. The occupation of Chitrál opened up a large area for fresh inquiry. Griesbach and Lydekker have examined its chief geological features. Leitner investigated the languages and ethnography of the Indus basin, and has written some learned treatises on the subject in the *Indian Antiquary*. But the best book on Kashmir for the study of the ordinary reader is by W. R. Lawrence ("The Valley of Kashmir"), which gives a comprehensive account of the chief features of the state in comparatively modern times. Kashmir is full of archæological interest. This subject is fully dealt with in the Archæological Records of India, and is referred to on broader lines in Fergusson's "History of Indian Architecture." For Himalayan studies the reader is referred to the standard works of Sir J. Strachey and Sir W. W. Hunter; to contributions to the *Royal Geographical Society's Journal* by Sir R. Strachey, Godwin-Austen, and Tanner. Oldham and Griesbach have written of the geological evolution of these stupendous mountains; Sir Martin Conway and Mr. Douglas Freshfield have made the extreme north-west and the extreme south-east familiar in more recent works.

# CHAPTER V

## THE GEOGRAPHY OF THE INDIAN PENINSULA

STATISTICS.—India, including Burma and the native states, possesses a total area of nearly 1,600,000 square miles, and 287,000,000 inhabitants; reckoned by the census of 1891.

SOUTH of the Himalayas India may be divided roughly into two parts: firstly, the area embraced by the great alluvial plains of the north, which include the Punjab, Rajputana, and Sind on the north-west, the United Provinces in the centre, and a great part of the Bengal province with the deltas of the Brahmaputra and the Ganges on the north-east; and secondly, the highlands of Central India and the low alluvial tracts of the south. The great northern area of low-lying plain reaches from the Himalayas to the Indian Ocean on the west, and to the Bay of Bengal on the east, and includes the main arteries of the great river systems of the Indus, the Ganges and the lower Brahmaputra. "The Indo-Gangetic plain comprises the richest, the most fertile, the most populous, and historically the most famous countries of India. It covers more than 500,000 square miles, an area as large as France, the German and Austrian Empires, and Italy, and it contains 160 millions of people." "The alluvial deposits of which it is composed are so comminuted that it is no exaggeration to say that it is possible to go from the Bay of Bengal up the Ganges, through the Punjab, and down the Indus again to the sea, over a distance of 2000 miles and more, without finding a pebble, however small."[1]

Differing widely in its physical characteristics from Northern India, the second great natural division comprises

[1] Strachey's "India," chap. i.

the provinces of Madras and Bombay, the Central Provinces, and some of the chief native states of India. It is separated by no sharply defined line from the north, the plains of the northern states gradually rising in broken and irregular steps to the crest of the Vindhya and Satpura Mountains, and maintaining an average of 1500 feet south of the Narbada across the central tableland to Mysore, where it attains to 3000 feet or more. These central highlands, which include vast primeval forests covering rugged hill tracts intersected by wide valleys with gentle slopes, is depressed towards the east, and is bounded on either side by well-defined ridges of higher altitude, which appear as ranges when viewed from the sea, and follow approximately the line of coast curvature, leaving a broad strip of level coast between their lower spurs and the sea. These bounding edges of hill country are termed the Eastern and the Western Gháts respectively. The plateau slopes to the east and south-east, so that the Eastern Gháts are of no great altitude, being about 1000 feet above sea-level, and there is little or no fall from their crests westward, but the Western Gháts adopt the formation of a distinct anticlinal with more decision ; and though irregularly piled together where they first commence to take shape south of the Narbada, they gradually consolidate and finally rise to an altitude of nearly 8000 feet in the south, where they culminate in the Sispára peaks of the Nilgiris. The deep blue tone assumed by these magnificent grass-covered hills, when the south-west monsoon sweeps across their crests and breaks on their western slopes, gives peculiar force to the name—Nilgiris, or Blue Mountains. South of the Nilgiris the Western Gháts continue in the formation of a mountain range, receding, however, from the coast, and leaving the low level state of Travancore between themselves and the sea, until they terminate near Cape Comorin.

The Eastern Gháts commence to round off westward from a point not far north of Madras, and with broken outline fall back from the coast until they merge into the southern buttresses of the Nilgiris, leaving the broad plains of the Karnatic to stretch almost unbroken to the Bay of Bengal.

To the north of the line of the Western Gháts, but thrown back at an angle which gives them a north-easterly and south-westerly trend, is an isolated range, flanking the eastern deserts of Rajputana and dividing them from the native states of Central India, called the Aravalli range, the primeval range of India. Mount Abu (the highest point of the range) is 5000 feet above sea-level, an altitude which ensures a climate suitable for the small hill-station which occupies the highest slopes and clusters round the ancient rock cut temples, overlooking vast stretches of plain to east and west. The Aravalli is but the most southern link of a system in which straight rocky ridges, more or less isolated by stretches of intervening sand, follow the same strike and crop up in parallel lines of small elevation through the length of Eastern Rajputana. In general appearance this formation is that of a range, connected and continuous, but which has been overwhelmed by an encroaching sand sea. The flood of sand has filled up its valleys, and drifted in long smooth slopes against its crest until it has left nothing but lines of narrow jagged peaks to mark its position. The Vindhyas, the Aravalli range, the Western Gháts, and the Nilgiris, with the final southern extension culminating in the Anamali Hills, are the chief mountain masses of the Indian Peninsula south of the Himalayas. Hidden amongst them are many spots of rare beauty, many a group of magnificent peaks clothed with an infinite variety of forest vegetation, the recesses of which are known but to the district official, the sportsman, or the forest officer.

The river systems of India may be grouped as follows:—

(1) The Indus system on the north-west.

(2) The Ganges and Brahmaputra on the north-east.

(3) The Narbada, Tapti, Són, and Mahanadi in the central group.

(4) The Godavari, Kistna and others in the southern, system.

Some of the upper affluents of the Indus have been already mentioned in connection with Afghanistan and Kashmir, so that west of the Indus we need but consider those western tributaries which are derived from the basins of the Kabul, the Kuram, the Tochi, and the Gomal. These are all closely connected with the military policy of our frontier ; all of them afford means of communication between India and the trans-border districts, and are much more important to us as military highways than as channels of commerce with Central Asia. As they drain the slopes of mountainous regions they run in fixed channels, passing over rocky beds, often as mountain torrents, and always with a rapid and dangerous current when under the influence of floods caused by melting snow or by heavy rain in the hills about them. On emerging into the open plain of the Deraját, the Kuram, Tochi, and Gomal pass through beds of alluvial soil which tends to a constant shifting of their channels ; but as the distance from their debouchment into the plains to their junction with the Indus is short, such changes are comparatively unimportant. The Kabul River and its mountain-bred tributaries, the Kunar and the Swat, also flow through well-fixed channels with little apparent variation from century to century. But when we examine the Indus and its great Punjab branches, we find that in their character as rivers of the plains they evince a constant tendency to shift their positions from one bed to another. So long as they are rivers of the hills they obey the same laws as are common to all hill streams. The spurs of the mountains hold them in their rocky channels, and not even the influence of vast landslips, blocking their way and forming deep reservoirs, has any serious disturbing effect on the course they run. Under favourable conditions they change their grade, filling up the valleys with detritus ; and, cutting back at their sources, capture fresh areas from the highlands. It not infrequently happens, indeed, that the entire flow of the Indus is held up by a mighty barrier of fallen rocks and débris, and the narrow channel above the fall rapidly deepens to a reservoir from which but a very small outflow permeates the retaining wall of débris into the lower course of the river. In due time this barrier gives way to the pressure caused by the influence of floods in the upper branches of the river basin, and with terrific violence the escaping torrents pour

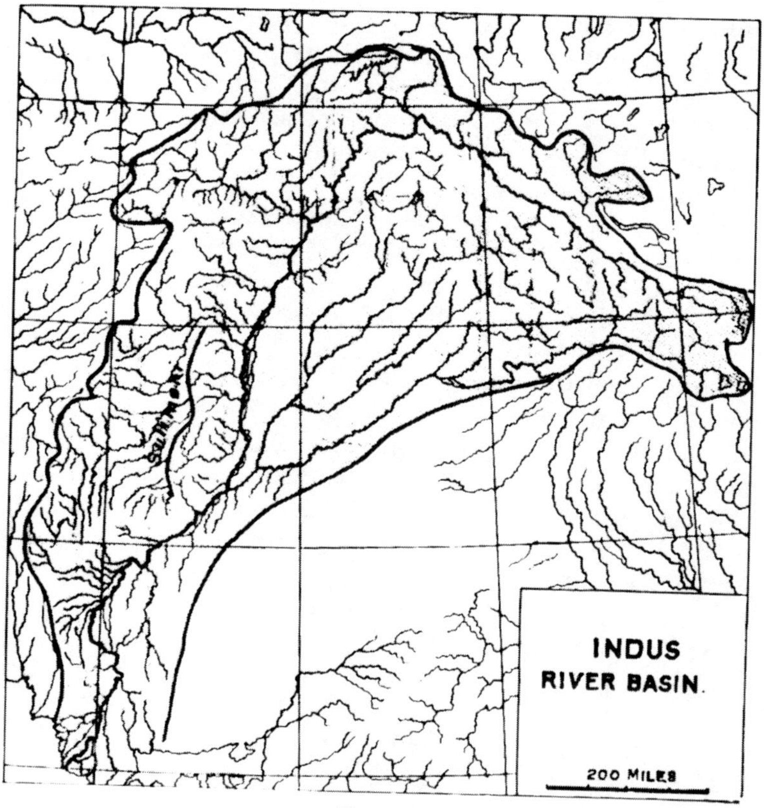


FIG. 40.

down through their usual waterway, carrying everything before them with resistless force. Then the lower valleys become inundated, and lives are lost and property destroyed ere the river resumes its normal level again.

The source of the Indus (as already pointed out) lies in a lacustrine region in Western Tibet, from whence also issue the first beginnings of the Sutlej and the Brahmaputra, and which is not far removed from the source of the largest affluent (sometimes reckoned as the main stream) of the Ganges. Enclosed between the Indus and the Sutlej, the three other great rivers of the Punjab, the Jehlam (Jehlum), the Chenab, and the Ravi rise; the head of the Jehlam (which is largely increased in volume by the Sind and Kishenganga affluents) lies in the heart of Kashmir, and the Chenab and Ravi take their rise from contiguous sources east of the little Rajput state of Chamba. All these rivers have one feature in common. They all lead off in a north-westerly direction before shaping their course to the south-west to sweep through the plains of the Punjab. We are so apt to regard the Indus as a gigantic waterway passing south-west through the alluvial flats of the Punjab and the sands of Sind, that we constantly overlook the fact that at least one-third of its course of over 1500 miles is towards the north-west.

All the Punjab rivers derive their main water-supply from the snows and mountain torrents of the Himalayas, and all are liable to their periodic seasons of flood when the snows melt off the higher ranges during the late summer, and the monsoon at the same time brings up its warm vapour-bearing currents to burst against the cool summits of the peaks overlooking their sources. Then (about July and August) comes the rush of life-giving water to the steaming plains; then is the anxious time for the engineer and bridge-maker; then the swelling brown torrent spreads across miles of river bed, curling and eddying with resistless sweep against piers and abutments, licking the neck of the bridge supports, and bringing down heavy batteries of floating timber and uprooted trees. The flood action of all these Punjab rivers is the same. There are no restraining natural revetments to keep the river within bounds, nothing set by Nature to prevent its carving out a fresh channel for itself in the soft alluvial soil, and forsaking its old waterway and discarding its bridges (if they prove obstructive), taking up an entirely new position. And this would happen yearly but for the artificial constructions which are engineered on its banks for miles above the bridges to keep the current in a permanent channel.

Occasionally an accident directs the destinies of the stream. A loop in the Indus was formed above Dera Ismail Khan some years ago, which, had it straightened itself out, would have cut the station in two. Houses were forsaken or sold for an old song, and it certainly appeared as if the place was doomed. But a tree fell in, up stream, some distance from the city, and the accumulation of drift sand and débris against the fallen tree formed a natural abutment which shifted the corroding current into a new direction, and saved the cantonment.

All the Punjab rivers east of the Indus, including the Beás, open out into a wide network of channels on leaving the hills, and maintain this formation to the end. In the early dry months of summer these channels are frequently nothing but wide white spaces of shimmering sand, with here and there a narrow ribbon of gleaming water permeating the width of river bed, and offering no difficulty to the passer by, except where the main channel, narrowed to the dimension of a rivulet, may perchance present an unfordable obstacle. Here the ferry is to be found, and flat-bottomed boats of picturesque construction assist the wayfarer. Crossing a Punjab river in the hot months, when a furnace blast stirs up the sand and sends it swirling across the river flats, is a dry and bitter experience. Crossing it when a wide torrent of rolling flood sweeps southward, carrying on its crest destructive snags and the circling evidences of dangerous eddies, is not so unpleasant, but it is more risky.

The network of the Punjab waterways is completed thus—the Beás joins the Sutlej near the historic field of Sobraon; the Ravi (the river of Lahore) and the Jehlam both join the Chenáb, and the three together unite with the Sutlej some 60 miles south of Multan (the city of the Chenáb), the whole system becoming one with the Indus about 48 miles south of the last junction. I have said that all the Punjab rivers east of the Indus flow in alluvial channels from the time they leave the hills. So does the Indus itself at first, for it spreads into a network of channels as it crosses the Peshawur Valley. But its channel is constricted again to one main stream after receiving the Kabul River at Attok, and the river thenceforward flows in a rocky bed (which narrows to a gorge below Attok) for some 70 miles, until it emerges from the defiles between the cliffs of the Kohat district on its western bank and the abutment of the Salt range of Rawal Pindi on the east, and passes the salt-built town of Kalabagh.

Throughout these enclosed reaches of the river the narrow rock passages are magnificent in the wildness and the weirdness of their scenery.

The road connecting our frontier post of Kohat with the railway system of the Punjab crosses the river by a bridge of boats about half-way between Attok and Kalabagh. South of Kalabagh the river again opens out into countless channels, which are constantly shifting and changing their position under the influence of the yearly floods. The general tendency of the main branch of the river is to shift westward, and it is this process which so nearly demolished the town of Dera Ismail Khan. From Dera Ismail Khan, southwards, the river is navigable for the flat-bottomed steamers of the Indus flotilla. The character of the Indus remains unchanged till it crosses the Sind frontier on leaving the Punjab, some 60 miles below the junction of the Punjab rivers, now united in the Chenáb. Here, at Kasmur, a great engineering scheme has arranged for the storage of the yearly overflow for distribution in the form of irrigation through that part of Sind which lies between the river and the Baluch Mountains. At Sukkur the channel is so enclosed and narrowed that, with the assistance of a rocky island in its midst, the river has been spanned by a magnificent bridge in two spans. This bridge carries the line of the North-Western Railway from the left, or eastern, to the right bank of the river, which it follows till it reaches Karachi.

From Sukkur southward the river again pursues an

open course in a wide bed of alluvial soil for about 600 miles till the Sind frontier hills touch its western banks. At this point the Indus has shifted as far west as is possible under the conditions of the hill conformation which there obtain, and it becomes confined to a more or less permanent channel until it enters the great delta south of Haidarabad.

The delta of the Indus is riddled with ancient channels to the east of the position of the present main stream, and it is almost within historic times that one of

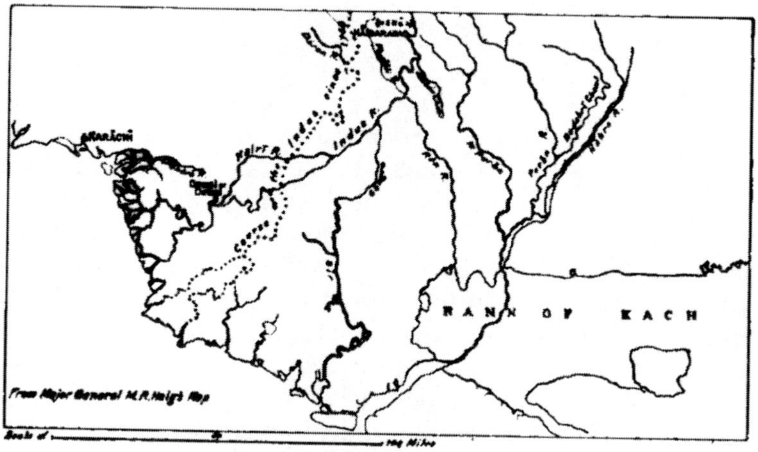


FIG. 41.—Indus Delta showing Ancient Channels of the Indus.

these, the Puran, carried the main waters of the river to the Rann of Kach, 70 miles to the east of its present debouchment. Very interesting are certain local legends that account for the rift in the beds of lime and conglomerate, the formation of which is said to have deflected the Indus into its present channel from the ancient bed of the Nara at Sukkur. "Hakro," says General Haig, "is a name in modern times restricted to the lower part of what has become a flood channel of the Indus, and is now known as the Nara (officially, Eastern Nara), but it once belonged to an entirely independent river of which the Nara channel formed a part. The course of this river may be traced throughout Sind, in the far north of which it bears the name of Wandan ; through Bhawalpur, where the name Hakro reappears, . . . thence through the north of Bikanir, and onwards beyond Rajputana to the foot of the Himalaya." Whether this river can be identified with an ancient course of the Sutlej, or can be connected with the Ghaggar east of the Sutlej (which now disappears in the sands of Rajputana), rather than with the Indus, may still be questioned ; but General Haig considers that "it is certain that the Hakro of lower Sind was formerly a part of the course of an independent stream, the drying up of which has been calamitous, not only in reducing thousands of square miles of once fertile land and inhabited country to waste and solitude, but also in forcing a vast additional body of water into the already overcharged channel of the Indus, thus enormously increasing the risk of desolating floods along the lower course of that river."

The risk of desolating floods is still further increased by the action of the river in depositing vast quantities of silt, which have a tendency to gradually raise the level of the channel. Thus the Indus and other Himalayan-bred rivers liable to yearly flood usually acquire a channel level which is considerably higher than the plains on either side of them, and the area of land subject to inundation is thereby enormously increased. The floods of the Indus extend to the foot of the Baluchistan hills, and it is no uncommon occurrence for the line of railway connecting Jacobabad with Quetta to be so deep under water as to render it impossible to maintain traffic. The remains of Indus-built boats have been dug up far to the west of Jacobabad, and these relics are old enough to indicate either that the deep-water Indus floods have spread through the Kachi of Gandava from very ancient days, or that there was once a western branch of the river.

In direct connection with the river systems of India we may well consider the general geographical conformation of those districts which they water and sustain.

The Punjab, the native state of Bhawalpur, Rajputana, and Sind are all of them within the Indus basin ; all of them are subject to similar climatic conditions at the same periodic intervals. There is also much similarity in their conformation, for they all form part of that great Indo-Gangetic plain which stretches from the Arabian Sea to the Bay of Bengal. The Punjab extends east and west from the frontier hills west of the Indus to the Jumna

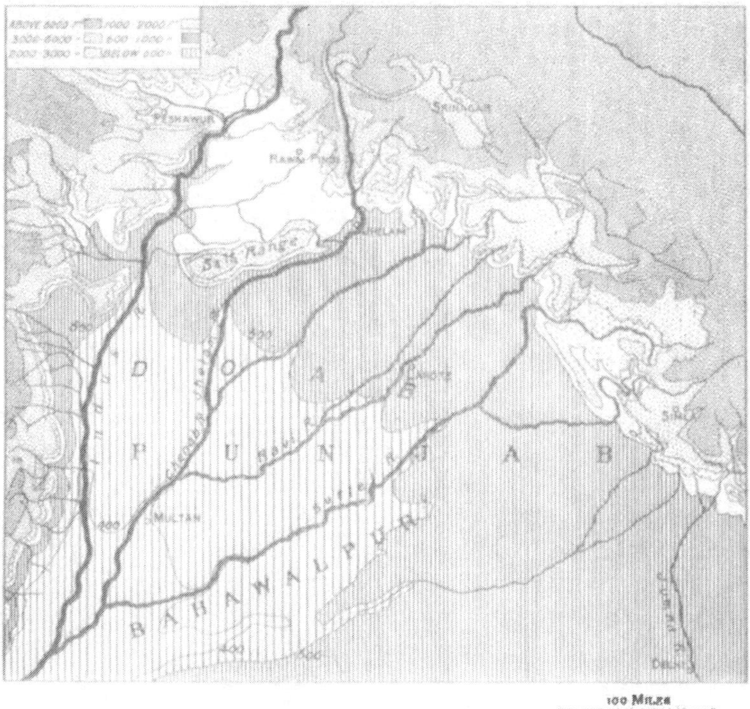


FIG. 42.—The Rivers of the Punjab.

River, and from the Himalayas on the north to the plains and deserts of Bhawalpur and Rajputana on the south. The city of Delhi is on its extreme eastern frontier, and Simla, together with certain hill states which lie to the north of Simla, is included within Punjab administration. Omitting these Himalayan states, the Punjab, within the five rivers, consist of a series of wide flat plains—called Doab—extending in unbroken succession to Rajputana and Sind. All the southern districts of the Punjab are flat: the eye rests on nothing but a wide vista of monotonous dust-coloured plain, or on vast stretches of wheat cultivation, according to the season of the year. Between Lahore and Multan a dreary expanse of sandy waste, supporting a scattered jungle of undersized trees and scrub (chiefly tamarisk), is the distinguishing feature of the country bordering the railway on either side. Similar characteristics prevail throughout the Doab tracts between the Punjab rivers from the Sutlej to the Indus. Only when approaching the riverain, or a district subject to flood or irrigation, is there any marked change in the scenery. Then indeed close set fields and a wealth of trees and hamlets indicates the productive nature of the alluvial soil when sufficient water for cultivation is available. Parts of the Chenáb and the Indus, near their junction, are so thickly bordered with trees as to remind one of the ancient tradition of forests on the Indus; and lower, about the Sind reaches of the river, are many square miles of tamarisk jungle which much more nearly approach a forest growth than do the scattered and ragged jungles of the north country.

In the extreme north of the Punjab, the districts of Rawal Pindi and of Peshawur, west of the Jehlam, as well as the northerly extension into the hills east of the Indus, which includes the Khagán Valley, are all hill districts with characteristics entirely distinct from the Doab. The dividing line is near the Salt range, which practically extends across the Indus from the southern Kohat district to Pind Dadun Khan on the Jehlam. North of this remarkable feature (which contains an unexhaustible supply of salt underlying multicoloured clays and sand-drifts of recent formation) there is a vast network of broken ground intersected by ravines and nullahs. These enclose the railway from Jehlam to Rawal Pindi, and surround the latter city with an almost impassable maze of intricate ground. Farther north the Peshawur Valley opens out into a comparatively level plain—a plain which is highly cultivated and covered with tree growth—

of which it is difficult to realise that it ever supported the swamps and grass jungles in which the rhinoceros was hunted less than four centuries ago.

Excepting this northern district beyond the Salt range, the plains of the Punjab retain their characteristic flatness until they merge into the sands of Rajputana and the Sind wilderness.

The general aspect of Eastern Sind is much the same as that of Rajputana, more inhospitable and waste than anything to be found in the Punjab, and subject to the scorching influences of the fiercest heat without the modifications of a fair rainfall. The desert nature of all this part of India culminates in the dreary expanse of the Rann of Kach, which may be described as a great salt waste struggling towards a final reclamation from the sea, not yet fully accomplished.

The Derajat, which forms the upper portion of that strip of trans-Indus territory which reaches from Peshawur to Karachi, and the trans-Indus districts of Sind have been largely brought under the influence of irrigation, and our frontier stations from Kohat to Jacobabad are all of them buried in trees and surrounded with an area of most highly developed cultivation. It would be difficult to imagine a scene of fresher luxuriance than may be found in the neighbourhood of any of these stations in the spring months of the year.

Of all the river systems of India the Gangetic is the most important, for it waters the most populous, the wealthiest, and the most famous provinces of the Indian Empire, including within its basin the North-West Provinces,[1] Oudh, and a great part of Bengal. Closely connected with it as a river system is the province of Assam, for the Brahmaputra, which is the central river and main channel of communication within that province, unites with the Ganges some 75 miles above its mouth, and assists it to fertilise lower Bengal. The chief tributaries of the Ganges are the Jumna, which rises west of it in the central chain of the Himalayas and joins at Allahabad ; the

[1] The North-West Provinces and Oudh are now the "United Provinces."

Ghágra, and the Gandak. The Gandak, which might almost rank as the main stream, joins the Ganges near Patna. The Ghágra, under various names, drains the western borderland of Nepal, and a branch of it forms the boundary between Nepal and Kumaon on the east of the latter district. The Jumna marks the western boundary of Kumaon and separates it from what are usually called the Simla hill states.

The Gandak, as already noted, rises not far from the

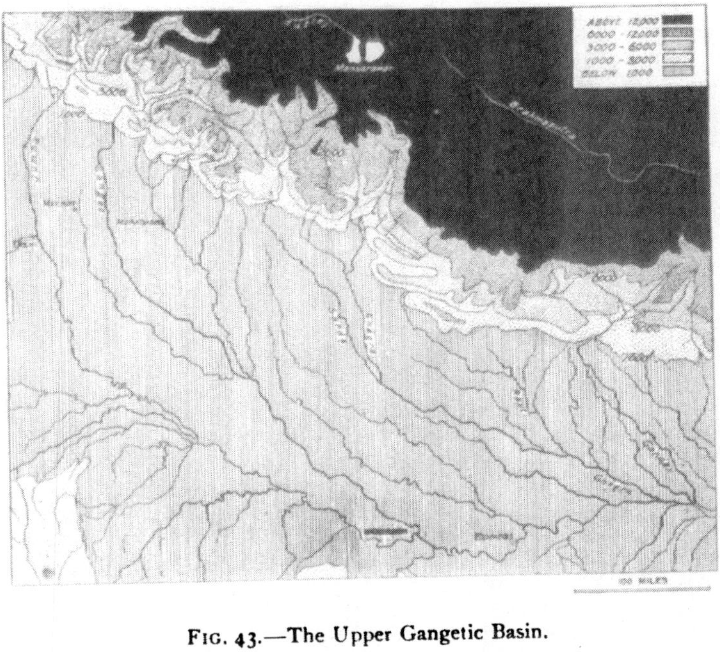

FIG. 43.—The Upper Gangetic Basin.

sources of the Brahmaputra, and carries more water to the plains than does the Ganges itself. Within the Himalayas both the Jumna and the many-headed Ganges are hill torrents, flowing over beds of rock and boulder, breaking into cataracts, and assuming all the picturesque phases of mountain rivers; but from where they enter the plains, and until they reach the sea, they pursue a wide and uneventful career of land-making and irrigation, spreading over the flat alluvial soil in times of flood, and narrowing to an intricate network of small channels circling round huge sand spots and islets in times of drought—yet never failing altogether. The Ganges still retains the sanctity that Brahmanism has accorded to it through all ages. Hardwar, at the point where the river leaves the

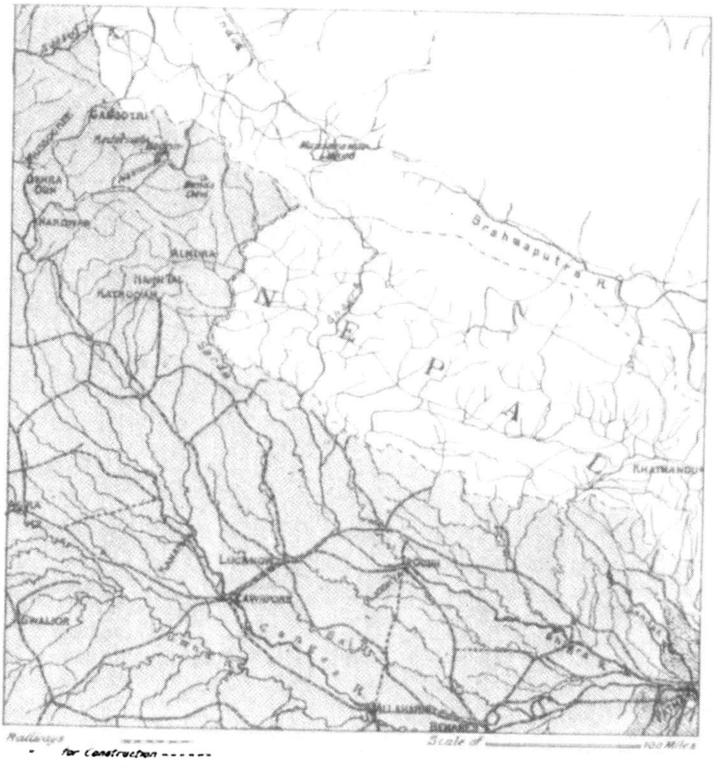

FIG. 44.—Northern India Railway Communication.

Himalayas, is still the sacred city, the great city of pilgrimage, and of that ablution which washes away sin. It is still the central attraction of vast crowds of worshippers who congregate at the yearly mela, or fair. But it is said that its days as the holy river of India are numbered, and that its saving graces are soon to be transferred to the Narbada.

The fall in the Ganges river bed from the Himalayan

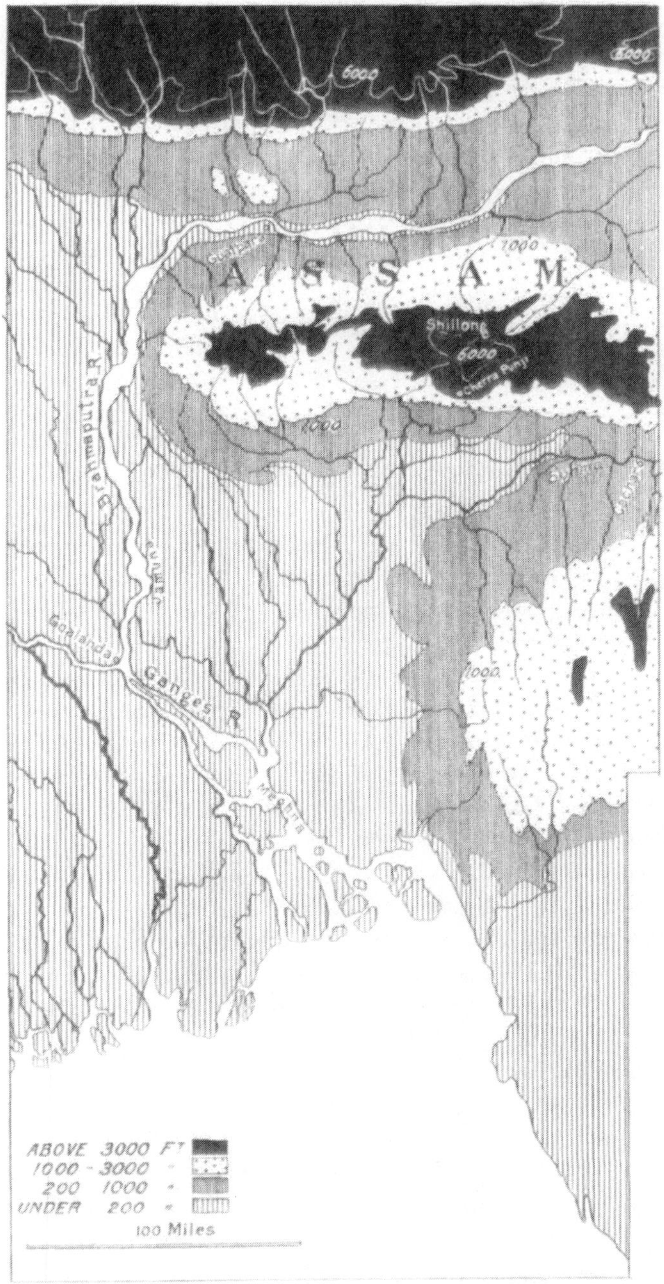


FIG. 45.—The Lower Brahmaputra and Gangetic Delta.

K

exit to the sea may be reckoned at 1 foot per mile, a gradient which does not interfere with the navigation of its lower reaches, and allows the river to slide in solemn majesty to its destination. The part which the Jumna and the Ganges take as fertilising agents, enriching the soil of thousands of acres of otherwise unproductive country by means of the magnificent canal system to which they give rise, will be dealt with elsewhere. In the lower part of its basin the level flats of lower Bengal are so freely watered by countless natural channels that artificial irrigation becomes unnecessary.

The Brahmaputra, from its debouchment into the plains of Assam to its junction with the Ganges, is very similar in its general characteristics to the latter river, although the districts which it drains in North-Eastern Assam, and (through the agency of its great tributary, the Megna) in Southern Assam, are widely distinct from the flat alluvial plains which border the Ganges. The Brahmaputra is a majestic river when it rolls in full flood down the comparatively narrow valley of Assam. The distance from bank to bank is often counted by miles; and the dense forest-clad slopes of the lower Himalayas to the north, beyond the wide swampy grass jungles of the Doars (the Terai of the eastern frontier), through which flow the Teesta from Darjiling, and the Monás from Bhutan, together form with the hills of the Khasia and Garo plateaux on the south, an impressive setting to its broad solemnity. Such effects are wanting in the sandy flats about the Ganges. That the channels of all the great rivers of the Gangetic plain are constantly shifting and changing hardly needs assertion, but there is no record of any general change of the bed of the entire river, or of its displacement for scores of miles, such as is apparent in the Indus. The Brahmaputra has no room for any large changes of this nature; but in the low-lying delta lands of the combined rivers, channels shift and change so often that it is probable that no general map would define them correctly for more than a year or two.

The United Provinces (which are drained and irrigated by the Ganges system) cover together 106,000 square miles, and include a population of 44,000,000. "There is no country in Europe in which the population is so dense; the average number of persons to the square mile in England and Wales is 446, in the United Provinces it is 460. No other Indian province is so thickly peopled; in Bengal, which most nearly approaches it, the average number to the square mile is 360." "This has been for ages the most famous part of India. In prehistoric times it was the Central or Middle Land, the Madhya-desha of the sacred books of the Hindus and of the ancient poets, the abode of the solar and lunar races, and of the gods and heroes of the Mahabhárata and Ramayána. . . . This tract contains the most holy places of India, Benares, Ajodhya, Kanauj, Muttra, and many others: it was here that Buddha was born, and preached, and died, and it was from this centre that his creed spread over a great part of the eastern world. In more modern times Hindustan was the chief seat of the Muhammadan power. Delhi and Agra became the capitals of the Afghan and Moghul sovereigns, and although the great majority of the population always remained Hindu, there was for many centuries no part of India in which Mussulman authority and organisation was so complete. In our own times this has been politically the most important part of our Indian Empire. 'To the native imagination,' as Mr. Keene has observed, 'Hindustan is still the centre of India, and Delhi is still the metropolis.'" Thus writes Sir John Strachey, who is perhaps the best living authority on the subject. In physical conformation there is no great difference between the Eastern Punjab and the United Provinces. They are all included in one vast alluvial plain, of which the unbroken monotony is a weariness to contemplate. But the flat ugliness of much of the Punjab plain scenery is relieved in the upper provinces of the Gangetic basin by the wealth of rich cultivation, which during the rains and in the winter season, covers the country in one continuous sheet. For 500 miles there is an unbroken succession of fields, orchards, and mango groves surrounding clusters of villages, as perfect a picture of rural prosperity as is to be found in the world. "It would be difficult to find in any part of the world, on so large a scale, a more striking prospect of industry and quiet contentment." The

FIG. 46.—The Deltaic Channels of the Ganges.

scenery in Behar, the northern district of the province (or lieutenant-governorship) of Bengal does not differ largely from that of the North-West. This is the land of indigo and opium, probably the only part of India where existing traces are still to be found of European social existence in the eighteenth century. The district of Bengal proper (or Lower Bengal), comprising the deltas of the Ganges and Brahmaputra, and the rich low tracts between those rivers, possesses a scenery which is unique. The land is intersected in all directions by the channels and estuaries of the two great rivers, and where it borders the sea the labyrinth of creeks is lost amidst the dense jungle and forests of the Sundarbans. When the yearly inundations occur an immense area is covered with water like a sea; the ordinary method of conveyance from one cluster of huts to another is by boat; nothing is to be seen of the rice crops but the "ears of grain floating on the surface." Rice is the great agricultural staple, and in this part of India forms the chief food of the people; but the products of lower Bengal are many and varied, and it ranks as the most productive part of the whole province. Sir John Strachey thus describes the scenery: "A constant succession of admirable pictures is afforded by the reaches of the river busy with traffic; the boats with their great sails; the cocoa-nuts and other palms, huge figs, tamarinds, and mangoes, bamboos and plantains; the villages with tanks green with slime and water-lilies; neat cottages covered with creeping gourds and cucumbers and melons; the delicate forms of the men and women in scanty but graceful costume—these, and a thousand picturesque details, and the colouring of its hot and steamy atmosphere, makes Bengal one of the most beautiful countries in India. Nor is it so disagreeable for Englishmen to live in as might be supposed. Although it has not the advantage of the pleasantly cold winter of Northern India, the heat of the summer is tempered by the greater moisture, and by the nearness of the sea. Heat like that of June at Agra or Lahore is unknown, and for three or four months in the winter the climate is very agreeable."

The Ganges with its tributaries covers an enormous catchment basin, reckoned at 391,100 square miles, between the Himalayas and the Vindhyas. Starting at 13,800 feet above sea-level the river drops to 1024 feet at Hardwar in the first 180 miles of its course. Here it discharges about 7000 cubic feet per second at its lowest, when it is almost entirely absorbed in irrigation. In another 1000 miles it collects drainage amounting to 1,800,000 cubic feet discharge in flood time, so that its maximum volume is greater at this point (400 miles from the sea) than that of the Mississippi at the end of its course. "About 200 miles of the sea-face of Bengal consists of estuaries of the Ganges intersected by low islands and promontories formed out of itself."[1]

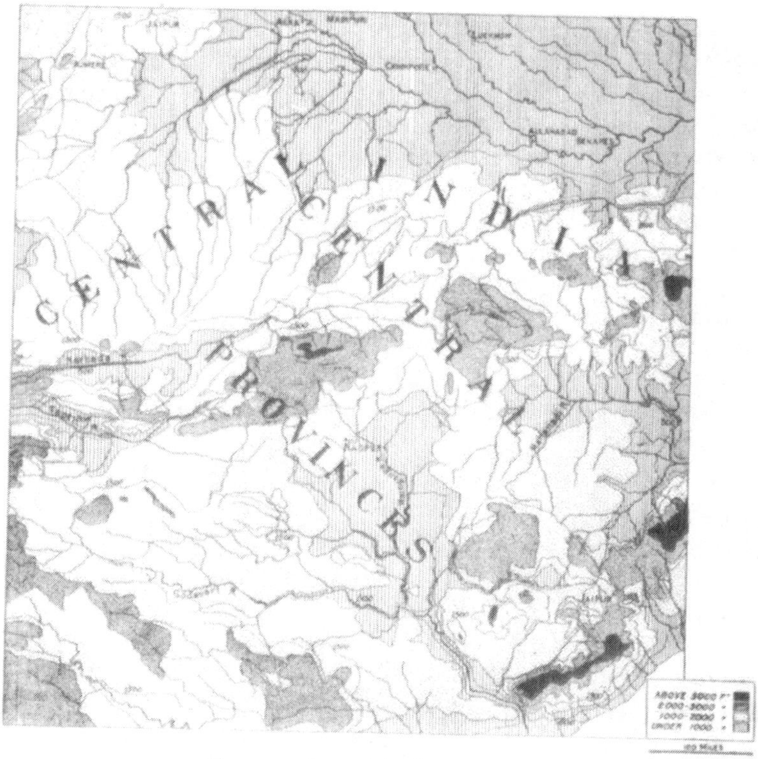


FIG. 47.—Central India Orography.

The most important (if not the largest) tributary is the Jumna, which starts at an elevation of 10,850 feet above sea at Jamnotri, not far removed from Bhágirathi, the source of the Ganges. Where the Jumna and the Ganges unite (near Allahabad) is the true Prayág, or place of pilgrimage, where devout Hindus assemble in thousands and are washed and sanctified. The Jumna

[1] Hunter, "India," vol. vi.

(which in prehistoric days was probably a tributary of the Indus) is an important factor in the agricultural development of India, and sustains an immense irrigation system; but neither the Jumna nor any other river of India approaches the Ganges in general works of beneficence. For not only does the Ganges exercise a great function as land maker and fertilising agent, but she has ever served as the great national highway of India from the Bay of Bengal to the north-west.

Between Agra and Allahabad many a large tributary joins the Jumna from the native states of Central India which occupy the long northern slopes of the central plateau; and one important river, the Són, unites with the Ganges near Patna after draining the north-western hills of the Chota Nagpur division of the Bengal province. The Central India tributaries all take their rise from the crest of the Vindhya hills overlooking the deep valley of the Narbada. The Són rises in the historic mountains of Amarkantak, from whence also the Narbada takes its rise and flows westward; thus these two rivers together form a transverse system right across India from Patna to Broach, which has practically no northern basin or "catchment area" at all. On the southern slopes of the mass of elevated tableland which culminates at Amarkantak commence also the headwaters of some tributaries of these great rivers, which find their exit in the Bay of Bengal, *i.e.* of the Mahanadi and the Godavari.

Central India and that part of the Bengal province which is included in Chota (or Chutia) Nagpur is infinitely varied in its general appearance and character. Here commences the forest country, which with occasional modifications covers the whole of the eastern highlands of India.

In Central India the hills are broken and separated into groups and clusters, rising some hundreds of feet (seldom more than 1000) above the general level of the tableland, which is itself from 1500 to 2000 above sea-level. Often these hills are marked by precipitous cliffs surrounding their summits, and rendering all efforts to approach them difficult and dangerous. Hundreds of fortresses have at one time or another in history occupied the tops of these hills, and each has its own tale to tell of the days when security was only to be found in such strongholds. But between the hills very wide stretches of land are cultivated—wheat, pulse, opium, cotton, and millet being grown much in the same proportion as in the north-west. Sugar-cane is also largely produced. The soil consists largely of a species of black loam called "cotton" soil, which prevails throughout the districts of Central India and the Central Provinces. This soil is undermined by flood in the rainy season, and broken into innumerable holes and pitfalls; the surface water during the rains usually finding a readier method of drainage straight through the friable soil than by collecting in rivulets and streams, and finally making its way to the rivers. The hills are almost invariably clothed in a thick tangle of acacia jungle, amidst which are many forest-trees, the well-known "pipal" and "banian" being conspicuous; with teak, sál, mahogany, tamarind, &c., in fair abundance. Central India, flanked, as it is, by the sands of Rajputana on one side and the dense forest-growth of the Central Provinces on the other, partially assumes the physical characteristics of both. It is not a forest-clad country, but there are many square miles of forest land to be found in it. The great cultivated flats of the Central India tableland are broken and intersected here and there with deep ravines and gorges (locally called "Kho"), which, by reason of their comparative isolation form most admirable game preserves. The big game shooting of Central India has always been famous amongst sportsmen, but of late years the chiefs of the native states which form the province or "agency" have adopted methods of strict game preservation which places it beyond the reach of all but a few favoured officials. Writing with some experience of the fascination of the hills and jungles of Central India we can say that no part of India contains more charming country, or is possessed of a more perfect climate than is to be found amongst those wild stretches of forest and plain during the cold weather months.

INDIA, SOUTHERN SECTION

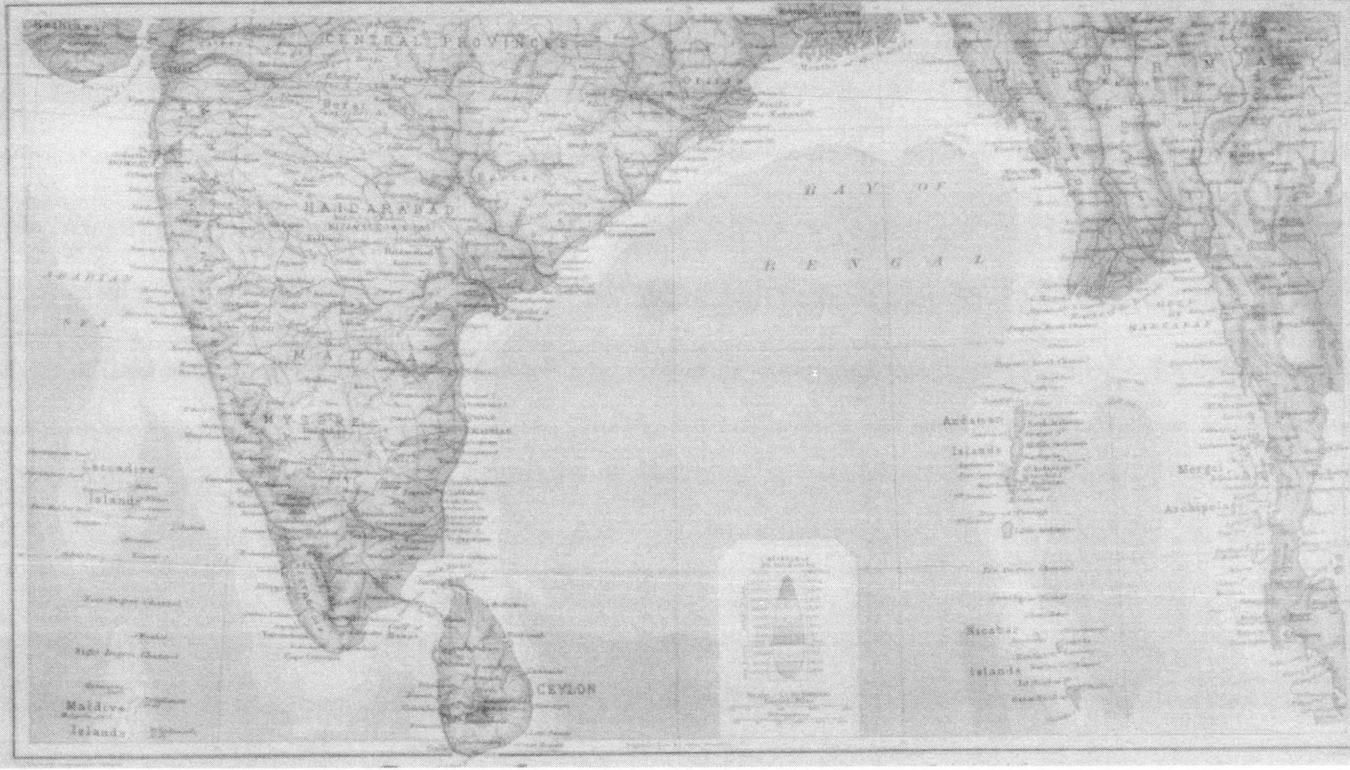

Parting the north of India from the south is the long trough of the Narbada and the valley of the Són. The latter belongs to the Gangetic system, but its characteristics are, at any rate in the upper part of its course, much the same as those of the Narbada. We have a graphic description of the Narbada (which holds its own straight course with little assistance from tributaries, either north or south) from the pen of Sir Lepel Griffin: "Through this country, which is but a network of hills, rising in some places to a considerable height, runs in an almost straight course the revered and miracle-working stream of the Narbada, which, in a few years' time, is to displace the Ganges itself in the religious estimation of the Hindus. Of all the rivers in India there is probably no one which is surrounded by more romance and mystic interest than the Narbada, whilst, for strange and fantastic beauty, it takes high rank amongst the celebrated rivers of the world; but its beauties are little known to English travellers. A few may perhaps see it where it falls into the Gulf of Cambay, below Broach; some may cross it at Hoshangabad or at Mortakka, where the branch lines to Rajputana, Bhopal, and Gwalior leave the main line of the Great Indian Peninsula Railway. A large number of tourists halting at Jabalpur, which is, as it were, the very centre and *omphalos* of India, spend a few hours in visiting the holy river, which here flows through marble rocks of some, though exaggerated, beauty, and beyond this the sight-seeing traveller knows nothing of the Narbada, although its course is everywhere beautiful from its rise at Amarkantak, at the southernmost point of the Rewah state in Central India till, dashing in a thousand rapids and whirlpools through the Vindhya and Satpura ranges in the Bhil country, it bursts in a broad stream into the Bombay plain below. From its birthplace to its grave in the sea the Narbada is an object of superstitious veneration, and in a country like India, where water, to the unscientific mind, signifies more than even the sunlight and heat, the vivifying principle of Nature which changes the desert into a flowering garden, the adoration of

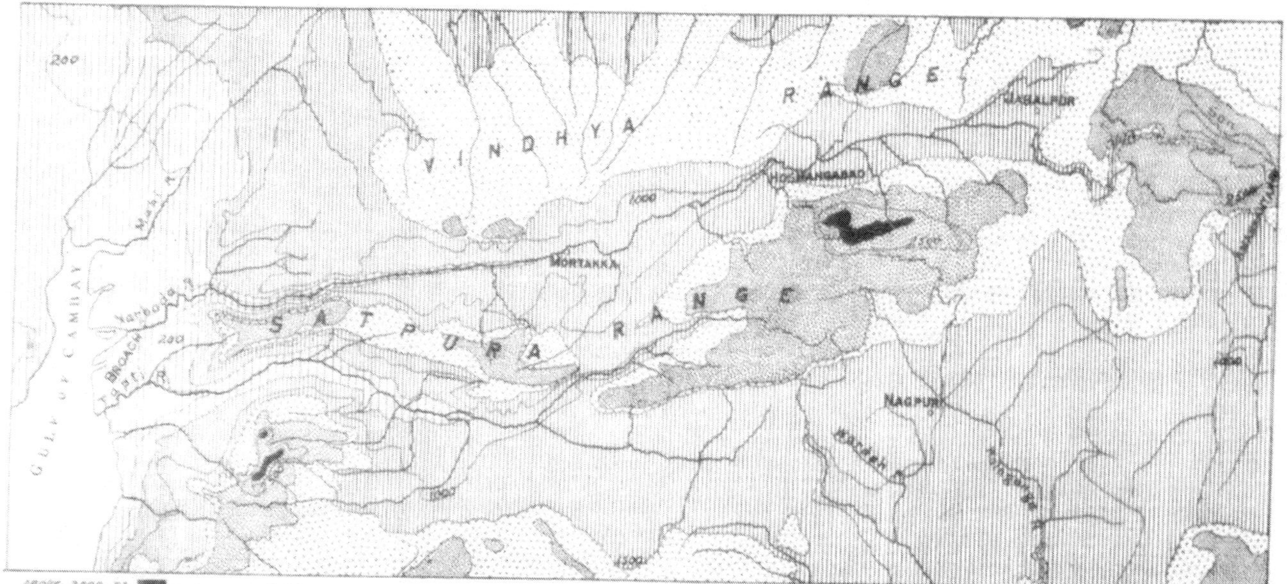


FIG. 48.—The Narbada-Tapti Basin.

streams is both natural and appropriate. Amarkantak, where the Narbada rises, is one of the most sacred spots in India, and in spite of its remoteness and its exceeding difficulty of approach, is visited every year by thousands of devout Hindus."

The northern or hill districts of the Central Provinces, culminating in the Satpuras, are in general physical conformation and appearance the same as the southern hill districts of Central India culminating in the Vindhyas; the former making the southern half, and the latter the northern half of the Narbada basin. Wild, picturesque jungle-covered hills, closely massed and drained by small but clear and rushing hill streams; inhabited by a wild and picturesque race of aboriginal people, unvisited by Europeans, and unknown to all but a few officials—these are the distinguishing features of the whole district. Farther south the Central Provinces (which are often confused with the Central India native states, with which they have no administrative affinity) open out into more extensive flats and tablelands, with a red gravel soil and outcrops of laterite, supporting a growth of forest and grass which is everywhere abundant and occasionally dense, but which often assumes a park-like appearance, with scattered groups of trees, and stretches of grassy sward. There is no wide extent of alluvial soil here, though the black cotton soil pervades the lower levels bordering the main streams. The districts around Jabalpur and Nagpur are all much of this nature; but as we move farther south, we rapidly pass into the jungle-covered area which stretches, with very little break in the endless monotony of ill-grown trees, indifferent grass, stunted bamboos, and all varieties of scorched and ill-nurtured vegetation, right across Eastern India from the Godavari to the Eastern Gháts. This is the region which may justly be called "darkest India." Into its recesses travellers never penetrate, and even its rivers are comparatively unknown.

Before touching those river systems which take their rise in the Western Gháts and flow across India to the

Bay of Bengal, we must refer to one comparatively minor system (although it drains an area about as large as France) which includes the waterways of two districts of the Bengal Province (Chota Nagpur and Orissa) and of the eastern half of the Central Provinces. This is the Mahanadi system, which is as complicated and as difficult to trace as that of the Narbada is straight and simple. The Mahanadi and the Brahmani combined find their exit to the sea by a labyrinth of channels intersecting the delta to the east of Cuttack. All the characteristics of the delta of the Ganges and Brahmaputra are repeated in the delta of the Mahanadi. Here, again, we encounter wide and water-logged jungles near the coast, backed by thousands of acres of rice fields, with all the steamy accessories of the lower Bengal climate. Here, again, we find a mild-mannered and enervated race of people, scantily clothed, and passing an amphibious existence from year to year, only stirred into occasional bursts of fanatical enthusiasm by the rites and ceremonies which attend the great Jagannáth festival. This most ancient centre of Hindu superstition is situated at Pori, on the coast due south of Cuttack, and though these prehistoric and mystic rites have been shorn of many of their most attractive horrors by the determination of an enlightened Government, thousands upon thousands of pilgrims still assemble periodically to do honour to an exhibition of Hindu symbolism which they do not in the least understand.

From the highlands immediately south of the Narbada, where the Wardah (an important tributary of the Godavari) takes its rise and flows southward through the Dekkan, another considerable stream also issues on the west, and flows parallel to the Narbada to the sea. This is the Tapti. Between the upper branches of the river, the northern abutment of the Western Gháts forms a high and distinct range running east and west to a height of 4000 feet above the sea. The southern spurs slope gently down to the general level of the Dekkan tableland, which extends from this range southwards, and, from the Tapti Valley southward, is flanked by the Western Gháts, which here run to about 3000 feet above sea, and about 1000 above the general level of the plateau.

Passing now to those river systems of the south which have their birth in the west and are finally lost in the eastern seas—the Godavari, the Kistna (or Krishna), the Kavari (Cauvery), and other minor rivers—we find a certain general similarity pervading the surroundings of them all. All of them flow through the Dekkan highlands for a great part of their course, and all of them make their final exit to the ocean through the flat alluvial delta bordering the coast.

The Godavari is by far the most important river of the central districts of India, and it is by far the most comprehensive in the structure of its upper basin. Its main branch rises on the west, not far from Bombay, and not more than 50 miles from the coast. It has another branch (the Wainganga) which rises not far from the centre of India, and hardly 50 miles from Jubbulpur; and it has yet another branch (the Indravati) which rises about 50 miles from the eastern coast, a little to the north of Vizianagram.

The Godavari is essentially the river of the Dekkan, and for two-thirds of its course it passes through the dominions of the Nizam of Haidarabad. The tableland which forms the upper part of its basin is comparatively bare of trees wherever the plain extends. The Western Gháts and the southern hills (which contain the sources of the Kavari) are well wooded, and some of the small valleys enclosed between the barren rocky hills which intersect the plain are highly cultivated. Black "cotton" soil again prevails over the whole surface of the plateau. During the rains it is a grass country, green with cultivation; but in spring and summer the bare, brown, level surface is only relieved by clouds of dust, which are whirled along by the furnace blasts of the hot wind. The heat is extreme.

Although for the most part the Godavari drains a country broken by hills, it is a comparatively wide and

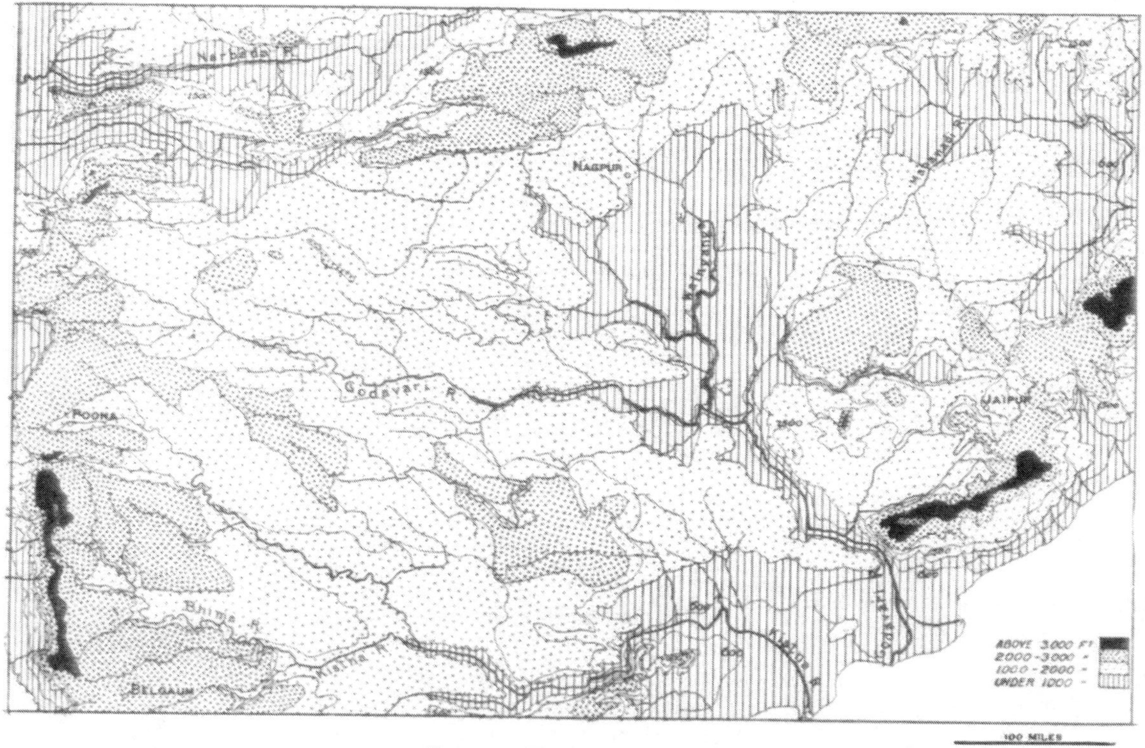


FIG. 49.—The Godavari Basin.

placid stream for some 200 miles of its course ere reaching the sea, with no violent fall, and only the obstruction caused by the shallowing of the river in crossing two or

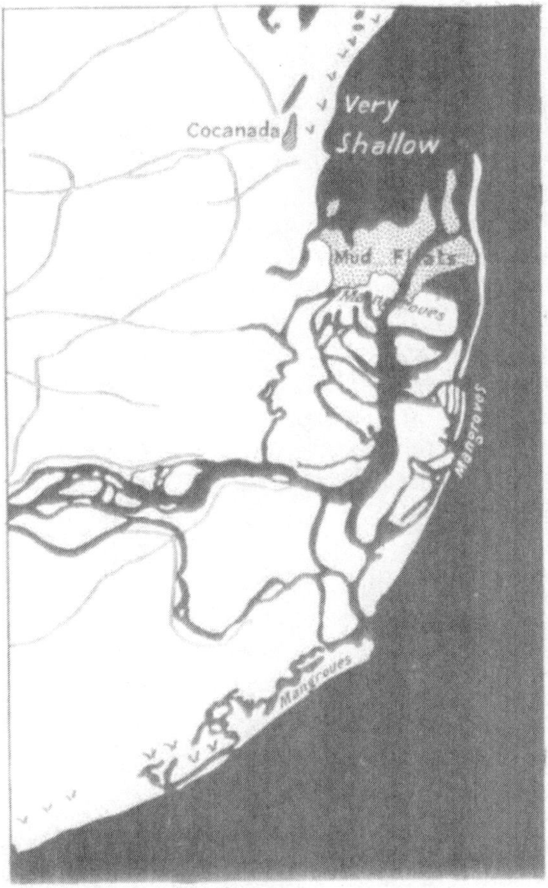


FIG. 50.—The Godavari Delta.

three sections of rocky bed (where it traverses the strike of the adjoining hills) bars the way to navigation when the river is low. About thirty years ago a scheme was initiated for making a permanent channel, navigable by the flat-bottomed steamers of the Godavari flotilla at all seasons of the year ; but the attempt was finally abandoned for uncertain reasons (though the frightful mortality which beset the European staff of engineers and workmen in these pestiferous jungles may have had much to say to it), and the Godavari is now only partially navigable when in flood.

It is only natural that amid the varied scenery which borders the river there should occasionally be points of great beauty. Perhaps the most striking is to be found some 50 miles above Rajmahendri (Rajamundry), where the Godavari is steeply enclosed between the Bison range (so called from the occasional visits of herds of bison) and the hills of Rumpa. Here the steeply-shelving cliffs and massed forests of bamboo, teak, tamarind, and fig, with scores of other indigenous trees which clothe the lower slopes and dip into the river, form a most striking series of pictures as the steamer strains up against the stream from reach to reach. No part of the Rhine is more picturesque, although it possesses the added charm (totally wanting in the Godavari) of human interest in the quaint castles and ruins which dominate the heights on either bank.

The Indrávati, which is entirely a forest-bound river, has the attraction of a waterfall of 90 feet where it drops into the valley of the Godavari from the highlands of Jagdalpur, but it possesses otherwise far more attractions for the sportsman than it does for the artist. Into the domain of the Godavari but few people, except sportsmen, penetrate ; and even the few usually confine themselves to the western branches of the river, where the Haidarabad plateau opens into a less dense continuity of jungle. Into the native states of Jaipur (not to be confounded with the Jaipur of Rajputana) and Jagdalpur (otherwise called Bustar), between the Godavari and the east coast, no European ever ventures except under official compulsion. These eastern jungles are deadly at nearly all seasons of the year. They form the home of the aboriginal Gond tribes—who will be described elsewhere.

With the limited facilities now afforded for navigation,

the trade of the Godavari is comparatively insignificant. Hides and gingelli nuts are the chief products of the lower basin, where a scattered population, which lives largely on the natural produce of the forest, grows hardly enough rice for home consumption. The wealth of the Godavari commences with the delta, through which a highly-developed system of irrigation has been matured, and has proved to be one of the most successful of all Indian irrigation projects. Here, once more, the natural lines of communication through the country are the waterways, and European officials travel chiefly in boats. Rice and tobacco are very largely cultivated, and the latter has achieved a reputation equal to that of the more southern Trichinopoli growth. Much of it is cultivated on the islands (or lunkas) of the river, and "lunka" tobacco has long been recognised in the European market as one of the best of Indian tobaccos.

The Kistna rises in the eastern declivities of the Western Gháts, and runs about 650 miles to the sea, carrying with it the waters of the Bhima from the north and the Tongabudra from the south-west. Both are important streams. The surface of the Kistna River is too low for irrigation purposes; the river carries but a small volume of water, and is unnavigable. Between its debouchment from the wild hill country which separates its lower course from that of the Godavari, and the Godavari delta, are districts which are annually inundated by a fresh-water lake called the Kolari, which occupies a deep depression about the centre of this low-lying tract. In the dry weather this lake is about 24 miles long by 12 in breadth; but when the annual floods from July to September raise the level of the two rivers, they overflow from both directions into the lake, which then becomes 40 to 50 miles long, and spills over the adjacent country. Its waters are used for irrigation during the dry season, embankments being formed to prevent the flood tides from the sea from reaching it. A small but navigable river connects it with the sea and carries off the surplus water.

The large commercial town of Machlipatnam (Masulipatam) is situated here, this being the only part of the eastern coast which is not subject to a surf. Shoal water, however, extends for some miles from the coast-line off the deltas of the Godavari and Kistna, and prevents ships of any size from anchoring near.

The Kavari (Cauvery) also rises in the Western Gháts, the source of one branch being within 30 miles of the west coast. For about one-fourth its course it traverses the south-west districts of the Maisur plateau, passing the famous stronghold of Seringapatam. It then winds through a mass of mountains till it reaches the great plain of the Karnatic. Here it takes up the Bhawâni affluent, a river which circles round the southern base of the Nilgiris, and thenceforward pursues a placid course to the sea. Below Trichinopoli it divides into several branches, the most southern and most important of which is called the Kalarun (Coleroon). Much of the water of the Kavari is exhausted in fertilising its delta, where a quality of rice is grown which is considered to be inferior in quality only to that of Burdwán. Throughout its upper course in the higher levels there is much that is picturesque in the river scenery; the falls of the river (which may be easily reached from Bangalore) are equal to any in India in point of natural beauty, though the falls of Gairspa on the western coast, near Honáwar, are higher.

The Karnatic, which comprises most of the old Madras presidency, extending from Cape Comorin to a junction with the Orissa division of Bengal, is a long strip of territory only averaging 70 to 80 miles in width and narrowing towards the north. It is divided (geographically) into a northern, central, and southern division, and is further recognised on the east and west respectively as Paian Ghát (or below the Gháts) and Balaghat (above the Gháts), where the line of the Eastern Gháts intersects the province through its two northern divisions. Above the Gháts (which word is a form of the Sanscrit "gati," a way, or path) the climate is modified by three or four thousand feet of altitude, and is not unbearable; below, it is hot,

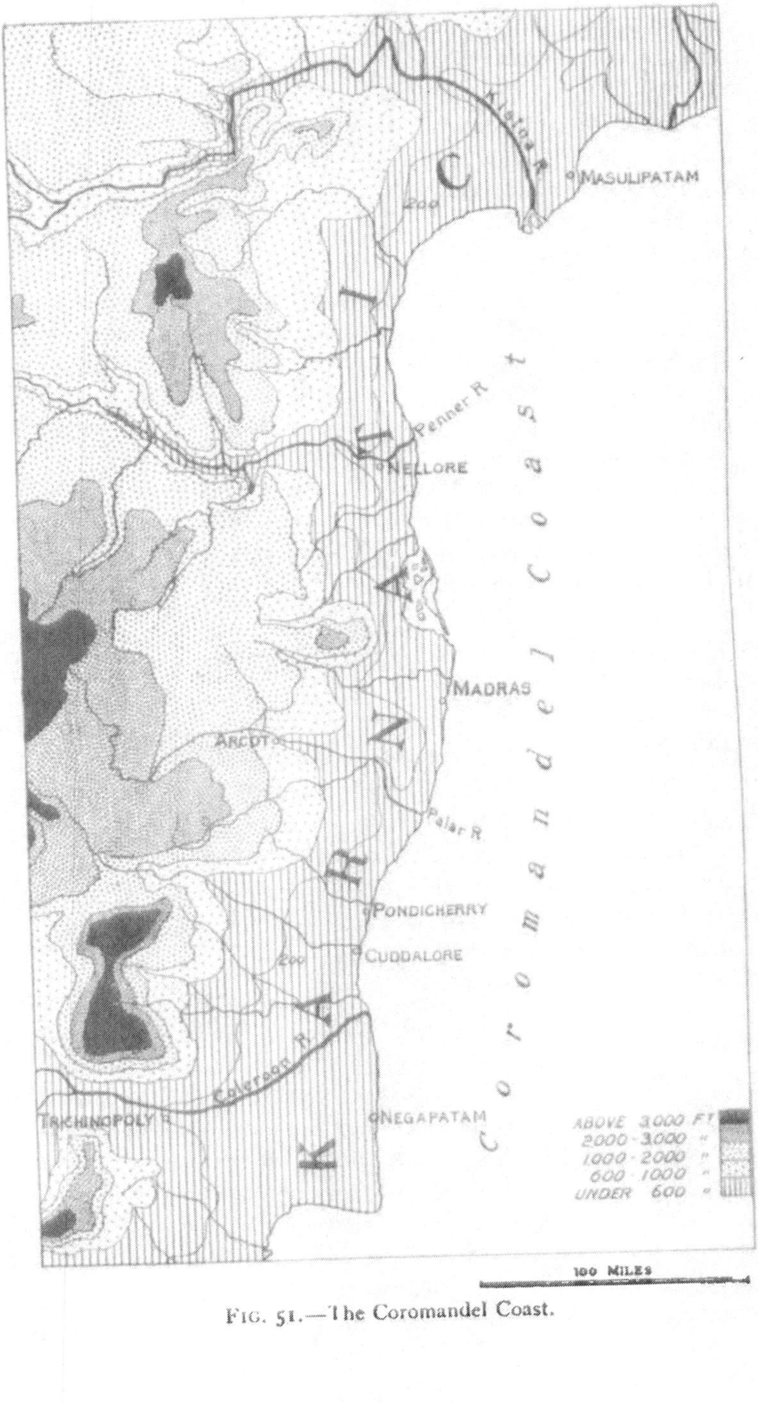


FIG. 51.—The Coromandel Coast.

moist, and enervating, and relieved only by the daily sea breezes.

There is no town of importance in the northern division of the Karnatic, which is but a narrow strip adjoining a coast whereon the surf beats continuously; but the central division includes Madras, Arcot, Pondicherri, and many other important towns; and the southern division maintains the chief wealth of the Madras presidency. Trichinopoli, Kadalur (Cuddalore), Nagapatnam (Negapatam), Tanjore, and many places associated with the history of our first occupation of India, are to be found in the south. Here also are the best examples of Hindu religious architecture, and the seat of much of the best art work of the country. The soil of the coast districts is an admixture of sand and loam suitable to palm growth; rice is the chief agricultural product of the low lands wherever irrigation is possible. On the highlands millet is raised as the staple for food. Sugar, cotton, indigo, and tobacco are all grown where the soil is favourable.

The plains of the Karnatic are connected with the flat coast districts of Western India by a gap between the south-western spurs of the Nilgiris and the southernmost extension of the Western Ghâts. This extension runs from the gap southwards to within 20 miles of Cape Comorin in one single range, dividing the native state of Travancore from the Karnatic. Through the gap (called the Coimbatore gap) the railway connecting the west and east coasts at Beypur and Nagapatam respectively now runs.

The narrow low strip which borders the west coast of India includes the official districts of Malabar (north of Travancore), North and South Kanara, and the Konkan. Its characteristics are very similar throughout. It is never entirely level excepting close to the littoral, and is covered with sand and overgrown with cocoa palms. Near the foothills of the Western Ghâts there is soil suitable for rice cultivation, and rice here, as throughout Southern India, is the chief agricultural product. The villages are mostly perched on the lower spurs of the Western Ghâts, which rise above them in forest-covered ridges where teak and sandal wood grow abundantly, and form a valuable part of the export trade of the west coast.

The chief towns of the west are naturally its seaports, which are still numerous, though they have lost the importance which was attached to them in mediæval days. South of Bombay the Portuguese settlement of Goa, and the port of Beypur, the western terminus of the Madras railway, are perhaps the most important. Goa is a picturesque town too little known to modern travellers. It is full of the interest of early Portuguese occupation, a relic of the past which has preserved reminiscences of Albuquerque and his energetic methods of propagating Christianity in Southern India even to this day.

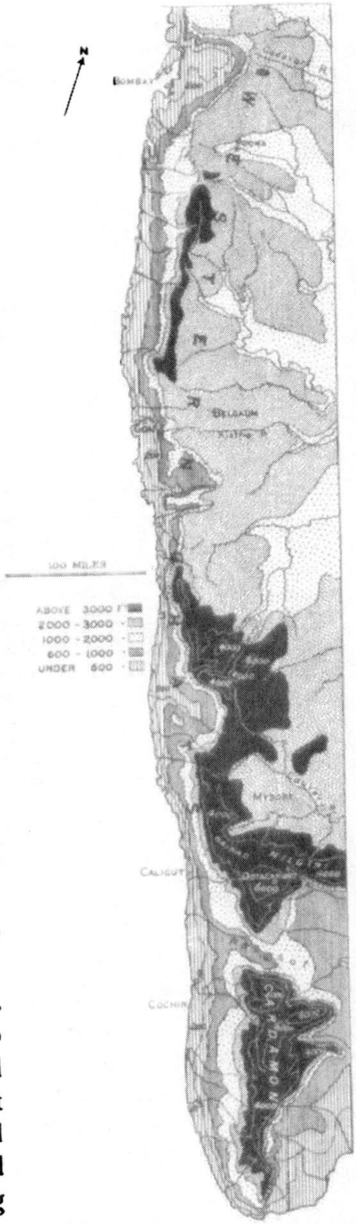


FIG. 52.—Malabar Coast; Western Ghâts.

That part of the central plateau of India which is called the Dekkan requires certain definition. Commencing on the north with the ranges which form the southern edge of the Narbada Valley it extends southwards to the Nilgiris. The Eastern and Western Ghâts which bound it are raised above the general level of the plateau, and descend steeply to the plains bordering the seashore on either side. The southern districts of the tableland including the native state of Maisur (Mysore) are the highest, and they are higher on the east than on the west; Bangalore (the capital of Mysore) being over 3000 feet above the sea. The greatest depression occurs in the regions drained by the Kistna and its tributaries, where the level drops to 1000 feet. The general surface of the tableland exhibits a level plain from which isolated hills

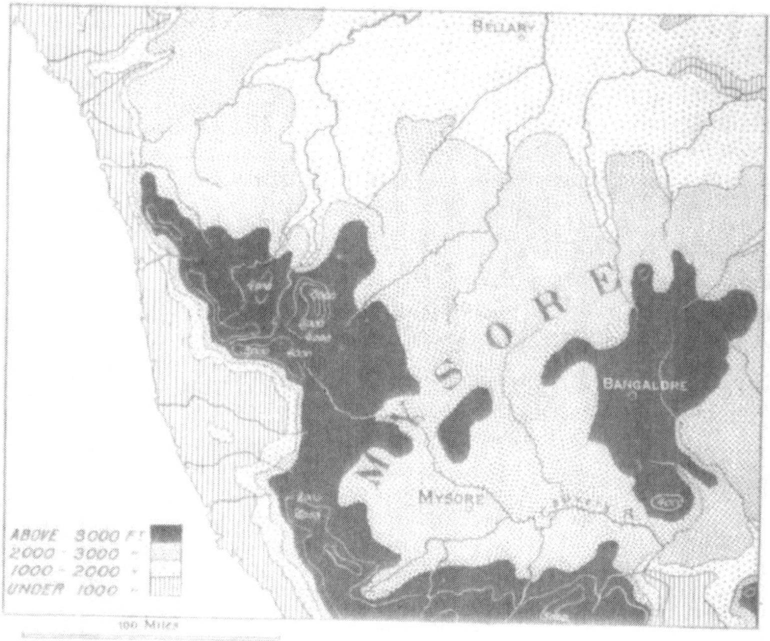


FIG. 53.—The Uplands of Mysore.

rise here and there, and run to 800 or 900 feet above the plain level. Towards the western edge of the tableland short spurs extend from the line of the Ghāts into the plain. These spurs and the isolated hills are often very steep and surmounted by precipitous cliffs. On them the fortresses (or "droogs") are built which figured so largely in Mahratta history. In the northern districts of the Dekkan, which enjoy a specially healthy climate, we have three sanataria—or hill-stations—well known to the

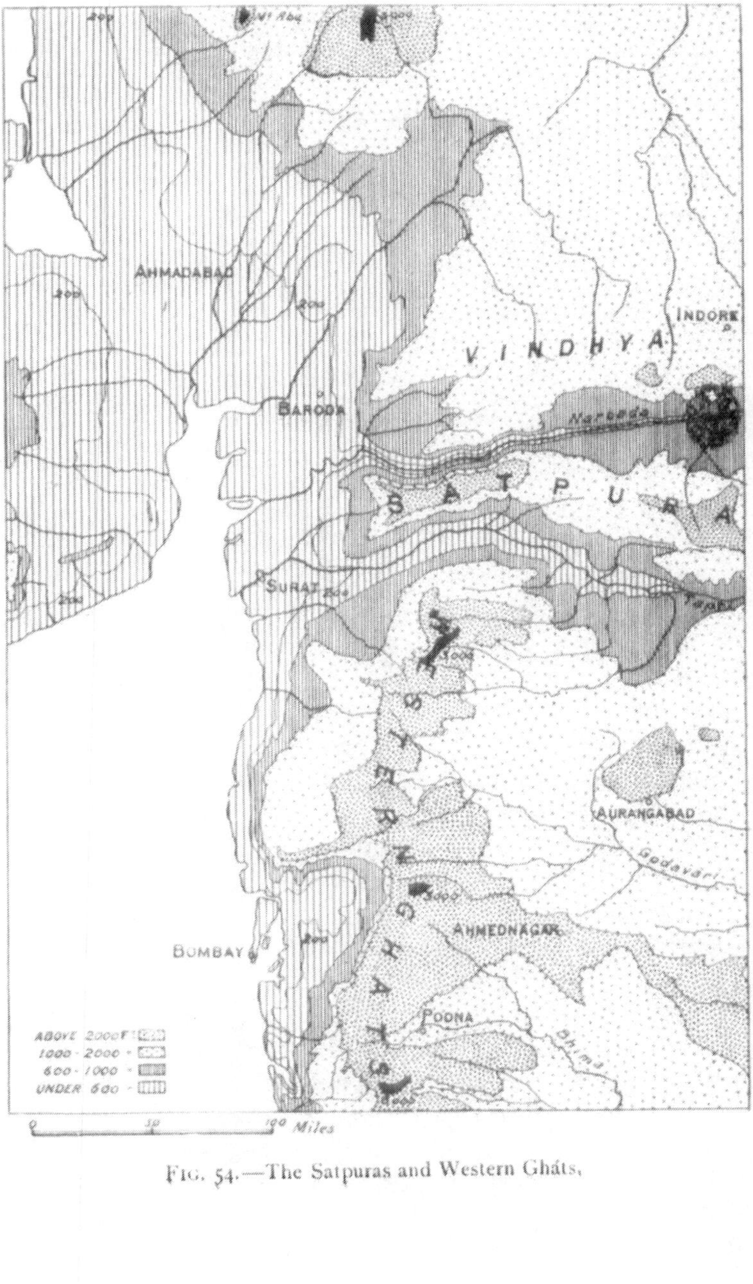


FIG. 54.—The Satpuras and Western Ghâts.

enervated residents of Bombay. Mahableshwar and Matherán are favourite resorts in the hot weather months, and Poona, the ancient Mahratta capital of the Dekkan, is perhaps the most popular station in Bombay during the rains. It lies below the level of the Ghâts, but like Bangalore is high enough to ensure a fairly cool and equable climate.

In the south the Nilgiris form the farthest abutment of this central plateau, and their elevation gives opportunity for the existence of a group of European colonies which are unmatched for the advantages of geographical position by any hill-stations in India. The summit of that elevated and somewhat restricted plateau, which is known by the collective name of Nilgiris, consists of rolling grass-covered downs intersected by clear streams, and broken by patches of dense jungle (locally known as "shola") which fill up its depressions and fit into the folds of the hills in beautifully moulded curves. The climate of the Nilgiris is far more equable than that of the lower spurs of the Himalayas. The annual rainfall is much the same as that of the Himalayan stations, but it is spread over more months in the year, because the Nilgiris fall within the influence of both north-east and south-west monsoons. Although fruit will not ripen well, flowers of every description flourish here as they flourish nowhere else in India, and the open grass downs are frequently a blaze of colour in spring and early summer. Road communications are easy, and the usual mountain drawback of narrow paths flanked by dangerous hillsides is almost wanting in the central station of Utakamand (Ootacamund). The scenery of the Nilgiris is doubtless tame compared to that of the Himalayas. This is owing in a large measure to the introduction of Australian trees (acacias and gum trees), which stiffen the landscape by the regularity of their planting, and never appear to be quite at home. But it is also due to the want of strong contrast between hill and valley. This flatness of effect pervades all but the western slopes of the plateau. There, indeed, as one looks across the blue sea of the Wainâd Hills to the lighter sheen of the Western Ocean, whilst deep-shadowed mists steal upwards over the western edge of the cliffs and stream across the rounded slopes of the plateau, one realises that Sispára has a right to the rank in beauty which Turner gave it.

Vast as is the amount of literature on the subject of India generally, it is not difficult to select standard works which may be quoted as authoritative. First and foremost is Sir W. Hunter's magnificent compilation, "The Gazetteer of India." Vol. VI., which deals with the physiography of India as a whole, is a model of generally concise and always lucid information. Sir John Strachey's "India" also treats of the physical aspects of the peninsula area, and gives us a picturesque conception of the plains of lower Bengal. Articles by Sir W. Hunter and Sir Alfred Lyall in the *Ency. Brit.*, and by Sir Lepel Griffin in the *Asiatic Quarterly Review*, will also be found to add something to the general view of the chief geographical features of the continent. For reference to the process of geological evolution, Oldham is again the authority quoted. But the continent of India, equally with its borderland, has only recently been accurately surveyed, and the records of the Indian Survey Department, with contributions from surveyors to the periodicals of the Royal Geographical Society, are the latest support for the views expressed in this chapter, which are mainly the result of personal observation.

# CHAPTER VI

## ASSAM, BURMA, AND CEYLON

"HAPPY is the land which has no history" might well be written of the province of Assam, which, since its annexation from Burma in 1826, has steadily added its growth of revenue to the Indian treasury, enlarging its agricultural borders from year to year in placid contemplation of those events which have stirred the peninsula and made modern Indian history. On the north the valley of Assam lies under the eastern ridges of the Himalayas, where Bhután and the outlying border of Tibet occupy the great mass of the hills, and include some of the most irreclaimable and uncivilised of Himalayan tribes. On the south the rough tableland of the Khasia and Garo hills intervenes between the valley and the Cachar districts of Eastern Bengal drained by the Surma, ere the Surma joins the Brahmaputra after the latter has turned the western flank of the hills. Assam is the valley of the Brahmaputra, and it owes its wealth of agricultural resources—even its very existence—to that silt-bearing river. The Brahmaputra rises, like the Sutlej, near the sacred lake of Manasarawar. For 800 or 900 miles it flows steadily eastward through Tibet as the Tsan-pu, passing to the south of Lhasa, the Tibetan capital. Then, turning the eastern flank of the Himalayas, and receiving a few Chinese tributaries, it twists into Assam under the name of the Dihang. At this eastern bend it takes up the Dibang from the north and another stream (which is also named Brahmaputra) from the east, and finally, as the "Son of Brahma, the creator" (*i.e.* Brahmaputra), it proceeds to increase and fertilise the valley of Assam. Its drainage basin is 361,200 square miles, and its mean low-water discharge at Gualpara, near the head of the

INDIA,

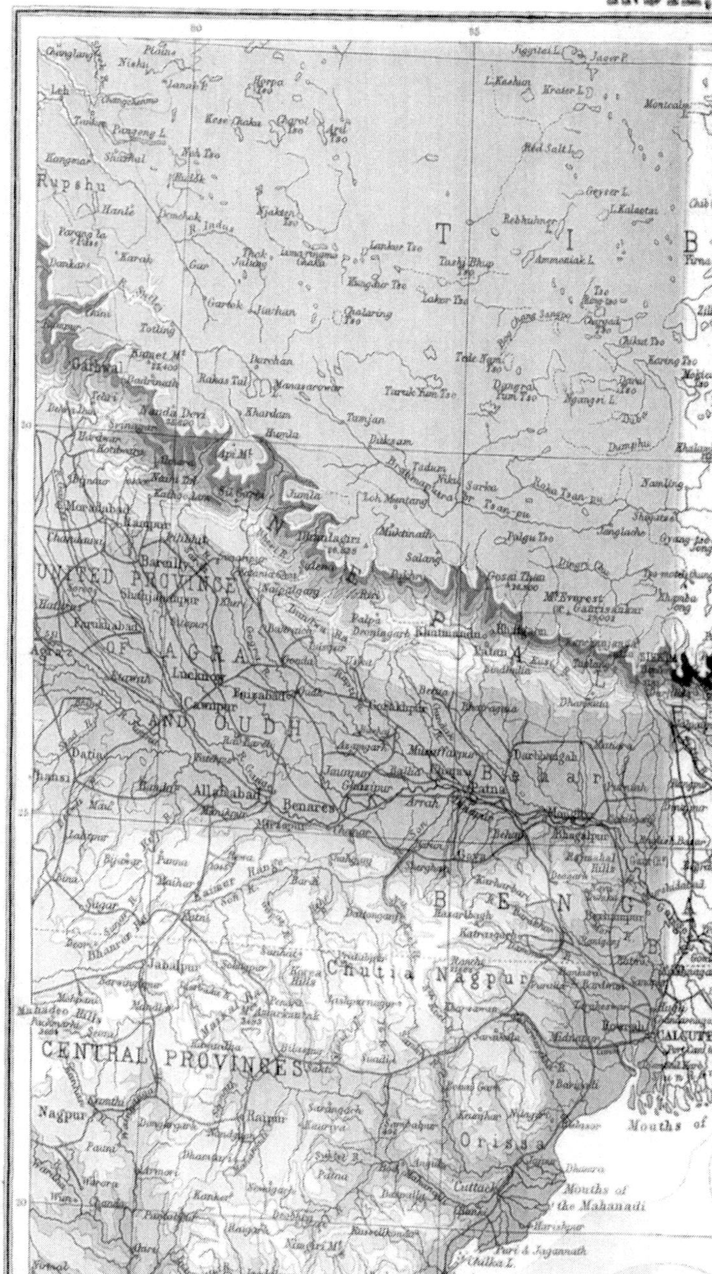


The Edinburgh Geographical Institute

INDIA, N.E. SECTION.

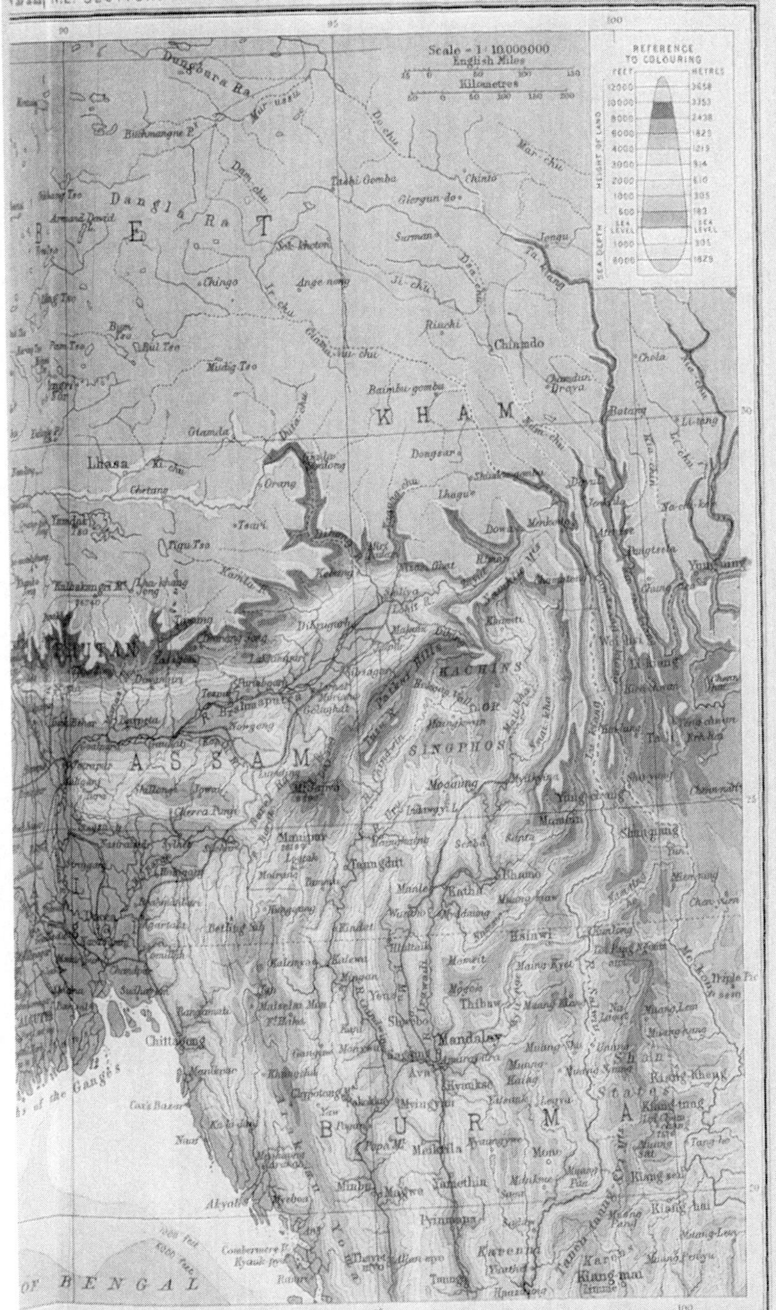

valley, amounts to 116,500 cubic feet per second. After receiving the Subansiri from Tibet the total flood discharge must be over 500,000 cubic feet.

"The Brahmaputra rolls down the Assam valley in a vast sheet of water, broken by numerous islands, and exhibiting the operations of alluvion and deluvion on a gigantic scale." The vast quantity of silt brought from the Himalayas is deposited in banks at the smallest obstruction, and islands form and re-form in constant succession. Broad channels break away, and rejoin the main river after wide divergences which are subjected to no control. The swamps which closely adjoin the elevated alluvial foundation of the river bed are flooded in the rainy season till the lower reaches of the valley are one vast shining sea, from which the hills slope up on either side. After 450 miles of open course the river turns the western flank of the Khasia Hills. Here it becomes the Jamúna for 180 miles of southerly flow across the flat plains of Bengal till it joins the Ganges at Goalanda. Then the deltas unite. After the Surma has joined from Cachar the united stream of the three great river systems takes the name of Meghna and rushes to the sea. Gualpara and Dibrugarh are perhaps the best known stations of the upper Assam valley, and on the Khasia Hills to the south stands the well-known hill sanatarium of Shillong, so lately, and so terribly, damaged by earthquake. The traffic on the river in Assam is maintained by exports of tea (to the value of 1½ million sterling per annum), timber, rubber, and cotton, with imports chiefly of rice for the tea-estate labourers. The tea industry of Assam now largely supersedes all other agricultural developments.

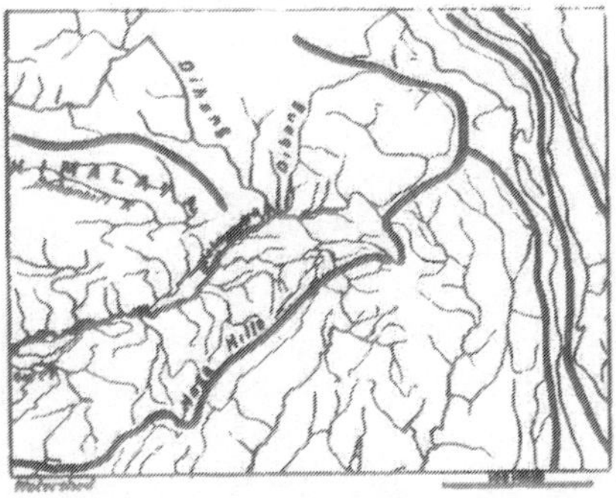

FIG. 55.—The Bend of the Brahmaputra.

Burma, the land of picturesque rivers and forest-clad

mountains; of light and colour; of laughter, song, and wooden pagodas, is almost as distinct from India in physical and ethnographical characteristics as Australia is from England. It has no recognised overland connection with India. Only by way of the sea can it be approached from the west, and this no doubt has contributed greatly to preserve its mixed nationality from recent floods of Aryan immigration. Not that the province of Burma (so lately the Burmese empire) is otherwise homogeneous in its ethnography. There are men of many races, speaking many languages, included within the red line that now defines British Burma, but they are all of one original stock—a stock which, whilst we class it under the general designation of Indo-Chinese or Mongoloid, offers far more evidence of the Mongolian element than the Indian. There is apparently no affinity whatever between the short, stout-limbed, indolent, ignorant, and gaily dressed (though not over-dressed) Burman, and the slight-limbed, long-headed Bengali graduate of the Calcutta University. And yet the two countries are not (geographically) far separated. Practically, however, they are separated by the deep sea, and the width of that sea is a matter of great consequence where a sea of any sort is a final and fatal obstacle to the personal enterprise involved in travel. Burma is shut off from Assam on the north-west by a mass of densely forest-covered mountains, running in steep and high ridges, intersected by deep and narrow valleys, inhabited by the wildest tribes of the aboriginal inhabitants of our north-east frontier; Singphos and Nagas on the north, Karens farther to the north-east, Lushais and Chins on the north-west; all of them secure in their almost impenetrable jungles, through which no right of way from west to east exists, or ever has existed.

This band of impassable hills is more or less continuous down the whole southern watershed of the Assam valley; it envelops the little independent state of Manipur, and reaches into the Khasia and Garo plateau north of Sylhet and Tipperah to the west. One long arm stretches away southwards, and gradually separates the coast district of Arakan from the interior of Burma. The extreme north of Arakan is lost in the southern abutments of the long parallel mountain ridges of Lushai, which run from north to south and end on the sea-coast. South of this, about the debouchment of the Arakan River, which joins the sea near the trading port of Akyab, there is a stretch of coast lowland some 40 miles or so in width. Then this southern arm of the mountains becomes definitely detached as a single range, and strikes southwards, approaching nearer and nearer to the coast, narrowing the width of the Arakan lowlands until it ends as a barren red rocky ridge at Cape Negrais. This is usually known as the Arakan range. The chief pass across it is the Aeng, of which the summit is about 5000 feet above sea. The western spurs of the mountains are covered with forests of fine timber, but on the east, where the range breaks down to the level of the Irawadi Valley in a succession of minor parallel ridges, bamboo is the principal growth.

East of the Arakan range are the great central plains of lower Burma, watered by the Irawadi and the Sittang. East of this again, extending through Burma from north to south, we find broken highlands and plateau, traversed by no definite mountain ranges, but forming one continuous chain of rugged tableland, stretching from the Kachin Hills on the north, through the northern and southern Shan states to the Karenni country on the south. This tableland is intersected by the trough of the Salwin River. Beyond the Shan states is China in the north and Siam in the south. But the province of Burma does not end with the Shan states. There is a long strip of coast land, averaging perhaps 20 miles in width, but occasionally narrowing to 10, which extends down the western edge of the Malay peninsula, and includes the districts of Martaban and Tenasserim. This is also part of the province under the administration of the Lieutenant-Governor of Burma. It includes the Mergui archipelago, and is chiefly remarkable for the long broken coast-line, extending through 16 degrees of latitude, flanked by hundreds of islands which once formed part of the peninsula. The total length of Burmese coast-line from North Arakan to South Tenasserim is not much less than 550 miles. The total area of the province is 171,500 square miles, and its population (in 1891) was 7,600,000.

Burma may be divided into four distinct areas or

FIG. 56.—Delta of the Irawadi.

districts, as follows: (1) the western or Arakan division; (2) Central Burma, or the basin of the Irawadi; (3) the Shan states, or the basin of the Salwin; (4) the Eastern Coast strip, which includes Martaban and Tenasserim.

The first and last of these natural subdivisions are comparatively unimportant. Arakan was acquired by the British, together with Tenasserim, in 1826. The value of Arakan was chiefly in its rice cultivation, and the products (tobacco, cotton, red pepper, hemp, and sugar) of the volcanic island of Ramri, where Port Kyankpyu is one of the two notable towns of its coast, Akyab being the other. The hot, moist, malarious climate of northern Arakan renders it unsuitable for European existence; but it is the happy home of the Mug, an offshoot of the Indo-Chinese race, who has specially developed a natural instinct for cooking. No large establishment in Calcutta is quite complete without a Mug cook.

Tenasserim is a long strip of country which, together with Arakan and Pegu, has been united with the Burman province since 1862. A continuous range of mountains, varying from 3000 to 6000 feet in altitude, separates Tenasserim (with which we include Martaban) from Siam. Its exports are inconsiderable, rice and teak forming the chief trade. There is, however, much mineral wealth in the country, which may be capable of further development. Gold, tin, iron ore, antimony, and coal are found in Tenasserim, the coal measures being worked on the banks of the Tenasserim River, and the coal itself being of excellent quality. The only towns of any importance are Mulmain, at the mouth of the Salwin (which river has no delta); Amherst, about 15 miles south of Mulmain; and the port of Mergui near the mouth of the Tenasserim River. The climate of Tenasserim is singularly equable. The thermometer never rises above 90° F., and in June (during the rainy season) it varies between 72° and 76°. October is the hottest month of the year.

Central Burma, the land of rivers and rubies, has only fallen to British sovereignty since 1885, when Mandalay was taken, and the emperor Thibau deposed. The province of Pegu in the south has been British since 1852, and, with Arakan and Tenasserim, formed the Burma that we knew and ruled before the days of Mandalay occupation. The annexation of the northern districts (or Upper Burma) has opened up a new and most important area for commercial enterprise, and has added a tract of country which differs in some most essential climatic conditions from the south, and is altogether far more suitable to European life. To understand the trade relations between Burma and the far east, which promises to develop into a question of national interest quite as great as that of the Nile Valley, certain broad features of the geography of this part of Asia should be noted.

In the high altitudes of Eastern Tibet, bordering on Chinese territory (or rather on China, for Tibet is itself a dependency of China), there is a central gathering of the sources of great rivers, similar to that which exists near the Manasarawar Lake in Western Tibet. From this great eastern point of departure two gigantic rivers start for China. One, the Hoang Ho, or Yellow River, drains and waters all Northern China, and is the great waterway from Eastern Tibet to Pekin. The other, the Yang-tse-Kiang, is the great commercial highway of all Central China, and it is by the Yang-tse-Kiang that half of China lives. It is the main trade artery from which subsidiary lines take off. Two other great rivers also find their beginnings near this centre—the Mekong, the river of Siam, which has lately assumed political importance in connection with French expansion from Tonkin; and the Salwin, the river of the Shan states of Eastern Burma. Neither of these two rivers are navigable for any great distance, and they are not in themselves trade routes, but they mark important points on the line of east and west connection, and their small tributaries are important, as indicating possible means of developing a continuous route across their main line of drainage.

For hundreds of miles in their upper courses, where they are lost in the mass of hills to the north-west of Burma, the Salwin, the Mekong, and the Yang-tse-Kiang travel on parallel lines in narrow troughs, separated from each other by what are apparently (for we only know this country imperfectly) single ranges of precipitous mountains. Between this triad of rivers and the great bend in the Brahmaputra north-east of Assam there is a massive (but not a broad) band of rugged, forest-clad mountains, and it is amongst the recesses of these mountains that the Irawadi rises. Nowhere is the progress in economic development of Burma since British occupation so marked as it is in the upper reaches of the Irawadi north of Bhamo. Bhamo is our most northerly cantonment, and it is 250 miles (as the crow flies) above

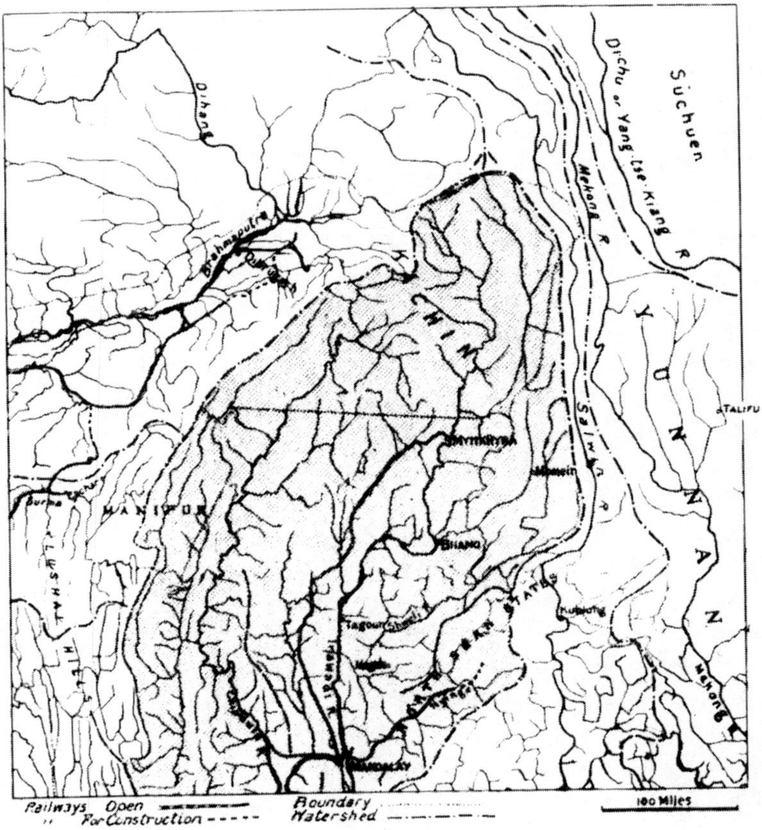


FIG. 57.—Upper Basin of the Irawadi.

Mandalay, and 20 miles west of the Chinese frontier. Above it the river passes through a craggy, forest-covered defile in the mountains, which is only navigable for half the year, and beyond this, for 150 miles farther, it still stretches, sometimes half a mile wide, to the confluence of its two northerly affluents, the N'maika and the

N'malika, which join from the north-east and north-west respectively. Beyond this confluence is the unmapped Kachin country of mountains and forests, about which exceedingly little is known.

Some 50 miles south of the confluence, and about 140 north of Bhamo, lies Myitkhyna (Mitchina), the river terminus of the northern railway extension from Mandalay, marking not only the terminus of civilisation, but very nearly the terminus of our geographical knowledge as well. The immediate banks of the river, for 10 or 12 miles in breadth on the east, and stretching across to the Mogaung River on the west, are fertile plains; but beyond the plains on the east to the Chinese frontier (which here runs north and south at a distance of 40 or 50 miles from the Irawadi) are Kachin Hills rising to 6000 or 7000 feet, amongst which lie the scenes of much of our hardest frontier fighting. But whilst Kachins occupy the hills, the plains are left to Shans and Burmans, who now hold what was once a prosperous and cultivated country, and what may soon be prosperous again. "The Kachin has forsaken his predatory ways, and promises to become a profitable subject; whilst the Chinese Shan and emigrant colonists from Yunnan are increasing in numbers, and are, as ever, the most industrious of people. Rubber, jade, and cotton caravans now pass through from China in safety, and no blackmail is levied on the Sadon and Sima routes." Bhamo has always been a great trading centre, and is still largely a Chinese town. It is still of importance (though left on one side by the line of railway), as it lies on the main road to Talifu *viâ* Momein.

At the point where the Salwin, the Mekong, and the Yang-tse-Kiang emerge into the regions of ascertained geography, two of them, the Salwin and the Mekong, are traversing the western districts of the Chinese province of Yunnan, the Yang-tse-Kiang having turned off eastwards to form the northern boundary of the province, and thus any route which connects either of the large trading centres of the Irawadi (Bhamo or Mandalay) with the Yang-tse-Kiang must cross the Salwin and the Mekong, and must strike the Yang-tse-Kiang somewhere north of the province of Yunnan.

The one great river system of Burma is formed by the Irawadi and its two affluents, the Chindwin, from the north-west, and the Myinge, from the north-east. All the smaller upper tributaries of the Irawadi, other than the Chindwin, are lost in the northern mass of mountains,

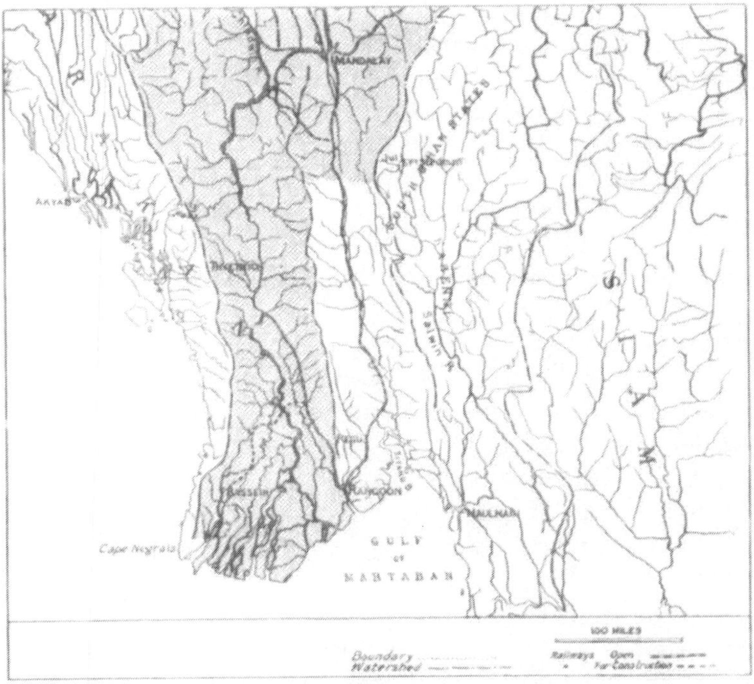


FIG. 58.—Lower Basin of the Irawadi.

which are ranged in narrow watersheds running north and south—the home of the Kachin. The mountainous character of the country extends through the Manipur state, on the right bank of the Chindwin, to within 100 miles of its junction with the Irawadi. The country to the east, however, becomes comparatively open, and there are broad, high-level valleys in that part of Upper Burma which lies between the Chindwin and the Irawadi to the north-west of Mandalay. The Irawadi itself is greatly shut in by mountains, which enclose the valley throughout its length north of Mandalay, and which closely border its left bank south of that capital. All Upper Burma may be called mountainous, although the Shan states which lie between the Irawadi and the Salwin are more regular in their conformation, which approaches that of an elevated plateau or tableland intersected by wide, fertile, and populous valleys.

A little below Mandalay (which is now the recognised official capital of Burma and is situated not far north of the more ancient capitals, Ava and Sagain) the Irawadi is joined by the Myinge from the Shan highlands to the north-east. The Myinge has always offered a fairly open route to Chinese and Shan traders from the Salwin, and it is this valley now which carries the railway (not yet completed) from Mandalay to the Kunlon ferry over the Salwin; the point where, for many years, the Eastern traders have been wont to meet, and from which they diverged westwards into various parts of the Burmese empire. From the Kunlon ferry to the Mekong, and from the Mekong to the Yang-tse-Kiang, are the next links in this great commercial chain which has yet to be bridged over by the steel line—a direct distance of less than 300 miles, which will finally connect Central China with Central Burma.

About 35 miles to the south-west below Mandalay the Irawadi and the Chindwin unite, and for another 30 the river continues its south-westerly course, leaving the ruins of another ancient capital (Pagan) on its left bank, and then runs south for 70 miles to Prome (passing Thyetmyo, 20 miles above Prome), which is the terminus of a branch line of railway from Rangoon. So far the Irawadi runs amongst hills, but the hills are of decreasing altitude, and are frequently separated by wide, well-cultivated plains. They are generally covered with forest-trees, amongst which teak is abundant. Petroleum is found in great quantities on the eastern banks of the river in this part of its course, and vast numbers of fossil bones are dug out of the hills near the petroleum wells, proving its recent conformation. Not far above Prome, which is itself 75 miles above Rangoon, the river emerges from the hills which mark the ancient boundary between Ava and Pegu (*i.e.* between Upper and Lower Burma), and spreads into the plains which thereafter conduct it by many channels to the sea. It is somewhat remarkable that Prome was never an ancient capital. Burma is a land of ancient capitals, and the site of one exists very near Prome, about 6 miles to the east of it, but Prome itself escaped the honour. The width of the river here varies considerably; at some points it is 3 or 4 miles across; at others it narrows to 600 or 800 yards. There are shoals and cataracts in the narrow places which interrupt navigation when the river is low; but the whole distance (500 miles) between Rangoon and Mandalay is ordinarily navigable without any great difficulty by steamers of light draught.

For the last 60 or 70 miles of its course the Irawadi splits into many channels, and reaches the sea by fourteen different mouths. About 60 miles from the sea the Bassein Channel takes off to the west. It joins an excellent harbour, protected by Cape Negrais, and is navigable for ships as far as Bassein, which is some 15 miles above the harbour; beyond that only country barges can navigate. The Rangoon, or eastern channel, offers advantages for navigation which have led to the concentration of nearly all the commerce of Burma at the Rangoon port. The tide ascends these channels for 50 miles in the dry season, and as far as its influence extends, the delta is covered with forest and grass plains. Above the reach of the tide tall reedy grass takes the place of the forest growth, without much underwood. Rice cultivation commences above the delta and beyond the grass jungles.

East of the Irawadi basin is that of the Salwin, and between the two is the comparatively small but fertile Sitang Valley, at the mouth of which the old Burman capital of Pegu is situated. The Sitang basin is flat, with all the Irawadi Valley characteristics. It is important, as it offers the best line of railway approach to the interior;

it is along the Sitang Valley that the Pegu-Mandalay line is laid. But the river itself is of little importance. It is blocked by sandbanks at its mouth, and is hardly navigable. The same may be said of the Salwin, which has

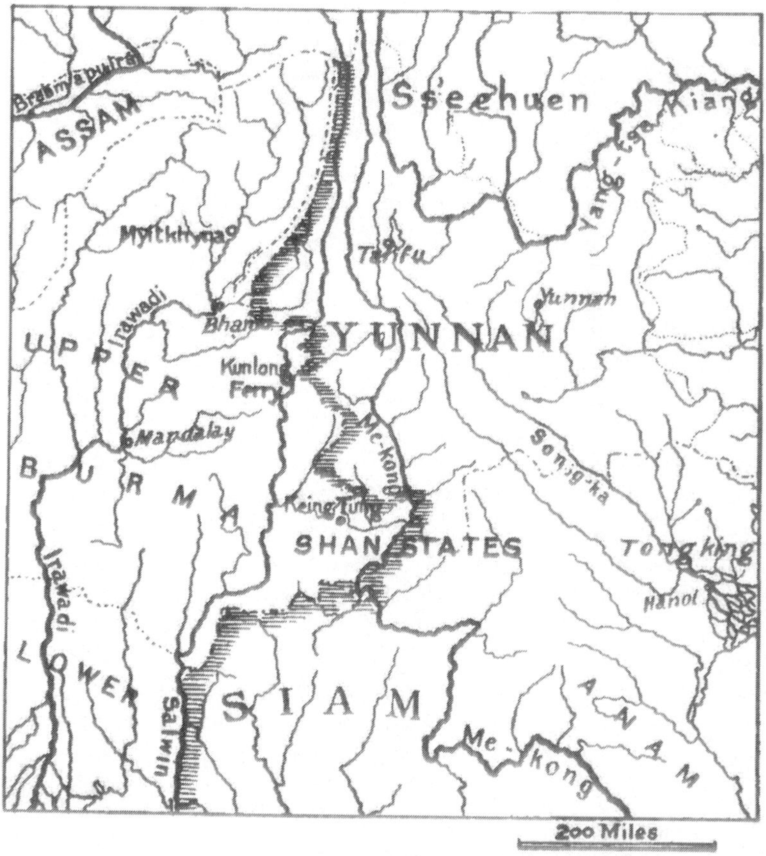


FIG. 59.—Between Burma and China.

no delta, and is only navigable in the near neighbourhood of its mouth, where the island of Bhilu divides it into two branches, on the eastern of which is Maulmain. The Salwin rises, as already explained, far to the north of the sources of the Irawadi, and passes through the western districts of the Chinese province of Yunnan. South of Yunnan it waters the Shan states, which extend on both sides of the river, and, for a part of its lower course, it serves as the boundary between Lower Burma and Siam. It is a broad rushing river, carrying more water than the Irawadi at certain seasons, but it possesses a rocky bed and many abrupt sinuosities.

The Shan states have been graphically described in recent years by many travellers. The states under British protection form the easternmost portion of our Burmese possessions, presenting a broad base towards the Irawadi, and narrowing considerably towards the east. To the north and east of them is the Chinese province of Yunnan, with Chinese Shan districts immediately on their borders. To the south are the Karen Hills and Siam.

"These states," says General Woodthorpe, "present a remarkable variety of natural features. The country to the west of the Salwin is a series of elevated plateaux—great rolling grassy downs separated by deep valleys and intersected by lofty parallel ranges, the general direction of which is north and south. These ranges, in contrast to the yellow downs, are beautifully wooded, and attain to great heights, some of the peaks rising to nearly 9000 feet above sea-level, the general elevation of the plateau being from 3000 to 5000 feet. Along the valleys flow swift rivers, now through dark and narrow gorges, pent between mighty cliffs, now through alluvial hollows, with terraced rice fields, among which they wind with many a curve. To the east of the Salwin the country is much broken up ; no clearly defined range of mountains presents itself, but the eye wanders over a confused sea of forest-clad hills and narrow valleys, relieved here and there by small oases, till Keng Tung plain is reached, beyond which the mountains rise again, range upon range, in tangled masses to the Mekong. Across the Mekong we have similar features, flat fertile valleys, or terraced uplands, lying amid intricate mazes of hills, the drainage system of which is the despair of the surveyor." In the northern Shan states the main drainage is into the Irawadi, but in the south several fair-sized streams join the Salwin.

Chief amongst these is the Balu Chaung, the river of Fort Stedman. "It rises to the north of this place, and flowing at first through forest loses itself in a huge swamp merging into the Jull Lake, a vast expanse of water, 13 miles long and about 4 miles wide, at its upper end, but narrowing towards the south. It is nowhere very deep, and the bottom is overgrown with long and tangled weeds which rise nearly to the surface. The lake dwellings of the Inthas—an amphibious tribe said to have been originally brought as slaves from the province of Tavoy—rise on poles out of the water in groups near the edge, and floating gardens on which are grown tomatoes, water-melons, gourds, and the panleaf vine, dot the surface of the lake around them. Many large villages are seen on either shore; monasteries, and clusters of white pagodas, built on the extremities of the spurs running into the lake, are reflected in its placid depths; and on the eastern shore, lying back from the water on some rising ground, are the houses and barracks of Fort Stedman." All writers agree that the climate of the Shan states is for a great part of the year delightful, and enough has been said to show that we possess here large possibilities for the development of European colonisation. The Kunlon ferry on the Salwin, which has risen into prominence as the present objective of the railway line from Mandalay by the Myinge valley route towards China, is on the western edge of Yunnan, and leads direct from Chinese to British territory, the Salwin being here the boundary. It is situated about 100 miles south-east of Bhamo (the valley of the Shweli and two ranges intervening), and 200 miles north-east of Mandalay by railway.

"The Burmese," says General MacMahon, "are probably the gayest and most light-hearted people in the world. Blessed with a happy temperament, a contented disposition and jocund spirits, which make light of the inevitable ills to which mankind is liable, they defy dull care," and live an easy life, but "they are proud, arrogant, and conceited," having been born and bred in the belief that they are the lineal descendants of celestial Brahmas who visited this earth and stayed there. According to Sir Arthur Phayre, "The Burmese many years ago were formed into a nation by the union of Mongoloid tribes who then occupied the land which is still the home of their race." Most authorities agree that the Burmese are closely allied to the Singphos on the north, and the Manipuris and kindred tribes on the west, and it seems probable (although there is a difference of opinion on this point) that they found their way originally from beyond the snowy ranges, through Assam, into the basin of the Irawadi. The true aborigines are to be found, as might be expected, in the southern districts of Pegu, and are known as Mons or Talaings (an equivalent for Telinga), which latter name the Burmans once applied to all strangers who reached their shores by way of the sea. Whatever their prehistoric origin may be the Burman Mongoloid has been very largely modified by the influence of the Aryan Hindu—who figures in Burmese traditions and in Buddhist legends as the founder of the Saverna Bhumi, or Golden Land in which the city of Thahtun was famous. The Golden Land is nearly identical with the province of Pegu, and Thahtun was visited by ships from Ceylon and India as late as the sixth century. So rapidly has the land gained on the sea in this part of Burma that the ruins of Thahtun are now twelve miles inland.

Aryan influence may be traced in the religion, language, and literature of the country, but the first principles of commerce were taught by the Dravidian races (Telingas), who traded from the Coromandel coast, and formed settlements amongst them. Thus Aryans and Dravidians have combined to mould the Burman into his present shape.

The Shans, the inhabitants of the great stretch of highlands which encompass the Salwin, are "the most widely diffused and probably the most numerous of the peoples of Indo-China." According to J. G. Scott, "They overlap all Burma, and extend so far into Yunnan that it is a question whether there are not more Shans than Chinamen in that province of the Middle Kingdom." . . . "As far as history goes back the Shans and Burmese have been connected either as rulers, subjects, or allies." They are everywhere Buddhist, and everywhere, to a considerable extent, civilised. "Mixed up with the Shans we find a wonderful variety of more or less wild tribes. These various tribes inhabit the hills and the wilder parts of the country, the Shans occupying the alluvial basins." Rice is grown everywhere, but our future interest in the Shans lies more with their capacity as traders than as agriculturists.

It is impossible to trace out the habitat of those wild Mongoloid tribes who live interspersed amongst the Shans, or on the borders of their territory. Chief amongst them are the Kachins on the north, the Karens on the south (about whom much has been written lately), and the Kakhyens (an uncivilised race of fetish worshippers), who occupy hill districts amongst the Shans. The latter are a "pushing race"—"so much so" (according to Captain Yate) that "not improbably the time will come when the Shan will be effaced before the Kakhyen."

The Karens (who are divided into Red and White Karens) are interesting as a fighting race of people who were subdued with difficulty, but who not only accepted British authority, but the Christian faith, when once they acknowledged the strength of our arms. The tradition amongst them that they were to "look to the west for their deliverers in the shape of white strangers, who would bring them a book, once theirs, which would make them acquainted with the true God, and free them from their oppressors," has led to the acceptance of English rule and the Holy Bible as a literal fulfilment of this prediction; and induced them "not only to receive the Word with joy, but also to become a law-abiding people." "They are absolutely distinct from the Shans," says Scott, "not less in language than in personal appearance," and their exact place in the family of nations has not yet been determined. They are as distinct from Burmese as they are from Shans.

In store of national wealth few countries in the world surpass Burma. Every description of timber known in

India is produced in the forests of Burma, together with sticklac and rubber. Cotton, sesamum, and tobacco are extensively grown in the lower provinces, though rice covers about five-sixths of the cultivated area. In Upper Burma rice, maize, millet, wheat, pulse, tobacco, cotton, and sesamum are chiefly grown. Burma is rich in minerals. Gold and silver are found in small quantities, marble (near Mandalay), coal, and petroleum, jade and amber are all produced in fair amount ; the mines of Mogok (forty miles north-east of Mandalay) supply the world with rubies ; sapphires are also found there, and in the Shan states. The silks of Mandalay ; the lacquer work of Pagan ; the gold and silver work of Rangoon, Maulmain, and most of the large towns of Burma ; Burmese wood and ivory carving (especially that of Mulmain) are celebrated all the world over. "The characteristics of Burmese art are vigour and novelty in design, but want of delicacy and finish in execution.

Burma is essentially the land of temples, pagodas, and of wooden architecture—and it is the latter, doubtless, which has led to the development of the vigorous forms of wood carving that are to be found in that country. The early capitals of Burma (Tagoun, between Bhamo and Mandalay, earliest of all ; Pagan, coincident with Pollonarua, the ancient capital of Ceylon ; and Thathun) are all full of the interest of early forms of architectural design, obviously drawn from Babylonian sources. The connecting links in India seem to have disappeared (possibly owing to the free use of wood in construction), so that Burma now stands alone as the modern exponent of fairly complete forms of architecture of which the prototypes are to be seen in ruins on the plains of Chaldæa.

Of one of the pagodas at Mengun, half-way between Mandalay and the old capital of Amirapura, Fergusson writes: "Had it been carried out it would have been the tallest building in the world. It was, however, shattered by an earthquake in 1839 ; but even in its ruined state it is as large and imposing a mass of brickwork as is to be found anywhere. Since the pyramids of Egypt nothing so great has been attempted; and it belongs to the nineteenth century!" King Mentara Gyé, who commenced it, died in 1819. The architectural interests of Burma require a volume to themselves.

Our national interest in Burma, however, lies chiefly in the possibility of future commercial developments, and for that we must look chiefly to the newly acquired Shan states and their geographical position relative to the great productive centres of the vast empire of China. It is indeed in this direction that England has more to hope for, more indeed to expect, than she has in any other part of the world. The wealth of the highly developed provinces of Western China bears about the same proportion to the prospective value of the yet undeveloped Sudan, for instance, as does the wealth of the city of London to that of any ordinary market town in England. The Shan states themselves are not as yet fully developed, but it is the opinion of competent authorities that the temperate climate, ample rainfall, and excellent soil which they possess, renders them fit for the production of almost any form of vegetable product—nor are they destitute of mineral wealth. That unrivalled authority on the subject, Mr. J. G. Scott, writes as follows of the country bordering the line which is now happily in course of construction between Mandalay and Western China: "Such a line would traverse a country which produces everything, from indigo to tea and opium, from potatoes and cabbages to forests of teak, and is moreover rich in ores of all kinds, so rich that an Indian mineralogist grows eloquent over a spot so singularly wealthy in metal that he calls it a solid mountain of iron, and records the absolute paralysis of his compass. Lead and silver have long been found in abundance, and the paltry holes dug by our new Shan subjects yield an amount which promises to skilled labour a return that will probably eclipse in interest the much vaunted ruby mines. Hot springs and mineral waters await the arrival of the speculator in table drinks, and the mines of sulphur may probably be as valuable as the seams of coal which have yet to be scientifically examined."

The Kunlon ferry, to which the railway is already projected, is at the foot of that "great descent" of which Marco Polo speaks as so easy: "If therefore the Chinese choose to connect, the proverbially wealthy province of Ssuch'uen might be reached from Rangoon well within the week by a goods train." The caravans from China "assemble at Keing Tung. A committee is appointed, and on a fixed day determines by what routes and at what intervals the various caravans are to make their way west to Mandalay or south-west to Maulmain. In this way the iron pots and pans, the grass woven and felt hats, the shoes, silk, gold leaf, orpiment, walnuts, and what not, brought by the traders are judiciously distributed, so that in no place there may be a glut and the merchants everywhere may make an equal profit." Manchester, Birmingham, and Sheffield goods are what the return caravans carry back with them to the Shan states. Mr. Scott foresees the day when the "miserable wattled bamboo clachan" (Kunlon) "will assume the proportions of a town; Manchester looms will grow busy and the hardware town will forget what it is to have a strike." "With the railway to stimulate the natural resources of the hill states, the wealth of our tributary Shan princes would soon outrival that of the most potent of the Indian Maharajas."

Murray's excellent guide-book introduces Ceylon to the reader with certain advice about the climate: "March and April are the hottest months in the year; June and August the wettest (on the west coast), and December and January the most disagreeable (on that coast) on account of the long shore wind." It is certain, however, that during the months of October and November also, there is present in the atmosphere an amount of moisture which is unequalled by anything of the sort known in India, and possibly only surpassed by that which is experienced during June and August. But the conformation of hill and plain in Ceylon divides that island into climatic spheres which are best recognised by a consideration of the action of the south-west and north-east monsoons respectively. Whilst the south-west monsoon is filling the western area with vapour, and clouds are hanging on the western slopes of the hills which culminate about the central portions of the southern half of the island, the eastern slopes and plains may be free from anything

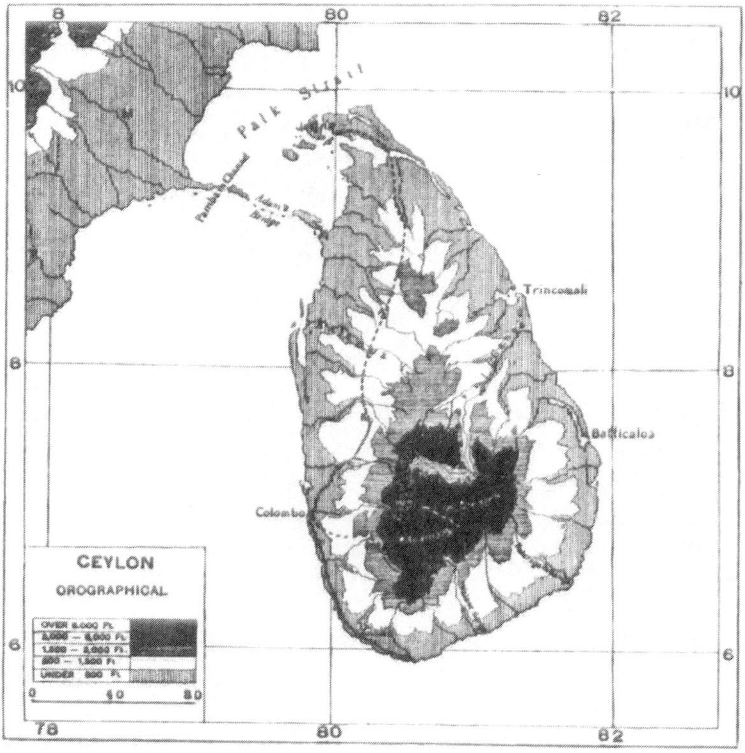


FIG. 60.

approaching to excessive rain; and the climate may be not only tolerable, but on the higher levels actually bracing. When the monsoon turns about, and in obedience to laws explained elsewhere in reference to India, brings with it sheets of rain from the Bay of Bengal, then it is that the western districts have a chance of respite from the prolonged vapour-bath atmosphere in which they have been enveloped. But the operation of the north-east monsoon is much modified by local atmospheric conditions, and thus it frequently happens that Colombo and west-coast stations are rained upon for many months in the year, lasting through the autumn to the middle of December. A study of the rain chart of Ceylon should be a preliminary to any attempt at permanent settlement in the country.

The island contains a total area of 25,300 square miles, and about 3,500,000 inhabitants. Of these latter 2,200,000 are Singhalese, 1,000,000 are Tamils, and about 6500 are pure-bred Europeans. Portuguese colonisation commenced on the island in 1505, with a factory built at Colombo. A century later the Dutch landed on the east coast, and in fifty years had dispossessed the Portuguese. About two centuries later again (1796) the Dutch were expelled by the English, and the maritime provinces of Ceylon were attached to the Madras Presidency for a year or two, after which Ceylon became a Crown colony. Ceylon now possesses a government of its own, including a governor, a commander-in-chief, and an executive council of five members, with an elaborate system of administration. It is about one-fifth the size of an average province of British India, being equal in land area to about six official districts. For purposes of administration the island is divided into five "provinces" presided over by Government agents.

The attractions of Ceylon to the traveller lie chiefly in its unrivalled scenery. "It is impossible to exaggerate the beauty of Ceylon," says Sir Edwin Arnold. "Belted with a double girdle of golden sands and waving palm groves, the interior is one vast green garden of nature, deliciously disposed into plain and highland, valley and peak, where almost everything grows known to the tropical world, under a sky glowing with an equatorial sun, yet tempered by the cool sea winds. Colombo itself, outside the actual town, is a perfect labyrinth of shady bowers and flowing streams and lakes. For miles and miles you drive about under arbors of feathery bamboos, broad-leaved breadfruit-trees, talipot and areca palms, cocoa-nut groves, and stretches of rice fields, cinnamon and sugar-cane, amid which at night the fireflies dart about in glittering clusters. The lowest hut is embosomed in palm fronds and the bright crimson blossoms of the hybiscus, while wherever intelligent cultivation aids the prolific force of nature, there is enough in the profusion of nutmegs and allspice, of the india-rubber and cinchonas, of cannas, dracænas, crotons, and other wonders of the Singhalese flora, to give an endless and delighted study to the lover of Nature." But this by no means exhausts the beauties of Ceylon. One need only travel by the train from Colombo to the station of Kandy, embosomed in mountains and overlooking the broad surface of a lake which reflects the varied beauty of the forest-covered hillsides, and thence pass on through the terraced spurs to higher levels, where acres upon acres of tea cultivation now spreads over the same soil which was not long ago devoted to cinchona and coffee, to realise that there is hardly any sort of scenery from that of the temperate zone to the tropics which is not to be found almost at its best in Ceylon.

On the north-west Ceylon is nearly joined to India by the island of Manaar, Adam's Bridge, and the island of Rameseram. There are two passages through the strait—the Manaar between Ceylon and the island of the same name, which was formerly not more than 4 feet deep at high water; and the Pambam passage which separates Rameseram from India. This used to be only 6 feet deep at high water. Both passages have been widened and deepened.

The eastern shores of Ceylon are rocky, and the water deep; the north-western and western shores north of Colombo are uniformly low and indented with bays and inlets. The general flatness of the coast districts has led to the formation of salt-water lakes or lagunes which have been connected by canals (said to have been constructed 300 years B.C.), which much facilitate traffic and communication between these maritime provinces.

The harbour of Trincomali on the north-east coast is

celebrated for its great natural strength and capacity, as well as for the beauty of its surroundings. It is said that all the navies in the world might find shelter in the harbour of Trincomali.

Galle harbour, on the south coast, is also well known to travellers as a port of call for ships bound to India. It has lately been superseded by Colombo, but is now under a process of improvement that may once again bring into prominence the quaint old Dutch town which dominates it. Colombo harbour is also undergoing extensive alterations, which will add greatly to its advantages. A heavy surf beats unceasingly on the coast at Colombo, and, under the influence of strong south-westerly gales, the approach to the harbour in its recent form was often dangerous.[1]

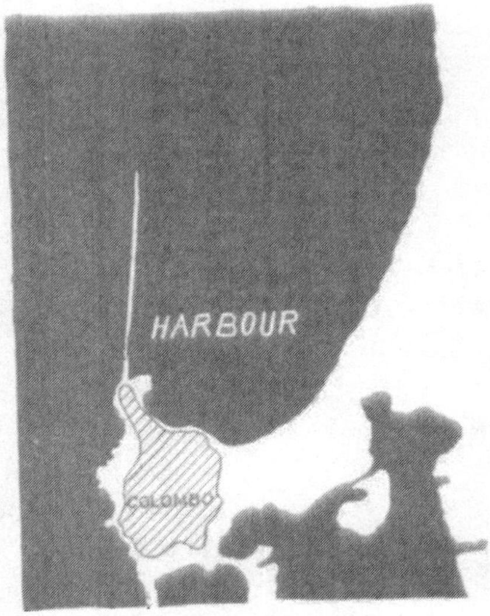

FIG. 61.—Colombo Harbour.

The northern half of the island is flat and forest-covered. The southern is about equally divided between hills and plains, the hills occupying all the centre of the island, and influencing the climate (as already explained) in a remarkable degree. It is about the hills and the southern and western plains that most of the planting which constitutes the wealth of the island exists. These hills culminate in the peak of Pedrotalagalla (8300 feet above the sea) close to the pretty hill station of Nuwára Elia (generally pronounced Nuralia), which occupies the highest plateau amongst them; Adam's Peak, which is much better known, and was for many years supposed to be the highest peak in the island, being only 7400 feet.

[1] New harbour works have already been constructed.

N

From the central mass of hills numerous offshoots are detached towards the coast from south-east to south-west. Nuwára Elia is above the 6000 feet level, and is the counterpart in Ceylon of Ootacamund in the Nilgiris. The surrounding of blue mountains, of stretches of green upland, the patches of uncleared forest filled with quaint and fantastic trees (amongst which the "Keena," a curious imitation of the stone pine, is prominent), the Australian importations (gum trees and wattle), the cloudy, humid atmosphere—even the flowers, arum lilies, heliotrope, and geraniums, which seem specially suited to the climate of Nuwára Elia, recall vivid impressions of "Ooty." Round about Nuwára Elia, are tea plantations which are carried over the hill slopes to a height of nearly 7000 feet. A recent and most admirable law has been passed by the Ceylon Government that the higher slopes of the mountains are in future to be reserved for forest growth, the absence of which after extensive clearings had been effected having a most appreciable effect on the rainfall. In amongst the lines of tea plants cinchona is still grown. It serves as a much-needed shade tree to the tea, but the over-production of cinchona in the island has led to this industry being partially abandoned. Tea has almost entirely superseded coffee since the year 1870, when the coffee plantations were destroyed and many wealthy landowners ruined by the appearance of a new fungus (*Hæmilia vastatrix*), which choked the pores of the leaves and destroyed the plant.

On the lower slopes of the hill districts cocoa plantations are now increasing. Nothing can exceed the beauty of some of these plantations set amidst the most lovely scenery in the island, and interspersed with a magnificent growth of shade trees—much needed for the cocoa plant. Cinnamon and cocoa-nut palms are indigenous, and the latter form the chief wealth of the Singhalese, who utilise every part of the tree for domestic purposes. But every species of spice is cultivated, as well as rice, sugar, tobacco, indigo, and a certain amount of cotton. A vast variety of timber is found in the forests, and is largely exported. Probably no country in the world of equal area possesses such natural wealth as Ceylon. Useful minerals and valuable gems are not wanting. Iron, tin, plumbago, copper, quicksilver, and coal are all in the island; and there is a cave from which the best Epsom salts are produced. The precious stones chiefly in repute are the ruby, cat's-eye, sapphire, amethyst, topaz, garnet, and beryl; but casual purchasers should beware of imitations, in which a large trade was for many years successfully carried on. Latterly, however, this trade has not proved so profitable, and it is attended with a certain amount of risk.

The two most interesting features of Ceylon to the visitor are its wealth of modern plantations in the south, and of ancient Buddhist ruins in the north. Amidst the natural beauty which he will find distinguishing the former, with all the enchantment of mountain and river scenery (for the rivers of Ceylon are very beautiful, even if they are economically unimportant), and all the comforts of home surroundings in this garden of the eastern world, he may well forget that the attractions of Ceylon once lay farther north, where there are relics of an historic past which surpass in interest anything of their kind to be found in India.

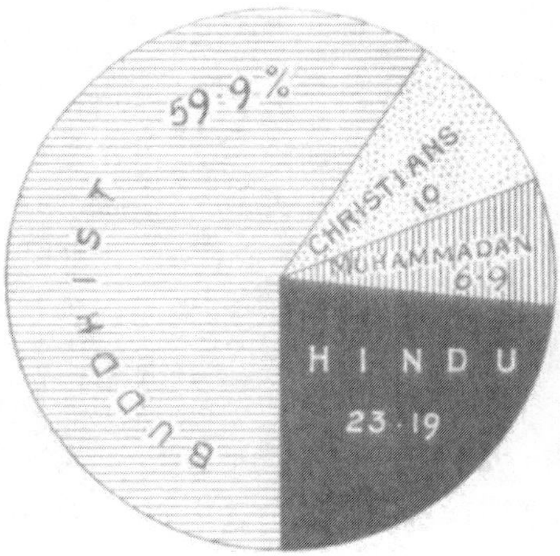

Fig. 62.

Ceylon is the land of Buddhists—even more so than Burma. The yellow-robed priest is always *en évidence*, and the bells of temples, and the chant of the scholar, learning his monotonous incantations and prayers as he sits under a hedge of sunflowers or the shade of the temple portico, is always in the air. Kandy is perhaps the centre of living, as Anuradapura is the centre of dead, Buddhism in Ceylon. The Malagawa temple at Kandy contains the Dalada, or sacred tooth, which was brought to Ceylon in the year A.D. 311, concealed in the hair of the Princess Sanghamitta. After many vicissitudes it was (according to veritable history) taken to Goa in 1560, and there burnt in presence of the Portuguese Viceroy and all his court. But another tooth, 2 inches long and less than 1 inch in diameter, now enjoys all the reputation of the original relic. To this has lately been added certain veritable relics of the founder of Buddhism discovered on the borders of Nipal, and the temple still remains the most important seat of the Buddhist hierarchy.

FIG. 63.—Buddhist Centres and Modern Railways.[1]

From the northern terminus of the Ceylon railway at Matalé, north of Kandy, the great highroad to Trincomali stretches away over the falling plateau, and through flat forest-covered plains till it reaches Dambulla. Here it branches, and leaving the ancient stronghold of Siguri, and the yet more ancient capital Pollonarua, away to the right, it runs north-east to Trincomali. A north-western branch takes the traveller to Mahintalé and Anuradapura. A short description would absolutely fail to give any impression of the magnitude and

[1] A railway is now under construction to the extreme north of the island.

the magnificence of the ancient Buddhist remains that are to be found in these old-world sites, even if it afforded a faint conception of the beauty of the highways that lead to them. The granite enclosed temple at Matalé and the cave at Dambulla are both typical, and attest strongly to the vitality of the still living faith, whilst the marvellous extent of the ruins, which occupy many square miles of country at Anuradapura and Mahintalé, now covered with the forest growth of years and buried beneath the accumulations of centuries, attest yet more strongly to the enormous wealth and influence of that faith in the past days of its highest development. At Anuradapura is the sacred Bo tree under which Gautama attained his Buddhahood, the dagoba of Thuparama, oldest and most venerated of any in Ceylon (although the pious devotion which led a wealthy disciple of the faith to smarten it up with a coating of "chunam" deserves scant acknowledgment from the archæologist); and here are sixteen square miles of ruins—grass-grown jungles in which the contemplative stone figures of Buddha stare solemnly through the ages; forests of lâts and pillars surrounding the ruins of tanks; foundations of monasteries, temples, walls, and edifices, which must once have been the glory of the Buddhist world.

Hardly less astonishing are the great tanks which retained the headwaters of an elaborate system of irrigation which has yet to be traced out to its full extent.

The great northern road leading to Anuradapura and Trincomali runs through the heart of the country. It is usually enclosed with forest on either hand, but occasionally strikes through long open stretches of grass land, sprinkled with clumps of trees of magnificent growth, reminding one of English scenery. In the winter months, when the rains are still in force, the vivid luxuriance of the landscape is very striking, and all Nature seems alive with animated beauty. Butterflies in countless thousands swarm in the woods till they appear like beds of flowers, and they rise in clouds as the traveller passes by them.

The chief river in Ceylon, the Mahavelli Ganga, drains northward from the mountains to Trincomali harbour. Its source is near Adam's Peak, and in its course of 200 miles it waters what was once the granary of Ceylon, but is now frequently pestiferous marsh country. About 80 miles of it might be made navigable if Trincomali were a commercial rather than a naval port.

The inhabitants of Ceylon are Singhalese in the southern districts, Tamils in the northern, Vedda aborigines in the wildest and most inaccessible parts of the forest country, Muhammadans, and Europeans. The Singhalese are probably of mixed Hindu extraction, and date their origin from the Hindu invasions of Ceylon about 500 B.C. The Tamils are the representatives of those periodic invasions from Malabar which are recounted in the history called "Mahawanso." The Veddas are rapidly disappearing. The European community is chiefly represented by a widespread class of settlers of Dutch extraction, who are locally known as Burghers. They fill all the clerkships and lower civil offices of Government, and answer much to the Eurasian element in Indian society. There is also a sprinkling of Malays and Chinese in the island; but it is to the developing character of Singhalese, who are now rapidly being brought under the influences of European systems of education, rather than to the effete and degenerate form of European existence as exemplified in the descendants of a once robust Dutch ancestry, that we must look for the regeneration of the social status of Ceylon. English planters are not, as a rule, settlers in the country, and Government officials never outstay their period of active service. The Singhalese combine

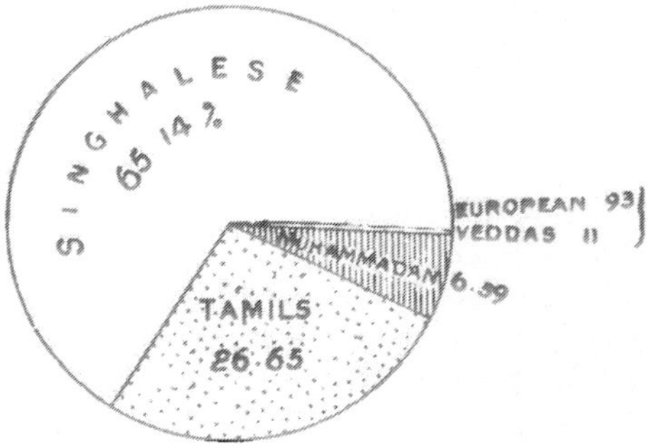


FIG. 64.

many qualities which entitle them to hold a higher place in this agglomeration of nationalities than they have ever yet taken. They are intelligent, industrious, and frugal.

The trade statistics of 1898 show the total value of exports from Ceylon at Rs. 95,000,000, and imports Rs. 97,900,000 approximately, the value of the exports to India being Rs. 7,300,000, and of the imports from India Rs. 61,400,000.

The physical characteristics of Assam and Ceylon have been generally described from personal observations in those regions, with such assistance as may be derived from Survey Reports (Indian and Ceylon) and Census Returns; but for Burma I have been dependent on the writings of such experts as Scott, Woodthorpe, Yate, and M'Mahon, and on the recently issued Indian Survey sheets of Burma, which illustrate a vast extent of country about which very little has been written.

# CHAPTER VII

## THE PEOPLE OF INDIA

"ONE of the greatest difficulties that exist," says Fergusson, "perhaps the greatest, in exciting an interest in Indian antiquities, arises from the fact that India has no history, properly so called, before the Muhammadan invasion of the thirteenth century. Had India been a great united kingdom, like China, with a long line of dynasties and well-recorded dates attached to them, the task would have been comparatively easy; but nothing of the sort exists, or ever existed, within her boundaries. On the contrary, so far as our knowledge extends, India has always been occupied by three or four different races of mankind, who have never amalgamated so as to become one people, and each of these races has been again subdivided into numerous tribes or small nationalities nearly, sometimes wholly, independent of each other; and, what is worse than all, not one of them ever kept a chronicle or preserved a series of dates commencing from any well-known era." Thus the history of Indian nationalities has had to be built up from such records as may be found in Indian architecture, in coins, inscriptions, and other forgotten relics, and the building is necessarily imperfect in construction and wanting in continuity. But although there is no ancient history there is abundant literature—"a literature extending, in fact, to some 10,000 or 11,000 works—and buried amidst innumerable and unreadable treatises on law, astronomy, grammar, metaphysics, and mathematics are two great epics, which, if rightly understood, appear to throw a certain amount of light on the developments of Indian ethnography."

All that can be deduced with certainty from such unpromising material is that at some very remote pre-

**INDIA**, ETHNOGRAPHICAL.

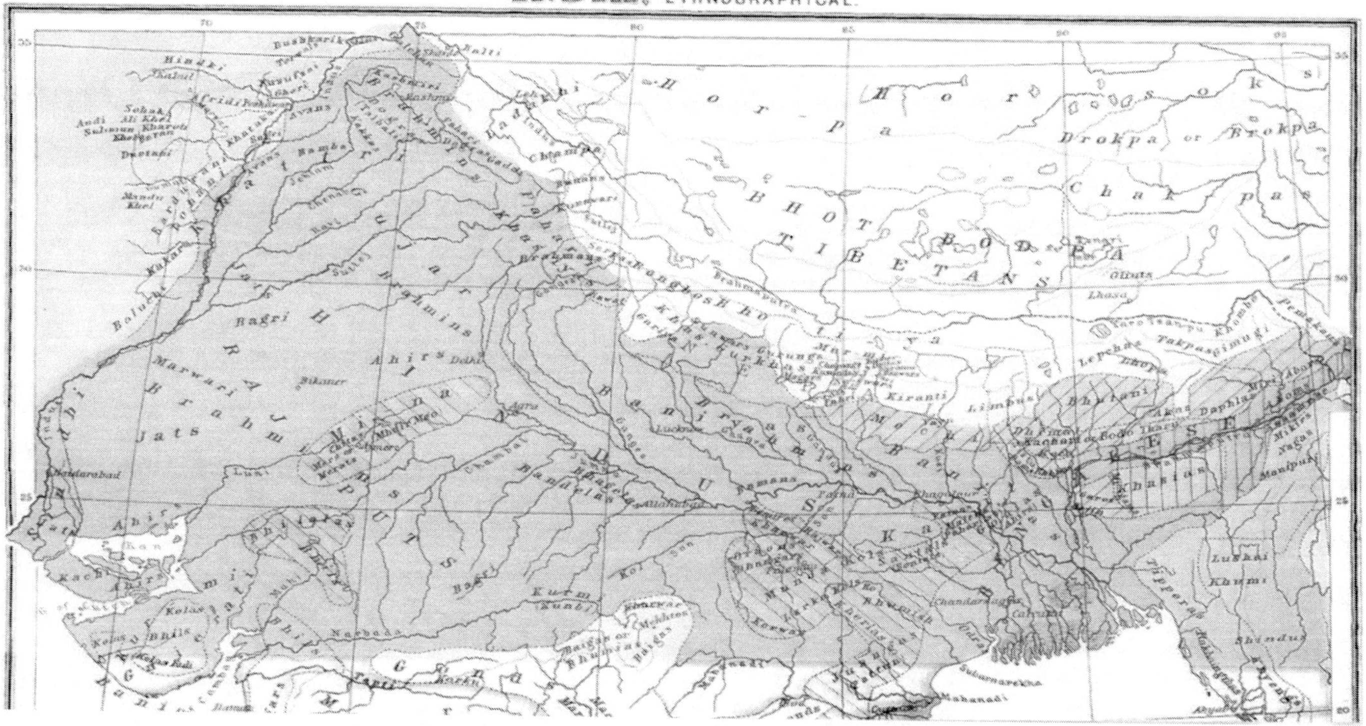

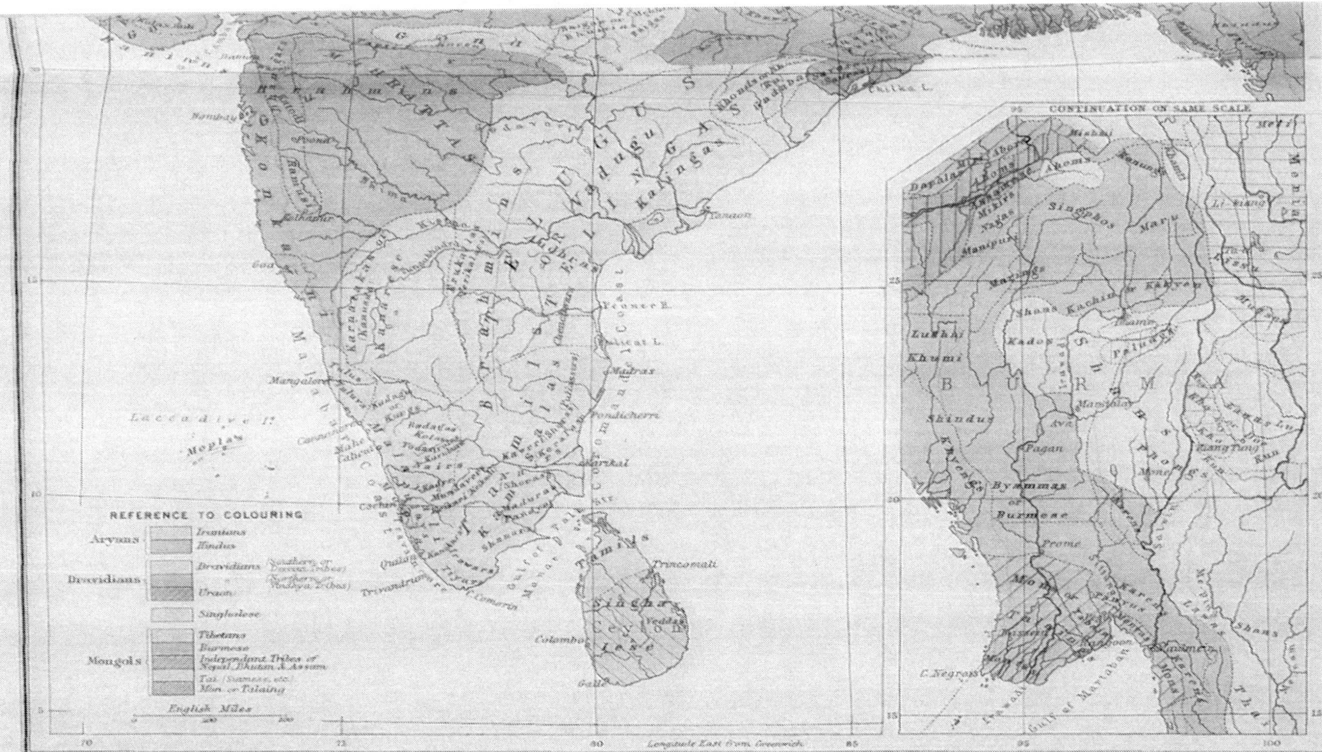

CONTINUATION ON SAME SCALE
REFERENCE TO COLOURING
Aryans
Iranians
Hindus
Dravidians
Dravidians
Uraon
Singhalese
Mongols
Tibetans
Burmese
Independent Tribes of Nepal, Bhutan & Assam
Tai (Siamese, etc.)
Mon or Talaing
English Miles
Longitude East from Greenwich
Bombay
Poona
Goa
Mangalore
Madras
Pondicherry
Karikal
Pulicat L.
Trincomali
Colombo
Galle
C. Comorin
Cochin
Trivandrum
Laccadive Is.
Moplas
Tamils
Ceylon
Singhalese
Veddahs
Kalingas
Chilka L.
Mishmi
Abors
Singphos
Maru
Nagas
Mikirs
Manipuri
Khumi
Kadons
Shindus
Shans
Mandalay
Pagan
Ava
Prome
Byammas
Burmese
C. Negrais
Gulf of Martaban
Mons
Karens
Li-siang
The Edinburgh Geographical Institute
J. G. Bartholomew

historic period a Sanscrit-speaking people, whom we call Aryans, came from Central Asia and settled themselves in the Indus Valley and the Punjab. About 2000 years B.C. they were well established in Ayodhya, and it is there that our best authorities consider that one of the great epics—the Ramayána—was written. The Ramayána appears to be an allegory recording in mystical language the conquest of Ceylon by this Aryan people. It was at this period that Brahmanism spread over the whole of Southern India. At a much later date (possibly about 1200 years B.C.) a second race of Central Asian extraction appear on the scene—a much less pure race than the original settlers, or possibly claiming more affinity with Tatar than the Aryan stock. They called themselves the Lunar race, in distinction to the original Solar race, and the Mahabhárata (the second great epic of India) relates in mythical form the result of the great contest between the two races. It was then, possibly, that certain sections of the original Solar, or Rajput, race were driven from the plains of India into the Himalayas and Indus valley hills. About the year 700 B.C. we find the Brahmans sharing power with the Kshatryas, or soldiers, and other than the priestly caste are asserting their position in the land. In the year 623 B.C. Buddha was born of the Solar race, and from this point there is a solid substratum of history.

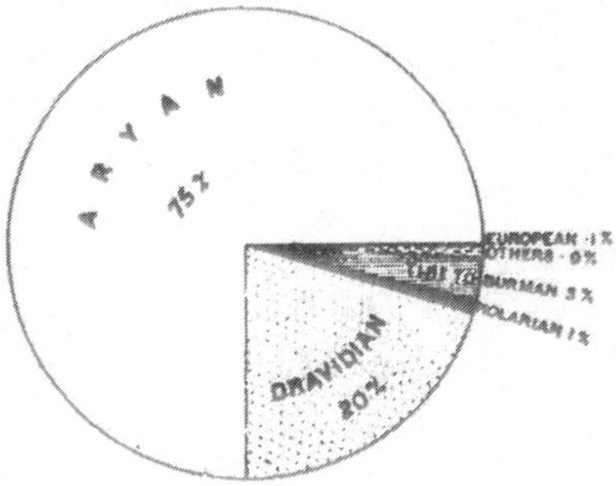

FIG. 65.

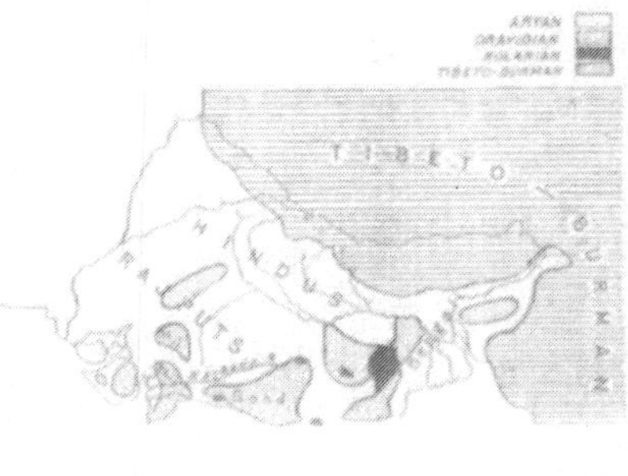
FIG. 66.—Race Distribution, Upper India.

The history of the Aryans, however, is not the history of India. The Turanian, or Dravidian element of the population appears to have been, in historic times, as numerous as the pure Aryans, and at present forms about one-fifth of the total population of India. They possess a lower intellectual status than the Aryans, but they "have preserved their nationality pure and unmixed, and, such as they were at the dawn of history, so they seem to be now." The advent of the Turanian element into India belongs to an epoch so remote that it is impossible to suggest even an approximate date. Recent explorations in Makrán and on the Persian coast seem certainly to confirm the view that the Dravidians passed into India across the lower Indus from the direction of Mesopotamia. The Brahui of Baluchistan appears to be the modern representative of that widely extended Dravidian people who occupied Makrán when Alexander forced his way through the deserts and passes of Southern Baluchistan to Persia. But the great mass of Dravidian people have ever been dwellers in the southern parts of the peninsula, and are now to be found in the lower districts of the Central Provinces and in Madras. Chief amongst Dravidian tribes are the Gonds and the tribes of the Nilgiris.

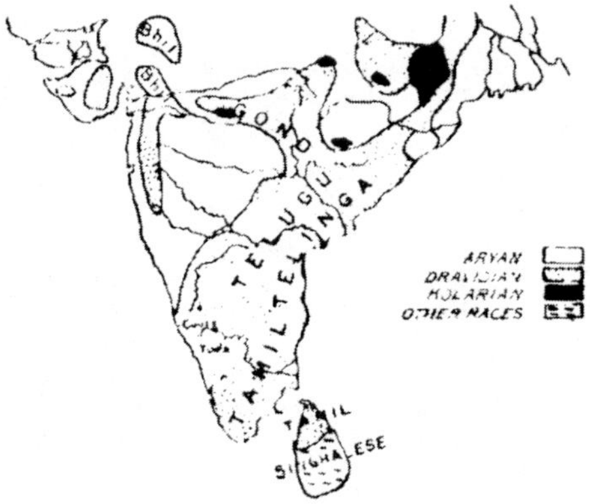

FIG. 67.—Race Distribution, Lower India.

Separate again from both Aryan and Dravidian stock are the aboriginal people, the ancient Kolarian tribes who once spread throughout India, and are now to be found under the name of Bhils, Kols, Santáls, &c., in the wildest fastnesses of Central Indian jungles. Their affinities appear to be with trans-Himalayan population, and they either entered India through the passes of North-

Eastern Bengal—which is unlikely, if we consider the nature of those passes—or they are a fragment of a great population that occupied both the northern and the southern slopes of that great chain of mountains at some very remote prehistoric period.

The Kolarian group of non-Aryan races now occupies the northern districts, and the north-eastern edge of the southern tableland of India.

A third and most important element in non-Aryan ethnography is that of the Tibeto-Burman group of tribes which clings to the skirts of the Himalayas and their north-eastern offshoots. Their prehistoric home was with Mongolians and Chinese. This group includes an immense number of tribes, the limits of whose habitat is at present but indefinitely known, although it is confined to the mountain districts of the north-east of Bengal and to Burma.

These are the people, at any rate, who finally accepted Buddhism, which was never an Aryan or Dravidian form of faith. In Bengal, Ceylon, Tibet, Burma, Siam, and China, wherever a Tibetan people exists, or a people allied to them, there Buddhism flourished and still prevails.

For the ordinary student of Indian geography and of the distribution of the castes, tribes, and peoples through the country these three great divisions, Aryan, Dravidian, and Aboriginal, may be sufficient to summarise the primary or original status of the whole population ; but the infinite variety and enormous number of even important subdivisions which take their place in modern history, waxing great as nations, and disappearing as scattered tribes, render it absolutely impossible to do more than select a few of the prominent representatives of each great division, and indicate their chief characteristics and geographical distribution.

Amongst the so-called Aryan races of Northern India the Rajputs are distinctly the oldest and the noblest. They belong to one of the greatest races of history, and their past extends through thousands of years in an unbroken record of valour and nobility. Unfortunately exact ethnology is a comparatively young science in India, and the absence of authentic history is productive of a host of ethnographical myths and misconceptions which can only be gradually cleared away. We do not even know precisely what is meant by the term "Aryan," or whether it is a true race term at all. The two great prehistoric races of Central Asia who have most influenced the destinies of Europe and of India are certainly Aryans and Skyths, but we are not yet able to say whether there was—or was not—any connection between them, whether either included the other either as a whole or in part. We are, however, safe in assigning to the Rajputs the chief place amongst the earliest of those Aryan immigrants of which we have already spoken. They were the Kshatryas, the warriors of Indian epic, distinct from the Brahmans, who form the priestly caste. But there was a time when the Rajput (whose name is an abbreviation of the Sanscrit Râja-putra or king's son) held spiritual pre-eminence in India, and to this day the Ranas of Mewar officiate as high priests in the temple of their guardian deity. To this day thousands of Brahmans, bathing in the Ganges, repeat a hymn every morning of which the author was a Râjanya and not a Brahman. Whether the Rajput can be identified with the Solar race and the Brahman with the Lunar race of Indian classics remains still to be seen ; further ethnographical inquiry may yet clear away the allegorical mist of the Mahabhárata, and throw light on many dark points of India's earliest records.

The Rajput is tall and well built, with well-developed limbs, which are generally described as of a "reddish" hue. He is by heredity and national instinct a warrior and a huntsman. Intensely proud of his descent, which he attributes to supernatural rather than historical origin, he is only just beginning to conform to those usages of society which govern other less illustrious communities, and to fit himself to the views of a government to which he is distinctly loyal, but which he doubtless regards as dangerously democratic in its tendencies. A Rajput cannot marry a woman who does not belong to a Rajput family, nor can he marry one of his own class; so that the field of matrimony is most inconveniently narrow. A poor man frequently cannot marry at all, and a rich man is "besieged with applications for his hand in order that the stigma of an unmarried daughter may at least be formally removed." Thus large dowries are usually necessary to enable a girl to marry, and suitable alliances may mean the ruin of a family. In order to avoid such catastrophes the crime of female infanticide became a fixed custom amongst Rajputs. Sir John Strachey says that "these people have gone on killing their children generation after generation, because their forefathers did so before them, not only without a thought that there was anything criminal in the practice, but with a conviction that it is right." Happily Government has been able to deal with this subject by a system of registration, and Rajput girls are to be found now where formerly no girl was ever known to exist; but "there can be no doubt that if vigilance were relaxed the custom would before long become as prevalent as ever."

The hereditary and central habitat of the Rajput is in Rajputana, one-half of which consists of waste sandy spaces, which, if not absolutely desert, are very closely allied to it. In the south-eastern half of Rajputana, where the desert merges into bands of rugged hills and of open cultivable flats; where sands and occasional oasis gradually gives place to plains watered by clear streams and rivers; where the desert well (often hundreds of feet deep), from which water is extracted by the bucketful with the assistance of a pair of oxen and a long rope, ceases to be the most prominent feature in the sandy landscape; there are the great cities of Rajputana. Jaipur, Jodhpur, Ajmir (a British possession), Chitor, and Udaipur still attest, with their lofty battlemented walls and scarped defences, the strength of those ancient strongholds which have witnessed centuries of stirring action and many a bold defence; whilst the magnificence of the relics of ancient architectural structure and art designs with which they abound attest equally to the high development of early Rajput culture. No towns or cities in India so amply repay a visit as those of Rajputana. There is nothing in India to exceed the beauty of the city of Udaipur, seat of the most ancient of Rajput races, with the white brightness of its towers and terraces reflected in the waters of its still clear lake, and its noble surroundings of hill and plain; nothing in the art of marble carving to beat the records of that race of sculptors which decorated Ambér, the ancient site of Jaipur; nothing historically so fascinating as the blood-stained courtyards and walls and towers of Chitor. No district in India can compare with Rajputana in historical interest.

Rajput races are, however, scattered and mixed with other classes of the Indian population all over India. Under the name of Dogra they are settled in large numbers in the Himalayas. The Himalayan state of Chamba is a Rajput state, and the seat of one of the oldest dynasties in existence. On the borders of Sind, in the districts of Las Bela, we again find Rajput clans, and there can be little doubt that many of our frontier tribes-people possess Rajput affinities, derived from some prehistoric reflex wave which was swept back from the plains of India into the bordering hills.

Distinct from Rajputs, the Brahmans have ever represented the priestly caste in India, and, like the priestly clan all over the world, they have directed the destinies of nations, and still exercise the most potent influence of any caste in India.

Into the history of early Brahmanism, when the faith was higher, nobler, purer than anything that at present exists, ere it was eclipsed for a time by Buddhism, we cannot enter. When Buddhism declined, Brahmanism again resumed its ascendency, and although it is not (or it claims not to be) a proselytising religion, Sir Alfred Lyall thinks that it probably claims more converts in these days than any other religion in the world. It is difficult to understand the ascendency of the priest over the people of India without a complete grasp also of their appalling ignorance and superstition.

Modern Hinduism may be described as the most contemptible religion in existence. "The term Hindu," according to Sir Alfred Lyall, "is not a national, nor even a geographical denomination, but signifies vaguely a fortuitous conglomeration of sects, tribes, hereditary professions, and castes." "The Hindu religion is a religious chaos. . . . I doubt if any one who has not lived amongst Hindus can adequately realise the astonishing variety of their ordinary religious beliefs, the constant changes of shape and colour which their beliefs undergo, the extraordinary fecundity of the superstitious sentiment. Hinduism is a tangled jungle of disorderly superstitions, ghosts and demons, demi-gods, and deified saints, household gods, tribal gods, local gods, universal gods, with their countless shrines and temples, and the din of their discordant rites, deities who abhor a fly's death, and those who delight still in human victims."[1] Sir John Strachey declares that the "sacred books of Sanscrit literature represent in no way the religion of the masses of the people." It is true that Vishnu and Shiva claim these countless devotees, and that the stories of Krishna and Rama are repeated as domestic fables in every household; but the everyday life of the ordinary Indian peasant is little affected by the pure tenets of his ancient faith. The rural population of India is governed through ignorance and superstition by a degenerate race of priests, and the priests are supported by the people.

No domestic incident occurs in a household without the tax of offerings or food for the Brahman. Nothing happens without the Brahmans being "feed and fed." "But with the spiritual life of the people" (says Mr. Ibbetson) "they have no concern. Their business as Brahmans is to eat and not to teach." "The universal acceptance of Brahmans, and the recognition of their divine right to be fed by the rest of the community, is the one link between the countless shapes of Hinduism; this, to the great majority of Hindus, constitutes in practice the chief part of their religion."[2] Here, then, is the opinion of

[1] "Asiatic Studies," p. 2.

[2] Strachey, p. 210.

some of the most competent observers in India, and it is difficult to comprehend the source of that strength which gives Brahmanism its overshadowing and overwhelming authority.

None but a people sunk to the lowest depths in a tangle of crude and grotesque superstitions could accept such a sacerdotal tyranny—nothing but liberal and wide-spread education can lift them out of it.

As for those sharply defined distinctions of caste which (so we have always been taught) separate Hindus into four distinct communities, they are unrecognisable in the present day. Exclusive of the Brahmans and Kshatryas, "caste means, for the most part, hereditary occupation, but it also often signifies a common origin of tribe or race." "In the enormous majority of instances caste is only the name for a number of practices which are followed by each one of a multitude of groups of men, whether such a group be ancient and natural, or modern and artificial. As a rule every trade, every profession, every guild, every tribe, every class, is also a caste; and the members of a caste not only have their special object of worship, selected from the Hindu pantheon, or adopted into it, but they exclusively eat together and exclusively intermarry."[1] Even Muhammadans have castes. There are said to be 1429 different castes in India, of which Brahmans, Kunbis (agriculturists), and Chamars (leather workers), are the only three castes which number more than 10,000,000. These three include nearly 15 per cent. of the inhabitants of India.

Of those repulsive aspects of Brahmanism which find expression in the obscene rites of Shiva worship, or in the fantastic eccentricities of wandering fakirs, yogis, and devotees, who consider a thin smear of ashes as a full and sufficient substitute for civilised clothes, and who live a life of indecency and beggary, there is no need to write. They are only useful to point a moral. No nation or people that can not only tolerate such nuisances, but look to them as a high and worshipful expression of a mystic

[1] Strachey's "India."

faith that they do not pretend to understand, can possibly appreciate any process of upward levelling in their social condition that might be introduced by education under a government that condemns such things. We must not look for any popular appreciation of English rule from a people who hug such a religious slavery as this, and who take delight in their own degradation. Consequently the popularity, or otherwise, of English government is not to be considered in taking the measure of its success.

Hindus greatly outnumber the followers of all other faiths put together within the limits of Hindustan. Out of a total of 287,000,000 in 1891, 207,000,000 were Hindus. But whilst the mass of the people are sunk in the lowest depths of a barbarous superstition, such as could never have been contemplated by pre-Buddhistic Brahmans, there are, of course, many noble exceptions to the general rule; and we find in all the great centres of civilisation high-minded and highly-educated Hindu gentlemen, equally distinguished in the courts of justice or the halls of science. Indeed the Hinduism of the cities may be said everywhere to approximate much more nearly to the religion of the Vedas and ancient Brahmanical ritual than it does in the agricultural districts.

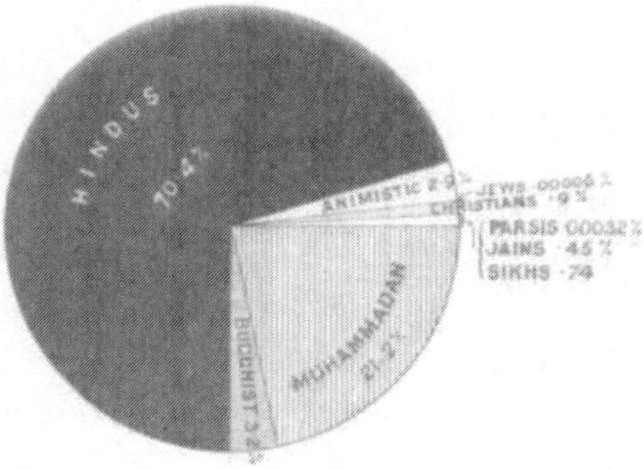


FIG. 68.

Hindus (Brahmans and Rajputs) formed the main strength of the army of India in pre-Mutiny days, but since the reorganisation that followed on the transfer of the army from the East India Company's service to that of the Crown, the proportion of Hindus has been very largely reduced. They are chiefly represented by Rajputs, Dogras, and Gurkhas, but the Hinduism of the latter is anything but orthodox. The hardy little Gurkha mountaineers are recruited from the hill districts of Kumaon and Nepal, and, with the Sikhs, they form the flower of the native army. They are a people of Indo-Tibetan or Mongolian extraction, small in stature, sturdy in frame, broad chested and broad shouldered, with the facial characteristics that distinguish all the Mongol race, and endowed with an aptitude for fighting and a spirit of enterprise that removes all surprise at the astounding successes of Chenghiz Khan and his successors in the Central Asian empire of six or seven centuries ago.[1]

The Sikh is allied to the Hindu by religion, and, as a soldier, he is as important a factor of our military strength as the Gurkha. He is of the Skythic race called Jat, and is usually of finer physique than the majority of north country plains men. Tall, straight, and manly; gifted with perfect manners and an unassuming address, a well-bred Sikh is, in the best sense of the word, a native gentleman. With the Sikh the profession of arms is hereditary; the traditions of the Khalsa uphold his pride in centuries of honourable warfare waged against his national foe, the Pathán; and we have ourselves found the Sikh soldier a sturdy enemy in the field, every whit a match for the best troops that the British army has ever placed in line against him.

The Sikh religion is a comparatively modern offshoot of Hinduism, with none of its debasing superstition and demonology. Its centre, or headquarters, is at Amritsar, in the Punjab, where is situated the "Golden Temple," founded in 1574 by Ram Dass, the Guru, or high priest, of the Sikhs, upon a site granted by the Emperor Akbar on the banks of a sacred tank, from which the city takes its name. Within this temple one may usually find the high priest reading the Grunth (the sacred book of the Sikhs), whilst pilgrims cast their offerings into a sheet spread on the marble floor before him. A copy of the Grunth is carried in front of the Sikh companies of a native regiment, placed on a cushion, with bearers waving "chowries" above it to preserve it from contamination.

We must now reckon with the Muhammadan popula-

[1] Or of the Japanese in the present age.

tion of India. Throughout the country are scattered between 57,000,000 and 58,000,000 Muhammadans, a number sufficient to justify the expression that the empire of India is the greatest Mussulman power in the world. As compared with the Hindu population, the comparatively small number of Muhammadans in India affords but little indication of their political importance. The strictly orthodox Muhammadan is only to be found on the frontier, or in the great cities of the plains. Although we hear much of Muhammadan factions and of the constant recurrence of civil conflicts between Mussulman and Hindu, such outbreaks are almost entirely confined to large towns, where the creed of Islam is upheld with something approaching to fanatical fervour. The great majority of Muhammadans in India are descendants of but half-converted Hindus ; and they are still in effect as much Hindus as their progenitors. Six million or seven million Muhammadans are to be found on the north-west frontier who partake more or less (for even on the frontier there are many half-hearted professors of the creed of Islam) of the fanaticism which is kept alive by the zeal of those upholders of the faith who dwell beyond our borders ; and if we add to the Mussulman strength of the frontier those descendants of former invaders or immigrants who live in the towns of India, we shall include the whole body of the faithful who uphold the orthodox tenets of Islam.

Fig. 69.—Upper India.

"One-third of the inhabitants of the large towns of the North-West Provinces is Muhammadan, and it is the religious animosity which exists between them and the Hindus that arouses such constant attention to the power of the Muhammadan faith in India. As for the great Muhammadan agricultural population (18,000,000 of whom exist in Bengal alone), it is remarkable for an absolutely superficial form of religious belief, and is no more to be counted as a political factor in India than if it were entirely Hindu. For the most part they are quiet peasants, the descendants of Hindus, nominally converted. The Muhammadan sovereigns usually treated them as subjects, in the matter of religion, with great tolerance; but more or less pressure was from time to time brought upon Hindus to induce them to embrace the faith of the ruling power. This was especially the case in the time of Aurangzeb, the most bigoted of the Muhammadan emperors. The change of faith was often little more than nominal, and took place to an extent just sufficient to save the joint property of the village community from molestation. One section of the brotherhood would become Muhammadan, while the rest remained Hindu. The change of religion had little practical result, nor did it affect the rules of caste or of social life in the community."[1] Thus the great majority of Muhammadans in India hardly deserve the name. "Local saints and Hindu deities still have their shrines, even in villages held wholly by Muhammadans, and are still regularly worshipped by the majority, though the practice is gradually declining. . . . The Hindu family priests are still kept up and consulted as of old, and Brahmans are still fed on the usual occasions, and in many cases still officiate at weddings side by side with the Muhammadan priests."[2] And the Hindu meets the Muhammadan half-way. It is no uncommon occurrence to find the ziarats, or sacred shrines and burial-places of the frontier, visited by devout Hindu pilgrims quite as frequently as by Muhammadan devotees. The well-known shrine of the Takht-i-Suliman is held in high estimation by Hindus; and it is a curious fact that one of the most popular shrines in the East, situated in Makrán, and visited by thousands of Hindus and Muhammadans alike every year, is really sacred to a Mesopotamian goddess who was worshipped before Brahmanism was known to India.

[1] Strachey's "India."   [2] Ibbetson.

In our army, however, the Muhammadan element is most important. The Punjabi Muhammadan is a strong addition to the mixed class regiments of the Punjab and the frontier, and takes his place alongside the Sikh in no unworthy manner. The Pathán tribes of the borderland, Kuttaks from the Kohat district, Afridis from Tirah, Afghans, Baluchis, Kakurs, &c., from the southern districts, contribute some of the best of the raw material for our native military service, and as our knowledge of the border people extends, and mutual confidence increases, we shall doubtless number more and more of these fighting races in the ranks of our native army. For the best

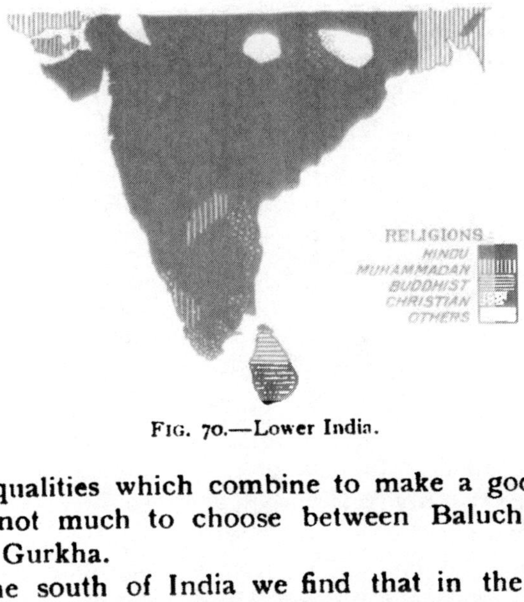


FIG. 70.—Lower India.

of those qualities which combine to make a good soldier there is not much to choose between Baluch, Pathán, Sikh, or Gurkha.

In the south of India we find that in the province of Madras, out of a population of nearly 40,000,000, nearly 35,000,000 are Hindus, and rather more than 1,500,000 are Christians. Southern India is the habitat of the Dravidian races, the Tamil and Telegu (Telinga) people, whose origin is to be traced to quite a different Asiatic cradle and who reached India in prehistoric times by quite a different route to that followed by the Aryan immigrants of the north. It has long been conjectured that Western Asia (Media and Mesopotamia) was the original home of these races of the south, and that they passed overland by the coast districts of Persia and Makrán (where, indeed, their representatives, the Brahuis, still flourish) to the western states of India. Gradually pushed southward by the influx of more highly-civilised races from the north, they have spread into Southern India, and filled up the waste spaces of the Central Provinces, where they may be found in almost aboriginal simplicity to this day.

The ancient glory of the Telinga kingdoms of Southern India has long been dimmed ; gone, too, is that martial spirit which once animated these southern races, and made them great in the annals of Hindustan, even to the days of Haidar Ali and the French occupation of the Karnatic. Never, perhaps, in the history of the world has the enervating influence of climate and geographical position over the energies of humanity been so fully illustrated as in the gradual decadence of the military instincts of this once military people since the early days of our struggle for supremacy with France.

The Madrasi is a man of peace, an agriculturist, a shopkeeper, an excellent man of business, and an admirable servant rather than a soldier. But there are races of fishermen and boatmen on the Karnatic coasts, descendants of the Telingas who crossed the seas and founded kingdoms in Burma, who are brave and enterprising in all that appertains to the calling of the sea, and who are certainly no whit inferior to the Bengali lascar as practical sailors.

In physical characteristics these southern races differ most essentially from the tribes of Northern India. The Tamil is usually a black-skinned man of small size, but with no want of muscular development. His features are of the Tatar type without the strong accentuation of the Mongol, and he seldom has hair on his face. The Telegu people differ from the Tamils in their superiority of general physique, and in the general lighter colour of their skin. The Telegu makes a better-looking soldier, but he possesses on the whole less stamina than the Tamil, who, under favourable circumstances, exhibits fine fighting qualities.

A marked feature in the Southern India population is the prevalence of Christianity. It is usual for the native servant in Madras to commence the enumeration of his many good qualities by the statement that he is, by religion, "same like master." The vast majority of Madras Christians are Roman Catholics, descendants of those who owed their conversion to the Christian faith less to the traditional preaching of St. Thomas than to the more stringent methods employed by the early Portuguese crusades, which enforced Christianity in the western districts of India by fire and sword. It is often but a superficial creed, accepted by the uneducated and ignorant as an intelligible alternative to the unintelligible Hindu mythology. The Virgin Mary is to them but a beneficent goddess, and the transition from Krishna to Christ is one which offers no material difficulty to their limited intellectual powers.

But it is good to witness the devotion of the Catholic priests to their scattered flocks in Southern India. Often in the early months of summer, when the scorching breath of the hot wind shrivels the jungle and sends whirlwinds of dust and dried leaves scudding over the sun-baked plain, the bullock cart (which is the travelling residence of the priest) may be found under the shade of the village banyan tree, and the priest himself, shrivelled, dried, sun-hatted, cheery, and happy, teaching and ministering to his little half-clothed congregation of puzzled Christian adherents in these depths of darkest India. And so he will go on teaching and explaining and hoping for the best till he dies and is buried—when a few sticks with rags tied to them will decorate his grave, and he will rank as a departed "fakir" or "yogi."

With the Tamils and Telegus of the southern provinces are associated other Dravidian tribes, more nearly "aboriginal," who form no inconsiderable part of the total population, but who possess no great political or economic importance. Probably the oldest of these

Dravidian races are to be found in the Nilgiri Mountains. There, on the rounded grassy slopes of the hills are collections of wattle-built huts shaped somewhat like elongated beehives with wooden ends, and inconvenient doors through which the house-owners pass and repass on all-fours. The people who build these huts (the lords of Nilgiri soil), recognised as the original landowners by Badagas, Kotas, and other tribes of mountaineers, are called Todas. They are lighter in colour than the Tamil of the plains, and their features are rather Semitic than Tatar; but they speak a dialect of the Dravidian tongue, and it seems to be probable that their affinities are Dravidian.

Scattered over the Nilgiris (as indeed in many places along the line of the Western Gháts) are stone monuments of a forgotten age and a lost race, to which the Todas make no claim, and in which they acknowledge no interest. Thus they are clearly the successors of a yet anterior race of cairn-builders—a race of higher civilisation than themselves, many of whose customs, however, have been adopted by them so far as we can judge by the evidence of such relics as have been brought to light. The Todas are never agriculturists. Like all Indian races claiming the rights of first possession, they live as herdsmen on the produce of their buffaloes. The Todas burn their dead, and offer sacrifices with much picturesque ceremony as a part of the funeral rites. One of the buffaloes sacrificed on these occasions always wears a bell, and it is this bell which connects the ritual of the Toda with that of the yet more ancient Dravidian who preceded him on the Nilgiri hills. They are not a large tribe, and there was some years ago a danger of their final disappearance from the face of India, but they are at present living witnesses to the fact that the advance of civilisation does not always tend to the extinction of an aboriginal population.

The picturesque accessories which surround this small but interesting tribe, the wild free hills, and the sweet grass-covered valleys which lie amidst their folds, the quaintness of the Toda "mands" or villages nestling under the lee of aboriginal jungle; their wildly fantastic rites and ceremonies amidst the grim relics of an age of rude stone monuments—all these combine to attract attention to the Todas. But politically they are not of the least importance; and even ethnographically they must yield in interest to those Dravidian people (the Gonds) who occupy the wildest recesses of jungle-covered India, and who to this day set up monoliths and a crude imitation of dolmens over the remains of their buried dead.

That part of India which lies east of the lower Godavari Valley, the wilderness of hills and highland that enclose the great tributary of the Godavari, called the Indravati, south of the Mahanadi, may well be called "darkest India." Here there are thousands of square miles of country belonging to the dependency of Bustar into which the European has seldom penetrated. Neither the fascinations of sport (for these districts swarm with big game), nor the exigencies of civil administration, are sufficient to attract the white man into those unvisited jungles if they can be avoided, for they are perhaps the most pestiferous jungles of India. The survey of that country was only carried out at a lamentable cost of life, both European and native. There, hidden away in reed-covered plains, in cane brakes and teak forests, often at a considerable altitude above sea (where the western flanks of the Eastern Ghâts are approached), are rude wattle-and-stick-built villages, hiding a people who wear but little clothing, and who flee from their homes into the rocks and stones of the nearest hills as soon as a stranger approaches. They live in the forest, and on it. There are spasmodic attempts at cultivation by the rude processes of axe and fire here and there, and, on the fringe of Gondwana, near the Godavari, or near the coast, there are open spaces of rice cultivation. But the mainstay of the central Gonds is the jungle produce—roots, berries, and the products of the chase. They are skilful hunters and excellent shots with bow and arrow, and as they find bison and buffaloes, spotted deer, marsh deer and other smaller species, with bears, tigers, wolves, and pigs swarming in plenty around them, there is no lack of interest in their pursuits, or of food in ordinary times.

The centre of Gondwana may be located north of the Indravati, in the Mardian hills. Here dwell the Mária Gonds. South of the Indravati, in the fork formed by its junction with the Godavari, are the Gotturs ; and south of them again, abutting in the low-lying provinces of the Godavari basin, are the Kois. These are all Gond tribes speaking a common dialect, but they differ a good deal in social customs, the primitive habits of the southern people being much modified by contact with the Hindus of the plain country. The Koi (otherwise Koiwar) is a small wiry man with Turanian features, dark skinned, lazy in habits, and physically wanting in muscle. His hair is twisted off his head into a knot ; he has no hair on his face, and his high-pitched (though not unmusical) voice and fancy for beads and ornaments (which are generally displayed in great profusion round his neck and arms) give him a particularly effeminate appearance. The dress of the Koi is usually limited to a single loin-cloth, and a vast quantity of beads round the neck, which represent more or less his wealth and social status. He is fond of aping the manners of his Hindu neighbours, when he has any ; and near the Godavari he is generally known as Koi Dora (or Koi gentleman), a distinction which is somehow admitted by the other tribes. His gentlemanly instincts are shown by his aversion to hard work, and he much prefers tending cattle and basking in the sun to any form of manual labour.

The Gottur is taller, fairer, and physically stronger. He is much more suggestive of the aboriginal yellow races of Chaldæa than any other Dravidian I have met.

The Márias are the wildest of the Gonds, and it is very difficult to establish intercourse with them. Many of the Márias are light in colour, and the absence of hair on their faces is not so universal as one would expect in the purest type of Gond. Living in the fastnesses of the hills they are exposed to great vicissitudes of climate, and their habit of sleeping between fires frequently leads to their being covered with the scars of burns, and adopting a grimy complexion of cinders. Beads and brass ornaments represent their wealth, but there is little of it, and they are usually sunk in the depths of extremest poverty. Their faith is simple demonology and witchcraft; the one great goddess that all of them recognise is Matadevi, the goddess of smallpox, whose influence is acknowledged as much for good as for ill, with a simplicity of reverence which says much for the hardness of life amongst them, and the insecurity of its tenure. Many a little swing with a few grains of rice as offerings is set up by the road-side to propitiate Matadevi. All these people erect monuments to their dead—monoliths where stone is abundant and slabs of gneiss are handy, and wood where stone is not available. The wooden posts are often curiously carved, and it is usual to find a rough imitation of a peacock as the headpiece, often clothed with decorative strips of cloth so as to represent the original bird more completely. At the foot of the post there is generally a slab of stone, which is used both for sacrificial purposes and as an altar for offerings made to the spirit of the departed. Their festivals, their customs, and their wild fantastic dances which form part of the recurrent rites of burial, would fill an interesting chapter; but we must leave the Gonds, and turn to a yet more ancient, more perfectly aboriginal people, who occupy another of the untraversed districts of Central India, and who represent those tree and serpent-worshipping races whom the Aryans found in possession of the plains of Hindustan when they first arrived from Central Asia.

The Bhils occupy a portion of the Mahratta state of Indore, and a section of Rajputana and Khandeish. Where the Narbada runs its straight course through a network of hills thrown out by the Vindhya and Satpura ranges to the point where, bursting through these enclosing mountains, it spreads itself out into a wide stream in the plains of Bombay—there is the home of the Bhil. For the shrines and temples that Brahmanism has erected on the banks, or the overhanging spurs of this sacred river, the Bhil cares little or nothing, although he is not untouched by Hindu influences; but the river itself he "regards with veneration and terror." "The Bhils" (says Sir Lepel Griffin) "are held by the Hindus amongst whom they live in profound contempt. The Brahmanical creed with its caste exclusiveness, and its insistence upon purity of blood in the male line, gives it a contemptuous air towards all aliens . . . which is the real cause of the estrangement between English and Indians, which is often erroneously attributed to the coldness and reserve of the former. But the attitude of the Hindu towards the English is rather that of the Pharisees of Jerusalem towards Pilate and the Roman legions. The contempt is mingled with a very strong proportion of respect, fear, and esteem. But towards the Bhil, the slave of slaves, the outcast of centuries, the very refuse and waste of the old world before the Aryans arose and gave it the rudiments of civilisation, the sentiment of the Hindus is unmitigated scorn." But the Rajput chiefs and their ministers who overlord the Bhils have been compelled by the British Government to relax the burden of their oppressive taxation, and to observe the rights of the Bhils, and there has thus sprung up a spirit of confidence in English justice amongst these savages which has gradually ripened into mutual respect and liking between English and aborigines.

In spite, however, of Rajput scorn for the Bhil, the original proprietary rights of the latter over the soil is recognised in a singular custom. The coronation ceremony of a Rajput chief in any state where there is a Bhil population is not considered complete unless the "Tika" —or mark of kingship—is impressed "upon the forehead of the new chief by the head of the Bhil family to which this hereditary privilege belongs. . . . The Maharana of Udaipur is the highest in rank and descent of all the princes of India, tracing his lineage to the Sun, yet on the day of his installation it is the despised Bhil who places the sign of kingship on his forehead."

The Bhil is as much a cattle lifter and thief as the Scotch borderers of 200 years ago. He "proclaims himself to be a thief by Divine decree as part of the curse pronounced upon his ancestors by the great god Mahadeo when he slew the sacred bull," but he is gradually losing his predatory habits and taking to agricultural pursuits. So long as his crops flourish and times are prosperous the Bhil is fairly well behaved, but in times of drought and famine, when streams run dry and there is no fish, and "when the wild animals leave his neighbourhood for distant and low-lying jungles where they can obtain water and shelter, then the Bhil in self-preservation turns with a light heart to the congenial occupation of cattle lifting."

Some years ago a military corps of Bhils was raised, which has done much to reclaim these people from their wild habits. The corps has proved a success. The Bhil soldier may not be much to look at when compared to the more regular sepoy of the Indian army, but he is an excellent policeman (as might he expected from his original trade); he is an adept at every sort of woodcraft, an excellent shot, and possesses marvellous powers of endurance. Withal he is most astonishingly truthful; his oath taken on the head of his dog is never known to be false; he is gay, light-hearted, and a sad drunkard. Like the Gurkha, he is savage in his cups, and nine-tenths of the crimes committed amongst Bhils are the result of alcoholic fury aroused by the spirit of the Mohwa, the fruit which is found abundantly in the forests of the Central Provinces.

The Bhil lives much on natural produce, collecting honey and roots and berries. It is a curious fact that years of drought and famine are usually years of special abundance in jungle produce; the bér (jujube) Mohwa, bamboo, and Corinda shrub contribute greatly to mitigate the effects of famine amongst these people. The Bhil worships the gods of the Hindus more or less, but his principal deity is the local village god; his idols are usually mere heaps of stones, and he never builds temples. Traces of tree worship are to be found amongst them still, and it is curious that the local name for the teak tree (Sag) should be also the name for a snake. They burn their dead, and have a profound belief in ghosts, witches, and omens.

Sir Lepel Griffin, who knows them well, believes that the Bhil country offers a fine field for missionary enterprise.

Yet more aboriginal, possibly, even than the Bhils are certain races which we find in the islands adjacent to India, notably the Andamans and Nicobars. The Andamanese appears to be a negritic race, with many of the more strongly marked characteristics of the true negro wanting in them. They are a race of small people, exquisitely moulded and of perfect figures, with curly, but not woolly, hair, dark skins, and the habits of savages. They have yet to be properly placed on the ethnographical scale of humanity. The yet more savage inhabitants of the Nicobars are ethnographically entirely distinct from the Andamanese, and their affinities are undoubtedly with the Malays.

Many of the races of Western India, who are of no political importance and who are never brought into contact with Europeans through the ranks of the native army are well worth the attention of ethnographers. Such, for instance, are the Coorgs, whose mountainous habitat is dovetailed in between Mysore and the Malabar and Kanara districts. The men are described as muscular, handsome, and tall, and the women fair, well-proportioned, and good-looking, although they are as a rule small compared to the men. The Coorg race has ever been noted for its loyalty, and the Coorgs afforded material assistance to the Government in the third Maisur Campaign against Tippu Sultan. They are permitted to carry arms, and are noted for their marksmanship and their prowess as hunters. They are, nevertheless, ignorant and superstitious, worshippers of "demons and ancestors, and dealing in charms and sorceries," and blood feuds are sustained amongst them with all the hereditary vindictiveness of the Pathán.

But the variety of nationalities is great in India, and ethnographic distinctions are as varied as the differences of social manners and customs. From the princely and arrogant Afghan to the artificial tail-wearing Naga (of the Tibeto-Burman group), who dances his war-dance on the top of a hill, and wags his tail as a symbol of defiance; from the highly-educated Bengali sceptic of Calcutta to the provincial landowner (not far removed from him) who will sacrifice a human victim in order to secure a favourable decision of the High Court, humanity may be found and studied in India in all its aspects and phases both of physical and moral eccentricity. It is impossible to refer to even a tithe of the ethnographic interests that will be found contained in the continent between the Indian Ocean and the Bay of Bengal. But we may well ask, Which of all the races of India have shown the highest aptitudes for upward development?—which of them can be claimed as affording really satisfactory evidence that the civilisation of England has had any decided effect in raising the moral standard of the people, or of securing a strong and intelligent body of political adherents? The most cultured races, and indisputably the most intellectually advanced, are the Bengalis (with whom may be associated the Mahratta Brahmans of Bombay) and the Parsis. But education so far has apparently conduced far more to political agitation and discontent than it has to social and moral improvement or material strength. One hears far more of the screams of agitators than of any satisfactory witness to a full and just appreciation of the advantages of British rule in India. Yet the appreciation undoubtedly exists, and exists widely, and with most strong vitality, but it does not advertise its existence in the native Press, nor air itself in the British Parliament. The fact is that political discontent is a profession in India just as it is elsewhere—men live by it, and advertisement is necessary to provide for its support.

Thus it happens that of all the many peoples of India the Parsi and the Bengali are perhaps the best known and the least understood in England, for individuals amongst them alone can command the ear of the British public, and these individuals are seldom really in touch with their own communities. The Parsi looms especially large with his portly figure, strange hat, and affable manners. He is the representative of the ancient Zoroastrian fire worshippers, who were driven from Persia by religious persecution in pre-Muhammadan times. Like other people of Western Asia, they found their way along the coasts, and have left evidences of their pilgrimage near the shores of the Arabian Sea. They maintain the rites of their ancient faith in their Bombay settlements, or wherever else they spread; keeping up the sacred household fire, and building their grim temples of silence, where the body which may not pollute the earth is exposed to the voracity of the birds of the air. They live the lives of hard-working, money-making men of business. The Parsi is essentially a shopkeeper, rivalling the Jew in his capacity for making and retaining wealth; but he is often generous and open-hearted, freely affording his assistance to the weaker brethren of his own faith, and prominent in those larger works of charity which enlist the votaries of all faiths. He is loyal (in spite of those occasional indications of a tendency to political agitation to which I have referred), because it is to his interest to be loyal. His communal existence depends on the stability of the English Government in India. Under its protection he can traffic and flourish, and multiply the race of those who add to the economic development of the country, without being called on to furnish any contingent to those defensive engines, armies and fortifications, which secure his continued existence.

The chief of his strongholds is Bombay. Here the Parsis hold all the best of the house property, almost to the exclusion of Europeans; but they may be found in scattered units through the length and breadth of India, and always in the capacity of the shopkeeper, the man of commerce, often holding high and responsible posts in the public interests. The strength of intellectual capacity, added to the material wealth which is possessed by this community, have given it abnormal prominence, the measure of which may be estimated by the fact that out of a total of 287,000,000 inhabitants of India, the Parsis do not number even one-tenth of a million.

Equal to the Parsi in intellectual capacity, but distinctly inferior in physique and the manlier attributes of the Asiatic races, is his Aryan brother, the Bengali. Like the Parsi, the modern Bengali is the result of the English occupation of India. Without that occupation his effeminate, indolent, and cowardly nature would long ago have led to his disappearance before the stronger races of the north. It is, of course, dangerous to deal in generalities, and notable exceptions may certainly be found to this general estimate of the Bengali character; but in a work like this it is only possible to deal in generalities, and no one acquainted with the Bengali will deny that nationally he belongs to a comparatively contemptible race.

Sir John Strachey, after quoting Lord Macaulay's judgment on the Bengali character, which marks him as "feeble, even to effeminacy," possessing a mind which bears "a singular analogy to his body," whilst, at the same time he is possessed of a certain "suppleness and tact," adds that what was true in the days of Macaulay is true still. "His (Macaulay's) description may be applied without exaggeration to the majority of the people of Western Bengal, and especially to those with whom Englishmen come most into communication in Calcutta and the neighbouring districts. The Muhammadan peasantry of the eastern portion of the province are men of robuster character. It has often been said, and it is probably true, that Bengal is the only country in the world where you can find a great population amongst whom personal cowardice is looked upon as in no way disgraceful. This is no invention of their enemies; the Bengalis themselves have no shame or scruple in declaring it to be a fact. Although it cannot be said that English education which has taken so deep a root has made any class of Bengalis more manly, it is, we may hope, encouraging the growth of this amongst other virtues. For a Bengali it is something to have begun to talk in grandiloquent English about patriotism, and manliness, and courage. Even the academic admiration of such things is perhaps a mark of progress. The people generally are acute and intelligent, patient and industrious, and when they get more knowledge they may become more self-reliant, less timid, and less helpless against wrong." Unfortunately these are the people whose purely intellectual progress under English encouragement have brought them into prominent notice by reason of their capacity to advertise what they believe to be their "national" grievances. The people of India, as a whole, are undoubtedly loyal to the British Government. Such sedition as exists is fostered by the so-called educated classes, who regard agitation as a recognised way to obtain notoriety, and a possible means of earning a livelihood.

I have often been asked what place is taken by the Eurasian amongst the social communities of India ; and I have often thought that but scant justice is done to an intelligent, sober, and industrious class which furnishes the material from which all the smaller wheels and springs of the Government machine are fashioned. Without the Eurasian element that machine would be most seriously disjointed, and it would be exceedingly difficult to find any other material so excellently well suited, to replace the Eurasian in its complicated structure.

When Europeans and natives intermarry the result is Eurasian, so that not only the English, but Portuguese, Dutch, Danish, and French have all contributed to the Eurasian stock of India, and are to be recognised in the names of their descendants. Da Souza, Almeida, Fonesca, Corneille are common enough in the west and south of India, and are probably borne rightly enough by their owners. Such names as Claudius or Cornelius betray a desire to conceal the true patronymic, which savours of the bar sinister. The last census returns of the number of Eurasians in India is 79,800, but this can be only an approximation. Native Christians often call themselves Eurasian, and Eurasians call themselves European; nor would it be possible to detect the mistake. There are probably many more Eurasians than appear in the census. One-third of the Eurasians belong to Madras. Bengal has only 15,000 and Bombay about 9000, many of whom are Goanese or of Portuguese descent. The North-West Provinces and Madras are the localities most favoured by Eurasians. In both provinces there are large communities or settlements (as at Dehra Dun in the north-west and Bangalore in the south) of an almost exclusively Eurasian class. Poverty and improvidence are unfortunately common amongst them. This is largely due to their possessing native proclivities in the matter of early marriage. Men marry from the age of sixteen, and girls from the age of thirteen, "and, like the patriarchs of old, they all beget sons and daughters, the average number of births being six per family, nearly half of whom die in early life." Very few Eurasians take to agriculture. The vast majority are clerks, and it is in this capacity that they develop their best capabilities.

In colour they range from black, through brown and yellow to pure white, but there are certain slight physical peculiarities which betray the admixture of native blood even in the third or fourth generation from its introduction. The average height of the Eurasian is 5 feet 6 inches, average weight less than 8 stone, and average chest measurement 31 inches. Nevertheless many of them are of exceptionally active habits, and some of the best rifle shots in India are to be found in their ranks. In physique they are inferior even to the Madras sepoy, but the Eurasian is nevertheless by no means a negligible quantity in estimating the strength of our national defence. He is absolutely loyal, amenable to discipline, fond of sport, and capable of endurance; so that, as a member of our Indian volunteer force, he fills a very important place in the Indian defensive line; and even in his own special civil capacity he often attains to positions of trust, dignity, and honour.

No central and comprehensive authority for all the ramifications of race distribution in India from the earliest time to the present age exists. Ethnographical science has not been officially recognised in India, and a compilation of all the views and opinions expressed by generations of writers on the subject is quite beyond the scope of such a work as this. The most recent authorities are Bellew (for the frontier), Hunter, Lyall, and Griffin for the continent generally, and the most condensed epitome of their opinions will probably be found in articles in the *Ency. Brit.* Recent Census Reports are full of information about the people of the continent, but they hardly throw much light on the frontier and trans-frontier peoples, amongst whom, after all, that evidence has to be sought which will establish the origin of many of the most important sections of the Indian community. Ethnography has been so much in the hands of amateur inquirers, that it is difficult to assess the relative importance of the many contributions on the subject which have appeared from time to time in the pages of the *Asiatic Quarterly Review*, or in pamphlets published under the authority of the Government of India. Undoubtedly a very large field for research is still open. Meanwhile it is only possible to collate such information as is to be found in the works of writers on Ancient India with the opinions of modern administrators who have had exceptionally good opportunity for local observation. Owing to the want of systematic supervision every fresh inquiry in the field of ethnography is at present conducted as if no previous inquiry into the same field had ever been made, and no lines of division had as yet been drawn between the main Central Asiatic sources of the Indian population.

INDIA,

The Edinburgh Geographical Institute

INDIA, POLITICAL.

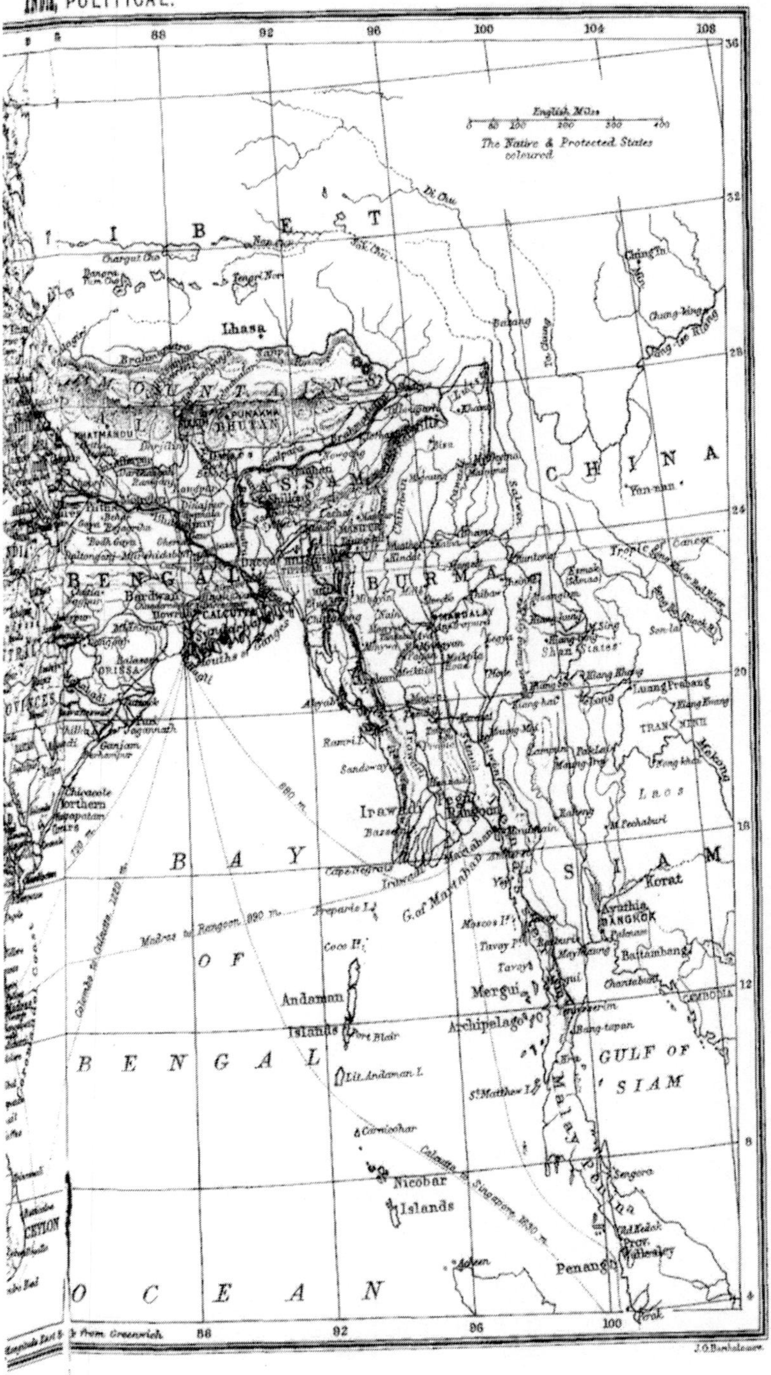

# CHAPTER VIII

## POLITICAL GEOGRAPHY

FOR purposes of administration the 965,000 square miles of territory which constitute British India are divided into eight leading provinces, each of which is under its own

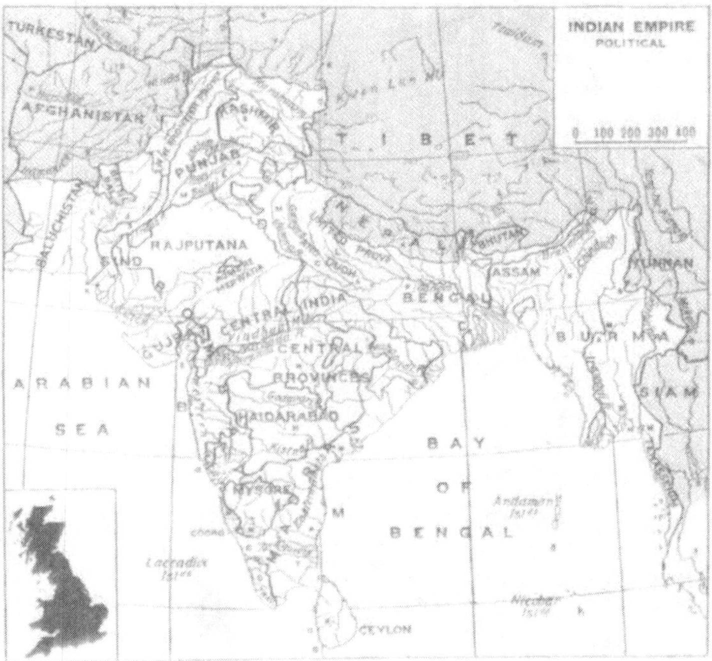


FIG. 71.

local government, and certain smaller divisions. The provinces include the old Presidencies of Madras and Bombay, the Lieutenant-Governorships of Bengal, the United Provinces (old "North-West" Provinces, with which the Chief Commissionership of Oudh is combined), the

Punjab, and Burma, and the two Chief Commissionerships of Assam and the Central Provinces. The minor divisions are Coorg, Ajmere-Merwara, British Baluchistan, the Andaman islands, and the new North-West frontier province, each under a Chief Commissioner. All are governed on the same principles, but they are not all on the same administrative footing.

Madras and Bombay are still officially regarded as

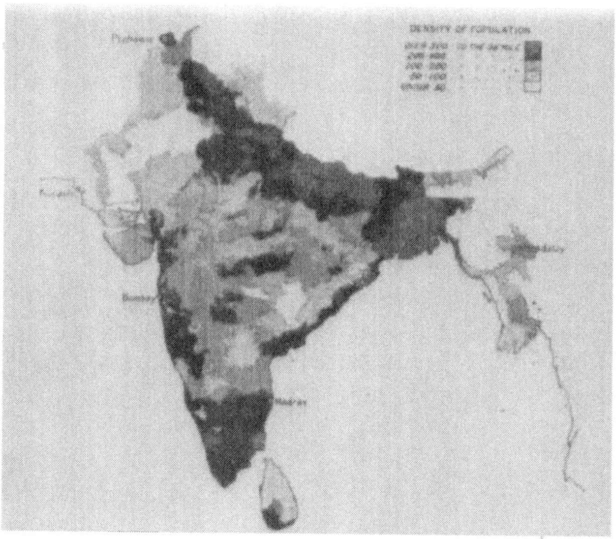

FIG. 72.—Density of Population.

Presidencies. Their governors are appointed by the Crown, and each of them has an executive council, consisting of two members of the Civil Service appointed by the Crown.

The Lieutenant-Governors are appointed by the Governor-General with the approval of the Crown. The Chief Commissioners are appointed by the Governor-General in Council.

Each province includes "divisions" under commissioners, and each division is broken up into "districts" under a collector-magistrate or a deputy commissioner, who has entire control of the district. There are about 250 of such districts in British India.

In area and population the provinces and commissionerships vary from 1583 square miles inhabited by

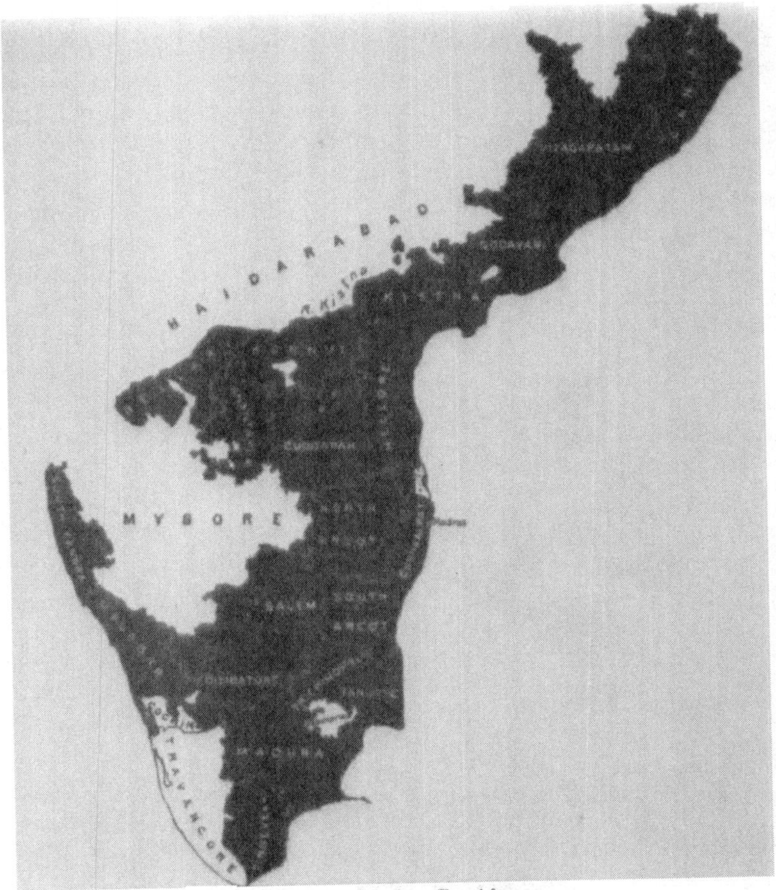


FIG. 73.—Madras Presidency.

178,300 people in Coorg, to 151,453 square miles and a population of 66,750,500 in Bengal. The administrative responsibilities of the Andamans (estimated by population) are even less than those of Coorg, but the area over which they extend is indefinite.

The governors of the ancient Presidencies of Madras

and Bombay, being appointed by the Crown, are usually men of high social standing in England (occasionally even of higher rank than the Governor-General himself), whilst Lieutenant-Governors and Commissioners are almost invariably selected from the ranks of Indian officials. These governors may almost be regarded as the last surviving relics of an epoch in India which is rapidly passing away under improved conditions of internal communication. Although Bengal, once the leading Presidency, has subsided to a provincial level, much of its ancient prestige still clings to it. Of the four army corps into which the army of India is divided, one is still called by the name of "Bengal," although it is doubtful whether there is a single Bengali recruit in its ranks, nor are its chief military stations to be found within the boundaries of the province.

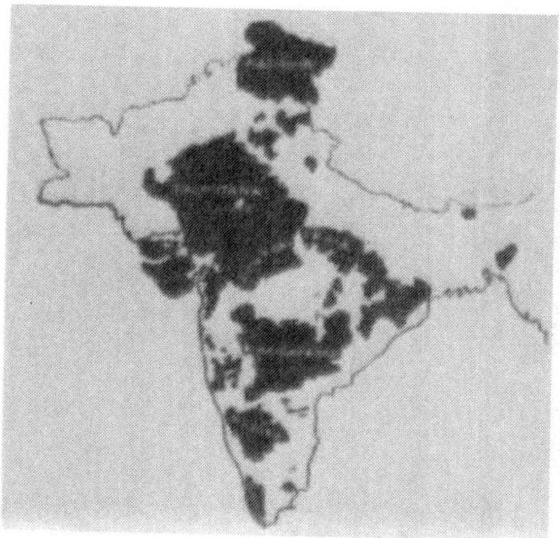

FIG. 74.—Area of Native States.

It is only lately that the great ruling class of India—the Indian Civil Service—has ceased to be distinguished in three great divisions as belonging to Bengal, Madras, or Bombay, and probably some little time yet will pass ere Englishmen in England cease to regard India (like Gaul of old) as "divided into three parts."

Besides, and apart from, the provinces of British India, there are nearly 600,000 square miles of territory included in the native states—states which are governed by their own rulers subject to certain definite control exercised by the supreme Government. These will be dealt with separately. At present we will define as concisely as possible the nature of that supreme Government in India—a Government which is the most astonishing, and in many respects the most successful administrative machine that the world has ever known.

Ever since the dark episode of the Mutiny in 1857–58 revealed the weak points in the old East Indian Company's administration, India has been brought directly under the Crown, the present form of the Government of the Indian empire being established by the Government of India Act, which received the Royal Assent on August 2, 1858. On January 1, 1877, the Queen of England assumed the title of Empress of India. As in the days of the Company, so also in these days the constitution of the Indian Government is dual—*i.e.* it is conducted by an Administrative Council in England, and an Executive Council in India.

The Secretary of State for India is invested with all the powers formerly exercised by the Company, and he is assisted by a Council of not less than ten members, appointed by himself, who advise on questions of finance and revenue, but have little to say to foreign policy or war.

The supreme executive authority in India is invested in the Governor-General in Council, often styled the Government of India. Since 1858 the Governor-General has also been Viceroy. He is assisted by a Council of five members appointed for five years, who represent seven different departments of Indian administration, as follows: Home, Foreign, Finance, Military, Public Works, Revenue and Agriculture, and Legislature.

In addition to the five ordinary members the Commander-in-Chief is usually appointed an extraordinary member. He is the executive rather than the advisory officer to Government in military affairs, the Government adviser being the military member of Council, who may be, and often is, of junior rank to himself.

Additional members can be added, up to the number of sixteen, by the Governor-General, for purposes of legislation only.

Thus there are practically four members of the Indian Civil Service, one lawyer, and two soldiers on the Viceroy's Council. In every administrative department there is a Secretary to Government, whose business it is to prepare all cases for submission to the Governor-General by the departmental member, so that they may be ready for decision. These officers are not secretaries to the members, but secretaries to Government in the various departments in which they serve, so that their position is analogous to that of permanent under-secretaries in England. In this distribution of administrative authority there is one striking omission. There is apparently no Member of Council for Foreign Affairs. This is explained by the fact that the Governor-General himself represents the Foreign Department, combining the functions of political member with his other duties.

But there is, of course, a Secretary in the Foreign as in other departments, who submits all questions of Foreign Policy direct to the Governor-General; so that, whilst all the internal affairs of the Indian Government demand the attention first of the Secretary to Government, next of the Member of Council whom they specially concern, and finally of the Governor-General, the Foreign Policy alone is matured by a secretary and sanctioned by the Governor-General, whose administrative attention has to be divided between the Foreign and six other departments.

The local Governments of Madras and Bombay still retain something of their former dignity and independence. Two members of the civil service and the local Commander-in-Chief formed the Council till lately. But the commands in Madras and Bombay have been reduced to a level in dignity with those of the Punjab and Bengal—which are undoubtedly more important—and the Commander-in-Chief in Madras and Bombay is no longer "His Excellency." In Ceylon, where the united military forces do not amount to half a brigade, he still retains this dignity. The Governors can add to their Councils from four to eight additional members for legislative purposes. Half of these members must be non-official.

The Government of the four great regulation provinces of India—*i.e.* Bengal, the United Provinces, the Punjab, and Burma—is administered by Lieutenant-Governors appointed by the Governor-General. They are always members of the Indian Civil Service, and they have a Legislative Council only. A secretary and an A.D.C. usually represent the staff of these high officials, who govern provinces as big as European countries, and guide the destinies of "men in nations."

In 1870 the Governor-General made regulations having the force of law for those provinces of India which had more recently come into our possession, and which not being considered fully ripe for the more complicated systems of administration which applied to the older and more settled districts, had been known as the non-regulation provinces. The chief difference between regulation and non-regulation as applied to the form of government, lay in the fact that in the latter executive and judicial functions were combined in one and the same person, fewer officers were employed, and the administrative staff were drawn either from the covenanted Civil Service, from the ranks of the Staff Corps, or from the uncovenanted service, and not from the covenanted service only. The Central Provinces and Assam are still known as non-regulation provinces, but there is in these days very little difference between the forms of government in regulation and non-regulation districts, the chief nominal distinction being that the latter are placed under the control of a Commissioner instead of a Governor or Lieutenant-Governor, and that the Commissioner need not necessarily belong to the Indian Civil Service.

Nothing, perhaps, is less understood in England by the public generally than the status of the civil servants of the Indian Government. We may divide them into two distinct classes: the "covenanted," and the "uncovenanted." The covenanted civilian is the man who takes his place in the service by the results of a competitive examination. He is, *par excellence*, the representative of the "Indian Civil Service," and he may, if he likes, place the letters I.C.S. after his name. To him belongs by prescriptive right the highest offices in the land, many of which can only be held by a member of his service. The Indian Civil Service is the governing class of India, and the testimony of a long succession of Viceroys witnesses to the success with which the high functions of this service are discharged. The Indian Civil Service is called "covenanted" because after passing an examination a covenant is made with Government in the person of the Secretary of State for India, "not to engage in trade, not to take bribes, to subscribe for pensions, &c."

The administrative offices in the regulation provinces are held almost exclusively by covenanted civilians, as well as a large share of those in the non-regulation provinces. In the covenanted class are included a certain number of the natives of India who may have attained their position either by direct competition, or by nomination and subsequent qualification under the rules laid down by Lord Lytton in 1879. These latter virtually belong to the Indian Civil Service.

Amongst "uncovenanted" civilians is included every public servant who does not belong either to the covenanted Indian Civil Service or to the Army. The great majority of civil servants belong to this category, and they fill some of the most important administrative posts in the empire. Sir John Strachey has pointed out that there are still many branches of the administration for which it is impossible to find duly qualified natives. Civil Engineers, Telegraph and Forest Superintendents, and the superior officers of the Educational and Public Works departments must still necessarily be Europeans. Appointments to the Educational Department are made by selection by the Secretary of State. The other departments referred to are officered by Englishmen who have been through a course of education at the Cooper's Hill Engineering College after passing a competitive examination for entrance. Excepting the above, all appointments to the civil offices of the Indian Government are made by the Government of India, the rule being maintained that qualified natives are to be employed in preference to Europeans in every branch of the service; so that in all the subordinate offices of the Secretariat and the Public Works, Survey, Telegraph, &c., natives and Europeans will be found working alongside each other. It is in this manner generally that employment is found for that mixed race known as Eurasians.

"Out of the total number of civil employees in India 90 per cent. are natives, but of course the great majority of these are in minor posts. Excluding the 765 offices held by covenanted officers, there are about 2600 persons in the superior grades of the executive and judicial branches of the service, and very nearly all of these are natives. Thus although the higher offices of control are held by Englishmen, the greater part of the actual administration is in native hands." Sir John Strachey wrote this in 1888, and during the ten years which have elapsed since then the proportion of natives has increased. Every post or appointment, except perhaps the very highest in the land, is within the reach of a duly qualified native so long as it is a purely civil appointment.

In this connection it is well to note the opinion of so eminent an authority as Sir John Strachey on the efficiency of the *native* civil service. After detailing the important part they take in magisterial and judicial work, he says: "I have already stated my belief that, as a rule, their work is quite as good as that of the English judges. Twenty years ago the native civil service was badly paid, comparatively inefficient, and not always trustworthy. In these respects there has been a great change. Nothing in the recent history of India is more remarkable than the change which has taken place in the standard of morality amongst the higher classes of native officials. Much of this has certainly been due to the fact that their positions and salaries are much better than they were, and that temptations to corruption have been removed. But I do not doubt that much has been due to their better education. Another powerful cause has been in constant and silent operation. The native officers have had before them, through a long course of years, the example of the irreproachable integrity of the Englishmen employed in the higher ranks of the public service.

Living in an atmosphere of official uprightness has made native judges and magistrates upright also."

But although a certain amount of statistical information is necessary to illustrate the composition of that corporate body in India which we call the British Government, it is more interesting to turn to the picturesque aspects of Indian administration, and to examine the actual working of the governing machine from the point of view of the native. What is it that the villager sees and knows of the "Sirkar"—that vague authority which from Olympian heights directs his destinies and shapes his ends? He never goes to Simla, to Calcutta, or any great central town. His narrow view of the flat plains that produce crops in rotation under the influence of a rainfall with the amount and disposal of which he is not quite certain that the Sirkar has not power to interfere; or with the rugged scantily-covered mountains that form the generality of his hill scenery, can scarcely grasp the compass of those inscrutable influences which, emanating now from Calcutta now from Simla, are hardly to be clothed in incarnate form. Pomp, magnificence, display, and all that is included under the generic term of "tamasha," these things he understands, although he sees but little of them; and indeed in these latter days there is but little to see.

Few, even amongst Englishmen in England, are inclined to concede that the Viceroy is but a hard-worked official, infinitely harder worked than any Secretary of State in England; and that he is supported by a band of equally hard-worked councillors and secretaries, men who rise early and late take rest, and eat the bread of carefulness in their Himalayan "Capua," just as much as if they were stockbrokers and merchant directors in London. It is curious that the popular view of Simla in England should be as unsound as it is. The native of the "flat plains" is, after all, not much more ignorant in regard to all that appertains to the greatness and dignity of the real builders and upholders of our Indian empire, than is the average "man in the street" at home.

What the agricultural class of native does see and know is his District Officer, and it is not too much to say that he often believes in him and venerates him more than his gods. The district is the unit of Indian administration, the head of the district is the District Officer. He may be a Deputy Commissioner in a non-regulation province, or he may be the magistrate and collector elsewhere; in either case his functions are much the same, and in both cases he is to the people for whom he lives and slaves the incarnation of the Sirkar, which is dimly recognisable in the distant background.

The magnitude of the areas and the numbers of the people that are governed by young English gentlemen who accept their responsibilities with a light heart in India is often insisted on, but never too strongly. Who knows what England as well as India owes to this systematic education of Englishmen in habits of government and command? Possibly two centuries of such practical education in India may have much to say to the extent of British empire elsewhere.

It is true that in these days the District Commissioner is more of a pilgrim in the land than he used to be. He lives always in hopes of an occasional short leave home, and he no longer looks to his life in India as the real objective of his existence. His surroundings have changed greatly within the last twenty-five years. He lives in a well-built house with a well cared for garden surrounding it, and his young wife (it is too often forgotten that official society in India is young) would be ashamed if her drawing-room were not as tasteful, and her receptions as well managed, as they would be in good English society at home. His home influences in fact are essentially English, and, so far, he is perhaps a little further from intimate touch with the people than was the case in those days when his domestic affinities were not always English. But the change is not a change for the worse. Intimate association in social matters is not what the natives of India ask for any more than they appreciate too subtle and too close an acquaintance with their own modes of thought or the ethics of their everyday life. The prejudice of caste is still strong, and the influence of neither District Commissioner, nor missionary, is extended by any effort to break through those social barriers which caste has recognised for centuries. So the District Commissioner takes the native as he finds him, and troubles himself only about his material welfare and his general good behaviour. "His duties, even with these limitations, are such as to call into action every faculty of observation that he possesses. There is nothing that occurs in his district that he does not know and provide for. In his functions as chief of the district he possesses a large share of administrative independence. He is the initiator of all new enterprise; he is the fiscal officer, charged with the collection of revenue from the land, just as much as he is sometimes criminal judge 'both of first instance and in appeal' as well. . . . Police, jails, education, municipalities, roads, sanitation, dispensaries, local taxation, and the imperial revenues of the district are his daily concern. He is expected to make himself acquainted with every visible phase of the social life of the natives, and with each natural aspect of the country. He should be a lawyer, an accountant, a financier, and a ready writer of state papers. He ought also to possess no mean knowledge of agriculture, political economy, and engineering." So says Sir W. Hunter.

But his multifarious duties do not oppress him, and few lives of men offer so much happy interest in the concerns of everyday life as do those of a deputy commissioner or "magistrate and collector." In the cool of the early mornings he is out with his attendant native satellites, and as he moves along the bordered and well-kept roads of the civil station, or through the crowded streets of the multi-coloured bazaar, his eyes are everywhere. He is a moving "court of appeal" for all the small affairs of each day's existence, whether it is in the matter of planting vegetables or of building a new court-house. The interest of his morning's walk or ride is quite sufficiently well sustained during the heat of the day, when for many weary hours at a stretch he has to sit in a heated atmosphere of physical and moral impurity to decide cases on evidence which can only be slowly extracted from the tangled mass of untruths which envelop it. His evenings are given up to those social functions which are rendered necessary by his position as the local leader of European society in the station. As a variation on his everyday home existence there comes the district cold weather tour, when he makes acquaintance with the farther limits of his kingdom and with people who probably see him only once a year, and who have amassed a pile of business for his attention that affects their well-being for the next twelve months.

Camp life, with its opportunities for sport in the jungles, and its sense of freedom and space in the open plains, is the life that renders existence in India not only endurable but delightful to Englishmen. It is this which makes India attractive, and which fills the memory afterwards with lively and happy recollections, when the business of the oven-hot "kacheri" or the more pompous functions of the Durbar have faded into obscurity. Such is the real practical everyday government of India, and it is only this outward and visible sign of it which is seen and understood by the vast majority of the 287,000,000 souls who make up India's population.

But besides the British Indian provinces there are 600,000 square miles of India included in the native states, with a population of 55,000,000. The native states of India are those states which are left to native rule. They are in a sense feudatory states, not absolutely independent, but with rulers exercising more or less autocratic authority, subject to as little interference with their internal administration as circumstances will admit. It is not always, indeed it is not often, that the ruling power thus constituted is so happily applied for the benefit of a people and a country that the English Government can stand aloof and leave the state to take care of its own concerns for any long period. As a rule circumstances will not admit of non-interference for a period much longer than the living authority of some prince whose strength of character is sufficiently exceptional to lift him above the temptations that beset him on every side, and whose governing powers are exercised in a spirit of justice and mercy. Too often a wise and beneficent rule is followed by the haphazard administration of the vicious spendthrift, and the ruin of a country is only to be averted by firm and judicious interference. But it is not until the internal affairs of a state have become scandalously bad that the Indian Government ever exercises its right of direct control.

There are, indeed, certain rights which the supreme Government must always assert. Political communications between the various native states or with any foreign power can only be carried on through its agency; and no native state can maintain an army which is obviously unnecessary for purposes of internal administration. Also any native chief can be arraigned and "tried for a crime of special atrocity by a tribunal constituted by the British Government," and it is unfortunately the fact that such rights have often had to be asserted.

"There is always much misunderstanding about the status of native states, and of the chief who governs them. It is often believed that they are principalities which for some reason or other have been omitted from the general confiscation attendant on our advance in India, and that they represent the rights of ancient dynasties, or the glorious heritage of a nobility whose patent is so old as to be prehistoric, and who have escaped, more by good fortune than anything else, the imposition of a rule which elsewhere has been forced on peoples who hitherto had been governed by princes of their own race. In the majority of cases nothing can be further from the truth. Some of them indeed have existed in something of the same form that they exist to-day for many centuries, and their chiefs represent a race of departed princes who trace their lineage back into the obscurity of the prehistoric past. These are the states that are thoroughly loyal and true to us, for their rulers know that, but for the protection afforded them by the British Government, they would long ago have succumbed to the fate which has befallen many greater and more powerful states who went to pieces in the general wreck which followed on the dissolution of the Mogul empire in the beginning of the eighteenth century, or who were swamped by Sikh ambition in the beginning of the nineteenth. Mahrattas or Sikhs, Sivaji or Ranjit Sing, one or the other, could have made them his own long ago but for us" (so says Sir Lepel Griffin).

The native states of India may be divided into five groups: Muhammadan, Hindu, Maratha, Rajput, and Sikh.

The geographical distribution of these states is not unimportant when considered in relation to the strength in arms and armament that is maintained in different portions of the Indian empire. The Muhammadan states are scattered. Excluding for the present Baluchistan and Afghanistan (not officially recognised as "native states"), there are those independent provinces on the borders of Sind, and between the newly demarcated boundary of Afghanistan and the British India line, over which we exercise political influence of a shadowy kind, although we refrain from actual interference with tribal government. Those on the border of Sind are controlled from Baluchistan. Those on the border of Afghanistan are now controlled from Peshawur as the capital of the North-West Frontier province. From end to end, from Karachi to Swat, the local form of government is tribal. There is no central authority with comprehensive influence, and the process of political negotiation is carried on between British officials and native "jirgahs," or collections of the chief men amongst the innumerable clans into which the tribes are subdivided.

In the wild mountain regions which form the barrier between the plains of India and the plateaux of Baluchistan and Afghanistan no other form of government has ever been found possible. Whether Afghans ruled at Delhi, or Brahmans reigned in Kabul, these frontier Patháns, through whose hills the connecting routes between Kabul (or Kandahar) and Delhi lie, have ever preserved their independence. And as an inevitable consequence they have always given trouble periodically, and armies and posts have had to be established to keep watch and ward

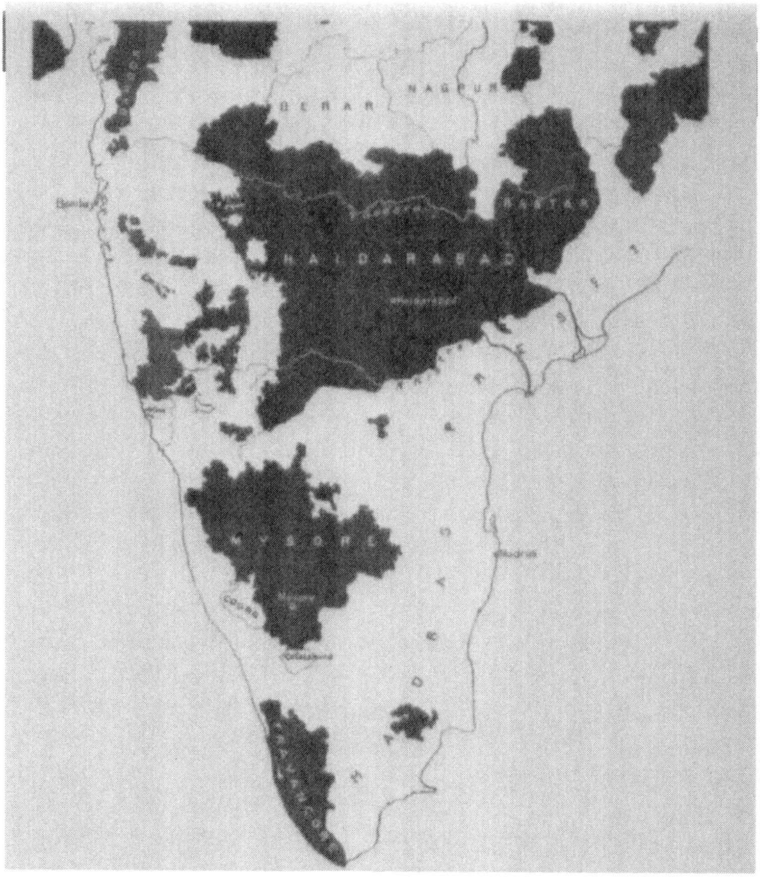


FIG. 75.—Native States, Southern India.

over their proceedings. The Baluch borderland is dominated easily from Quetta; and it may now be treated geographically as an integral part of the "State" of Kalát or Baluchistan. The Pathán borderland farther north is not really dominated from anywhere, and a large section of the Punjab Army Corps is employed in watching it.

After the frontier, Haidarabad (Muhammadan) is the largest, and politically the most important, of all native states. It includes an area of 82,600 square miles, stretching from the border of Bombay on the west to the Godavari and Madras on the east, with Berar on the north. The best part of the Dekkan highlands belongs to Haidarabad. The Godavari and the Kistna flow through it and fertilise it; and it possesses 11,500,000 inhabitants, a large native army, and a State railway of its own. The Hindu state of Mysore (Maisur, 28,000 square miles and 5,000,000 inhabitants) lies to the south of Haidarabad, occupying all the central portion of the peninsula, and is next in political importance. In the extreme south is another Hindu state (Travancore) which occupies a wide strip of the western coast, but which is politically unimportant. East of Haidarabad, and dovetailed in between the Godavari and the coast province of Madras, are the wild Gond highlands divided between two Hindu native States, Jaipur and Jugdulpur (or Bustar), whose remoteness and insalubrity render them comparatively unimportant items in the scheme of Indian administration.

Thus we see that Southern India is very nearly divided between British and semi-independent territory, and that so long as the independence of these southern native states is emphasised by the maintenance of local armies it is necessary that we should preserve a considerable force in the south (as in the north) to preserve the balance of military power.

Rajputana and Central India are (like Baluchistan) political agencies (answering to provinces) under the Foreign Department of India, and are administered by an agent to the Governor-General, who ranks much the same as a Commissioner in the non-regulation provinces. He is assisted by a staff of residents and political agents, who are officers drawn from various sources, both civil and military, attached to the Foreign Department. These two great central agencies comprise the chief Rajput and

Maratha states—Jaipur, Jodhpur (or Marwar), Udaipur (or Mewar), Gwalior, Indore (Bhopal), Bikanir, and many other smaller states, which, with Baroda on the western coast, and the Muhammadan state of Bahawalpur on the Indus, occupy an enormous area stretching from Sind and the Indus to the Narbada, and from the west coast to

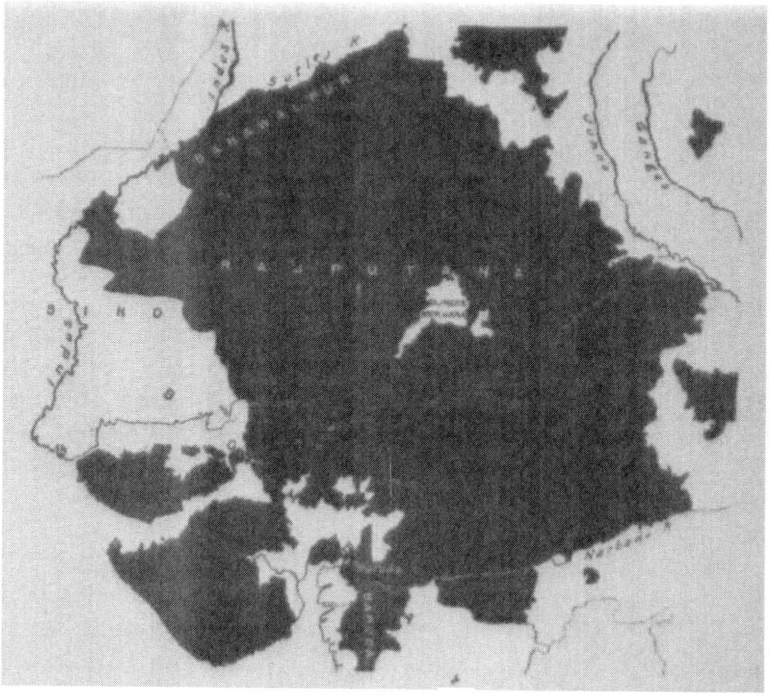


FIG. 76.—Native States, Central India.

the Jumna. In the midst of this vast independent tract, about half of which is desert—the other half including some of the loveliest tracts in the central highlands—the little British district of Ajmere is set in the map like a red island in a yellow sea.

The Sikh states—Patiala, Kapurtalla, &c.—are collected in a group in the north of the Punjab under the Himalayas, and some of the smaller Rajput principalities are enclosed (like Chamba) within the hills. Simla is itself surrounded by small independent tracts of hill country which can hardly be classed as states.

Amongst this large number of independent (or semi-independent) states, the form of government varies as much as does the measure of their independence. According to Sir John Strachey, the Muhammadan and Maratha states (Haidarabad, Bhopal, Bahawalpur, Gwalior, Indore, and Baroda) enjoy the largest measure of independence although they are all comparatively recent creations, and have all of them called for British

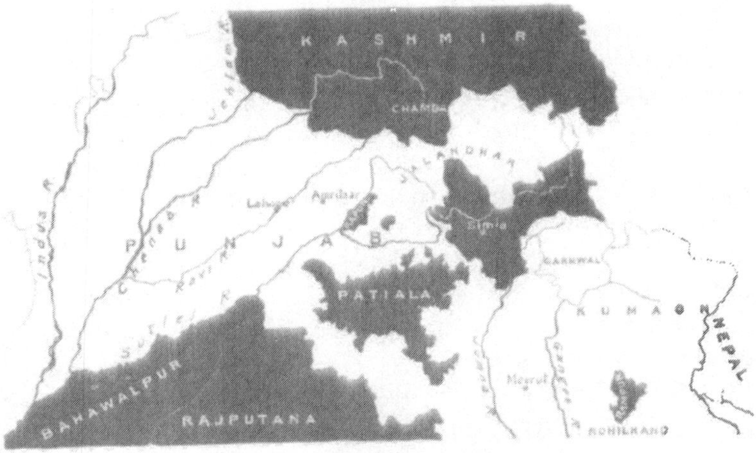


FIG. 77.—Native States, Northern India.

interference at one time or another. None of them are much older than the British rule in India, and none of them possess ancient dynasties or an historical nobility. The rulers are as foreign to the people as the English Residents at their courts, the nobility are but high officials of the state who owe their position to their chiefs, and their armies are composed of foreign mercenaries. It is a mistake to suppose that the vast population under Muhammadan or Maratha rule is governed by native chiefs who have any more right or title to their high position than has the English Government; and it is quite an open question whether they prefer the foreign administration of a native court to the foreign Government of the English "Sirkar."

The Nizam of Haidarabad is chief among the native princes of India. He is the representative of a dynasty which was founded by a Lieutenant-Governor of the Moghul court in the time of Turk (or Moghul) supremacy in India, and he rules a population of 9,000,000 Hindus and 1,000,000 Muhammadans. "No Government in India has been more shamefully corrupt than that of the Nizam," says Sir John Strachey, and the testimony of Sir Lepel Griffin, who knew the native states well, is much to the same effect. The Maratha states (Gwalior, Indore, and Baroda) date from last century, and their chiefs are "the representatives of the predatory hordes which, until crushed by British arms, turned the fertile plains of Central India into a wilderness. The Maratha dynasties have nothing in common with the people they govern. Their race is different and their language is not understood." Except the rulers and their followers there are no Marathas in these states.

In order to find ancient dynasties and time-honoured political institutions amongst the native states we must turn to the Rajput principalities (of which there are about twenty altogether) in Rajputana and Central India. These are states which have been preserved by the British Government from destruction by the Marathas, and the constitution of their governing power is entirely different from that of the Muhammadan and (so-called) Maratha principalities. The Rajput chief is "the hereditary head of a military clan, the members of which have been for centuries lords of the soil." He claims the highest descent in the land, but yet it is hardly higher than that of his chief officers and nobles. They are bound together by ancient ties of kinship, as by common interest, in times of danger; but the individual power of the head of the clan is much restricted in times of peace. In these Rajput states there is often a strong bond of sympathy between ruler and people. Ruler and ruled alike refer back to the days of antiquity for their origin, claiming descent from the sun and the moon, and if the chief represents a dynasty which has governed for 2000 years, there are many of the leading families amongst the people who can boast a descent no less ancient. Jaipur, Jodhpur, Udaipur, and Rewah are the greatest Rajput states, and it may be said of all of them that their loyalty is unquestioned.

Chief amongst Hindu states is Mysore (Maisur), with a population of 4,000,000 souls. Mysore, equally with Rajput and Sikh states, owes its existence to the British Government. During the last century Haidar Ali dispossessed its Hindu Rajas, and it remained under his rule and that of his successor, Tippu Sultan, till Seringapatam was taken in 1799. Then it was restored (like another Hindu state in Southern India—Travancore) to its former Hindu owners, and has remained Hindu ever since.

The native states of the Punjab (thirty-six in number, with a population of 4,000,000) would have been swept by Ranjit Sing into one comprehensive net fifty years ago had we not intervened. These Sikh states (amongst which Patiala and Kapurthala are pre-eminent) are always loyal, and their administration is usually fairly good. Thus the modern construction of all the native states in India is more or less due to the break-up of the power of Maratha and Sikh by the British. There is not one of them that has a right to claim that it would have maintained its present vitality had English arms not supported it through the struggles which closed the last century and lasted through the beginning of this.

On the borders of North-Western India are three great Muhammadan states to which we have already referred, *i.e.* Afghanistan, Baluchistan, and Kashmir. Although Afghanistan and Baluchistan are not usually included amongst the feudatory native states, they are both of them subject to British political control, Baluchistan being administered by an agent to the Governor-General, assisted by a staff of political officers, exactly in the same way as Rajputana or Central India. A portion of Baluchistan has been leased to the Government of India by the Khan of Kalát, and within the area so held lies Quetta and Peshin, with all those defensive works which protect the road to India from the side of Kandahar; but beyond this recognised province under British administration, the whole of Baluchistan, from the borderland of Persia to the boundaries of Afghanistan and the Gomal River, is directly subject to British jurisdiction. Not so very long ago the Khan of Kalát was deposed by the Indian Government for certain atrocious crimes, and the reigning Khan installed in his place. The south-western province of Las Bela loyally recognises British supremacy. In a bright little garden, not far from the ancient capital of that small state, is the tomb of Sir Robert Sandeman, the man who first brought Baluchistan under British rule, and developed the dormant capabilities of that country until the Baluch wilderness became green with crops and orchards. No impress on the land could have been made more significant of British supremacy to the eyes of the natives of Baluchistan than this shrine (for it is already recognised as a sacred place for pilgrimage) of the dead "Feringhi," whom they not only honoured, but loved.

In the outlying districts of wild Makrán, bordering the Arabian Sea, there is at present no direct and visible political authority; but it can hardly be long before this one-time highway into India from the trade centres of Khorasán, as well as the sandy steppes which lie to the north bordering the Helmund, are brought directly under the eye of the British political officer. The appointment of a consul for Seistán will, in fact, seal the fate of South-Western Baluchistan, so far as its absolute independence is concerned.

Kalát, and all the smaller native states which comprise Baluchistan, are just as much under the supreme control of the Indian Government as are any of the native states of Central India. The old rough and ready systems of administration, which were at first best suited to the idiosyncrasies of the wild border clans, are already giving place to the exacter and more rigid methods of civil "Regulations." The injured tribesman now fights his enemy in the court of law instead of on his own hill-side, and it may be doubted whether, in every aspect of its adaptation to the tribal politics of the frontier, the change is a change for the better. The more intellectual but physically inferior Hindu is gradually shouldering the Mussulman out of all the inferior posts under the central administration, and we may yet be edified with the sight of a brave and vigorous Muhammadan community practically subordinate to a clique of grasping Hindus.

But whatever may be the exact status of Baluch independence, there can be little doubt about that of Afghanistan. Sir Lepel Griffin is inclined to range Afghanistan alongside the feudatory native states of India on the grounds that the Amir is within the sphere of our political control, although he neither admits a British Resident to his court at Kabul, nor does he permit a British officer to pass into his country from India. The Amir himself would, however, have much to say on the other side of the question. We pay him a subsidy which goes a long way towards maintaining his army (reckoned at 60,000 regular and 100,000 irregular troops) in its present state of efficiency—for it is well armed and well equipped with mountain artillery. But the result is inevitable. The great mass of the ignorant tribespeople of Afghanistan regard our subsidy as tribute, and believe in the Amir as a sovereign ruler. He pays us nothing in return. What we really receive in exchange for the eighteen lakhs of rupees which yearly find their way to the Kabul treasury from India, is a certain confidence in the interposition of a well-armed buffer state between India and Russia, which is undoubtedly justified by the spirit of determined independence which animates every section of the heterogeneous elements of which the Afghan people are composed.

Thus the Amir maintains an army which is far larger than that of any native chief in India (not even excepting the Nizam of Haidarabad), and is probably quite as efficient; and we impose no limit on its extension. Neither can we interfere, even though crimes are committed at the court of Kabul which would sink any native prince within the limits of British India from his throne to a prison, or at least to a state pension and honourable confinement. The Amir is distinctly independent—more independent than the Khedive of Egypt or the Sultan of Zanzibar; and there must be many radical changes in the political relationship between Kabul and Simla before Afghanistan can be reckoned as a "native state" of India.

Amongst the most interesting of the social problems which arise out of our position as an educating, as well as a governing, influence in India is the question of the effect that European civilisation, and the example of English methods, may have had on the character of those princes and chiefs who govern the native states. Below the throne and the court the mass of the people, agriculturists and traders, are much on the same educational level on whichever side the border they live. You will find quite as many (or as few) who can talk and write English within our own borders as within the boundaries of a native state. The manner of life, the modes of thought, the ethics of everyday existence, do not vary greatly amongst the ignorant masses on either side; but amongst the rulers of the people, the princes, chiefs, and nobles, there is often a wide divergency of mind and manners. The divergency arises chiefly from the greater or less adoption of European habits whilst under tuition at the Government colleges (or at the hands of a European tutor), and subsequent association with Englishmen.

Amongst the Rajput princes of the plains of India there are many who live the lives of their forefathers amongst their people, uninfluenced and untouched by the glitter and unrest of western civilisation, although they may be well educated after European methods, and quite able to take their place in any western court society with dignity and ease. Intensely proud and jealous of their position in the scale of precedence, they prefer not to risk the social dangers which arise from too small a measure of appreciation of their dignity amongst a society of democratic tendencies. They live on their ancestral estates and administer their ancestral laws, surrounded by nobles who never transgress the strict rules of etiquette, and betray no hankering after the fascinations of foreign cities. This is a phase of Indian society that the Englishman in India hardly sees; but it is the most picturesque phase, and in many ways the most interesting. Amongst the smaller native chiefs there is often the wish for a reputation as men of the advanced world which includes western sport and many western vices, but not the means to maintain it; and one may find most ludicrous attempts at imitation of this unattainable Europeanism in their surroundings. They are nearly all sportsmen—these minor nawabs and rajahs—and in the matter of arms and ammunition there is usually nothing wanting in their equipment. They have, moreover, all of them (whatever position they occupy in the scale of precedence) learnt the value of game preservation; and it is not possible now to find any considerable area of jungle country over which the European sportsman can range at his own will in Rajputana or Central India; though there are still thousands of square miles of unwholesome jungle in the southern districts of the Central Provinces and in Madras where he would be right welcome.

The disadvantages of too liberal an English education are often illustrated by those chiefs and nobles who have so completely adopted the fashions of the western foreigner that they are no longer in touch with their own people. There are some (and they are amongst the best known of Indian princes) who do not conceal the fact that their social sympathies are with the European rather than with the native. They even occasionally marry white girls of an inferior class, thereby raising up an extensive field for domestic intrigue, if not for actual crime, amongst those who are interested in the question of succession. They wear European clothes, adopt European habits and manners, and draw a line between themselves and the people they are expected to govern and whose interests should be identical with their own. All this cannot possibly tend to make them better rulers or improve their chances of successful administration. The best that can be said of them is that they are usually good sportsmen.

Of the loyalty of those chiefs who are more intimately associated with the ruling powers in India there can be no question. There are many of them who would not only stand up against England's foes in the East (European or native), and take their share in the perils of a campaign with the hereditary eagerness of soldiers born of a race of soldiers, but who would fall with the English Government, if need be, and make no sign. But even in this matter of political and social sympathy with the English in India the geographical position of the native states plays no unimportant part. Those Sikh states which lie in and below the Himalayas, which exist, as it were, under the shadow of the Simla mountains, are loyal to the last unit. Constant personal association with Government officials leads to a bond of union in official action. If discontent and criticism of our methods of government, and a tendency to stir up awkward questions at inappropriate seasons are to be found in India, it is in those states which lie farther away from the direct influence of the Viceregal Court, and chiefly, no doubt, amongst those princes and chiefs who are under the influence of the fanatical spirit of Islam.

Such a very general description of the geographical distribution of administrative units throughout the great continent of India as the above chapter contains may be found in almost any elementary treatise on India. Sir John Strachey, Sir W. Hunter, Sir Alfred Lyall, and many others have written clearly, forcibly, and conclusively on the subject of the magnificent administrative machinery of the great provinces of British India. Sir Lepel Griffin and Sir William Lee-Warner have equally well illustrated the nature of its relation to the self-governing institutions which are fostered in the native states. The reader who would wish to know more of the most successful system of administration applied to a dependency that the world has ever seen would do well to consult these high authorities.

INDIA, SURFACE FEATURES.

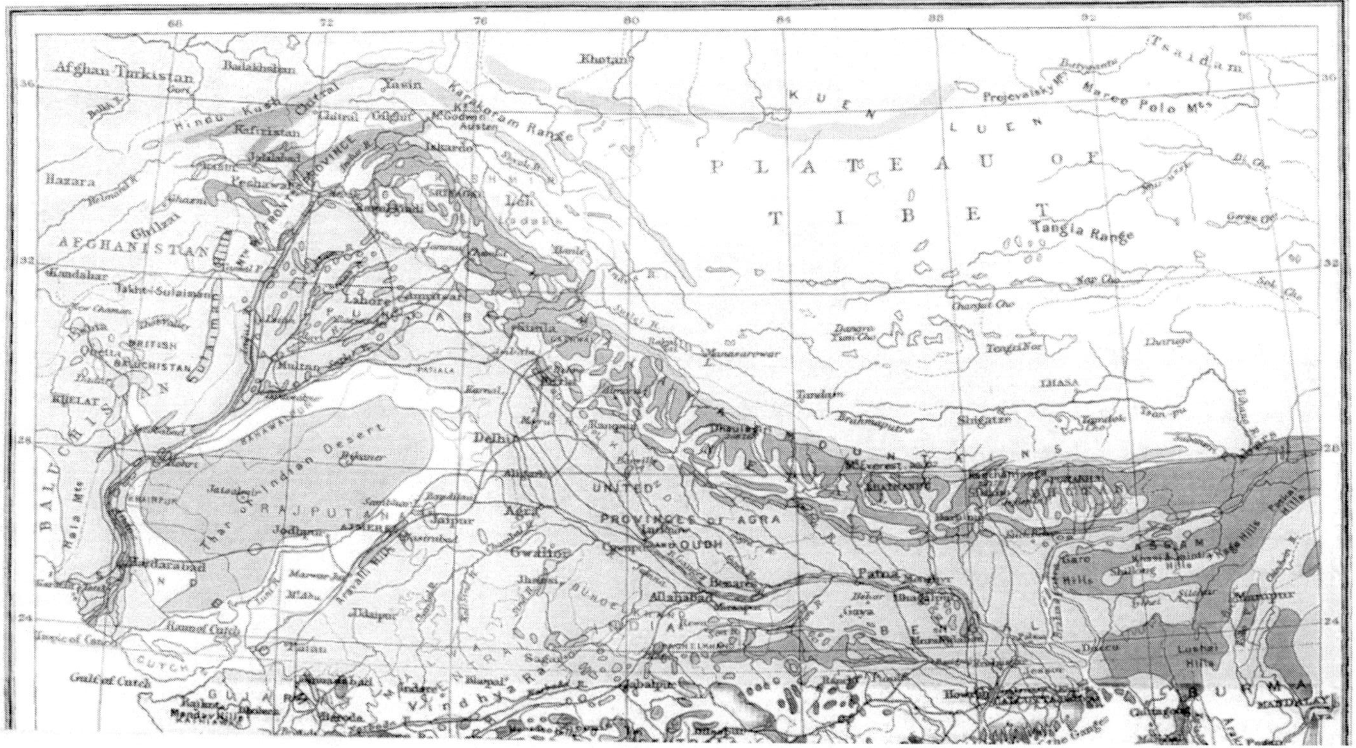

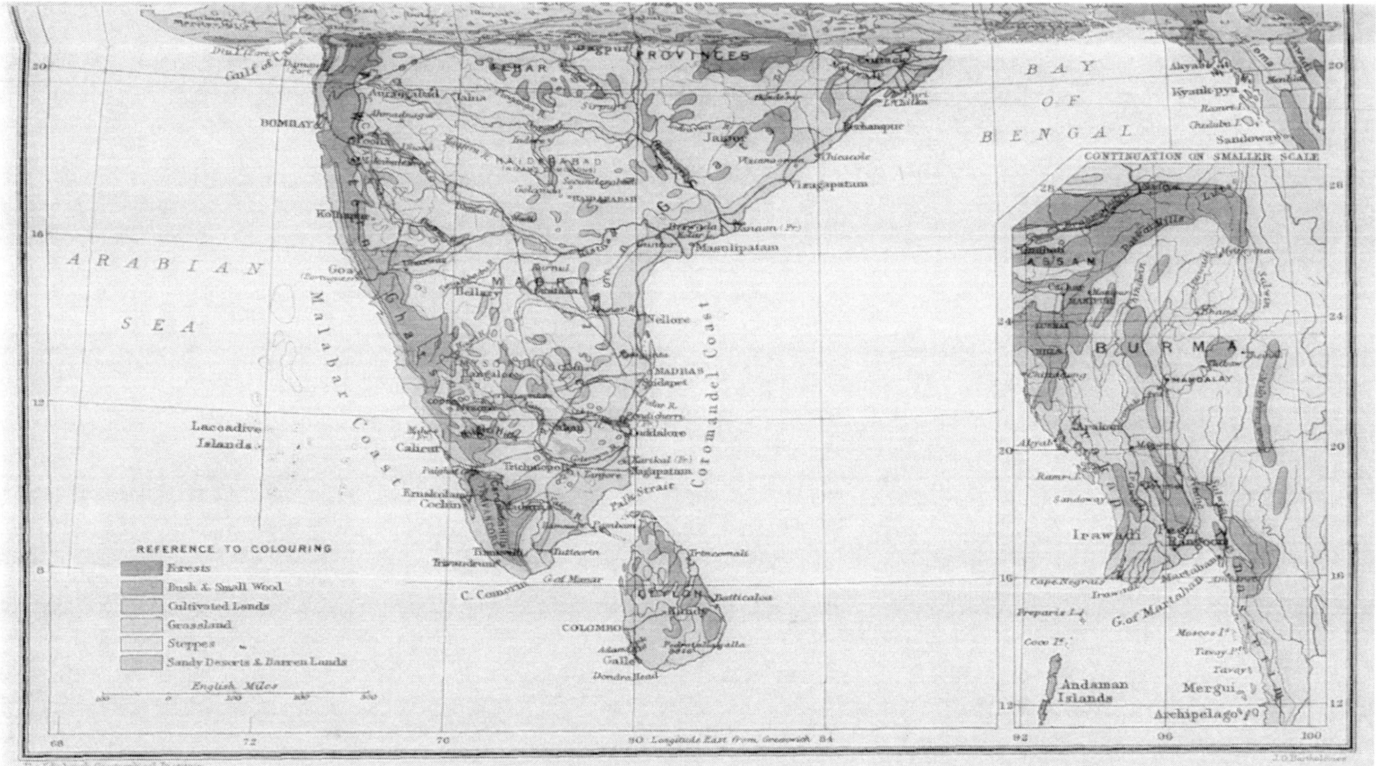
ARABIAN SEA
BAY OF BENGAL
Malabar Coast
Coromandel Coast
PROVINCES
MADRAS
BOMBAY
Goa
Bellary
Nellore
MADRAS
Masulipatam
Vizagapatam
Calicut
Cochin
Trichinopoly
Negapatam
Cuddalore
Palk Strait
C. Comorin
G. of Manar
Trivandrum
Tuticorin
Trincomali
Batticaloa
Kandy
COLOMBO
Galle
Dondra Head
CEYLON
Laccadive Islands
REFERENCE TO COLOURING
Forests
Bush & Small Wood
Cultivated Lands
Grassland
Steppes
Sandy Deserts & Barren Lands
English Miles
Longitude East from Greenwich
CONTINUATION ON SMALLER SCALE
ASSAM
BURMA
MANDALAY
Irawadi
Rangoon
G. of Martaban
Andaman Islands
Mergui Archipelago
Akyab
Kyauk-pyu
Sandoway
Preparis I.
Coco Is.
Tavoy
The Edinburgh Geographical Institute
J. G. Bartholomew

# CHAPTER IX

## AGRICULTURE AND REVENUE

THE diverse character of Indian geographical features and climate admits of most of the agricultural produce of both temperate and tropical zones. In the north of India the climate is dry, and the long winters are cold. On the Himalayas it is both cold and moist; in the low Himalayan valleys it is temperate and occasionally tropical; and in Southern India and Ceylon we find all the usual tropical conditions—a heavy rainfall at periodic intervals, and a moist, hot atmosphere.

Agriculture is the pursuit of about 75 per cent. of the Indian population, and the changes of season and variations of rainfall affect the conditions of life so closely and so seriously that in no country in the world are the meteorologic variations so anxiously watched, and the promises of the future so minutely balanced as in India. When we leave the peninsula area and pass into the rainless districts on the west and north, where irrigation is the basis of crop production, we find much less anxiety about weather conditions. There the worst effects of famine are unknown, and the people live in contented security from this most dreaded of all visitations. Scarcity may prevail from time to time, but the gaunt spectre of actual starvation does not trouble them.

In Northern India the cold weather is usually reckoned to last from October to April, and during that period the temperature occasionally falls below freezing point at night. Excepting in December, when rain is expected for a week or two, the sky is usually clear, and the sun is hot towards the middle of the day. Bright sunshine is the usual condition of the weather from one day to another during the cold weather months. It is then that the crops called "rabi" are cultivated, which depend chiefly upon the short winter rains for their proper development. Wheat is the cereal mostly cultivated in all Northern India during the cold weather. More than half (60 per cent.) of the crop-producing areas of the Punjab and United Provinces are taken up with the growth of wheat. With barley and millets 97 per cent. of the soil of the United Provinces is absorbed. Wheat exportation from the Punjab is already the chief feature of Punjab trade with England, the Punjab growing twice as much wheat as Great Britain, and equalling the total of the United States of America. But wheat is also largely grown in other parts of India, where the climate is favourable. It is much cultivated in Central India, the Central Provinces, parts of the Dekkan, and in Bombay, and there has quite recently been an extraordinary development in wheat cultivation in the highlands of the Shan states east of Burma. Wheat and barley are mostly consumed by the wealthy classes in India, the poorer agriculturists subsisting on millets, which form the real staple of the country. What is usually known as "ata" in India is the flour of any of these grains. It is made up into thin unleavened cakes called "chupattis," and eaten with a variety of condiments by the mass of the population of Northern and Central India. Probably three-fourths of the entire population of India live on the grain of millets, either Joár (*Sorghum vulgare*) or Bájra (*Pennisetum typhoideum*) or various kinds of pulse. Besides wheat and barley the cold weather crops include tobacco, opium, linseed, and mustard, with some of the many pulses.

In the highlands bordering India, Baluchistan, Afghanistan, and Kashmir, winter is a period of rest for the agriculturist. His irrigation canals are frozen, and his fields lie under snow. The wheat and barley crops are much at the same point of development as they are in England. There is little of them to be seen above ground. The rice "khets" (when they exist) are dry and hard, and even the "kerbi" stalks (the straw of the millet crops) has been gathered in for fodder for the cattle.

This, indeed, is all that the cattle get during the winter in many parts of the northern frontier, and it answers admirably for fodder. In Baluchistan, and indeed in most parts of Afghanistan, where wheat (or rice in small quantities) is cultivated, the straw is collected and beaten small, and is packed for winter consumption as "bhusa." Every frontier officer knows the value of "bhusa." It is the commissariat stand by for all frontier expeditions and takes the place of compressed hay and other fodders fairly well, but it requires large transport.

During winter in the highlands the fruit trees (mulberries, walnuts, and apricots) are bare and rigid; the dreary expanse of flat terraced fields is brown and hard. The wild roses and hedgerows take on a copper hue, and the stony hills betray hardly a trace of green under the stiff brown pines. This is the border time for action, for raids on the nearest British settlement, for squaring accounts with the wealthy "bunniah"[1] of the plains, for holding "jirgahs"[2] and arranging risings, which, however unsuccessful they may be, keep the young tribesmen occupied, thins the overgrown population somewhat, and finds opportunity for the trial of the latest imported (or stolen) weapon. Then the frontier tribesman stuffs his pockets full of dried mulberries and walnuts; slings on his back as much of the thick Pathán "roti" (a very serviceable form of bread, thicker than "chupatties," and more like English bread) as he can carry in addition to his sheepskin coat and his ammunition, and follows the warpath. He leaves nothing for an enemy to destroy excepting his easily-built house. Thus do the climatic and geographic conditions of the frontier combine to keep the military officials at Simla invariably busy in the winter time.

The hot weather crops of India (called "kharif") are as varied as the winter "rabi." The latter are generally reaped by the end of April, earlier or later according to the latitude. For about two months, till the end of June, when all the glory of early summer is about the highlands; when the plains of Afghanistan are a waving

[1] Shopkeeper. [2] Clan meetings.

field of well-grown wheat, or deep in rank lucerne; when the canals run full with snow-fed streams, and the bordered bypaths are scented with the willow and adorned with wild rose and clematis—then is the period of desolation in the plains of India. The scorching west wind passes over the northern districts; every blade of green vegetation disappears from unirrigated or unwatered spots; grass tufts grow yellow and stiff in the bare and withered fields; only the spreading banian, the pipal, and others of the genus *ficus* amongst trees, hold their own against the universal desiccation.

The hot weather of the Punjab and of the frontier is the hottest of all hot weathers. Southern Indian heat is tempered by sea breezes, and modified by a tropical vegetation, but this does not exist in the north. Not till the first burst of rain follows the blinding dust storms, does the land wake up to a new birth; and then indeed the process of wakening is startling in its rapidity. Then again does the labourer return to the fields with his plough and his oxen, and the season of agriculture makes a new departure.

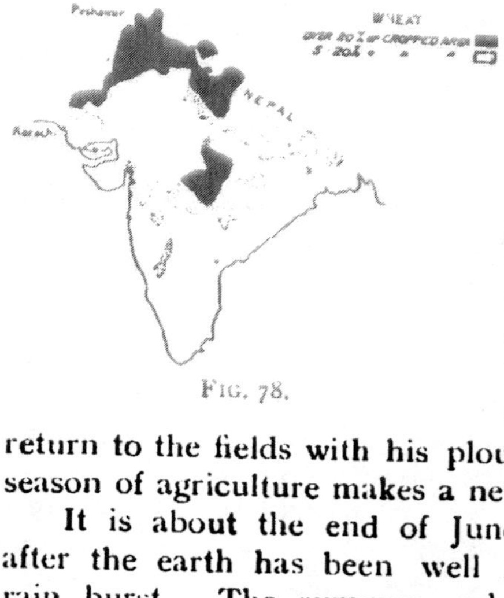

FIG. 78.

It is about the end of June that ploughing begins, after the earth has been well moistened with the first rain burst. The summer and autumn crops comprise chiefly the different kinds of pulse and maize, sugar-cane, cotton, and indigo. Rice is grown nearly all over India, but a hot, moist climate is the most suitable for its production. In Lower Bengal, and in parts of Madras and Bombay, in Burma and Ceylon, rice is the staple food of the people. In British Burma and in Lower Bengal from 80 to 90 per cent. of cultivated area is under rice. Elsewhere it is reserved for the consumption of the wealthy. But wherever irrigation exists and water is abundant in a warm, moist climate, there rice is grown during the hot weather months. In Kashmir, in the Peshawur Valley and its borderland, Swat, and even in the valleys leading up to the Afridi Tirah, rice is cultivated. In the Bara valley of Tirah indeed the rice is reckoned to be of a specially fine quality, and is in much demand in northern markets. Rice is also cultivated in the valleys of Baluchistan, but not so much in Afghanistan, where the water-supply by means of irrigation is plentiful, but the air is dry and the hot weather short.

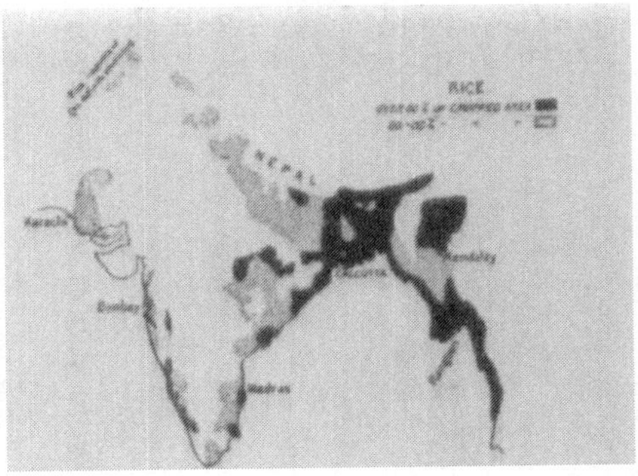


Fig. 79.

Amongst the most important agricultural products of India tea, coffee, fruit, and jute must be included. Jute is grown chiefly in Bengal; tea and coffee in such positions as will ensure a fairly equable temperature, with plenty of moisture. Tea can hardly be said to be a product of the plains of India, although it grows at comparatively low altitudes in Ceylon. It is cultivated in the Dun, or valley, that lies between the foothills of the Himalayas and the Siwaliks; in Kangra (also a Himalayan valley of low elevation); on the lower slopes of the Himalayas below Darjiling; in Assam and in Ceylon. It will flourish at an altitude as high as 7000 feet above sea; and it is notable that tea grown at the highest altitudes is reckoned the best in point of flavour, though the yield is inferior to that

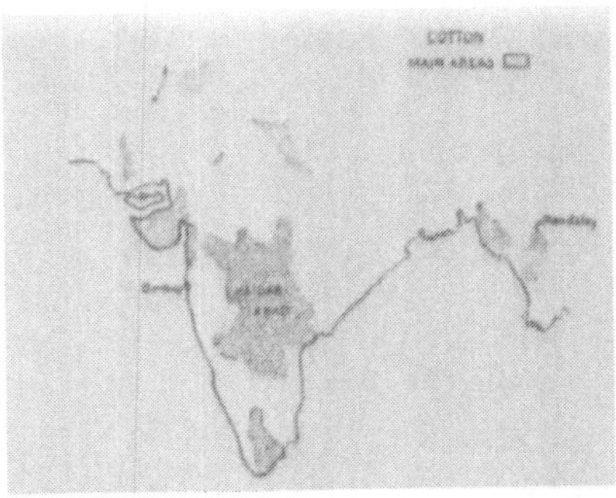


Fig. 80.

of the lowlands. Coffee is grown at comparatively low altitudes in the Madras hills. In Ceylon it has been superseded by tea. Cinchona was grown with such success both in Ceylon and the Nilgiris as to lead to over-production, with the result that the cultivation of it is now restricted.

No country in the world is so largely dependent on irrigation for its food-supply as India, and in no country

Fig. 81.—Chart of Irrigation by Canal.

have irrigation works on a larger scale been so successfully carried out. Chief amongst them are the canal-systems of the Ganges, Jumna, and of the Godavari, all of which have carried life-giving water to millions of acres of unproductive land. In the winter and spring months, when the snow lies unmelted on the Himalayan slopes, the great rivers which find their sources in these mountains run low, and carry comparatively little water to the plains. It is just at this season that water is urgently required for agricultural purposes, consequently whole rivers are at this season diverted into the fields.

India and Ceylon are full of ancient and long disused irrigation systems. In Ceylon at the present moment there in a project for restoring the old tank system of irrigation of centuries ago, the full extent of which has

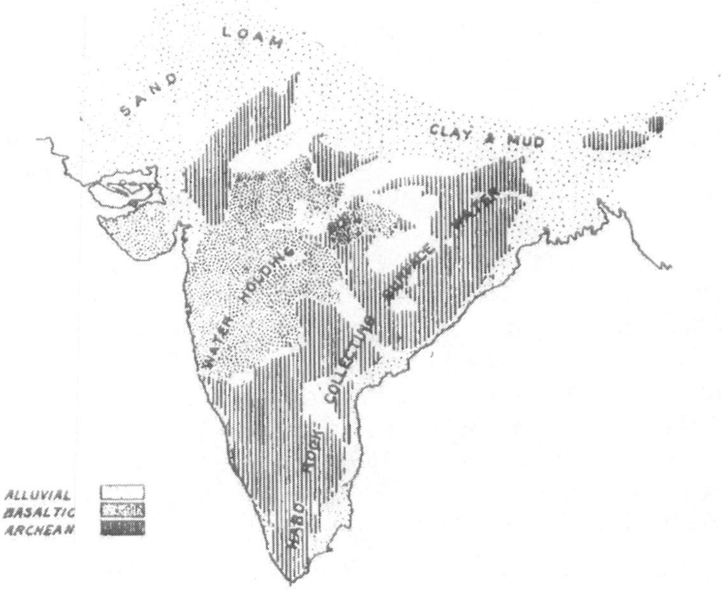


FIG. 82.

hardly yet been traced out. In parts of Persia, Baluchistan, and Afghanistan the water-supply derived from irrigation is the only supply available, and a system of underground tunnelling has been developed (called "Kanát" in Persia, and "Karéz" in Afghanistan) which utilises sources lying deep below ground-level. The practical engineering shown in laying out these underground canals is of a very high order. Makrán and south-west Baluchistan are full of the remains of ancient storage works, built in the middle ages during the days of Arab occupation, which are marvels of constructive skill; and to this day every drop of water in the Kabul River and in the Hari Rud (the river of Herat) is at certain seasons of the year carried off to the villages and fields.

But no such gigantic systems as the English have initiated were ever known in India before our advent. The entire volume of the Ganges at Hardwar (where it issues from the hills) is, during the season of low flood, diverted into a canal, and carried by a series of engineering works, sometimes above, sometimes below, the lines of drainage crossing it from the lower Himalaya to the level flats of the United Provinces. Through its agency the Doáb, or plain, intervening between the Ganges and the Jumna is watered. Twenty miles below Hardwar, where the Ganges has again developed into a river, it is again diverted into a second great canal. Either of these two canals discharge a volume of water which is double that of the Thames at Teddington. Three smaller canals tap the Jumna, and distribute its waters over a vast area. The Són River also provides an irrigation system, which is further developed in Bengal and Orissa in districts where the network of natural waterways does not extend.

In the Punjab the development of canals for the watering of the broad plains intervening between its great rivers is still in progress, and every river in the province is laid under contribution. So large is the expected extent of fresh cultivation that new "Districts," demanding an increase of administrative staff, are already contemplated. In Madras the Godavari and Kistna irrigation systems have been in force for many years, and the profit to Government realised therefrom, independent of the development of enormous areas of delta country and the salvation of millions from periodic scarcity, has been immense. Here the head of water required is obtained by building a weir, or anicut, across the river. In Sind, again, the Indus floods are utilised for irrigation, and the dry, arid plains of Sind are now fairly prosperous, and support 2,000,000 to 3,000,000 of people.

All these systems have proved to be on the whole a great financial success. The Punjab canals last year (1896–97), taking major and minor works together, gave a return of 9½ per cent. on the outlay. The returns of the Madras canals for the same year must also be considered satisfactory, although they were very unequal. The Godavari, the Kistna, and the Kavari gave returns respectively of 16½, 10½, and 46 per cent., but many of the minor systems (although the minor systems as a whole paid better than the major) sank to 1 per cent. or less. One canal only is classed as an "unproductive" work. Yet even of this canal it is stated that "the canal has proved itself a perfect godsend in this year of drought, and in the direct and indirect benefits it has secured to man and beast within its influence it has fully justified its existence." Similarly in Bombay, the Dekkan, and Gujrát, where irrigation is based on the tank, or storage, system, although irrigation cannot as a whole be quoted as a financial success, it proved to be "indirectly of great use in those districts where the general scarcity amounted to famine." In Bombay (as in the North-West) the cultivator only makes a voluntary demand for water when he needs it. In Madras certain areas are always irrigated, and rated accordingly, and the returns are consequently more even from year to year. But the cultivator who only uses canal water in dry seasons naturally makes his demand precisely at the very time when storage

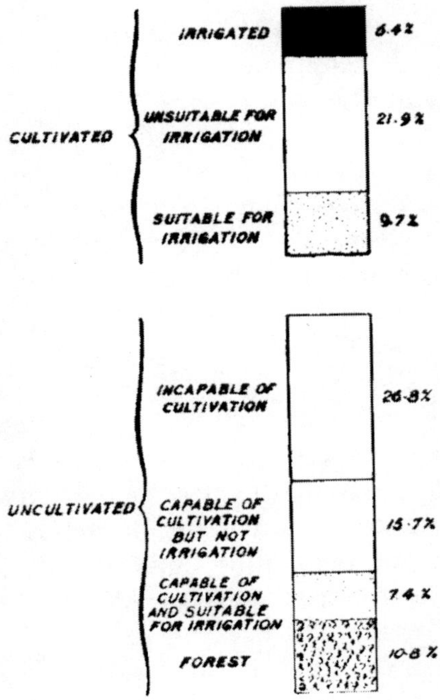


FIG. 83.

is most likely to fail; the position being that when the rainfall is favourable the cultivator does not need and will not take canal water, and when the rainfall is deficient he cannot get it. Thus storage works have rarely, if ever, stood the test of sound financial conditions. Within the last ten years the revenues derived from irrigation in India have increased from a million and a half to three millions sterling.

A few statistics are necessary to illustrate the economic development of India during the last half century; but as this is a geographical treatise, and not a statistical compendium, they shall be made as general as possible.

In the year 1840 the gross revenues of India amounted to twenty-one million sterling, in 1886 they were seventy-seven million, in 1896 they reached ninety-four million. Out of this ninety-four millions only twenty-nine millions are derived from taxation. Thus taxation does not supply one-third of the total revenues at the present time, although that source of income has somewhat increased in proportion to the gross revenues since the year 1886. In England taxation supplies five-sixths of the revenue. India is probably the most lightly taxed country in the world; the average tax per head of the population amounting to something less than one rupee (1s. 4d.) per annum, and this is chiefly derived from the taxpayer as a salt consumer. Were the rent included for the land he occupies (which is of course inadmissible as an item of taxation) it might perhaps be doubled.

The extraordinary increase in gross revenue which is shown in certain decades of our Indian history is usually due to the increase of land revenue as we gradually acquired fresh territory and extended British dominion. Within the last ten years very little of the increase represented by the difference between seventy-seven and ninety-four millions is due to this cause. Six million of it is due to the increase in railway receipts, a million and a half to irrigation, and more than seven millions to increased taxation. Receipts under the head of "opium" alone show a marked decrease, the diminution amounting to about two millions and a half.

But figures such as these do very little towards illustrating the growth of wealth or of general economic development in India. The growth of population, whether by natural progression or by the extension of British rule, may counteract the effects of increased material prosperity, and the problem whether India is virtually richer and its people more contented is not to be solved by any reference to statistics independent of personal observation. Where wide divergence of opinion exists on this subject it is usually due to want of such observation.

The ryot, or agriculturist, who represents the vast majority of the Indian population, is, as we have already said, lightly treated in the matter of direct taxation. Referring back to the last half century, Sir John Strachey writes that "the immense growth of the revenues has been in no degree due to increased taxation. If . . . we compare the revenues of British India in 1886 with those of twenty-five years before, we shall find that almost under every head there has been a diminution rather than an increase in the public burdens. The land revenue . . . is everywhere lighter than it was. The salt duties were generally higher than they are now. Heavy customs duties were levied in the former period on every article of import and export, whereas there is now almost absolute freedom of trade." This was written in 1886, and now requires some modification, especially as regards the salt tax, which has, in some parts of India, increased, but is still far lower than it was twenty-five years ago. As regards the chief support of Indian finance, the land revenue, Sir John Strachey quotes Fawcett and Mill in support of his opinion that the rent of land cannot be regarded as a tax on the people when claimed by Government, any more than it would represent a tax if paid to any private landlord ; and he shows that the share of the rent claimed by Government has decreased enormously under British rule. The Moghul Government took one-third of the land produce, and believed themselves to be "practising a wise moderation." The Marathas, the native rulers of Bengal, and the Sikhs, took one-half or more. The demands of our Government are regulated on different principles altogether to those of native rulers. The latter often hardly recognised the existence of a private property in land, and deemed themselves entitled to the whole of the surplus profit after the expenses of cultivation had been paid. Thus the cultivator was considered as "entitled to a bare existence; everything else went to the State." "Instead of sweeping off the whole or the greater part of the surplus profits of the land our Government never takes more than a fixed share, which falls at an average rate of from 3 per cent. to 8 per cent. of the gross out-turn."

There is, however, no need to enlarge on the advantages of a government which has brought to India a reign of law, order, and justice, and which ensures that every man shall at least possess his goods in peace, and be able undisturbed to develop such instincts as he possesses for the betterment of his own condition in life. But the very efforts that are made by the State to improve those conditions amongst the poorer class of natives (*i.e.* the 75 per cent. who gain their living direct from the land) lead to difficulties, if not to actual political dangers such as were unknown, or uncared for, in the time of the Moghuls. Civil war, famine, and pestilence are either suppressed altogether or met with the full resources of a civil organisation, and so successfully combated that but comparatively few lives are lost in the conflict. The direct result is an enormous increase of population. The Indian native (whatever his nationality) looks on the business of reproduction as one of the great ends of existence, and so long as his environment supports him, he sets about it without a thought of political economic results. The owner of a few square yards of paddy field, or of half a cocoanut tree, will leave his scanty property to be divided amongst a dozen children with exactly the same results, in a minor degree, that have filled the pages of history with perpetual records of civil strife and bloodshed amongst his betters. The wonder is, not that there should be poverty in the land, but that there should not be an increase in crime out of all proportion to the increase in population. In Ceylon, where a single cocoa-nut tree is possibly the disputed possession of fifty co-heirs, it is said that about one murder per diem represents the average rate of mortality arising directly from family disputes over small inheritances.

An increase of say twenty million souls in ten years represents the success of the Indian Government in dealing with those periodic visitations which in the days of the Moghuls thinned the population, and ensured there being room enough for all. Wild animals alone have so far defied the Government, and maintain a loss to humanity that is appalling, from whatever point of view it is considered. Twenty-one thousand people lost their lives from snake-bite in 1897, and four or five thousand more from wolves, tigers, and other animals; but such numbers tell little in a sum total of millions, and do not affect the difficult question of providing for the wants of such an increase in population as Indian statistics deal with.

There is no doubt a vast sum of human misery distributed through the lower agricultural classes of India. There are districts where insufficient food is the normal condition of the people, and there is not a single district probably where the indebtedness of the ryot is not a notorious evil. But this will always be the case in India, just as it is, under other conditions, in London and all over-populated places. Improvidence is not to be removed by legislation. Against this we must set the gross accumulation of wealth and prosperity in India. Who are the people who chiefly benefit thereby? The answer, in India, is that it is the well-to-do classes; the merchants and middlemen, the bunniah and shop-keepers, and in certain districts (especially Bengal) the large landowners who appropriate most of it.

Still, it must be apparent to every one who has lived long in India, who has moved about the country and amongst the people, that very large sections of the agriculturists are certainly better off than they were twenty-five years ago. They live in better houses, wear better clothes, have more brass pots and cooking utensils, and their wives and daughters go about decorated with more bangles and ornaments than formerly. I have already pointed out that, under stress of circumstances, the aboriginal people of the jungles, the Bhils and the Gonds, will revert to the natural resources of their forefathers, and live on jungle products—wild fruit and roots, bamboo shoots and grass seeds. There are, indeed, tribes in Gondwana who habitually live on this sort of fare to this day. In the days of the Moghuls it is probable that the percentage of the then comparatively scanty population who thus supported life was enormously larger than it is now. We have no reliable source of information about those days, and no direct comparison is possible ; but we may quote what the Abbé Dubois has put on record as the standard of living which prevailed at the beginning of British rule in India: "In most provinces those who cultivate rice do not eat it, but sell it to pay their taxes. During the four months the Sukha Kala (the time of prosperity) lasts, they live on the pulse and millet which they cultivate in their fields. During the rest of the year their only daily sustenance, in almost all cases, consists of a plateful of millet seasoned with a little pounded salt and chillies. When, after paying their taxes and debts, they come to the end of their store of grain, supposing there has been any remnant, they are reduced to living from hand to mouth. Some of them borrow grain, which they promise to repay with interest after the next harvest ; others explore the woods and the banks of the rivers and tanks in search of leaves, bamboo shoots, wild fruits, roots and other substances which help them to exist, or rather prevent them from dying of hunger." This was the standard of living amongst the cultivators ; below them was a class comprising, perhaps, a half of the entire population, "whose standard of living was even more abject. They go and seek for food on the banks of rivers and tanks, where they find leaves and shrubs, roots and herbs. These they boil, as often as not without even salt or any kind of condiment ; and this primitive food forms, for the greater part of the year, the most substantial part of their meals." There may be poverty and indebtedness in these days, but it is not the poverty of the pre-British era.

That India is undoubtedly amassing material wealth can be verified by certain trade statistics, especially by noting the enormous imports of gold and silver. What becomes of it? Gold is not coined in India ; it is not a legal tender ;[1] and of the silver imported, only a portion (perhaps half) finds its way to the mints. What becomes of the remainder? It is hoarded, turned into ornaments maybe, or actually buried, but not much of this amassed wealth is distributed amongst the great striving population of tillers of the soil.

But although, under the benign influence of the Pax Britannica, there is a steady development of material wealth in India, it is only right to point out that this does not directly improve the position of the 168,000 Europeans who live in the country. Year by year does it become more difficult to balance income and expenditure in such a manner as will ensure the attainment of that "something over" at the last which will ease off the roughness of life's declining years in England. Europeans who are but pilgrims in the land can usually live fairly comfortable on their incomes, but they can carry little away with them. No "Pagoda tree" has been known in India for many years. Even the best paid and most lucrative appointments involve expenditure in proportion to their prominence in the social scale which severely discounts their financial advantages. There is, indeed, more of the European style in general mode of living, more of incessant leave-taking and travelling to and fro, more care taken in keeping up presentable houses and surroundings than formerly ; but there is, on the other hand, less free hospitality, and far less expenditure on oriental luxuries.

[1] Written in 1898.

There is, indeed, little difference between the life of the official Englishman in India and his life in England ; and nearly the whole of Indian society is official. It is this fact, and the exact knowledge of the social circumstances which surround each unit in Indian society, which leads to that freedom of intercourse which is one of its greatest charms. If Indian society is official, it is also young, and it is mostly happy. In a community in which all people are living in much the same style there is little social rivalry, and there arises, on the other hand, much warm friendship and mutual good-fellowship.

Into the intricate question of the depreciated rupee we will not enter except to note a few of the general effects of its depreciation. Amongst natives and permanent residents, who spend their incomes in India, there is, perhaps, but little corresponding depreciation in their usual manner of living. It is true that prices have permanently risen almost all over India for foodstuffs ; but the wage-earner finds his wages higher, and has more rupees to spend, and the cultivator finds a more or less even balance between what he gets for his produce and pays for his scanty clothes and his seeds. The middleman and the bunniah gain largely, and the same may be said of European merchants, who buy produce in India to sell in English markets, and to be paid for in English gold. But the Government, which has large payments to make in England, and the European official who has to remit the best part of his income home for educational or other purposes, loses. To the Government of India a fall in the value of the rupee equal to one penny represents the actual loss of a million sterling per annum. To the official struggling with a growing family and the demands of a proper official *entourage* in India, the result of depreciation is almost disastrous. It is true that the rupee, in certain directions, still represents nearly its original purchasing capacity ; but for other reasons than its depreciation prices have undoubtedly risen on the whole. Wages, food, and nearly all the necessaries of life cost more in India than they did twenty years ago, whilst the straitened finances of Government have led to customs duty on imported European goods, to income tax, and other inconveniences, all of which tell on the narrowing income of the English civil or military officer, and reduce his means.

Taking it all round, the undoubted development of wealth in India generally is not reflected in the increasing value of that return for life's labour and ability which is represented by an Englishman's pay. The falling rupee has not distressed India: it has only hampered Government, and made life less worth living to Government employees.

A few trade statistics may be quoted to illustrate the extent to which India is gradually widening her area of commercial enterprise. The chief exports of India have already been noted—wheat, rice, cotton, oil seeds, hides, and jute, with tobacco and opium, figure most largely on the list, and the value of them varies from year to year with the variations of financial conditions between England and India. The value of the wheat exports, for instance, vary between one million and five millions, the amount exported depending on the value of the rupee, and the amount of grain which a year of exceptional plenty or otherwise can throw into the market. Nothing else varies so much as wheat; the exports of rice, tobacco, &c., remaining pretty even from year to year.

The imports are chiefly clothing, metal (manufactured or free), with gold and silver. Material for clothing forms about a half of the sum total of imports. The people of India can find nearly all else that they require to meet their very simple wants within the limits of India itself; consequently the value of imports are invariably less than that of the exports by many millions of pounds. Five or six years ago something akin to perfect freedom of commercial intercourse was established between England and India.[1] England maintained her duties on Indian tea and coffee, and India imposed duties on imported salt, on liquor, and on arms and ammunition only. But financial

[1] Written in 1898.

straits in India have led to the reimposition of duties on cotton and on most articles of European manufacture, and there has always been an export duty on rice.

The expansion of trade in India has been very rapid. Between the years 1873 and 1884 it increased 60 per cent. In 1886 it amounted to seventy-three million, value of imports, and ninety million, value of exports. In 1897 it was eighty million, and one hundred and nine million respectively. The difference in value between exports and imports is returned to India by a process which requires a little explanation. India has to meet many charges in England. There is interest on debts incurred by English investments of capital in India ; interest on railway capital ; army charges, civil pensions, and the cost of the India office and Secretary of States administration. Now the difference between export and import values represents a sum that has to be paid in India for produce consumed in Europe, and this can only be done by sending silver to India, or by purchasing bills on India in London. The Secretary of State makes the chief demand for remittances from India, so he draws bills on the Government treasuries in India, and it is by means of these bills that the balance is struck between merchants' payments in India and the funds needed by the Secretary of State in England. There is no drain on Indian resources to enrich England in this process. England only gets paid for investments made in India, or for other services performed. India, indeed, only pays for her Government, and for the enormous amount of English capital invested in the country for the country's benefit.

There is very much misconception about the financial value of India to England. Financially the relations between the two countries are those of ordinary business. India pays for nothing for which she does not receive a fair equivalent. The cost of the army, the civil charges for pay of her administrators and their staff, the charges for pensions, or for interest, are all represented in India by such good value as security, peace, order, and justice, and the benefits of economic development in railways, roads, telegraphs, &c., all of which are a source of wealth which remains in India and makes her rich. If the increased wealth of India does not meet with fair distribution, if it is apt to accumulate to the advantage of certain classes, and does not reach the working masses of the people in fair proportion, this is only what happens in all countries ; this may be found in England, just as much as in India, leading to the same results, stirring up the same spirit of discontent, allied probably with much more real misery. Political economists have yet to discover a remedy for these things. As for the money bags which Indian officials are supposed to carry with them to England on retirement, they are but the dream of fancy ! English officials take little with them to India, and it is certain that they can carry little out, nowadays.

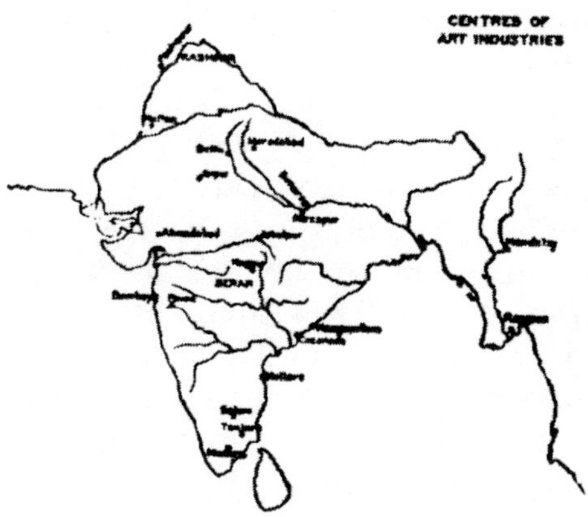


FIG. 84.

A far more interesting subject for consideration in connection with the economic development of India than financial statistics is to be found in her industrial arts and manufactures.

Here we touch the threshold of the inner life of India, and we realise something of the patient endurance of her people through countless ages, which has developed such visible manifestation of that intricate and careful thought which has directed hands gifted with hereditary skill. If art is sacred anywhere, it is sacred in India. Much of the religious mysticism which envelops the Hindu religion finds expression in the symbols of Hindu art. "No mediæval artist working on his knees can exceed in devotional spirit the potter working at his clay in the village street, and the gold worker fashioning his bangles with images drawn from the Hindu pantheon." So at least says Sir George Birdwood, who commences a most fascinating book on this subject with a full exposition of the outward signs and symbols of the faith of the Vedas. They are so intimately and unalterably associated with Indian art design that a comprehension of one is a necessary preliminary to an understanding of the other. Many of the outward and visible symbols of these principles which govern Indian design are exceedingly old. They may be found in Assyrian monuments,[1] in Biblical text, in a thousand other sources which were old when Greek architecture and sculpture were yet young.

We can hardly understand the reality of that life of intimate association with the supernatural which is to be found everywhere through the length and breadth of India. It is not only the suggestion of art design which is furnished by the quaint eccentricities of Hindu pantheology. "Everything that is made is for direct religious use, or has some religious significance," says Sir G. Birdwood. "The materials of which different articles are fashioned, their weight, and the colours in which they are painted are fixed by religious rule," and inasmuch as everything in daily use in an Indian household is (or was until European manufactures were introduced) made by hand, every Indian workman is a religious artist. Designs for purely decorative art are derived from many different sources, and amongst them the representation of Dravidian deities (Swami) are chiefly prevalent in Madras and the southern districts of India, and the primitive Aryan forms of decoration, such as the "Knop and flower," the "tree of life," &c., reduced to conventional forms, is the prevailing characteristic of the art industries of the north, where they have been introduced through Persia and Turkestan. Muhammadan art is not less indicative of religious symbolism than that of the Hindus. Every one knows the "prayer carpet," although every one does not recognise the meaning of the debased conventional form

[1] So much so that it is often maintained that India possesses no original art.

of the old Aryan symbols that are to be found interwoven in the pattern of it.

The worst enemy of ancient forms of Indian art are the manufactures of Europe and what Sir G. Birdwood calls the "irresistible energy of the mechanical productiveness of Birmingham and Manchester," which floods India with cheap designs and stifles native intelligence. In architecture, as in art design, mongrel styles are now taking the place of the traditional forms which combined perfect adaptation to climate and surroundings with admirable success in meeting the exact requirements of the building. The reason of this is to be found in the fact that the genius of the Indian artist is purely imitative and not creative. He will copy anything which he believes to be an emanation of a higher form of civilisation than his own with admirable exactness. He will paint miniatures with minute accuracy and painstaking care, but of original pictorial art he has no idea. It is true that the Bombay art schools are educating natives to paint pictures on European methods, and with some success; but at present this school of native art is in its infancy, and it will never make much impression on the mass of Indian art workmanship. The less that it makes, perhaps, the better.

Another enemy to Indian art is to be found in the European globe-trotter—the casual visitor with wealth enough to tempt the artisan into cheap and unfinished productions for the sake of quick returns. A good example of this may be found in the Simla bazaars, where wood carving has degenerated into a half mechanical process, which results in a vast out-turn of work of most inferior quality executed with a cheap rapidity which was unknown and quite impossible to the artist of fifty years ago.

In spite of modern deterioration the industrial arts of India form so prominent a feature in the productions of the country that they cannot be disregarded when dealing with any question of general economic progress, and a short reference to a few of the best known will not be out of place.

In the handicrafts of India, *i.e.* gold, silver, and metal work, enamels, jewellery, and household decoration, the art of India is still pre-eminent, especially in those branches which are in least demand. The gold work of India is perhaps best known in the forms produced in Southern India, and generally called Swami. Swami work is the representation of the Puranic gods in gold ornaments, such as bracelets, armlets, &c., and very much of it finds its way to Europe. In India the demand is chiefly for household idols in gold and silver—certain gods being always distinguished by embodiment in gold, and others in silver. Situla, the goddess of smallpox, for instance, is always silver. The silver work of India is famous all over the world. Kashmir parcel gilt silver (said originally to have been derived from a Mongol source), with its Lucknow imitations, as well as Katch, Gujrat, and Burma "sarais" and bowls in silver repoussé, generally exhibiting bold relief combined with intricate detail in design, are familiar in almost every English household with an Indian connection.

A vast amount of Indian jewellery still retains its primitive barbaric forms, some of which are of almost prehistoric origin, and most of them have furnished the basis for modern European patterns. English ladies will be pleased to learn, on the authority of Sir George Birdwood, that the "heart and serpent" form of European bracelets is probably derived from the silver fig-leaf (the heart-shaped leaf of the "pipal" or Indian fig), which still forms the sole adornment of the women of some of the wild tribes in Central India, and which is usually suspended from a serpentine form of waist-belt. The same authority mentions that a curious form of brooch worn by the Ladaki women in the Northern Himalayas is identical with one found in certain Keltic remains in Ireland. The form is evidently derived from symbols of serpent and phallic worship. The subject of Indian jewellery is so extensive and so varied that the reader who wishes to study it must be referred to the pages of Sir G. Birdwood's most interesting book. It is an increasing industry, which employs many thousands of Indian artisans.

The same may be said of the brass work (which centres chiefly in Benares), while engraved brass is a widely recognised speciality which is in vast demand both in India and in western markets. All Hindus use brass utensils for domestic use, and Muhammadans as a rule use copper, and it is by the fashion and extent of these vessels that the wealth of the proprietor is best known. At Moradabad tin is soldered on brass and cut through to form foliated patterns, which are often coloured. At Poona, Ahmadabad, and many places in Madras, workers in brass are to be found. The quaint little brazen figures which are so popular come chiefly from Vizagapatam, but perhaps the finest brass work in India is to be found at Madura and Tanjore.

The art of damascening, which consists in encrusting gold wire on steel or silver, is a speciality of Kashmir, and Sialkot in the Punjab. It is usually called Kuft work. Jaipur is famous for enamelling, and Nagpur for its inlaid arms of steel, the steel being obtained from the valleys of the Narbada and Tapti.

But it is in the production of woven goods, cotton, silk, lace, embroidery and carpets, that the industries of India are most appreciated locally and best known abroad. Immense cotton manufacture still exists in India, equal probably to the whole export trade of Manchester; and it would be impossible to enumerate all the centres of this enormous trade. Weaving would appear to be the chief employment of all the women in India. In the remotest village of the north-west highlands where the stony, steep hillsides afford a few feet of level terrace; under the shade of the banian trees and palms of the Dekkan; in the side alleys and slums of the great native cities; anywhere and everywhere in short, you may see the web extended in its rude frame, and women engaged in its management. The Punjab is especially famed for its weaving. Perhaps Multan, of all the Punjab cities, does the biggest trade in woven cloth, as the Povindahs, the

Afghan merchants from the highlands, find their market here, and carry off huge bales on the backs of their shaggy camels to bring them profit in the bazaars of Kandahar and Kabul.

Peshawur is famous for its "lungis," the head-dress of the Pathán frontier man—Sind, Rajputana, the United Provinces, all boast their specialities. In Bengal there is still a great trade ; but Dakka has fallen from its high estate, and the market for fine muslin (which takes its name from the Mesopotamian Mosul) is hardly in demand nowadays. In the time of Jehangir a muslin was manufactured of so fine a quality that when laid wet on the grass it disappeared from sight. This was called the "dew of the morning" (Subhnam), but there is none like it now.

In the Central Provinces (at Nagpur), in Berar, Bombay, Madras (Cocanada, Vizagapatam, and Nellore) are found centres of the cloth trade. Silk weaving flourishes chiefly in the Punjab, and for lace one must go to Ceylon.

Hardly less universal than the Indian weaver is the Indian potter. Outside every village he is to be seen, where the dead level of the plain rises to a small mound, and the accumulated débris of decades of rejected pots forms a point of vantage for his trade, moulding the clay with hands perfected by the transmission of hereditary skill, and surrounded with rows and circles of "ghurras," "sarais," and pans. The potter's trade is as old as civilisation is old, and in India it may be studied in its primitive forms. As for the art applied to pottery, beyond the traditional lines of form it is comparatively crude. The Bombay and Jaipur pottery turned out in "art" schools is generally much admired, as is also the blue and white patterned glaze of the Multan productions. The latter is a very ancient trade ; the former comparatively new. But the Indian potter is not easily stirred to attempt western design in decoration. He cares not for wealth, for he cannot change his caste or his social position. So long as his simple wants are provided for he would rather not extend his business to inconvenient limits. All decorative pottery of the best class in India depends much more on form than on colour or glazed decoration for its effect. Where imitation of European art is attempted it is usually a ludicrous failure. The best glazed pottery of Sind and the Punjab boasts of a prototype in the glazed tiles of Nineveh and Babylon. No modern innovations can much improve it.

The production of carpets of wool, cotton, and silk is another industry of India the antiquity of which is lost in the mists of tradition. In this branch of art manufacture, however, India can boast no originality. Colour and design are all borrowed from Persia, from Assyria, and even from Turkestan. The carpets of Kermanshah and Kirman in Persia are unrivalled by any Indian product. Even the stiff-patterned Turkoman work that is woven by women near Panjdeh in the Merve district, exceeds in excellence of workmanship and material anything to be found in India. Besides Persia there are extensive districts near Herat in which carpet-making is the chief industry. In Baluchistan, Afghanistan, and some of the Central Asian states carpets are turned out which, whilst they cannot boast the matchless combination of colour and form which are found in the best Persian products, are still admirable in quality and pleasing in effect. The carpet trade in India has received great impetus since the Exhibition of 1851, but in proportion as it has developed in extent deterioration in workmanship and design has set in. For much of this the jail schools of industry are responsible. "The mongrel manufactures of the Indian jails" still find warm support amongst the inartistic section of the English public, and jail influence has doubtless had a pernicious effect in all directions. Haidarabad and Masulipatam have suffered much. "Crude, inharmonious masses of unmeaning form" was, according to Sir G. Birdwood, a characteristic of Masulipatam carpets in his time. It is, however, only fair to add that twenty-five years has made much difference in the appreciation of true oriental artistic skill, and much of the corruption in design that was noticeable twenty-five years ago—especially in Kashmir—has disappeared. Many of the Kashmir carpets manufactured under European supervision in these days are true works of art. Multan, Mirzapur, Jubbulpore, and Malabar are all centres of the carpet trade besides those already mentioned. Silk carpets are made at Tanjore and Salem, but they are not to be compared to the silk carpets of Kirmán in Persia.

Apart from the convincing testimony of pages of statistics which are to be found in the "Statistical Abstracts Relating to British India," which are published from time to time, officially, by the Government of India, every writer of note already referred to, who deals with India generally, has much to say about the marvellous development of the resources of India ; its gradual progress as a manufacturing country ; and the place it takes as a source of food supply to the centre of the British Empire. But this is a subject which very largely interests the Indian public, and the leading Indian journals are consequently full of it : noting the variations which occur from time to time, and summing up results with the announcement of every Budget. A general review of Indian economics is perhaps better gathered from the pages of the Indian "dailies" than from any official statistical columns. I have, at any rate, to acknowledge my indebtedness to this source of supply ; and such opinions as I have ventured to express are but the reflection or echo of innumerable articles which have appeared in the pages of the *Pioneer* on the infinite variety of economic development which is peculiar to the land of the Hindu. It is to be regretted that since this book was written three or four years of progressive development have already passed. Three or four years in modern India is a period which must necessarily be marked by great and perhaps radical changes. It will, however, stand as a record (however slight) of the condition of things at the close of the nineteenth century, which is perhaps a useful epoch to mark in Indian history. In one particular, however, we need not expect any very great change to have occurred. In its arts and industries India is conservative, and the standard work by Sir George Birdwood on this fascinating subject will be authoritative for many years to come.

# CHAPTER X

## RAILWAYS

PROBABLY nowhere in the world can the traveller by rail move with more comfort than in India. Such at least have been the experiences of railway travel until quite recently. There are, however, signs that the extent of European passenger traffic in future may exceed the limits of space that has hitherto been possible to accord. When journeys lasting through several days and nights continuously are the constant experience of all Indian officials, it is necessary that accommodation should be both sufficient and good, and certainly in neither respect has Indian railway traffic failed so far. Nor are the arrangements made for food and supplies generally deficient. There are, of course, exceptions. There are lines on which the improvident traveller may starve if he does not hedge against such calamity by making his own arrangements ; but taking them all round, Indian railways compare favourably with those of England, or of the Continent, in the matter of personal comfort.

When complaints are heard (and they are often heard) of overcrowding and discomfort, it is generally the case that the passengers have themselves to thank for it. Liberal margin is allowed by the railway authorities in the matter of personal baggage, and the result is that an unnecessary amount of such baggage is packed by each individual into the carriage along with himself. In India, as is well known, it is usual for every European traveller to carry a full complement of bedding about with him ; from this he is never separated, and it is a part of his creed to observe all the formalities and the accessories that would accompany bedtime retirement in an English home. So that he starts with a recognised accompaniment of luggage which is both bulky and inconvenient. The accessories of a night's rest, however, are only a small portion of the usual impedimenta of the British traveller in India. I have seen a whole camp equipment, with the result of two or three days' sport, all massed together in one first-class compartment, together with several dogs. Moreover Indian railway officials of the higher grades travel in special carriages, sumptuously appointed and fitted which serve as permanent quarters, and which are very necessary in the wilder districts.

Thus it happens that first-class traffic on the Indian railways does not pay, nor has it, so far, been expected to pay. It is too vicarious and too intermittent for steady returns on most lines. With the increasing influx of European travellers, however, during the cold weather, it may in future add its quota to the excellent dividends earned by Indian railways in the more populous districts. It is the extraordinary development of the third-class, or native, traffic that sustains the ever-increasing returns for passenger service, and this is perhaps one of the most striking features of modern Indian travel. For it must be remembered that fifty years ago there were neither railways nor good road communications in the country. Fifty, or even forty, years ago India was the India of the previous century in the matter of communications. For two centuries and a half India had stood still, and all the conditions of European life in that country in 1850 were much the same as in 1650. The Europeanising of India has developed with the railways. The English atmosphere which pervades the house and household arrangements, the adaptation of Englishmen to the requirements of civilised existence in manners, in dress, and in morals is coincident with the advent of English women and English daily newspapers; of clubs regulated on English principles, and the constant interchange of ideas with fresh arrivals from English soil. It is railways and roads which have effected this change. Soon the weary monotony of the jolting progress of the palankin will be an unknown and forgotten experience, the lumbering dàk ghari will be found only in museums, and it will only be on the outside fringe of civilised existence that the far more handy and practical "tonga" will still be running. Railways will ascend the mountains and pierce the frontier barriers. India will be linked up with Russia, and Afghanistan will be no longer permitted to outrival China in the persistency of a benighted isolation. It needs no spirit of prophecy to forecast such certainties as these.

Colonel Chesney, writing of the days of the East India Company, says: "The Court of Directors, almost to the termination of their existence, did not recognise the prosecution of public works as a necessary part of their policy. The construction of a road or a canal was regarded by them, in their earlier days, much in the same light that a war would be—as an unavoidable evil, to be undertaken only when it could not be postponed any longer, and not, if possible, to be repeated." Yet it was before the final disappearance of the Company that the grand trunk road from Calcutta to the north was laid down nearly to the limits of the North-West (now called the United) Provinces; and the greatest irrigation project in the world, the Ganges canal, was completed by 1854. A year previously the advantages of railways in the general scheme of commercial development were urged by Lord Dalhousie, and it was not long afterwards that three great main lines—the East Indian, from Calcutta to the north; the Great Indian Peninsula, from Bombay to the east; and the Madras railway—were commenced. These lines were constructed by private companies under a Government guarantee of 6 per cent. on the invested capital.

There are now (March 31, 1899) 22,491 miles of line open to traffic representing the property of three guaranteed companies and thirteen "assisted" companies, as well as twenty-five "state" and twenty-four native state lines. The East Indian is now a State line, Government retaining the power to purchase a guaranteed line at certain periods under the original terms of the contract. As comparatively little capital has been invested by English capitalists in Indian railways, Government has raised the funds required for their construction and for guaranteed interest by loans, applying to railways the same process as was originally applied to irrigation works. These loans form part of the State debt. The net earnings of all the railways in India (including the West of India Portuguese line, which is worked at a dead loss) are about fourteen and a half million (expressed in tens of rupees), the net earnings of

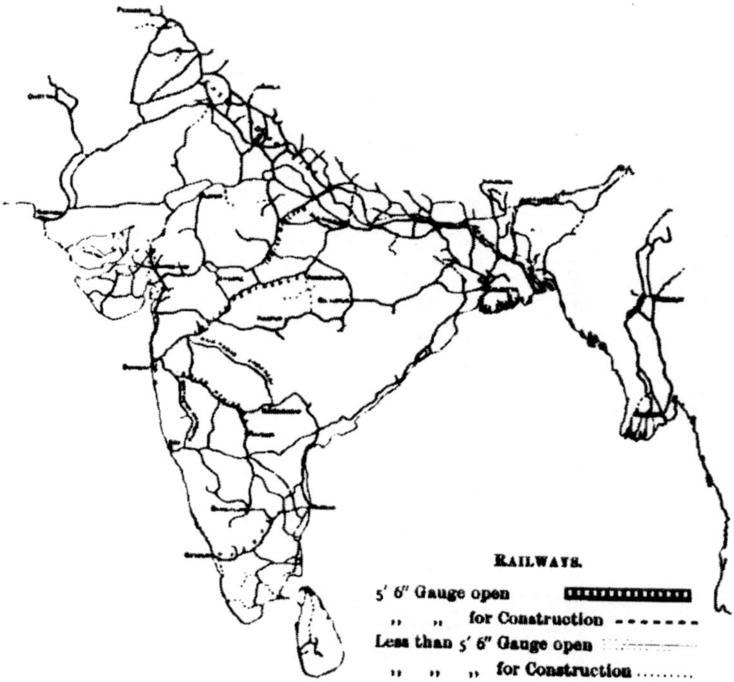


FIG. 85.

the East Indian line alone being four millions. Next to the East Indian ranks the North-Western system with a million and a half. The gross earnings in 1898 were twenty-seven and a half millions.

In no way can the vast variety of topographical and ethnographical conditions that exist in India be more forcibly impressed on the mind than by the simple process of a railway journey across the length or breadth of the peninsula. The one can be read and marked by looking out of the carriage window as the train moves forward, and the other by a study of the swarming hordes of idle humanity that cluster about the stations when the train stands still. In this way, too, we get glimpses of the great cities of the East, and can emulate in the course of a single week the record of those saintly or commercial pilgrimages which occupied years, and which have left us the story of these same cities in the mediæval days of history. The danger of such a process is the danger lest we forget that a superficial view of men and cities is as a glance at the illustrations of a great book without reading its pages; and that to read the pages of such a book as that represented by the continent of India requires attentive study before we can even master the rudiments of the language in which it is written. The majority of Englishmen and Englishwomen leave India knowing as much about the under currents of native existence and native thought as they knew when first they arrived in the country. To them one native is as another native, and all natives are of one great alien family sharing a common stock of doubtful principles, and living but to prey on the European. Yet even the intelligent use of their eyes, as they travel day by day from west to east, might teach most Englishmen that there are more different "sorts" of natives of India—by a great many—than there are of natives of Europe.

Approaching Karachi from the west, long after the Manora light has been sighted, nothing is visible of India but that which stands on its immediate borderland, *i.e.* the hills which divide Sind from Lus Bela. After a little while Karachi itself is indicated by one solitary square tower, dominating a flat, sandy plain; and presently the plain breaks up into the irregularities of outline which betoken the existence of a town round about. This tower belongs to the parish church of Karachi, and was built as a landmark for sailors, in architectural emulation of an Italian campanile. But it is the campanile without Italian environment, and is as much in its right place as the "Taj" would be in St. James's Park. The town of

Karachi was not so very long ago a collection of buildings grouped in a waste of sand, with a few gravel hills standing seawards, against the base of which washed the ever-restless waves of the Indian Ocean. But the introduction of water from the Malir River has changed all that. It is now quite sufficiently supplied with trees and vegetation. The neat stone houses stand in pretty compounds, in which flowers and rare shrubs are not wanting, and there

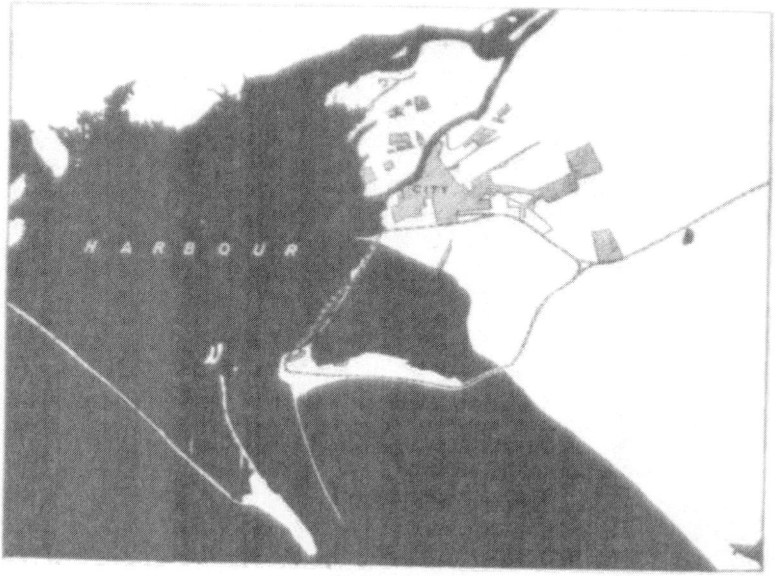


FIG. 86.—Karachi Harbour.

are here and there expanses of green lawn that would be a credit to England. An overgrown native city, a long straggling cantonment, and the harbour which has made of Karachi a great commercial port, are the chief features of the place. Much land reclamation has been accomplished, and more is in progress. The value of land has risen enormously in the course of the last fifty years; and it is hardly necessary to add that most of the land is in the hands of the Parsis. Many of the leading merchant houses in Europe have their representatives in Karachi;

so that at the Karachi Club one may meet men of most of the Western nationalities, just as in the streets of Karachi city one may find men of as varied Eastern origin. But Karachi possesses little of oriental attraction. To many of its European commercial inhabitants the cantonment limits bound the horizon of India. They never pass that horizon, but spend the best part of a laborious existence in anxious anticipation of that happy time when they can again recross the seas.

Leaving the dry, warm atmosphere of Karachi (an atmosphere which is more dry than that of Bombay and more warm than that of the Punjab) by the evening mail, the traveller loses much of the interest of Sind during the night hours, when he will probably (if he is well advised) be asleep. He will still have the opportunity of studying the idiosyncrasies of the Sindi, however, before he reaches Ruk, the junction for Quetta. At Ruk he will find the neatly clothed and gaudily hatted merchant of Sind giving place to the turbaned Punjabi and the greasy, ringletted, Baluchi, the voluminous folds of whose dress are usually held together by a strap supporting his little round shield, and a belt which becomes a small armoury whenever he is permitted to carry arms. There is not the least affinity between the Baluchi and the man of Sind. No Frenchman and German standing together on the same platform of a European railway station could be farther apart in all national proclivities than these two, although both acknowledge the representative of the same *lex Britannica* in the person of the blue-coated and yellow-trousered Punjabi policeman.

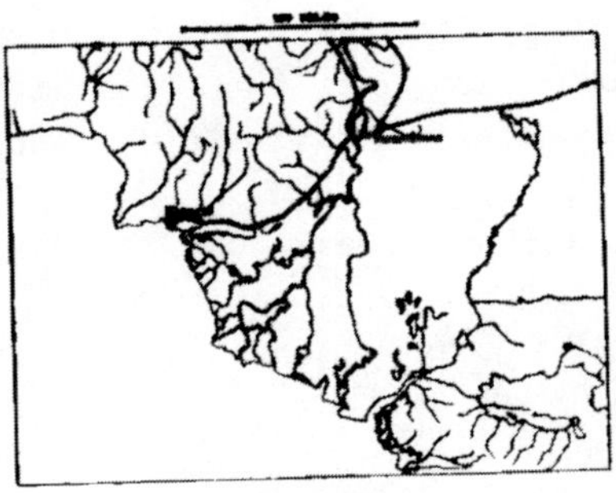

FIG. 87.—Karachi Port.

From the hot and dusty station of Ruk the branch Sind-Peshin railway strikes across the hot and dusty desert of Kach Gandava, first passing the outlying station of Jacobabad. Not thirty years ago Jacobabad was on the borders of Sind, where Sind and Baluchistan meet. It was our "frontier" station in that direction; and when the war-worn old frontier soldier, General Jacob, was buried there (to live for ever in Baluch legends as the founder of one of their most holy "ziarats"), there was little expectation that ere long, two days' journey by rail would separate Jacobabad from the advanced frontier—the modern frontier—which finds expression beyond the Khojak mountains in the little new-born oasis of New Chaman.

The history of the two lines of rail which carry the traveller from the foot of the Baluch hills to Quetta is written large enough in the recent annals of Indian public works. The Harnai route and the Bolán route have much in common. They are both mountain lines with steep grades, and both depend on powerful engines, running on metals laid at an ordinary gauge for their haulage. Each has had its special difficulties to contend with. The Harnai route, which, passing through the valley of that name, taps a direct highroad to the valleys of the Zhob and Gomal half-way to Quetta, is liable to be overwhelmed by periodic avalanches of clay or mud loosened by the effects of heavy rainfall. There is no engineering out of this difficulty. There are mountains of this clay formation, and when the avalanche descends there is nothing to be done but to dig out the line and start afresh. On the Bolán line the original alignment carried the railway up the Bolán river bed—a stony, shingly ramp, which in ordinary dry seasons is easily traversable, and which requires no great elevation above the water channel to avoid flood level in ordinary rainy seasons. But the Bolán is subject to intermittent floods of most extraordinary violence, which cannot be foretold or foreseen. One such flood completely destroyed the line when it was nearly complete. So terrific was its power that bridges, metals, revetments, and permanent way were all washed into space over long stretches of the line, leaving "not a wrack behind." Since then a new alignment has been adopted, avoiding the lower reaches of the Bolán, and the line now follows a subsidiary valley called the Mushkáf, rejoining the Bolán near its

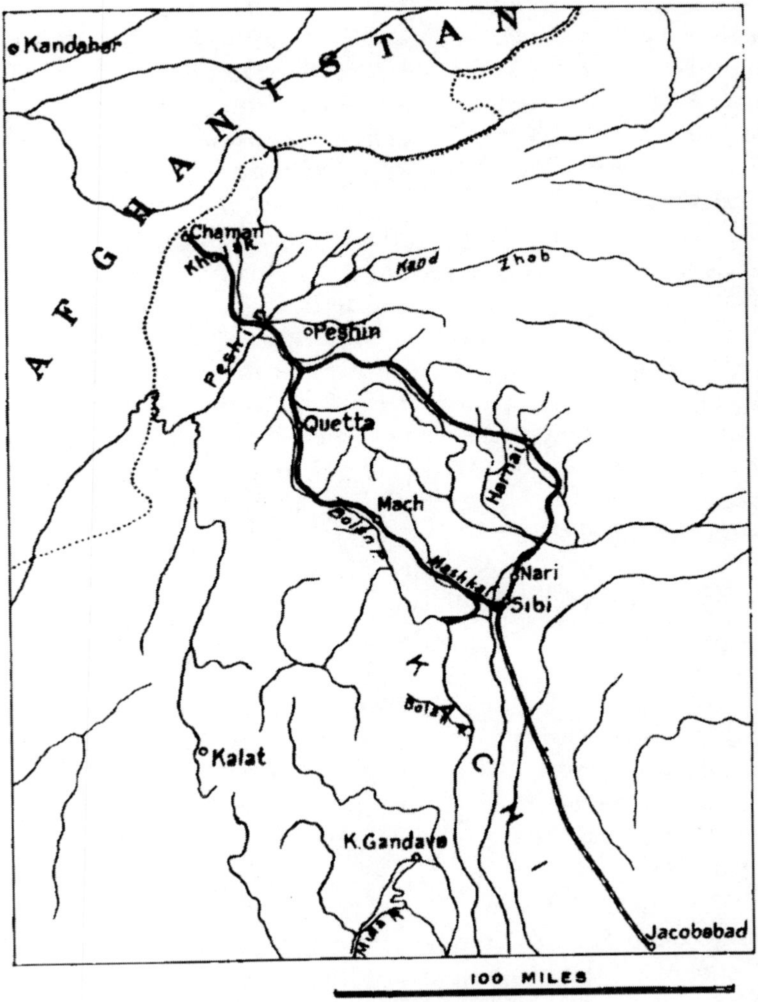


FIG. 88.—Sind-Peshin Railway.

head. The steepest grade on the Bolán is steeper than any on the Harnai.

Both routes are picturesque in a high degree. There is

a want of green freshness about all Baluchistan hill scenery, in spite of the luxuriant growth of oleander and other shrubs near the running streams, and of many a stretch of rice or wheat cultivation which surrounds the villages and orchards of the agriculturalist. Stern, frowning buttresses of rock, and jagged-edged lines of hills, mostly shut in the narrow metalled way. Here and there the line passes hundreds of feet above the bed of a local torrent, and twists itself into the sinuosities of a mass of hard limestone. Sometimes suspended high in the air, sometimes burrowing through tunnelled rock, the train works its way upwards to the open plain of the Peshin Valley, into new scenery and a new climate. No stronger contrast can be pictured than the fiery, oven-baked heat of the stations near the foot of hills in summer, where even flies and lizards cease to live, and the intensely cold blasts of the winter blizzard on the upland water-parting which marks the change of grade, when the powdered snow drives in wreaths through the chinks of closed doors and windows, and the uncoupled engine is set to tackle the snowdrift alone.

Nor is the least difficulty which presents itself to the Quetta mail that which is occasionally supplied by the flight of locusts in the early autumn. The power of the locust to bring a heavy train to a stand in an upward grade is derived from the disposition of hundreds and thousands of greasy bodies over the wheels and along the metals, and it is sometimes irresistible.

We have already given some short account of the great strategic station of Quetta, and of that farthest advanced post, which lies beyond the great Khojak tunnel called Chaman. Here then, for the present, 124 miles beyond the Quetta station, the Quetta-Kandahar line ends. Who shall say for how long? Seventy miles intervene between Chaman and Kandahar; 300 more will take any railway by easy stages to Herat; 60 or 70 miles farther (across the only considerable watershed in the whole distance) link up Herat with what will soon be the Russian Trans-Caspian rail head. Five hundred miles of easy line, tapping two such centres of Asiatic trade as Kandahar and Herat, would connect Europe with India, without any intervening deserts, no hot plains, no shifting of cargo from rail to steamer, and would pass through an admirable climate and over easy grades.

Returning to the main north-western line, which crosses the Indus River by the Lansdowne bridge at

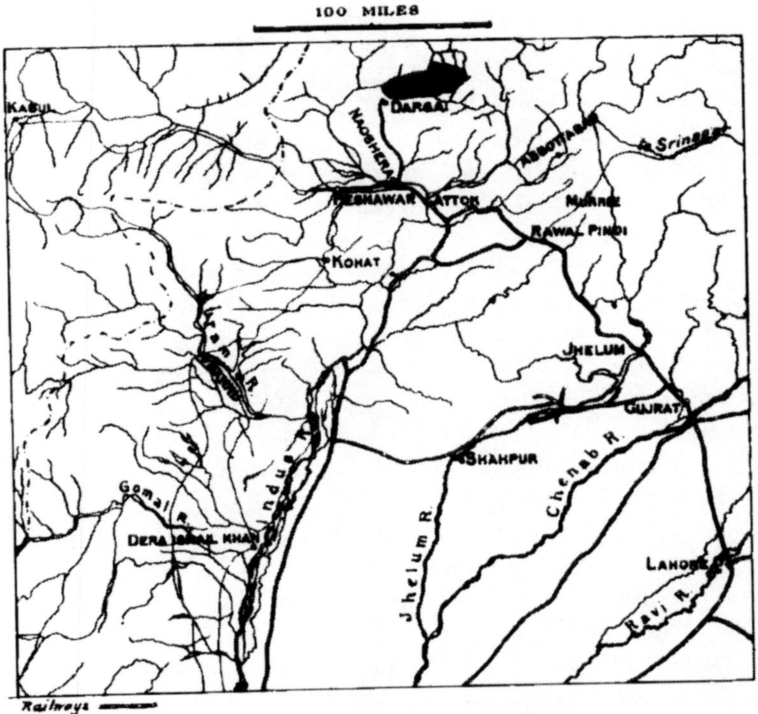


FIG. 89.—North-West Frontier—Railways.

Sukkur, we arrive at a very interesting group of old-world cities, which are worth much more than a passing notice. Sukkur came into our possession in 1842, and the present town is comparatively modern. It is connected with Rohri on the left bank by perhaps the most remarkable bridge in India, the construction of which has already been noticed. From the island of Bhakkur, near the middle of the river, to the river bank at Rohri, a single span of 840 feet completes the railway connection with the left bank, which is thereafter followed to Multan. About 5 miles east of Rohri, and off the line of railway, are the remains of the ancient city of Alor, the capital of the Hindu Rajahs of Sind ere the Muhammadan conquest under Muhammad Kasim in A.D. 711. At that period the Indus washed the walls of the city, and it was not till about the year A.D. 962 that an earthquake split the limestone ridge at Rohri, and diverted the main stream into the new channel. The old bed of the Indus is crossed by a bridge about 600 feet long, the ruins of Alor standing on the left bank.

Between Rohri and Multan the railway passes from Sind to the Punjab, but the change of province does not involve much change in the dreary monotony of one of the most tiresome journeys in India. The western Baluch hills have faded from sight, and the flat expanse of tamarisk jungle, or broken scrub-covered plain, is unbroken. Here and there a few patches of cultivation are springing into existence, giving promise of a brighter future for all these regions; and whenever the banks of the river are approached, these trees and jungle enjoy a luxuriant existence. Whilst crossing the Sutlej near Bhawalpur, the traveller (hot, dusty, and thirsty) gets a glimpse of the fresh green luxuriance which encompasses the capital of the Bhawalpur native state; but it soon disappears, and, with the exception of the Multan surroundings, there is nothing again to refresh the weary eye until he reaches Lahore.

Multan, the city of the Chenab, is one of the most ancient, as well as one of the most interesting, cities (historically) of India. The red sandstone walls of the city stand as they stood when we captured it in 1849, after the murder of our two emissaries under the dome of the Idgah. The fort is picturesque. Here was once the ancient temple of the sun, and here now is a red brick octagon, covered with the blue and white tiles—the shrine of Rakhnu-din. Next to Jacobabad, Multan is perhaps the hottest station in India. We are still in districts that lie beyond the full influence of the south-west monsoon, and the total rainfall here is only 7 inches.

All around us now are Punjab influences. The character of the people has changed with their dress and their manners. The Sind shopkeeper disappears with the Baluch borderer, and the Punjabi Mussulman, turbaned and loosely clothed (polite enough when encountered about the dusty, sun-baked little roadside stations; but often truculent and disagreeable in the crowded byways and alleys of the great Punjab cities) has taken their place. Multan, Lahore, Rawal Pindi, and Peshawur have all a common stock of humanity. It is a useful stock, filling the ranks of the army and police with recruits, and finding workmen for most of the public enterprises of India; and politically, it is a most important one, for the enormous gatherings of mixed ruffianism (including more and more of the worst Pathán element as one approaches the border) which gathers in these great towns must ever be a source of uneasiness in times of difficulty, and demands constant watchfulness even in times of peace.

Lahore, the city of the Ravi, is the capital of the Punjab, and in its streets and buildings are gathered 176,000 people. To reach Lahore we have travelled more than 800 miles from Karachi. The journey has been slow, indescribably dusty, and the scenery monotonous; nor should we have improved it much had we struck off from Multan and journeyed by the Sind-Sagar line (which follows the Indus to Dera Ismail Khan, and then runs eastwards to Jehlam) to our destination. We should have seen a dim silhouette of the Sulimani Mountains, tinted in grey, against a glaring western sky; and, if lucky, might have distinguished the dominating peaks of the Kaisargarh; but such distance as intervenes between the Indus and the crest of the Sulimanis lends little enchantment to the view, and on the whole the shorter route is the more profitable. Lahore (or Lahawur) is doubtless a very ancient city, but we find no mention of it earlier than the seventh century A.D., when it was in the hands of the Chauhán Rajputs. From them it passed to Mahmud of Ghazni early in the eleventh century, but it did not rise to magnificence till the reign of the Moghul Emperor Akbar. The mausoleum of his son Jehangir at Shahdara, on the banks of the Ravi, with the fort and the Shahimar gardens, is the chief attraction of Lahore. Lahore is surrounded by gardens, and the sweet luxuriance of verdure—still fresh when most of India is parched and withered—is due to the long cold weather of the upper Punjab. In April, and even in May, the climate is not only endurable, but often delightful. But the hot weather, if it sets in late sets in vigorously, and in July and August the heat is often terrific in this "city of dreadful night." About four miles from Lahore is the military cantonment of Mian Mir. Whatever advantages of position may have existed formerly in Mian Mir to recommend it as the site of a military station have so long disappeared as to be unrecognisable at present. There are certainly none apparent in the bleak and dusty plain which surrounds this cantonment.

From Lahore to Peshawur is a journey through the historic fields of the Sutlej campaigns, and through a country which, in many respects, differs from that of the Indus Valley. It is broken into a picturesque network of steep-sided ravines as the train approaches Rawal Pindi, where the general level rises to nearly 2000 feet above sea. It is traversed by three mighty rivers, the Chenab, the Jehlam, and the Indus, all of which are crossed by magnificent bridges, triumphs of engineering skill, and it is within sight of the snow-line of the Himalayas, the lower spurs of the mountains reaching southward towards the line, and appearing, in the still clear atmosphere of winter, almost to touch it. At Jehlam and Rawal Pindi they are, however, still far distant. Beyond Pindi, which is an overgrown military station (the headquarters of the Punjab Army Corps) with a huge seething native city lying low on its northern flank, the undulating country is never monotonous, and after passing the Indus there is at times a certain resemblance to the Scottish lowlands in the flat hills covered with purple flowering plants which faintly recall the heather and the braes. Rawal Pindi is the recognised point of departure for the hills of Murree (Mari) and Kashmir, which are connected with the station by an excellent road. At Hassan Abdal, between Rawal Pindi and Attok, another road branches to Abbottabad and the Black Mountain, and a third connects Naoshera (between Attok and Peshawur) with Mardán, Malakand, and Chakdara.

Of all the remarkable points on this journey perhaps the Attok bridge and the view therefrom is most striking. The stern grandeur of the white waters of the Indus sliding between black and broken cliffs fringed with gleaming strips of sand, seems rather to partake of Himalayan or of Tibetan scenery than that of the plains of India. It is as if the Indus had carried down with it a reproduction of one of its own reaches from the mountains about Gilgit; but Indus scenery never lapses into prettiness anywhere in its course. Even its beauty, where the river breaks through the salt ranges into the plains of the Deraját east of Bannu, is significant of strength and sterility rather than of landscape loveliness.

Peshawur, the most important of our northern military frontier posts (like Rawal Pindi), possesses a two-sided character. There is a pretty cantonment, beautifully laid out, and rich in all the charm of varied garden vegetation which its northern climate favours. Round about are the everlasting hills, the peaks which overlook the Khaibar and the Kabul River on one hand, and the hills of Swat on the other, with the triple-headed mountain of "Mor" over-topping them. This is the mountain of the "wild vine and the ivy," where Alexander sacrificed to his gods; at the foot of which dwelt the Nysæans of classical history. No wonder that the Amirs of Afghanistan still regard with longing eyes this, the fairest of cities that ever was an Afghan possession—the jewel of the Durání empire—the winter capital of the Durání emperors.

The other point of view is towards the city, where an overcrowded and much-mixed population of the Indo-Afghan borderland rivals Rawal Pindi in the criminal annals of the Punjab. It is, however, a most important trade centre, and carpets, furs, skins, and clothing of "pashmina" and of sheepskin are gathered in the Peshawur bazaar which are not to be found elsewhere in India. Nor is the fruit of Peshawur—grapes, apples, and "sardar" melons from Afghanistan—to be overlooked, nor its curious speciality in cloth beflowered with patterns in wax; nor yet its quaint pottery—which latter, indeed, is more quaint than beautiful. From the strategical point of view Peshawur is on the north what Quetta is on the south—the guardian outpost of the gates of India. No advance into India on any intermediate line would be possible which left these two positions untouched. But there is a wide difference between Quetta and Peshawur as to the manner in which this guardianship is exercised. Quetta faces west and south, dominating all lines of approach from Herat, Kandahar, or Seistán equally, and exercising a wholesome influence on the ever-restless border tribes which lie behind her. These tribes are still independent in the security of their mountains, but they are cut off from participation in any scheme of amalgamation with an advancing foe. Peshawur dominates the Khaibar route—the most important of all routes from Kabul; and, with the assistance of Rawal Pindi, also holds the Indian ends of all possible lines of advance from the north and north-west. But the independent border tribes-people are here in front of our defences, ready to assume the offensive on their own responsibility, or to act in concert with more powerful adversaries beyond them—as occasion may give opportunity. The position in Afghanistan most analogous to that held by Quetta in Baluchistan would be Jalalabad, in the Ningrahar Valley, near the junction of the Kunar and the Kabul rivers. So limited is the capacity of Peshawur for the defence of the Khaibar that it was lately reckoned impossible even to protect that route from occupation by the Afridis when they raided northwards from the Tirah.

From Lahore to Peshawur we have travelled 278 miles, but we have hardly changed our climate. The long but never severe winter at Peshawur is balanced by a short but more than genial summer. Peshawur can hold a record for heat during two or three months of the year against almost any city in India. It is, as we have before pointed out, along the north-west frontier and under the border hills that the great heat record, year

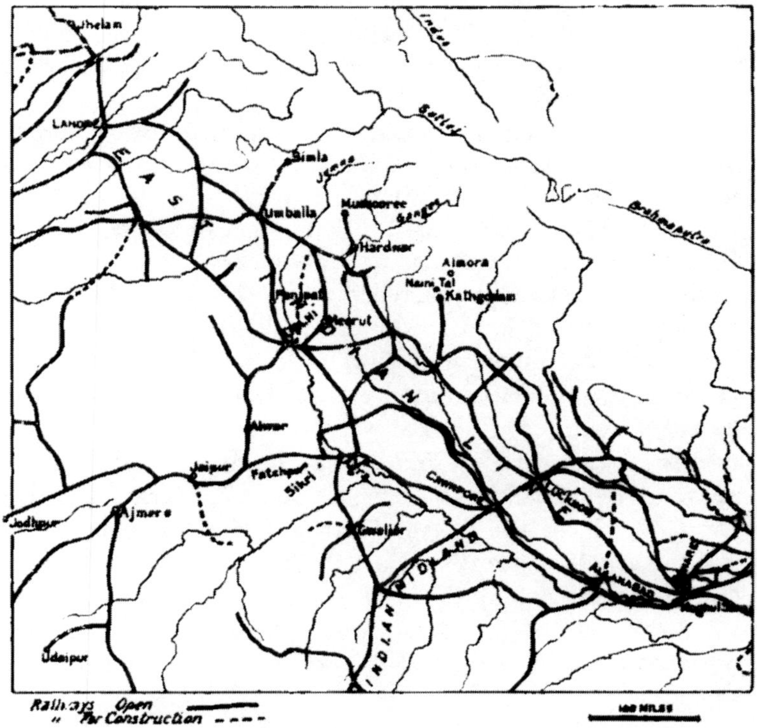


FIG. 90.—East Indian Railway.

after year, is registered. There is no hot weather in the plains elsewhere to be compared to that of the plains of the Punjab; and there is, at the same time, occasionally an intense and searching cold. This inequality of temperature doubtless augments the tendency to fever generated by the irrigated cultivation (and, we may add, the water-logged cantonments) of the north-west, and tend to place

Peshawur high on the list of undesirable stations in spite of its many undoubted attractions.

Beyond Peshawur we cannot at present travel by rail, although an extension to Jamrud at the foot of the Khaibar is contemplated. The connecting links that are to bring Kabul within a day's journey of Peshawur, and drop passengers at Jalalabad for the Kunar route to Chitrâl, are as yet in the future. The natural terminus of the North-Western railway system will doubtless eventually be formed at Kabul.

If we continue our journey through the Indo-Gangetic plain by rail, returning to Lahore from Peshawur, and starting thence for Calcutta, we shall witness the most complete development of the railway system that has yet permeated any part of India. There are singular natural facilities for railway construction in this flat expanse, and a singularly rich field for commercial enterprise, for it is here that the most important cities of India have been grouped from time immemorial. Delhi and Agra, Allahabad, Cawnpore, Lucknow, and Benares, all either lie on the Great Central East Indian line or on its northern supplement of "Oudh and Rohilkand." The chief wealth of India is within the Ganges basin, and it is a matter of small surprise that the East Indian, now a State line, should be financially the most successful line in India.

From Lahore to Calcutta is a distance of 1250 miles, of which the first 187 only are on the North-Western system.

From Umballa (which is important only as a military station pointing the road to Simla) the East India line carries the trade of the north through Delhi, passing *en route* the field of Paniput (where the destinies of India have been decided more often than destinies equally great have been decided on any field in the world's history) and following a direct line west of the Jumna. Delhi, the ancient capital of Afghan and Moghul emperors, now an important railway centre, is in the eyes of Hindus still the metropolis of India. Its position, just on the edge of the Punjab, however, practically reduces it to a secondary provincial status. It is no longer the seat even of a local government. We are told that within the area of 45 square miles round Delhi there are the remains of no less than seven cities, each of which represented the capital of Hindustan in its time. To us it is not the extraordinary wealth of Muhammadan architectural remains, nor the

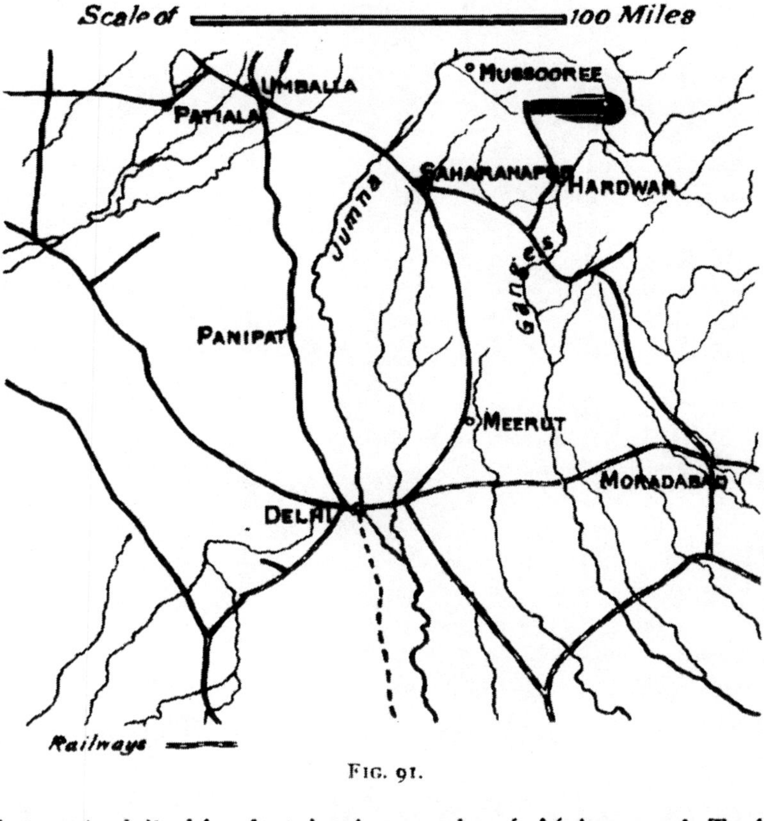


FIG. 91.

interest of its blood-stained records of Afghan and Turk sovereignty, but the recent story of its capture during the dark days of the Mutiny that keeps Delhi in national remembrance. Like Cawnpore (the next great native city which we pass on this route) it is hallowed to us by the blood of our countrymen. Cawnpore (Kanhpur) is better known by the glorious memorial of a ghastly sacrifice than by any of its architectural beauties ancient or modern.

Allahabad is the modern seat of the Government of the United Provinces, and it is the great central junction of the Indian railway system. From Allahabad the Great Indian strikes south-westward to Bombay, so that here we find an immense central railway establishment. The city is about equal to Delhi in size, both including something

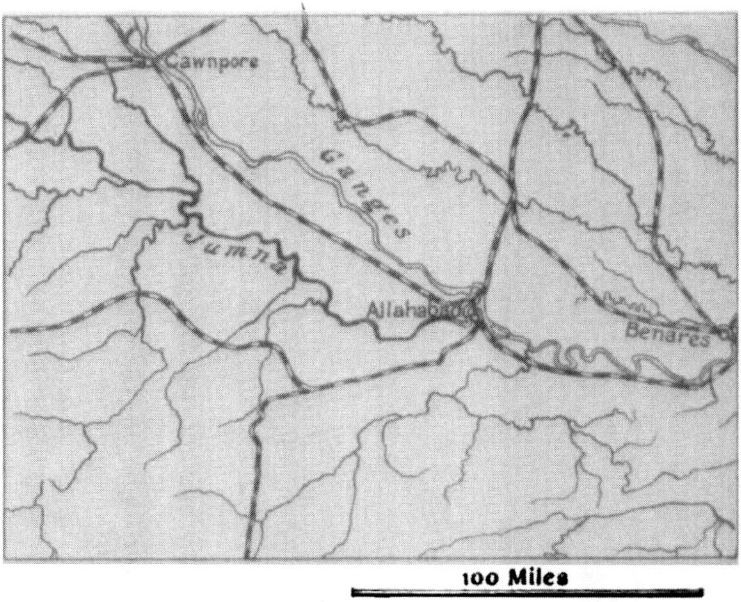


FIG. 92.

less than 200,000 inhabitants, and much inferior in architectural interest. Allahabad may be said to mark the division between the climate of the north and that of the south of India. It is from Allahabad, northwards, that the general fall in temperature is usually marked. The ancient name of Allahabad is Prág, and its situation at the confluence of the Jumna and the Ganges has always secured for it the foremost position amongst the sacred cities of the Hindus. Here are special evidences of the strong vitality of the Brahmanism of the present; and here too there is much to be admired of Muhammadan architectural design of the past. The station (civil and military) covers a vast flat expanse chequered with straggling compounds; and, like most of the large cantonments of the plains of India, its huge extent is out of all proportion to the population it embraces. It may be quoted as a typical Indian station of Northern India, and as it enjoys a fairly extended cold weather, it is distinctly popular.

Another important city of the Gangetic basin, Lucknow, we have left behind us. It lies some 50 miles to the north-east of Cawnpore on the Oudh and Rohilkand branch. Lucknow is perhaps, by virtue of its climate, its surroundings, the interest of its Mutiny records, and its attraction as a centre of sport, the most popular of all Indian up-stations. Agra and Benares are two other cities of unfathomable record and endless interest (if no longer strategically or politically important) connected with the East Indian system. To reach Agra it is necessary to leave the main line at Toondla, half-way between Delhi and Cawnpore. To reach Benares one must branch off from Mogul sarai, some 100 miles beyond Allahabad towards Calcutta. Either city is so full of the beauty of architectural design, each can boast so many specialities in art and industry, that it is sacrilege to treat them simply as geographical points of more or less note in connection with a utilitarian railway system. But the ancient traditions in which their history is lost; the mediæval romances which hang around them; the glory of that Indo-Italian architecture which finds eternal expression in the Taj at Agra, and the grand creations of Hindu and Jain workmen at Benares; the sacred veil which is drawn round the latter, her Ghâts and bathing-places, her temples and palaces, her art work in brass, copper and silver —none of these things tell much on the traffic returns, or make largely for that economic development of which the railways are the main instrument.

The travelling sightseer (the tourist) as a first-class passenger does not "pay" (as we have before intimated), and it is only the thronging crowd of natives, contented with little in the way of comfort, rather preferring hard seats and a chattering mass of close-packed compatriots, which adds any profitable returns to the gross earnings of the state or company. And in this connection the traffic returns which are directly due to the attraction afforded by religious festivals, "mélas," and fairs, are worthy of note. On the occasion of the great fair at Hardwar, for instance, pilgrims in hundreds of thousands collect on one line and for one purpose from all parts of India. Then indeed are the resources of the railway officials (and their temper) taxed to the uttermost. It is not possible to convey the crowds that silently mass themselves at the stations awaiting their turn for forward movement. Whether that waiting involves one hour or one week, seems a matter of indifference. Natives will sit in patient uncomplaining rows, unmarking the lapse of time, so long as their turn may come at last—that turn which will enable them to reach the sacred banks of the holy Gunga, to plunge in regardless of possible drowning, regardless indeed of all except this one great washing of themselves clean from their sins; and possibly the necessity of paying handsome fees to their priests afterwards.

So far as we have travelled south-eastwards from Delhi along the length of the Gangetic plain, there is not a city which we have encountered which cannot boast of some distinguishing attraction. It may have been dignified by architectural art, by antiquity, or by history. Something of living oriental grandeur still clings to them, and something of the pathos of a magnificent past. A Brummagem air of contented commercial prosperity has never been theirs. It is only when we pass from the north-west into Bengal that we find dull utilitarianism prevailing—no architecture, no art, no manufactures even, beyond the products of village handicraft.

Calcutta, with its 800,000 or 900,000 inhabitants, is the second city of the whole British empire, but there is nothing but wealth to make it famous. There is not a public building worth looking at. Even the historic Government House can only be described as the ugliest

Viceregal residence in the empire ; the wealthy European inhabitants live in "marble palaces" that are usually let in flats. There is not one really good hotel, not a building with more than a recent history, not a native residence that is remarkable for beauty either of outline or decoration. The most conspicuous monument is that of "Ochterlony" in the midst of the wide maidan, or plain, round which European Calcutta clusters, and which is indeed the "people's own." To the Bengali "babu" alone could this monument be a thing of beauty. The native quarter of Calcutta is in every sense abominable, and in as marked contrast to the native quarter of the sister city of Bombay as is the personality of the Calcutta native to that of the inhabitant of the western city. A Calcutta crowd is as dull and unlovely as only a crowd composed entirely of men can be—the plain white clothing draped round the smooth rotundity of the Calcutta "babu," surmounted by a close-cropped black head without head-dress, and crowned with a cheap and dingy Birmingham umbrella, can be but unpicturesque either in the unit or the aggregate. Nevertheless Calcutta is healthy and wealthy, and in spite of the expense of residence in that city, it is so full of visitors during the short cold weather when the Government of India resides there, that no city in India has so many social attractions to offer, or such a varied programme of amusement. Hence it rivals Simla in popularity, and easily maintains its position as the first and greatest city of India. At Howrah, on the right bank of the Hoogley, opposite Calcutta, is the terminal station of the East Indian railway, and here the Gangetic central system of communication comes to an end. It pays as no

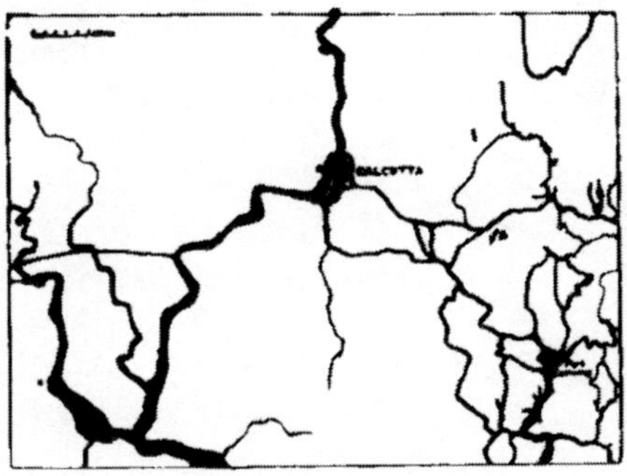

FIG. 93.—The Position of Calcutta.

other line in India pays, and as a suitable corollary, it is perhaps the most comfortable and the best found line in the country. The remarkable growth of the Indian coal trade has lately led to a large increase of rolling stock on this line and to the doubling of its carrying capacity.

Changing our point of departure to Bombay we find

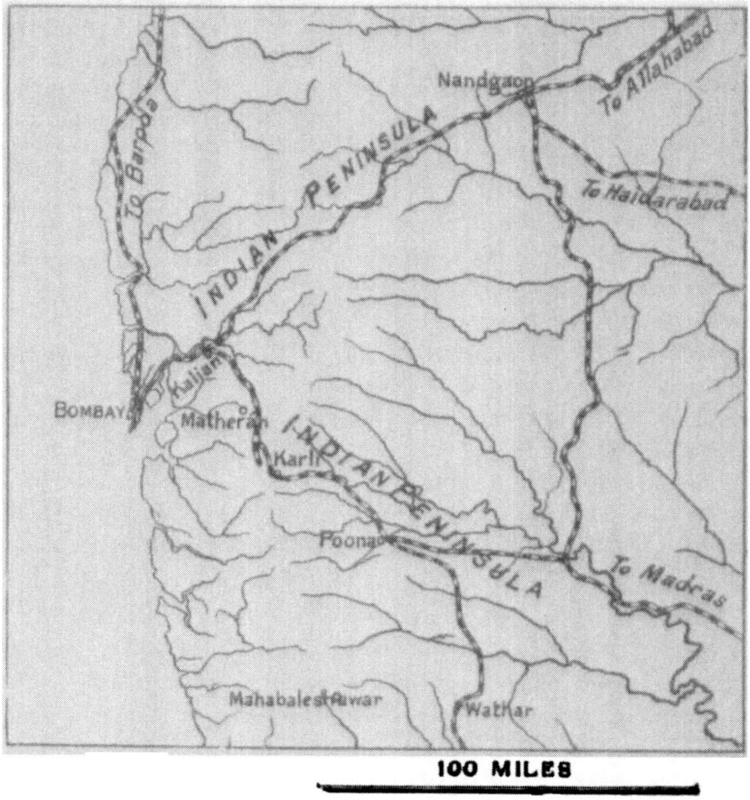


FIG. 94

spreading abroad over India two important railway routes to the north, centring on Delhi ; two to the east, with Calcutta as the terminal objective ; and two to the south-east, reaching to the Coromandel coast. There is no direct line northwards to Peshawur (which is not far removed from the meridian of Bombay), because no line yet has been carried through the northern portions of the great Rajputana desert lying between Bikanir and the Sutlej. Not long ago the recognised route to Delhi was by the west coast to Baroda, and thence across Rajputana, touching the capitals of the Rajput states of Jaipur and Alwar; nor could a line more strikingly illustrative of the variety of Indian climate and physiography have been selected.

From the moist sea border districts of the west, deep in rice cultivation and shadowed by palms; with the diminishing line of the Western Ghâts, green and grey with the luxuriance of an almost tropical vegetation, on one hand, and the moisture-laden sea-breezes sweeping inland on the other, the traveller is rapidly transferred to the sand plains of Rajputana, streaked by lines of rocky hills and breaking now and then into a green oasis where water can be found at no unmeasurable depth from the surface. He has passed meanwhile through some of the most lovely scenery of Western India, the lowlands surrounding Baroda and stretching through Eastern Gujrât, and he will have made no mistake if he has taken advantage of the change necessitated by the break of gauge at Ahmadabad to visit that historic town—a town which is second only to Delhi and Agra in the beauty of its architectural reminiscences of Hindu and Muhammadan rulers.

A narrow gauge line distinguishes the Rajputana railway system, but the comfort of travelling is unaffected thereby, for the carriages are quite sufficiently roomy to be both convenient and cool. In Rajputana we find a wealth of historic interest. All the best of India's ancient traditions centre in Rajputana, nor is there anything in the whole world of historic narrative more stirring than the chivalrous romances of Rajput valour and Rajput achievements. The voluptuous oriental loveliness of Udaipur; the blood-stained history of Chitor; the prehistoric antiquity of Ujain; the beauty of Jaipur, its unrivalled arts, and antique marbles; and the antiquities of Ajmir, of Alwar, and Indore, are all to be studied in this home of the solar race, and most of them are within reach of the Rajputana railway. Indore and Ujain are perhaps more easily reached from Bombay by a branch line which leaves the Great India Peninsula railway at Khandwa. Agra, too, is touched by this narrow gauge line which thus includes within its network a galaxy of historical and architectural points of interest such as no other line in India can rival. In financial importance the Rajputana line stands third only to the East Indian and North-Western lines.

But the traveller who would speed his journey, or the merchant who would avoid the inconvenience of expense of a break of gauge, now takes the other line to Delhi and the north-west—the line which, branching from the Great Indian Peninsula at Itarsi, makes for Delhi on an almost directly northward track *viâ* Jhansi. This is the Indian Midland, and it is not without its points of interest either, for it passes by the city of Bhopál through the old centre of the Buddhist faith at Bhilsa. The caves of Ellora and Ajanta, most remarkable of all surviving evidences of the former vitality of Buddhism in India (which, to this day, elsewhere numbers more votaries than any other religion in the world) are reached from the station of Nandgaon on the G.I.P. railway, about half-way to Itarsi from Bombay.

It is not to matters of antiquarian interest only that the G.I.P. (Great Indian Peninsula) railway owes its wide reputation amongst railway systems. It is its service to the country as the carrier of mails, its connection with Calcutta across the width of the Indian continent by linking with the East Indian line at Allahabad, that makes it great. A few hours' run carries one from the sea coast up through the winding passage of the Gháts on to the central plateau. Once at this elevation the line never descends again till, after crossing the Narbada and passing Jubbulpore, it drops by easy gradients into the Gangetic plain at Allahabad. Although there is a shorter and more direct route connecting Bombay and Calcutta than this—one which is shorter by about 125 miles, and which does not touch Allahabad—no time is gained by making use of it. The mails at present invariably follow the Allahabad route, and the direct line *viâ* Nagpur, Bilaspur, and Assensole is a commercial line only.

It is by this latter line that a traveller through India can gain the most comprehensive idea as to what is meant by Indian jungle. Hour after hour he will be shut in by close and occasionally dense forest of undergrown trees which never rise to the magnificence of European or American forest growth, but which are nevertheless of considerable commercial value. The direct Nagpur route to Calcutta is about 1275 miles in length—the Jubbulpore-Allahabad route is 1400 miles.

The lines from Bombay across Southern India to Masulipatam and Madras need little description. Up the Bor Ghát and as far as Kalian (33 miles) all lines eastward from Bombay follow the same track. From Kalian the Madras lines diverge and run south-east past the hill sanatarium of Matherán through Karli to Poona. Poona is 120 miles from Bombay. At Wadi, which is nearly central between the east and west coasts, there is a branch line to Haidarabad and Masulipatam, but the G.I.P. continues south-east to Raichur where the Madras line meets it. Madras is 793 miles from Bombay.

Three or four great cities claim our attention in this part of India, and they are cities as diverse in physical characteristics as in geographical surroundings. They have this in common: they are all hot. Between the cities of Bombay and Madras there is little to choose in the matter of temperature. The enervating climate of Bombay (which averages about 80° F.) is perhaps a trifle more enervating than that of Madras, which includes a double monsoon. Bombay possesses a magnificent harbour set amidst such lovely surroundings as to rival even the charms of Trincomali in Ceylon, or of Sydney in Australia. It might almost be compared to that of Rio de Janeiro in South America. Bombay is the greatest trade centre in India, for it gathers together the ends of all the great railway systems except that of the north-west. It is the funnel through which commerce pours from India to the sea.

Madras possesses no natural harbour whatsoever, and it is still a surprise that, before the construction of artificial works Madras should have risen to the position of a great coast port. But as we have already pointed out, there is no harbour in the east coast of India between Ceylon and Orissa. It cannot be said of Madras that it is the natural outlet of a trade basin extending over an area that has any parallel to that of Bombay; but it does, on the other hand, tap a very large canal system which reaches both north and south.

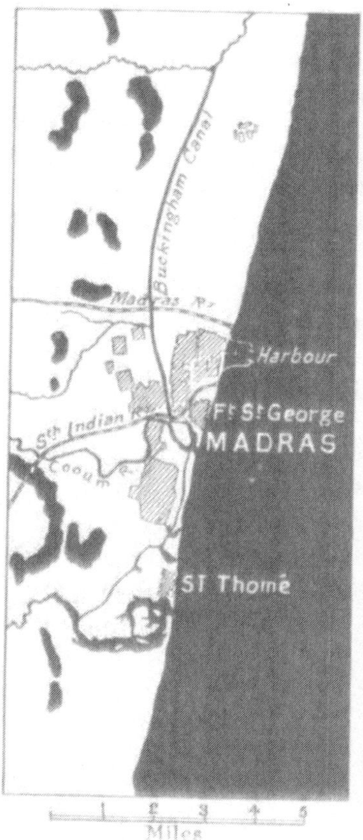


FIG. 95.—The Port of Madras

We have already referred to the marked architectural ugliness of Calcutta, an ugliness which is redeemed only by such charm as may be gained by viewing the town from a distance across the width of the central "maidán," when there may be detected a certain spirit of beauty which is never absent even from the flattest of river scenery. In Bombay, on the other hand, it is worth while to arrest a traveller's attention in order to assure him that never elsewhere in India will he behold a city so typical of oriental life, and so teeming with oriental colour. Every corner of that city, even to the very slums, possesses the charm of variety. A dirty picturesqueness (which is almost Italian) pervades most of the back premises of Bombay; Portuguese design is still apparent in the quaint mouldings and devices which adorn the houses in many of the streets, though the Portuguese have not been there since the early part of the eighteenth century, when they were ejected by the Mahrattas.

Every race and nation in the East is represented in the streets of Bombay; every shade of colour and of complexion, from blackest negro to the "café au lait" of the Parsi woman, is there set off by an array of positive hues in dress such as would make a colour theorist shudder were it proposed as an abstract study. Combined, the effect is brilliant beyond measure. It is worth a journey to Bombay to see what a Parsi girl will dare in the matter of dress. A Bombay crowd is as brilliant, as lively, and as interesting as a Calcutta crowd is ugly and depressing. Nor is the variety and beauty of the city streets discounted by the public erections of Government. It would be hard to find a more impressive array of buildings than those which face Back Bay and stretch away to Malabar Hill.

It is well that the eastward voyager should be introduced at starting to a city adorned with architecture which is worthy of the Government of an Indian Empire, for his impressions may possibly last. They have but little chance of being renewed as he travels farther eastward.

As a concession to statistical geography it may be mentioned that Bombay is an island which includes an area of about 22 square miles. The suburbs of the city occupy about 4 square miles, and into this space a population of nearly one million is squeezed. Little wonder that cholera is endemic, and that plague threatens to imitate cholera. From the island of Bombay the lines of rail are carried by causeways over the narrow channel which separates the island from the larger island of Salsette, and from Salsette they pass to the mainland by other causeways.

The points of interest which surround Bombay are innumerable, but for a catalogue of them the reader is referred to that excellent work—"Murray's Handbook of India."

Madras has nothing of the cosmopolitan air of Bombay. It is essentially Indian and Madrasi, and its charms (for it has many of them) lie chiefly in the local colouring which pervades it. There is no such wild and restless surf beating on any shelving beach as that of

Madras; no sea-breezes sighing amongst casuarina trees such as those which put daily life into the heat-worn European sojourners in Madras. It is not so very long since the days when the voyager was cast headlong from a masulah boat on to the shore. He can now step out of his ship on to a pier. Madras is notable for the "black town" (or native quarter), for its bright red streets, and for the broad avenues which connect the

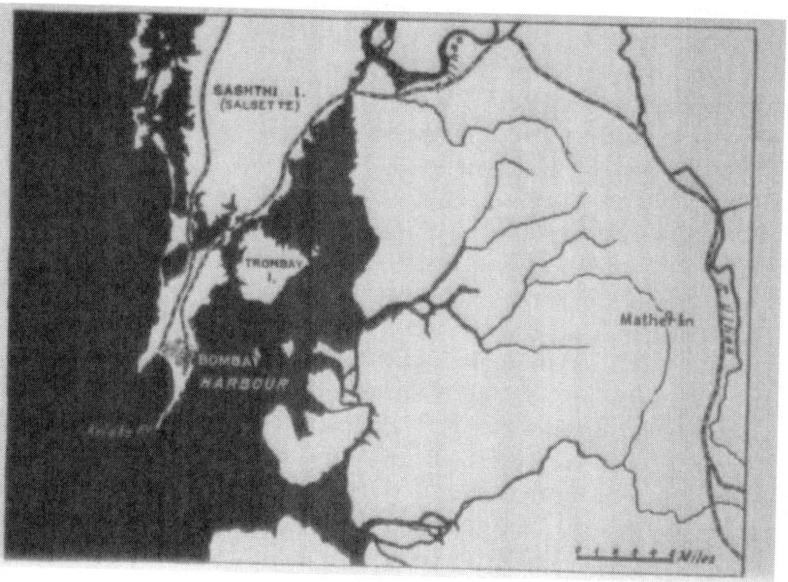


FIG. 96.—The Port of Bombay.

city with the European quarters; for its "marina" or sea promenade, and, above all, for its early association with the apostle St. Thomas, who is supposed (on authority which Sir W. Hunter shows to be quite untrustworthy) to have been martyred near the hill which now bears his name, about the year A.D. 68.

About equi-distant from Bombay and Madras, but edging towards the east coast, is the great native state capital Haidarabad. In climate and in surroundings this city and the overgrown series of military cantonments which lie beyond it does not differ largely from Poona and Bangalore. They are all in the central highlands ; high enough (about 2000 feet to 3000 feet above sea) to preserve them from the fierce heat of the low-lying plains, but still in all the general characteristics of their environment belonging to the plains and not to the hills. Haidarabad is important for nothing except its position as the capital of the largest native state in India, and the headquarters of an overgrown native army of 40,000 men (recruited chiefly from the northern borderland and from Southern Arabia), which is considered necessary to preserve the dignity and authority of the Nizam. This army is a picturesque assemblage of half-disciplined troops, reviving the traditions of a bygone age, and it may be seen to best advantage on the 10th day of the feast of the Moharram (for Haidarabad is a Hindu state governed by Muhammadans), when the procession called the Langar takes place. The admixture of Afghan and Pathán ruffianism with gaily-clad Arab soldiery is interestingly suggestive of the nature of those armies of the past which used to strike terror into the heart of the agricultural population of India, and which would do so again instantly were our rule withdrawn.

To keep check on this riotous force a brigade of British and native troops is cantoned at Sikandarabad, a few miles north of Haidarabad, and a special contingent (paid for out of the revenues of the Berars) of about 7000 men, called the Haidarabad contingent,[1] is maintained with its headquarters at Bolárum hard by for the same purpose.

Poona and Bangalore (which are now directly connected by the Southern Maratha railway) belong to the Sanatoria of India, which are elsewhere described. The connection is of geographical interest because it introduces us to the western districts of India, and touches the Portuguese settlement of Goa.

Sixty-eight miles from Poona and about 187 from Bombay is the little station of Wathar on the Southern Maratha line, from whence a carriage drive may be taken to Mahableshwar. This is a favourite resort of

[1] Now part of the regular Indian army.

Bombay residents in the months of October and November, when the dying efforts of the south-west monsoon leave the washed-out plateau fit for habitation. It is not till the end of the rains that it is possible to live there. Passing Belgaum (which is of some historic account, and a military station) at 244 miles from Poona the line runs to a junction with the West of India Portuguese railway at the roadside station of Castle Rock, 292 miles from Poona. Here we have an interesting item in the statistical list of Indian railways, and a curious little line on its own account. The West of India Portuguese railway, which runs to a terminus at the coast at Marmagoa (the seaport of Goa), is 51 miles long, and runs through ten tunnels cut out of solid rock in the course of the first 12 miles. Some of these tunnels are of considerable length. Like the great G.I.P. it has to negotiate the Western Gháts, and like it also passes through magnificent scenery. But here the parallel ends, for the G.I.P. only ascends the Gháts to gather in connecting links with nearly all the great lines of India, whilst the Portuguese line begins on the top of the Gháts and ends at the sea. It is a matter of small surprise then that its working expenses are out of all proportion to its earnings, and that it should figure on the statistical list as the only line in India whose net earnings are a minus (and a considerable minus) quantity.

There are two Goas, the old Goa, and the new. Old Goa derives its special interest from the fact that it is a fallen monument of European greatness, the disintegrating relic of a great Christian community. Founded in 1510 by Albuquerque, it became the wealthiest city in all India by the middle of the sixteenth century. Here St. Francis Xavier achieved a success in Christian missionary enterprise such as has never been equalled since; though it is but just to remember that Portuguese missionary methods are not our methods; and here today in the midst of ruins so complete that "the stranger approaches it unawares, and drives into its midst unconscious that he is traversing streets," there are still a group of magnificent churches in a state of perfect preservation. But old Goa has long since subsided as an inhabited city, and the Goanese "boys," with names of Portuguese nobility, so well known as the best of all cooks and waiters throughout India, come from the new town of Panjim. They are mostly the descendants of Hindus converted by Jesuits. It is indeed impossible to imagine that they can claim descent from those heroes of old who navigated unknown seas and fought Arabs, Turks, and Indian Muhammadans wherever they met them.

The network of Indian railways is gradually extending all over the continent, and it is already so complete in those parts that are commercially important that it would be impossible to enumerate the many different lines that have sprung into existence within the last quarter of a century. Vast as has been their commercial success, and important as is their influence in those civilising processes which are to weld the masses of the people of India into a homogeneous nationality by the application of an universal pressure born of self-interest, it should never be forgotten that Indian railways serve two purposes. The one purpose is civil and the other military, and the interests of the two are less easily separated than most Englishmen imagine. The same line of metal which serves to carry tons of wheat and cotton to our coast towns for export, serves also to move thousands of soldiers into a field of action which may be all-important to the interests of those who grow the wheat and the cotton; and it is in this connection chiefly that the great discussion arose, which was not inaptly called the "battle of the gauges."

If we look at the map we shall see at a glance that of the two great ports of India on the western coast, Bombay and Karachi, Bombay serves the commercial turn of India, and Karachi the military. It is inconceivable that so long as England dominates the sea, her power in India can ever be seriously threatened from any other quarter than the North-West. It is on the North-West frontier that in time of danger troops would certainly be massed. Now Bombay would be largely hampered in assisting in this process by the break of gauge that occurs in Rajputana, involving delays in the transfer of men and material, not from one line to another, but from one set of conveyances to another. It was this danger—a danger which has been greatly lessened by the opening of the midland line connecting the G.I.P. with Delhi and Lahore—which influenced those who opposed the introduction of the narrow gauge construction. Troops from Bombay and Western India could now be moved to the extreme North-West without disjointing the internal traffic, and paralysing the commercial intercourse of Central India; but the extreme North-West is not the only part of our frontier which is important strategically in the interests of India's security, possibly not even the most important part. For the Baluchistan section of the frontier, for the defence of Quetta, or for advance on Kandahar, Karachi is the only port of debarkation, and the North-Western line with the Quetta extensions the only line of communication. Great as are modern improvements in the harbour works at Karachi (into the development of which it is not necessary to enter), it must be remembered that its entrance channel is extremely narrow, that it is kept open with difficulty, and might be easily closed. And much the same might be said for the double line of approach to Quetta from the Indus—the line of the Mushkáf and that of the Harnai. They are both of them lines subject to periodic interruption from landslips or from floods, just as surely as are all other mountain lines whatsoever. Moreover, between Sibi, at the foot of the Baluch hills, and Sukkur on the Indus, there is but one single line (liable to periodic flooding from the Indus overflow) to feed both. On the maintenance of the Karachi harbour channel and this single line then, the possibility of rapid concentration of troops and material appears to depend, and this leads us to the last section of our study of the railway geography of India—the question of strategic extensions.

Although we may call them strategic, we may remember that the whole North-West system was strategic only in the first instance, but that it has developed a most surprising commercial value. It is probable that every line on our frontier that tended either to facilitate traffic, between two great centres of strategy and com-

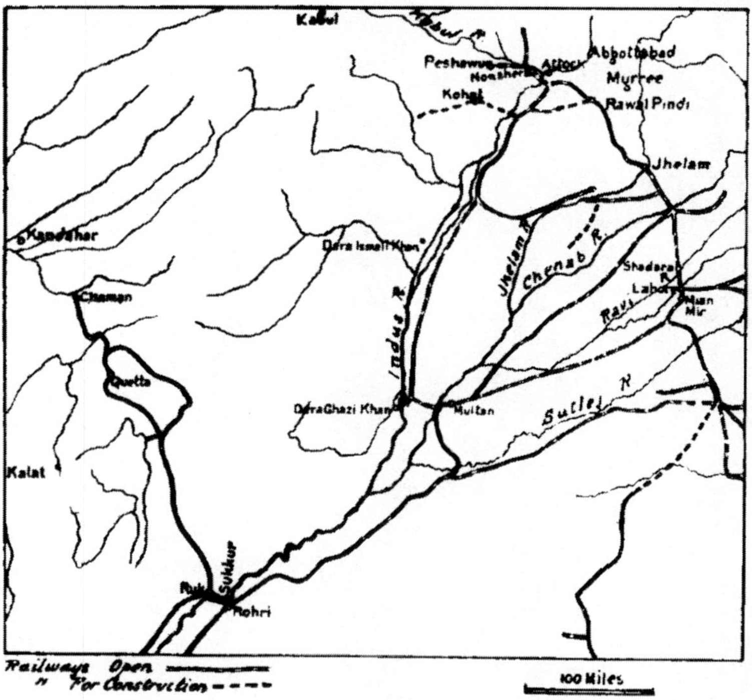


FIG. 97.—North-Western Railway System.

merce, or to push their way towards the great Central Asian marts, would inevitably follow what has become the rule of the North-West system (*i.e.* provide for strategy first and commerce afterwards) if the cost of construction was not absolutely prohibitive. Further into the financial aspect of the question this is no place to enter, but no suggestion here made as to possible extension is made without an amount of local knowledge which justifies us in maintaining the cost would probably *not* be prohibitive. The most obvious from the strategic point of view is the connection between Palanpur, or Decca, on the Rajputana line, with Sukkur on the Indus. This would at once bring all Western India into direct connection with Karachi and Baluchistan. But 300 miles of desert is not to be lightly negotiated. It was not easily spanned, even in Egypt; and Southern Sind would present far more difficulties than Egypt. Still there is every probability that this line will finally stand the test of construction, although it is possible that commercial views may indicate Haidarabad in Sind, rather than Sukkur, as the first point in the Indus Valley to be brought into direct connection with Bombay.

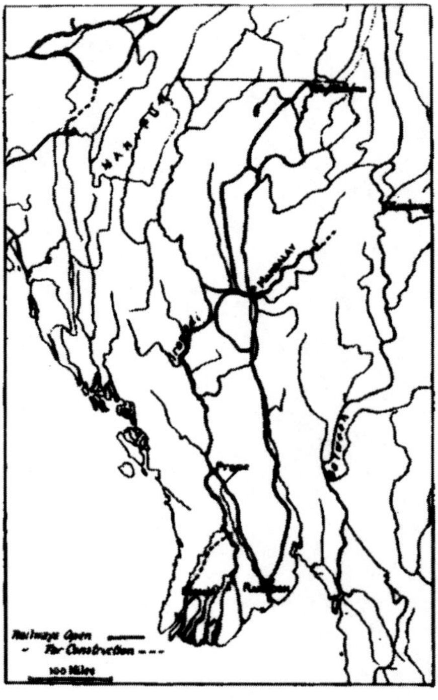

Fig. 98.—Burma Railways.

Equally obvious is the value of direct communication by rail between Lahore and Quetta, for which the long line of the Zhob Valley, debouching into the Indus plain at the mouth of the Gomal River, gives opportunity. Only in this way can we obtain a second line of approach to our defensive position in Baluchistan, or an alternative to the low level railway which crosses the Indus flats between Sukkur and Sibi. I have already alluded to the Kandahar-Herat extension as forming the shortest, simplest, and cheapest overland connection with Europe. Strategic reasons, however (if not commercial ones), will probably long stand in the way of the construction of this obvious link in a great international system.

Far more to our purpose it would be to extend westwards from Quetta through the Helmund desert to Seistán, and thus secure an important and rapidly increasing trade which the construction of the new caravan route has opened up, whilst at the same time it might very easily prove to be almost imperative that we should have the power of concentrating troops in that direction. It will not be long before the question of the Nushki-Kharán extension will reach an acute stage, and will demand a definite answer.

From Peshawur to Kabul there is a well-known and much-traversed road, down which there already pours a very considerable Indian trade; nor can there be any reasonable doubt that this road will be replaced by a railway ere many decades have passed. Afghan conservatism, like that of China, cannot last for ever. This is the most important, both on commercial and strategic grounds, of any future railway project connected with India west of Burma.

Much has been written, and much has been said, about the connection between Calcutta and Mandalay. The value of it needs no insistence; but the difficulty of it is great, and the cost would be excessive. From the present northern terminus of the Burma state railway at Myitkyina (Michina), the valley of the Irawadi stretches northward for 150 miles in comparatively open plain. At the end of the 150 miles lies nothing but primeval forest and an unmapped country—but at this point it would not be much more than 50 miles from the head of the Assam system west of it, and separated from it by a wild hill country, through which, however, a possible connecting line has already been traced. The connection no doubt will ultimately become a *fait accompli*, either by the route indicated or by way of Silchar and Manipur.

Railway statistics are to be found *in extenso* in the pages of the Statistical Reports relating to India, and in a more condensed form in the recent authoritative writings in such works as the *Ency. Brit.* Such reports speak for themselves. The beginning of the twentieth century has seen considerable extensions of railway traffic within the borders of British India, but no very great developments in the borderland, where in some directions (between Mandalay and the Kunlón ferry, for instance) the recent period has been one rather of retrogression than otherwise. In the direction of Seistán, the Quetta-Nushki extension should give a certain impetus to a slackening trade ; but it is not a short projection of the line from the Indian system here and there which will produce any radical effect in improving trade communications. A time will come (it may not be far off) when the necessity of an agreement with Russia will be acknowledged as the only means of opening up the overland avenues of approach to India from the west, and with a definite policy of peaceful intercommunication there will come such a vast impulse to railway traffic as could be achieved by no other projected line in the world.

# INDIA, GEOLOGICAL.

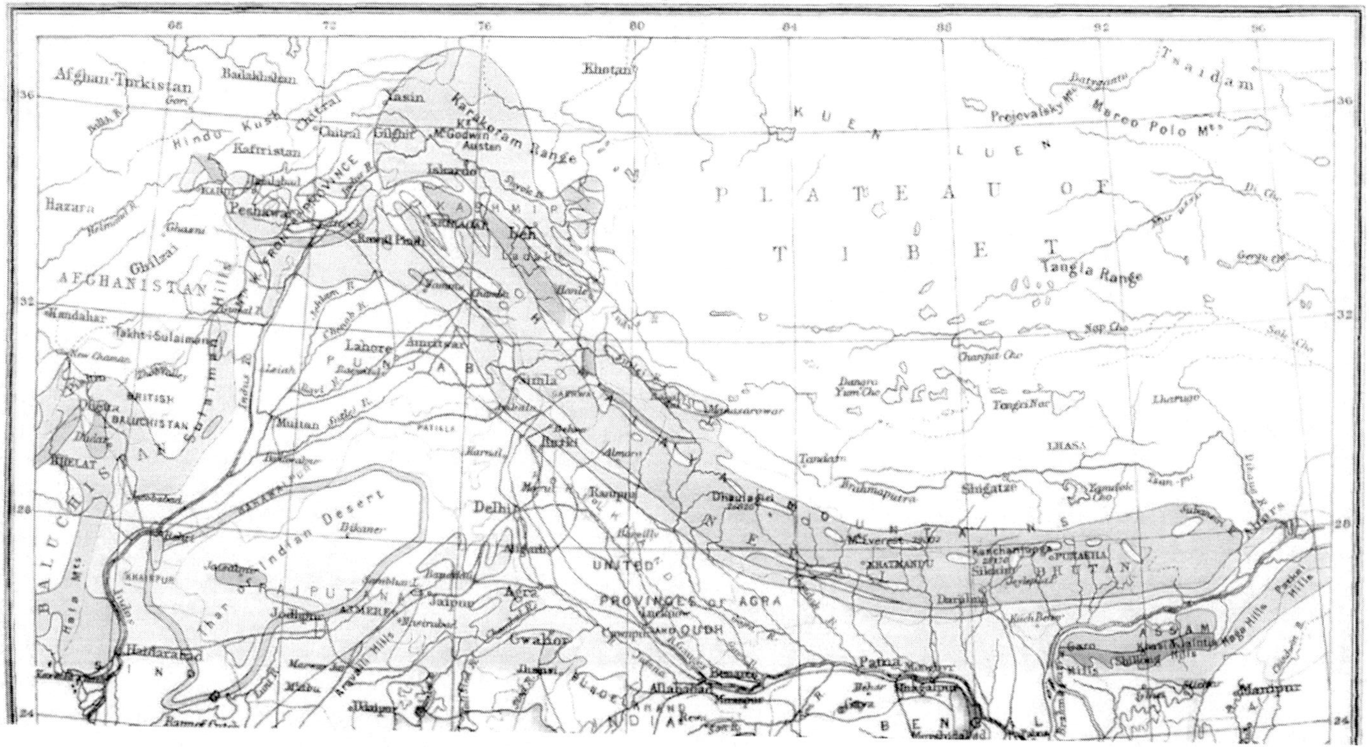

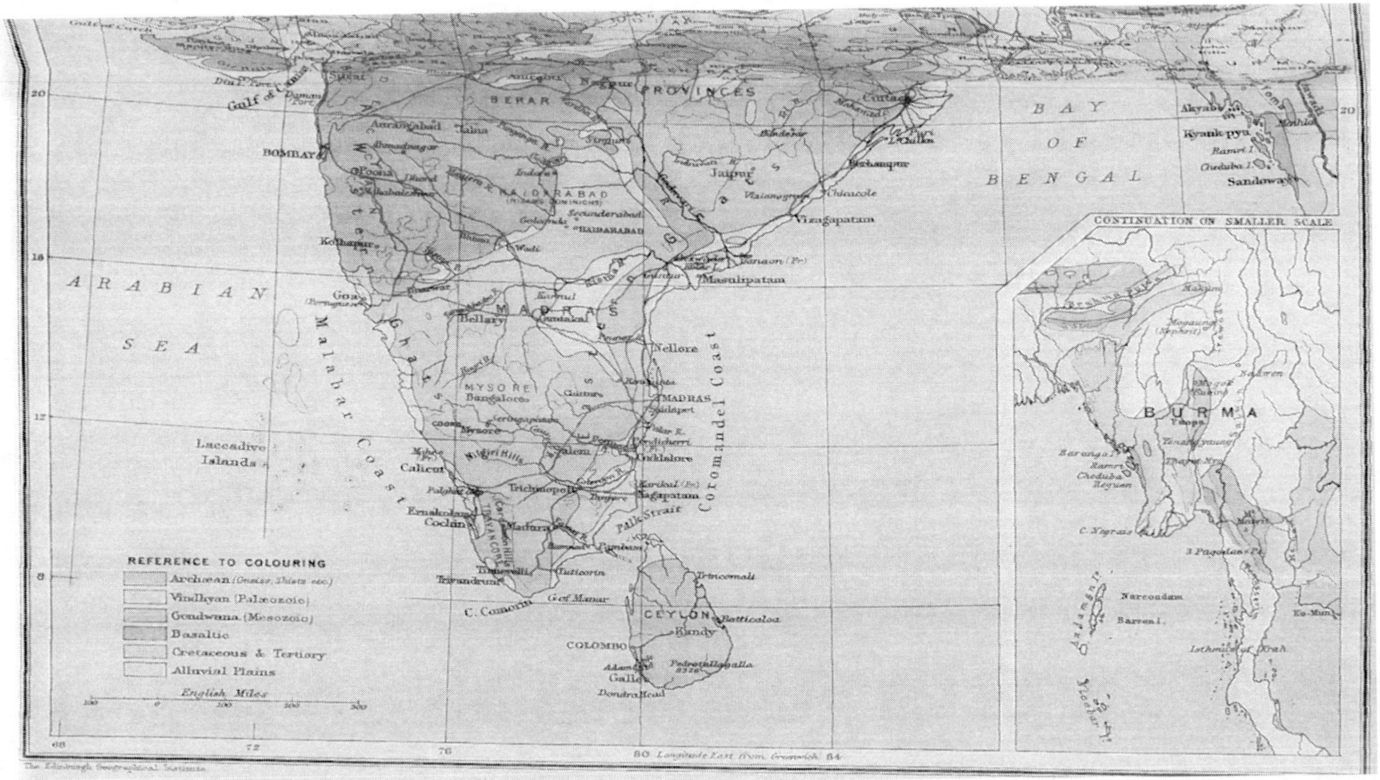

BERAR
PROVINCES
BOMBAY
Aurangabad
Poona
Kolhapur
Goa
Bellary
MADRAS
MYSORE
Bangalore
Mysore
Calicut
Cochin
Trivandrum
Tinnevelli
Madura
Trichinopoli
Salem
Cuddalore
Nellore
Masulipatam
Vizagapatam
Berhampur
Cuttack
Jaipur
Secunderabad
HAIDARABAD
Kurnul
Nagapatam
Tuticorin
Palk Strait
G. of Manar
C. Comorin
CEYLON
COLOMBO
Kandy
Trincomali
Batticaloa
Galle
Dondra Head
Gulf of Cambay
ARABIAN SEA
Laccadive Islands
Malabar Coast
Coromandel Coast
BAY OF BENGAL
Akyab
Kyauk-pyu
Ramri I.
Cheduba I.
Sandoway
CONTINUATION ON SMALLER SCALE
BURMA
C. Negrais
Narcondam
Barren I.
REFERENCE TO COLOURING
Archean (Gneiss, Schists etc.)
Vindhyan (Palæozoic)
Gondwana (Mesozoic)
Basaltic
Cretaceous & Tertiary
Alluvial Plains
English Miles
0
100
200
300
20
16
12
8
68
72
76
80 Longitude East from Greenwich 84
The Edinburgh Geographical Institute

# CHAPTER XI

## MINERALS

FAR into the field of Indian economic geology it is of course impossible to enter. We can only skirt round the edge of it, and note the geographical distribution of a few of the most important of these mineral productions which from earliest history have made India famous, and Indian trade the desire of the nations. Recent examination of the gold-bearing fields of the peninsula only serve to prove that we know but little more about them than was known many centuries ago. Ancient mines have been driven through the upper strata of the soil in some parts of India to an extent which renders many acres of land analogous to a huge rabbit warren. Sometimes shafts are sunk straight and deep through beds of quartz, with sides so truly vertical that it is difficult to conceive what the class of instruments may have been with which they were constructed.

Gold and precious stones were accumulated and hoarded in India from so early a time that it is probable that for very many centuries of the world's existence India was regarded as the only source of such treasures. We are now told that the ophir of Solomon was in Western India, chiefly for the reason that it is associated with ivory and apes and peacocks as articles of commerce. However that may be, it is in connection with precious metals and precious stones that ancient history and tradition chiefly concern themselves with the mineral wealth of India. The far more valuable economic products, such as coal and salt, created no demand in Old Testament days. The star of India's natural wealth has paled in later years before the magnificence of gold finds in Australia, in

Africa, and in Alaska, against which India never has competed, and never could compete.

There is little mineral exportation from India now. Such wealth as is acquired direct from the rocks of which her soil is composed, is valuable chiefly for purposes of internal development, and in this capacity its value can hardly be over-estimated. The peninsula of India is infinitely old, older than the Himalayas, though possibly not so old as Ceylon. It is interesting to reflect that there was a time when the Himalayas were not—when the crystalline rocks which form the axis and backbone of that mighty mass of mountains had not as yet protruded themselves above the general level of the world's surface, whilst they remained crushed beneath the stratified bed of an indefinite ocean. Since they were upheaved, and the more recent strata above them has been washed down southwards towards the plains of the peninsula carrying with them many of the mineral deposits of the original crystalline matrix, other vast variations in Indian geography have occurred which have all tended to distribute the wealth of the ancient beds into modern channels. There was probably a time when the Brahmaputra, instead of making its placid way to the Bay of Bengal, swept round the base of the Himalayas right across India, and possibly joined the Indus before it found the sea. This was in days when its banks were lined with a tropical jungle and gigantic mammals stalked through the land and left their bones in the Siwalik system of recent deposits. The delta land of Lower Bengal is all comparatively new. It covers an area of 55,000 square miles of alluvial deposit, 450 feet deep, and it is growing still. Successive deltas have formed south of the Khasia Hills, and have in turn been submerged beneath fresh deltas of alluvium washed down from the mountains.

Throughout the alluvial formations of the Indo-Gangetic basin we may search in vain for that mineral wealth which only lies embedded in ancient rock formations; but some of it (gold, for instance, and precious stones) may be found (and is indeed chiefly found) in the detritus washed from the Himalayas, or from the old rock formations of Central India, and is scattered amongst recent deposits or in river beds.

Geographically, the old geological formations of Central and Southern India are cut off from the elevated regions that lie to the north and west by the broad alluvial basin of the Indo-Gangetic plain, which is fringed on the far side by a series of recent deposits forming the foot-hills of the higher ranges of older formation. Amongst these the Siwaliks are the best known, and they are the most interesting because of the amount of palæozoic remains which they contain ; but they are not in themselves the seat or origin of any great mineral wealth. The Siwaliks usually occur as minor ranges flanking main watersheds, parted by a broad valley from the lower spurs of the mountains which they overlie geologically, and in this form they are easily accessible and readily recognised.

Looking southward from the Himalayan station of Mussoorie across the chequered blue and yellow expanse of the valley of Dehra (usually called Dehra Dún) the Siwaliks appear as a serrated ridge, thickly clad with pines, which may be traced distinctly as far as the eye can reach eastwards and westwards against the faint blue of the distant plains some thousand of feet below them. Very different indeed is the same formation when viewed from the summit of the Takht-i-Suliman Mountain on the trans-Indus frontier, nearly opposite the station of Dera Ismail Khan.

Looking eastwards, here, towards the Indus, there is a wonderful geological panorama spread outward. There is no vegetation except such as scantily clothes the summit of the magnificent pile of coral limestone rocks on which one stands, just a scattered sprinkling of weird and wintry junipers clustering round the peak of Kaisargarh which towers over the surrounding cliffs at a height of 11,300 feet above sea-level. On the terraces at the foot of the Kaisargarh peak, lying between it and the eastern ridge of the mountain (but parted therefrom by the terrific precipices of a gulley which splits its northern end and drops sheer to

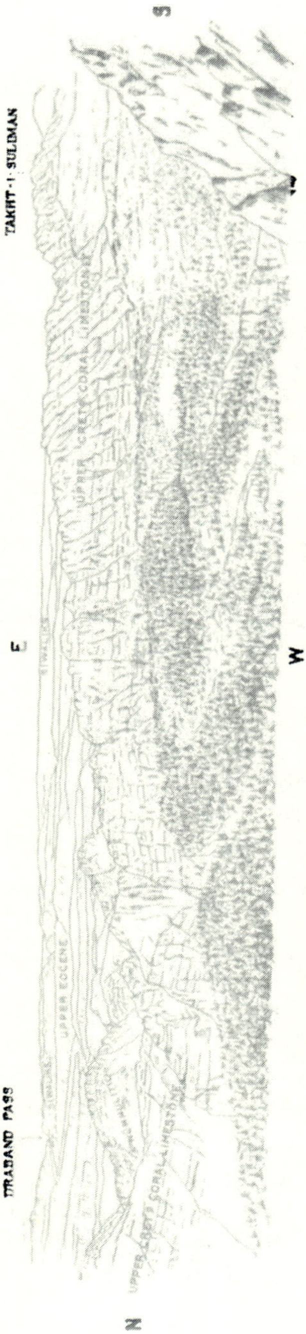


FIG. 99.—Geological Panorama from the Kaisargarh, by Major C. L. Griesbach, C.I.E.

the bed of the Draband torrent 5000 feet below), the chilghosa (edible pine) grows. The eastern and western ridges are connected at one point by the plain which is rifted by these gullies to the north and south, and which is besprinkled with huge masses of displaced limestone, but easily traversable. From the summit of the Kaisargarh, looking beyond the scarred cliffs of coral limestone which form the eastern ridge of the mountain, and over a secondary range of distorted and twisted nummulitic rock, the long flat edges of a whole series of ridges, narrow backed and serrated, with scarped sides facing west and long flat spurs sloping east towards the Indus plains, tier after tier, and range upon range, bleak, barren, and desolate, form a "middle distance," whose enchantment is of a most weird and fantastic character. Far away the faint blue meeting of earth and sky is marked by the dim black horizontal line of the Indus fringe of trees. Here and there the band of serrated ridges (of which the axis is nearly north and south, parallel to the axis of the great central upheaval of the Takht-i-Suliman Mountain) is broken across by the drainage from the Baluch and Afghan highlands which lie behind to the west, and the passage of these torrents through the successive gates of the hills can be very clearly traced as ridge after ridge is split asunder to let the waters pass. Nearest of these frontier ridges, beyond the nummulitic rocks, are those of eocene formation, and farthest, just breaking the expanse of the plains, are the "recent" Siwaliks. Here, on the frontier, they are represented by hard conglomerates, and a stiff mixture of clay and rounded boulders which is very difficult to deal with in matters requiring engineering skill. In general terms this represents the character of the western frontier geological conditions, and consequently nothing is to be looked for on the frontier which might be of economic value such as those minerals possess which, emanating originally from crystalline rocks, are washed down in river-beds or found in recent accumulations of detritus.

Neither is coal to be found in paying quantities on our frontier, although coal in India is found associated with far more recent deposits than is generally the case in England. With the exception of the coal which is worked on the Sind frontier, about Sharigh and Khost (stations on the Sind-Peshin railway), and which is locally useful for consumption in Quetta after passing through a process of compression, but which has practically no market beyond that which is afforded by the local railways and commissariat, there is no mineral trade on our frontier which is worth investigation. Petroleum exists on the Harnai line of the Sind-Peshin railway, but has proved to be deficient in quantity, and is, I believe, no longer regarded as a profitable field for investment.

A general inquiry into all the mineral resources of India is far beyond the scope of this work, but the following notes on the geographical distribution of a few of them may be usefully included as an illustration of the gradual process of economic development which has attended our rule in the country. Whatever is dug out of the bowels of the earth, or is found deposited on its surface, in India, may be said to exist for purposes of internal consumption, with the notable exception of its precious stones, and possibly of saltpetre. India does not supply the world with coal, or iron, or gold, or silver. The value of her imported metals largely exceeds her exports, and even in the matter of treasure only about half as much gold, and about one-third as much silver found its way out of India, as is represented in the list of imports of 1896–97. Owing, no doubt, to Government legislation the import of silver has largely decreased during the last few years, and there have been years (1892–93 and 1894–95) when the export of gold was four or five times the value of the imports.

Of all developments of mineral resources that which has occurred in coal is perhaps the most striking and the most satisfactory. So great has been the late growth of the Indian coal traffic as to create a demand for extension of existing means of railway conveyance on the East Indian line. Last year (1897) all records were surpassed; the total increase in the value of the traffic on that one line being upwards of one million (expressed in the conventional ten rupees unit), and the increase in earnings being 21 per cent. This is sufficient to assure us that we may look to Indian coalfields in confidence that they will eventually meet the full demands of India without English importations. The output of Indian coals last year reached four million tons, and the percentage in consumption of Indian coal has as largely increased as that of English coal has diminished. The quality of Indian coal varies very greatly, the best being that obtained from the Karhabari colliery in Bengal, and this coal is adopted to give the standard of comparison for other varieties.

The geological age of the carboniferous strata in India is very much younger than that of English measures; the best coal measures being found between the permian and lower jurassic formations within the area of the peninsula; but coal occurs in younger deposits beyond peninsular limits, *i.e.* in Sind, Afghanistan, Assam, and Burma. Although the coal usually found in the newer deposits does not as a rule exist in quantities sufficient to be of any economic value, exceptions to the rule are to be found, notably in Assam and Burma.

The chief coal bearing areas of India are as follows:—

1. The basin of the Godavari River.
2. The basin of the Són River.
3. Orissa.
4. Assam.
5. The basin of the Narbada River.
6. Damuda.
7. Rajmahal.

Thus it will appear that the whole coal bearing area (which may be reckoned at about 30,000 square miles) lies more or less in the central districts of the peninsula, and chiefly in the Central Provinces. Throughout this extent of possible field for coal mining there are scattered about a dozen collieries, a number which may be largely increased when railway communication is further developed. Although the provinces of Madras have been searched diligently, and there have arisen many reports of coal discoveries, and much correspondence has resulted therefrom, the net result may be expressed as correspondence only. There are no important workable seams in Madras. In Haidarabad one colliery (the Singareni) has risen to importance. This is situated in the Godavari basin to the east of Haidarabad, and is associated with the same group of rocks (Kamthis, Talchirs, &c.) as predominate in connection with all the coalfields in the peninsular area. The Singareni mines produce about 1000 tons per diem. The Orissa province

FIG. 100.—Coal Distribution.

(*i.e.* the basin of the Mahanadi) contains a comparatively large area of inferior coal measures, none of which are profitably worked at present.

The largest coalfields of India exist in Bengal, and the most important colliery is that of Karhabari, in the Hazaribagh district, about 200 miles from Calcutta. This, with the Ranigange mines (120 miles from Calcutta), furnishes the East Indian railway with all its coal. The Karhabari and Serampur collieries between them put out 450,000 tons of coal in 1897. Ranigange is probably the largest and most important of all coal areas in India, covering 500 square miles. Coal has been worked here for more than a century. It constitutes the "Black Country" of India, and the supply seems to be practically inexhaustible.

The Central Provinces possess two important collieries in Warora (near Chanda), south of Nagpur in the Godavari basin, and Mohpani, which is 95 miles south-west of Jabalpur, in the Narbada basin. The latter is a comparatively small field which, in 1879, turned out only 12,400 tons. It has now risen to 20,000 tons, but the mine is chiefly interesting from the nature of the galleries, which open on to the face of a cliff. The Warora mine put out 111,600 tons last year. The coal mines of the Salt range, in the Punjab, which are worked from an altitude of nearly 2000 feet above sea-level, are not productive of a very good class of coal, but the 90,000 tons of coal which they can produce per annum are exceedingly valuable to the N.-W. Railway.

The Umaria colliery, which, like the Warora, is worked by Government, is a valuable resource for the Indian Midland and the Great Indian Peninsula railways. Its output is 124,000. In Assam there are five or six coalfields in the valley of the Brahmaputra. The coal differs from that of the peninsula in possessing a homogeneous structure, and is of distinctly superior quality. The Tikak and Ledo mines put out 171,000 tons last year, a large contribution to the total value of the coal industry to India. In Burma there are coal measures of variable quality in nearly every district of the province. For more than fifty years attention has been bestowed on the seams that are found in Arakan, Tenasserim, Pegu, and Upper Burma, but without any great profit to explorers. A colliery has been established at Letkonbin (or Lek-ope-bin) in Upper Burma which is within 5 miles of the Irawadi, and which will certainly prove to be of commercial value; but the flooding of the mines reduced the output from 23,000 tons in 1896 to 10,000 last year. New workings have now been commenced, and a superior quality of coal is being raised.

But Burma (especially Upper Burma) must be regarded at present as in the initial stages of development so far as coal possibilities are concerned, and the value of workable seams which will undoubtedly be found in future must largely depend on facilities of transport and railway extension.

It is curious that in the matter of salt, as of coal-supply, India, although possessed of large resources, is still dependent to a certain extent on importation. Cheshire salt still supplies the local markets in Bengal, although the production of salt by the evaporation of sea water is largely carried on along the coast districts of Eastern India. Of all the mineral productions of India that of salt is of greatest economic importance. The revenue derived from salt amounts to nearly eight millions per annum, and the tax imposed upon salt is the only tax which directly affects the masses of the people of India. Special legislation in order to equalise this tax, and to insure a fair distribution of it throughout the length and breadth of British dominions, has been constantly necessary. There was a time (Lord Lytton's time) when a huge artificial barrier stretched through India and offered a stout physical obstacle to trade and traffic of all sorts in the interest of the salt duties. This, happily, has been removed, and no artificial salt barriers of any great extent now exist; but changes are constantly necessary in the application of Government monopolies to meet the constant changes in the sources of supply, and the salt tax, equitable and necessary though it may be, will always be a fruitful theme for grievance-mongers anxious to saddle Government with the responsibility of local disturbances. The tax now amounts to Rs.2½ per maund for India; *i.e* about one-halfpenny per pound, and to one rupee for Burma—less than a farthing per pound. At these rates its value to Indian revenues is maintained at from seven million to eight million per annum, the consumption apparently varying but little from year to year.

There are three distinct sources of salt-supply in India—*i.e.* sea water evaporation, salt lakes, and salt mines. Along the coast of Madras salt is obtained from the sea by evaporation in shallow pans, which are prepared on the coast districts for this purpose as soon as the rainy season is over. These pans are about two-thirds of an acre in extent, and require nearly a month of preparation by the introduction of a small amount of sea water and a constant succession of "puddling," or treading down processes, until the floor is ready to receive the highly condensed brine which is finally run in for evaporation. Salt is manufactured in a similar way near Karachi, and on the Orissa sea border, but not generally on the western coast of India. It is a curious fact that there is a large trade in salted fish from the coast of Makrán to the Malabar coast provinces, where one would naturally suppose that salt fish would be a drug in the market, but where the process of salting is expensive.

FIG. 101.

In Rajputana there exists a series of salt lakes, of which that of Sambhar, on the borders of the native states of Jaipur and Jodhpur, is the largest and most important. The lake is about 20 miles long and 4 to 5 broad. It fills a depression in the desert, protected partly by outlying hills of the Aravalli system and partly by high sand ridges, or dunes, from being filled up by wind-blown sand, and it is not more than a few feet deep in its deepest part. No one knows what the origin of the saline deposit in this or other Rajputana lakes may be. There may be underlying beds of salt, or (and this hypothesis is favoured by geologists) there may be nothing more than those saline principles which exist in all lakes which have no outlet except by evaporation. Beyond India, in Afghanistan and Persia, there are huge depressions in the general level of the plains, which are almost invariably associated with widespread stretches of sandy soil, and which contain thick saline deposits whenever the heat of the sun's rays has dispersed the water in which they were dissolved. These salt flats appear white and shimmery in the heat haze, stretching over miles of country, and are called "kavirs" in Persia, "kaps" in Makrán, and "hamúns" in Baluchistan. But the salt of these wastes is not usually the salt of commerce. There is, however, one such depression to the north of Herat (north-west of Panjdeh), which is an apparently inexhaustible source of commercial salt to the Turkoman and Afghan districts adjoining. It should be noted, however, that even running water is usually brackish throughout these districts.

In India, when land becomes water-logged from excessive irrigation or other causes, a saline efflorescence (called Reh) frequently appears on the surface, and is absolutely destructive to all vegetation, although the irrigating water is reckoned as "sweet." The Rajputana lake supply is sweet water, but the saline sediment is pure salt, which crystallises on the surface of the black lake mud to a thickness of 8 or 10 inches in the middle of the lake. It is quite possible to cross the lake on the surface of the salt in exceptional seasons. Magnificent pink cubes of salt, of 1½ inch sides, are obtainable from the lake centre; but the salt taken out for purposes of trade is usually taken from near the edges, where the pink colour is less pronounced, this colour (which is caused by a microscopic fungus growth) being reckoned an impurity. The glistening white lake shores surrounding the central, rosy-hued expanse of crystal salt, streaked here and there with an outcrop of black slime, and backed by the rough-edged and sombre-hued Aravalli ridges, is a striking spectacle ; especially when enlivened by flights of flamingoes, whose pink and white plumage barred with black on the wings seems a special provision of Nature for purposes of adaptation to local surroundings.

The most important of all sources of Indian salt, however, is found in the north country—in the Salt ranges of the Punjab and Kohat. Here there is no doubt about its geological age. The rock-salt of Kohat, which is literally piled up in mountains and is quarried as if it were stone, is at the base of all geological sections whatsover, no older rocks being seen. It is placed in the eocene period.

Bahadur Khel is an uninteresting halting-place near a small fort and straggling village, on the road between Kohat and Bannu. After passing Bahadur Khel southward the wayfarer at once plunges into the intricacies of the Salt range which intervenes between it and Latammar, the next halting-place beyond the range. Dry, barren hills, with a very scanty and ill-grown vegetation, surround him, but the clays and marls which overlie the salt vary infinitely in colour from pale grey to bright orange, and lend a weird sort of charm to scenery, which is accentuated by the fantastic shapes of the hills. The principal quarries have been worked from time immemorial, that near Bahadur Khel having been known twelve centuries ago. The chief outcrop lies rather to the east of the pass, and from it the salt is detached in slabs by pickaxe and wedge. It is roughly chipped into squares about 12 inches by 4 thick, and in this shape transported on camels all over the trans-Indus northern borderland. Strings of camels carrying salt may be met with on the eastern Afghanistan roads. It is carried across the Safed Koh Mountains by the Zakka Khel Afridis into the Jalalabad Valley. It is taken into Swat over the Malakand, and some of it finds its way westward to Kandahar.

The Salt range of the Punjab, which extends across the Indus at Kalabagh, is another inexhaustible source of salt-supply. It is the "oldest known deposit of salt in the world. As it underlies beds containing silurian fossils, it belongs to a period not younger than Silurian;" so that it is older than the Kohat salt. The salt is here worked from mines which are relics of Sikh industry in earlier years, when the original workings were pushed forward with a reckless disregard for safety. The Punjab Salt range mines have been so repeatedly described that no further account of them is necessary here; but the enormous advantage of the systematic mining introduced under English supervision over the erratic methods adopted by the Sikh workmen of past days is well illustrated by what remains of the salt mines elsewhere.

In Kishm (an island on the Persian coast) the interior of a mountain side has literally been scooped out, until the unsupported upper layers forming the roof of the mine crashed inwards and stopped further working. The result is very curious. The interior of the mine is a large dome-shaped cavity about as large as St. Paul's, in the centre of which the débris from the roof is piled in a ragged heap. The light of the sky breaks in where the mountain side has fallen through at the apex of the roof, and lights up the striated bands of salt, coloured in tints of delicate salmon, yellow, and green, or deep maroon (differing in this from the colouring of the Kohat salt, which occurs in layers of black and deep rose colour), with a weird and chequered lustre. The central pile of débris is capped by a gigantic pillar of salt, and all around are twisted columns, pendant from the roof or growing from the floor, sometimes continuous, sometimes broken. These are the stalactites and stalagmites formed by deliquescent salt. Behind them, arranged, as it were, round the base of the walls supporting the dome, are side chapels hidden behind veils of the most delicate salt tracery that ever imitated Brussels lace; and leading outwards from the dome under the foot of the hill till it opens on to the sea-shore, is a gallery so full of the quaint devices which salt can assume that it is difficult to make one's way along—impossible, indeed, without the aid of artificial light. So much beauty of natural design compressed and multiplied in so narrow a space I have never seen elsewhere, excepting, perhaps, in the tracings made by frost upon glass in the early mornings of a hard winter. The beauty of it is past description, but the economic result of unscientific mining is only too obvious. The mine is unworkable, and has been abandoned for years. It is reported to be the abode of mountain spirits, and indeed it requires no great effort of imagination to picture them amidst such surroundings. The salt mines of the Punjab are beautiful, but all picturesque illusions vanish before clean-cut galleries and tramways and scientific engineering.

Iron is an economic product of the soil that cannot be overlooked, although it is no longer one of any great value, regarded as a contribution to the wealth of India. Local iron industry has long been superseded by iron importations, nor is it likely that it will ever revive to any great extent; yet there was a time when it found employment for thousands of workmen, and less than two centuries have passed since iron was welded and forged in a fashion quite unknown to the western world, and which is hardly surpassed even in the largest foundries of to-day. There is a mass of wrought iron weighing six tons or more which stands as a monument to the capacity of India's workers in iron near the Kutb at Delhi—a solid iron pillar measuring 23 feet 8 inches in length, with an average diameter of more than 14 inches above its base, expanding to 2 feet 4 inches below. To this day it is a puzzle to those scientists who endeavour to account for its production. Scattered through India there are to be found enormous "tòps," or cannon, relics of the forgotten skill of the past races of Indian iron-workers.

Iron ore is distributed through India in great abundance, indeed Central and Southern India may be said to be red with it. Near Salem, in Madras, "whole hills and ranges" seem to be formed of the purest variety of hæmatite, and throughout India, wherever metamorphic rocks prevail, there are to be found beds and veins of magnetite.

Iron ore exists in the Ranigange coalfields, where it is associated with certain beds of shale, and there it is reckoned to be in fuller development than anywhere else in India. The beds of laterite, which are such a conspicuous feature in most parts of the Central Provinces, is very rich in iron ore, which has been largely worked by native smelters from time immemorial ; but the primitive methods of working which remained undeveloped in India throughout the mediæval ages no longer suffice for its production at a cost which can compete with English importations, although it is a mistake to suppose that the ancient systems of working were entirely devoid of science, or guided by mere rule of thumb. Few people are aware that the once world-famous Damascus blades were fashioned from iron brought from a remote Indian village which once figured in the world as the source of the finest steel in existence, and which has since passed into obscurity.

That distinguished Indian geologist and writer, Mr. V. Ball, attributes much of the decadence of Indian iron-working to the gradually increasing want of fuel, a want which is not likely to diminish, and he considers that Indian-made iron can never again compete successfully with European production, nor does he hold out any hope in the future of a revival of the industry under European supervision. "The best that could be hoped for by any one firm having constantly the same materials to deal with, would be to be able to turn out regularly a particular quantity which would steadily reach a recognised standard, so that consumers of iron in India would probably still find it necessary to order from Europe iron having particular qualities for special purposes, to which the Indian iron was not applicable. That a single factory could ever supply all the different qualities of iron required in any one province in India is not to be expected. . .

Supposing, on the other hand, that iron factories were established in the different provinces of India, their immediate effect would probably be to lower the price of English iron, since India is one of England's largest customers, and thus the margin of profit would probably be swept away."[1] This was written more than twenty years ago, but no recent developments have occurred to modify the opinion thus expressed. What the effect of State influence might have been had Government started the manufacture of iron on a large scale when railways were first introduced it is impossible to say. The conflicting interests involved would have presented a formidable array of difficulties.

What is true of iron is also true of most of the other mineral industries of India. With the exception of saltpetre, which is easily manufactured in the Indian climate, and has maintained its position as an article of export, representing a value of half a million or more in the export trade, the greatness of India's national wealth in mineral products is but a dream of the past. Before the days of scientific training in the arts of mineral development, whilst men were yet gathering in what lay on the surface ready to their hands, or, at most, but grubbing a few yards underground with insufficient tools and no knowledge of the natural causes which led to the effects which interested them, India was doubtless far ahead of her world's geographical contemporaries in the amassing of such barbaric wealth as was represented by lavish display of ornament. Gold, silver, precious stones—these were reckoned the staple of a country's wealth and greatness long ere architectural art and the work of the loom exercised men's brains as well as their bodies; and it is consequently no matter of wonder that in a country where climate and soil involved but little labour in the production of food and clothing, we should find that from the very earliest ages the surface of India has been riddled with the superficial scratchings and delvings of gangs of slaves, who were made to search for the precious metals

[1] "Geology of India," part iii. p. 344.

at a cost which was practically nothing to the land-owners.

That wealth which first made India the "desire of men's eyes" long before the days of Soliman; which has been the curse of the country from the attraction it offered to countless hordes of warlike savages who have swarmed eastwards and southwards from high Asia; and finally has assured to the civilised nations of mediæval Europe commercial pre-eminence so long as Indian trade was in their hands, was distributed chiefly in Indian soil. And, although much of it has disappeared from the surface of that soil, there is no reason to suppose that its sources have been seriously impaired. The peninsula of India is a vastly old, but not an exhausted, country, and we must look to other reasons than the gradual emptying out of her natural treasuries to account for her loss of prestige in that particular phase of economic development which is associated with production of precious metals and minerals.

One great reason is the enhanced cost of labour now that all men are free, and the undoubted necessity for digging deeper and employing more expensive mining agencies in order to secure quick returns. Native chiefs of ancient times were content with the accumulation of the small gatherings that were effected by thousands of men searching over the surface of large areas. The English shareholder wants a definite percentage on the cost of tapping the original sources of supply—by which process alone can sufficient quantity be realised to render the enterprise a paying one.

But the chief reason, no doubt, is the fact that other and newer countries have developed a wealth of resources such as India never possessed, and the most that India can now claim is the modest (and somewhat doubtful) position of being able to "pay her way." There is doubtless still a vast and almost immeasurable store of wealth hoarded above ground in that country which at present lies idle and takes no place in any scheme of commercial economy. India is still enormously wealthy, but her wealth is that of the miser.

In almost any part of India, excepting the north-west frontier, where (as already explained) there are no channels of communication leading up to crystalline rocks and deposits from which gold may be derived, the gold industry still continues on the old, old lines of prehistoric days. In the Godavari jungles I have watched a patient family of gold-washers (aboriginal Gonds) sitting contentedly by the banks of a small local stream, scraping up the sand into their shallow wooden pans, and performing the apparently simple process of swishing the water round with a circular motion till all the light particles had disappeared, and nothing but a sediment of black "iron sand" remained. No mercurial process was resorted to in order to capture the infinitesimally small particles of gold which existed in the sediment. The sand was examined, and if the examination proved satisfactory washing was resumed, until finally a small (ridiculously small) pinch of free gold particles remained. The net result of the day's "take" when the family of four had finished their work might, when spread out very thin, have covered a four anna bit; and it was valued (probably over valued) at eight annas, or, say, one shilling. But this was enough, and no persuasion would have induced these native vagabonds to work longer than was necessary to secure this amount of return. They wanted little. Their clothes were few and simple (in fact, two of the four individuals possessed none), and their food was probably found in the jungle. A shilling a day would find all the rest of their requirements, and to work when work was unnecessary was not in their creed.

FIG. 102.

On the banks of the Indus, where it still courses through the mountains and washes the scanty cultivation of various Himalayan valleys, I have seen the same process repeated, with much about the same result; and indeed, wherever a river runs down from a central source of the oldest geological formations, there may almost certainly be found searchers after gold working on primitive methods. It is said that every river in the Punjab (except the Ravi) contains gold, and certainly there are few streams that find their sources in the oldest formations of the Central Provinces in the basins of the Mahanadi and the Godavari that are not similarly blessed. But the gold-bearing sands of rivers do not necessarily obtain gold from any one abundant source. Gold is disseminated through a vast mass of geological material, apart from quartz reefs, which occasionally do not contain gold at all. So that the geographical area over which gold may be found in India is very widespread, and the sources of it in different districts very various. All along the foot of the northern hills of India, from Afghanistan to Assam, gold is found in tertiary deposits; but it is all detrital; it has been washed there from crystalline metamorphic sources far away in the Himalayas. In Ladak quartz reefs occurring in the carboniferous age are the source of supply; about Kandahar auriferous reefs belong to the cretaceous deposits.

Within the peninsular area, the Madras province is probably the richest in gold. The Wynaad gold mines, which have been opened up in the rolling plateau which lies between the Malabar coast districts and the Nilgiris, are on the site of certain ancient mines which were found in great abundance—mines which have been sunk with very considerable engineering skill, and which must have been worked for centuries. Reports on the gold wealth of the Wynaad have been intermittently submitted to Government ever since the beginning of this century, and so late as 1880 one great authority reported that the reefs were more numerous, richer and wider there than in any similar area in Australia. But the gold is found in exceptionally hard material—granite and gneiss—traversed by quartz reefs, and in spite of estimates based on the results of unusually successful prospecting, mines have proved unproductive owing to the cost of plant and working. Gold mines have been started by half-a-dozen companies in Mysore, where the rocks all belong to crystalline or metamorphic groups interlaced by quartz reefs, and the Kolar mines have been successful—perhaps the most successful—of all. Rocks of the Kamthi age in the Gondwana system appear to be exceptionally auriferous. To them may be traced the source of the gold washings in the Godavari affluents of Haidarabad, where again gold mining has largely developed lately, and where (as in Kolar) ancient workings carried to a considerable depth have exhausted all the most profitable sources of supply. The Kolar mines have quite recently far exceeded the original expectations of their founders. In the year 1899 the production of gold in this part of India amounted to no less than 447,397 ounces, the production in Burma, Madras, and the Nizam's territory (Haidarabad) bringing up the total to 457,020 ounces, the value of which may be taken to represent about £1,828,000.

In Chutia Nagpur and the eastern districts of the Central Provinces, all more or less on the line of the Bengal-Nagpur railway, is situated a large group of gold fields. In the districts of Manbhum and Singbhum, north of the Mahanadi basin; and in Gangpur, Jushpur, and Udaipur, within the limits of that basin, as well as at Sambulpur, which is on the Mahanadi, gold industry flourishes. The gold of these districts occurs in schists, slates, and quartzites of sub-metamorphic series. The gold washings of the Ib and the Mahanadi are still carried on by the aboriginal Gond people, with the assistance of the primitive pan and scraper, just as they may have been twenty centuries ago.

In Upper Assam the gold of the Dihong River has long been famous. It is said that all the rivers in these districts of Assam contain gold. It was estimated that £10,000 represented the value of the revenue derived from the sonwals or gold washers of Assam before we took possession. The ultimate source is probably to be found in crystalline rocks which occur on the upper reaches of the Brahmaputra. The Brahmaputra, as we know, rises in Tibet, a country which has been known for ages to possess extensive gold fields, about which at present we have only the record of travellers who have not been scientific prospectors. The immediate sources of gold in the Brahmaputra of Assam are tertiary deposits and the alluvial beds of rivers.

In Burma gold is found in the sands of the Irawadi at Bhamo, and in the Chindwin River, where it is collected in a primitive fashion by pegging out the skins of animals in the stream. The minute gold particles carried down by the current adhere to the hair. When the skin is dried, the gold is shaken out of it and collected. This is a system entirely suited to the indolent character of the Indo-Chinese races. An automatic process of gold accumulation, involving no labour, would appeal so strongly to their idiosyncrasies that it is surprising that they should adopt any other process. They do, however, work for gold as well. Much gold is used in Burma in temple decorations, but most of it is imported.

The ancient gold industry of Tenasserim has lately been revived, and at the head of the Tavay River, where gold is found associated with the tin, washing on the Portuguese system has been introduced, and mines are being opened which promise fairly well.

Some indication of the economic value of the gold industry in India may perhaps be gathered from the fact that the exportation of gold in 1897 amounted in value to a little over two millions sterling. In 1896 it was nearly two million and a half, and in 1895 (the record year) it was no less than £6,700,000.

Something must be added about the diamonds and rubies of India and Burma which have assisted to enhance the fame of eastern wealth through past ages, though perhaps they do not promise in future to add much further lustre to this "brightest jewel of England's crown."

It may be interesting to know that the mines of Golconda never existed. There is a fort near Haidarabad called Kala Kanda, and here, in early days, stood a great central mart or market for diamonds, which were found afar off. The Kistna and Godavari basins were the real Golconda in ancient times, and indeed they are so still. There are three great diamond tracts in India, *i.e.* the Kistna-Godavari tract, the area between the Godavari and Mahanadi, and Pannah, in Bundelkand. In the first two tracts diamonds are found in what are geologically known as the lower Vindhya beds; in Panna they occur in a conglomerate, which is analogous to the diamondiferous rocks of South Africa. Diamonds are found in small quantities elsewhere in the Madras provinces, but the industry is entirely in the hands of natives, who declare that British ascendency in India is displeasing to the presiding deity of the mines (their geological goddess Lakshuri) and account in this way for the decline of the trade. The mines at Panna seem to be the most systematically worked. An interesting account of them occurs in vol. iii. of the "Geological Manual for India." Panna is situated amongst the hills of Bundelkand, not more than 180 miles to the south-west of Allahabad. The mines are scattered over a large area of country, and the diamonds obtained therefrom, though small in size, are of good quality. The diggings near Panna itself do not cover more than 20 acres. Irregular pits are excavated through the overlying strata, often to a depth of 30 feet, in order to reach the diamond conglomerate. In this pit the miners work almost naked and knee-deep in water. The stuff excavated is hauled up by hand in small buckets, then placed on stone slabs and examined. Both the examiners and the miners work under a guard. Various attempts have been made by Europeans to compete with the natives in the diamond fields of India, but never with success unless associated with gold mining. Native labour as utilised by native chiefs is a cheap commodity, and no European could hope to work on the financial principles which govern native mining. Then again there must always be large opportunities for diamond stealing, and it is impossible to rival native methods for preventing this constant source of loss. Also the unhealthiness of the districts in which diamonds are chiefly found is in itself fatal to much European enterprise. There is no part of India (possibly no tract in the world) more fever-ridden and unwholesome than the Godavari basin.

Yet it cannot be supposed either that the original sources are exhausted, or that the field for enterprise has greatly narrowed. There must be vast areas untapped as yet lying beneath the Vindhyan rocks of the Central Province. The most celebrated diamond of India is the Koh-i-Nur, now a British possession. This was apparently (for there are many histories attached to it, and they do not by any means agree) found on the Kistna River at Kolar, to the north-west of Masulipatam, and is probably identical with the Great Moghul diamond which was shown to Tavernier by the Emperor Aurangzebe in 1665. He describes the Kollur (or Kolar) mine as being about 100 years old, and records that 60,000 people were then employed in the diggings. Mining in this district (which was the true Golconda of mediæval history) has lately been revived in connection with gold digging.

Rubies and occasional sapphires are the outcome of the well-known, and perhaps over-rated, ruby mines of Mogok, in Upper Burma, whilst sapphires and occasional rubies are found in Ceylon. Within the area of peninsular India (especially towards the south) rubies are not unknown, but they are not systematically collected. The mines of Mogok are not the only mines in Upper Burma, although they are the chief. There are mines also about 16 miles from Mandalay, in the Sagyin Hills, where the red clay-covered limestone rocks are split and fissured with cavities containing the detritus out of which rubies, sapphires, and amethysts are washed. But the rubies are of inferior quality; all the best are found at Mogok. These mines are about 70 miles north of Mandalay, concentrated in a small area at the foot of the Shwe Doung or Golden Mount, which is a spur of the Central Burmese chain east of the Irawadi. The mines were captured in 1886, after a stout defence on the part, not of the miners, but of the traders and robbers who had lived by illicit traffic in rubies. These people collected the best fighting men of the Shans within reach to dispute possession.

The Mogok mines are from 4000 to 5000 feet above sea-level, and are flanked on the north by the rolling hills of the Shan plateau—hills which rise to 6000 feet in elevation, and are covered with forests of oak, chestnut, and fir, decorated with numberless varieties of rare orchids. The northern route to the mines must be a dream of beauty. The valleys of the mines themselves are lovely, surrounded with hills of granite, gneiss, and limestone, disintegrating masses of which form the lower spurs and foothills, and close in the narrow line of central plain. It is here, near the streams, that the ruby beds are found, beneath layers of clay, gravel, and sand, which thicken to 20 feet or more. The ruby-bearing sand is generally about 2 feet thick. This sand on being brought to the surface is full of minute rubies, from amongst which the larger are picked out after washing. The primitive methods of 1886 have long given place to scientific working, and rubies are evolved from the mass of disintegrating material forming the lower hills as well as from the flats adjoining the beds of the streams. The lessees of the mines under the Burmese Government paid £20,000 annually for the right of working, and gave up all the biggest rubies to the king. The company formed soon after our occupation of Upper Burma originally leased the mines for an annual payment of £30,000 to Government, and one-sixth of the net profits on the workings. Great as is the promise of such an undertaking as the working of the chief sources of ruby supply for the whole world, the difficulties that surround it are not inconsiderable. Malaria, illicit smuggling, and local labour disturbances have all to be reckoned with, to say nothing of the enhanced cost of production, which the introduction of expensive plant and machinery necessarily involves.

Taking it altogether, the economic prospects arising from the mineral resources of India (enormously scattered as they are) must be considered to be poor in comparison with those of newer countries. Development in the production of all the principal metals is crushed by English competition; and as regards the precious metals, gold and silver, India is nowhere in a field which includes Africa, America, and Australia. In coal and salt and some other useful mineral commodities she may rise to the level of dispensing with importation, and has already become self-supporting. Diamonds, rubies, and other precious stones are her heritage, and the source of them is apparently unexhausted; but it still remains to be seen whether the European mining engineer, with his scientific methods and latest machinery, will effect very much more than the unlimited labour resources of past ages of native proprietors.

The Geological Survey Reports are naturally the best authorities for all relating to India's capacity for mining developments. But this, as an economic feature in India's progress, is also watched and measured by journalists in that country, and is the subject for constant speculation and inquiry in the Indian periodicals. Most of the information given above is obtained from special sources, but there is a good deal to be learned from the usually careful statements and the correspondence relating to Indian mining progress which appear from time to time in the leading newspapers. I am indebted to the *Pioneer* for a great deal of such general information.

# CHAPTER XII

## CLIMATE

THE laws which govern the Indian climate and the succession of its seasons are now fairly well ascertained. In India and on the borders of India almost any extreme of

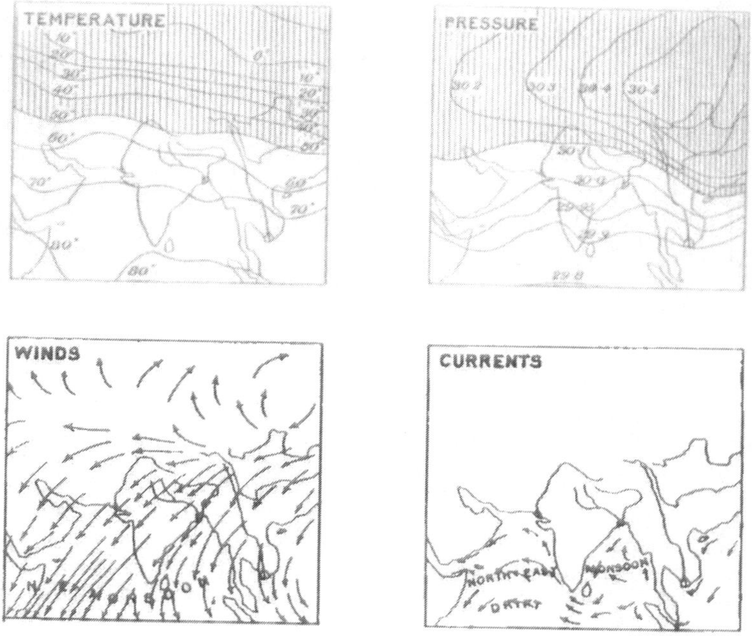


FIG. 103.

climate that is known to the tropics or the temperate zone may be encountered, half of the continent lying actually within the tropics. A line joining Dakka in Bengal to Ahmedabad on the north of Gujrát is approximately the line which divides the two zones.

It is, however, remarkable that the greatest extremes of heat are experienced within the northern zone, as well as the greatest extremes of cold, the climate of all the southern part of the continent being far more equable than that of the northern. It is in Sind and in the highlands of Baluchistan that the range of temperature between extreme limits is most marked. It is a matter of no infrequent occurrence for the thermometer to record a rise or fall of 70° Fahrenheit within twenty-four hours on the elevated plains about Kalát, ranging upwards from 20 degrees of frost during the nights of early autumn, when

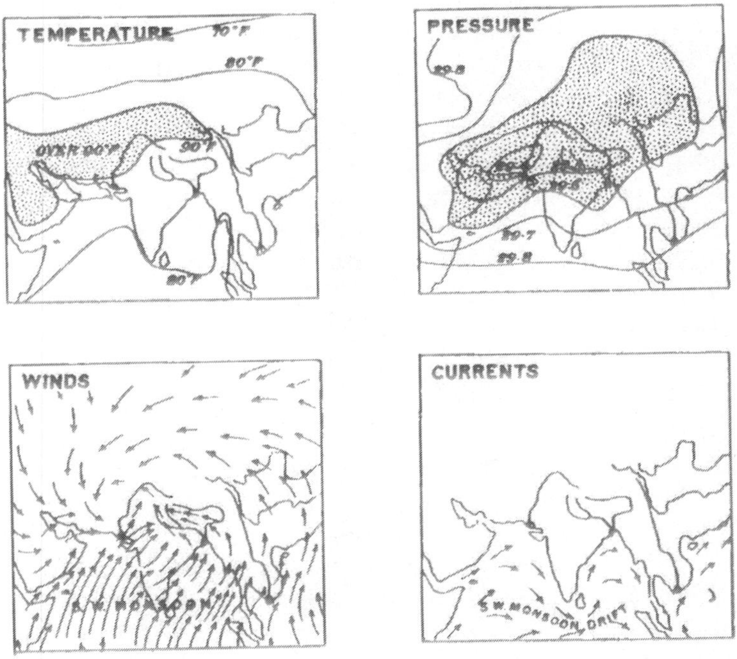


FIG. 104.

the heat acquired from a still powerful sun is radiated from the barren rocks and sand under a clear sky with inconceivable rapidity. Then the cold at night, enhanced by 6000 or 7000 feet of elevation, becomes almost unendurable by contrast with the scorching heat of the sun's rays by day. Quetta, which is less than 100 miles north of Kalát, but situated at a somewhat less elevation, and rather more protected by its surrounding wall of mountains, experiences a good deal of this extraordinary thermometric variation, and it is to this in great part that we must attribute those periodic outbreaks of fever which occasionally place the garrison *hors de combat* at the changing seasons of the year.

The cold of the Afghan and Baluch highlands, which is very severe in winter, is much accentuated by the periodic blasts of north-westerly wind which are particularly noticeable on the western borders of those countries. These wind currents may be traced through Western Afghanistan, Turkestan, and Persia to the Caucasus and the Caspian deserts. They reach the frontiers of India in Sind and the Punjab in full blast, bringing with them a peculiar haze caused by minute particles of dust held in atmospheric suspension, and enveloping the landscape in a mist which lasts for days. In the Turkestan deserts these icy blasts (more icy there than on the Indian border) are locally known as "Shamshir" (or the scimitar) from their cutting intensity. In the Persian Gulf they are called "Shumal" or "northerly" gales; but wherever they are met their character is the same. They are not healthy, rain-bearing currents from the sea, but dry, icy blasts generated in high altitudes (possibly in the Russian steppes), and they sweep across the high plateaux of Western Asia unchecked by any formidable ranges and unmodified by the influence of forests or cultivation. They have a distinct influence on the climate of the Indian borderland, but gradually become lost in the low altitudes of the plains.

But if Baluchistan can produce an exceptional record of cold in winter, it is no less remarkable for the heat of certain of its low-lying tracts in summer. The actual registered record of high temperature belongs to Jacobabad in Sind, where the thermometer for days together occasionally descends no lower than 108° F. in the shade. But there are certain well-known points on the Sind border near the line of railway connecting Jacobabad with Quetta, in which the temperature becomes even more intolerable than it is in Jacobabad, where it is modified to a certain extent by a well-developed growth of trees and a considerable extent of irrigated cultivation. Farther west, throughout the low valleys of Makrán as far as the Persian border, the heat of summer is also extreme—so much so that on the Persian border it is maintained locally that an egg may be cooked on the open ground under a summer sky. Here, however, there is practically no cold weather whatever. In Sind and throughout the Punjab there is a winter which extends through a greater or less period according to the latitude, and which does much (especially in the Punjab, where there are eight cool months in the year) to modify the effects of the exceptional heat of summer. The climate of the Punjab, where the extremes of temperature range far apart (if not so far as in Sind), is a possible one for continued European existence; and although statistics show a greater mortality amongst Europeans in the Punjab than in other parts of the Indian empire, it is on the whole a popular province for residence on account of the long cold weather.

Throughout the north-west the winter climate is as nearly perfect as climate can be. Bracing, without any bitterness of cold, bright and clear, it forms one of the great charms of Indian existence, and even when the fierce heat of early summer has passed and the monsoon rains succeed, it is by no means unendurable. Farther south, as we reach the tropical area, the average temperature increases; but the variation diminishes, and with this diminished variation there is no doubt diminished risk of many of those ills which are the bane of Anglo-Indian existence. Calcutta, Bombay, and Madras all possess the equable climate that is induced by proximity to the sea. Calcutta, however, enjoys a distinct period of cold weather which is not to be found in the other Presidency towns. The average temperature of the air in shade at Bombay is about 80° F., and at Madras somewhat higher; but the damp enervating atmosphere of these low-lying coast ports enhances the effects of the recorded heat, and the result of long residence in the south of India is undoubtedly a degree of physical deterioration such as is not experienced in the north. Throughout India exception must be made to those stations which enjoy the cool atmosphere of high altitude. There are hill-stations scattered through the length and breadth of India, all of them possessing local attractions, which render them delightful resorts for many months of the year. India, indeed, possesses every sort of climate, and it may appear difficult at first sight to account for the extraordinary modifications (if not actual contradictions) which occur even within a comparatively small area. Many of these

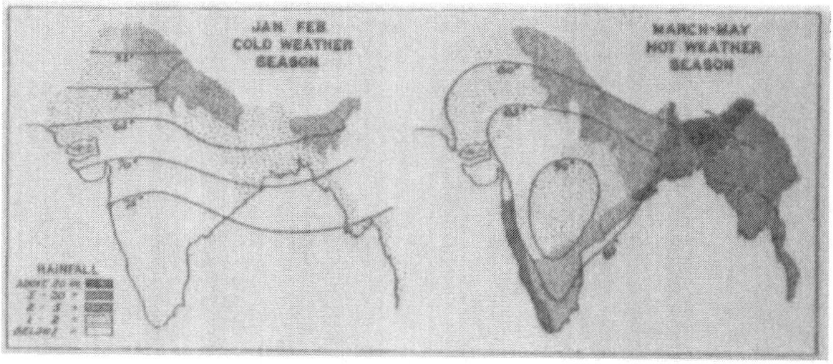


FIG. 105.

weather anomalies are due to the influence which the physiography of the country exercises on the monsoon currents, to the periodic return of which all India looks for that all-important rain-supply which yearly waters the parched plains, and renders its deserts green with abundant fertility.

The monsoon is the yearly salvation of the millions that live on the fruits of the soil. A good or bad monsoon is the criterion of plenty or of famine. By it India lives ; without it there is starvation, death, and misery. The anxiety, therefore, with which all, from highest to lowest, look out for the first warning telegrams from the Seychelles or Mauritius of these indications which are the forerunners of the yearly rain-supply may well be imagined. The explanation of the natural phenomena which precede and accompany the monsoon are simple enough. During the winter months, when the meridional sun is low, the surface of the earth throughout the Southern Asiatic continent cools down by the radiation of its heat into space until its temperature is below that of the adjoining sea. Atmospheric pressure rises over the ocean and falls over the land ; but after March, as the sun strikes with more direct rays, and the daily period to which the earth is exposed to them grows longer, this

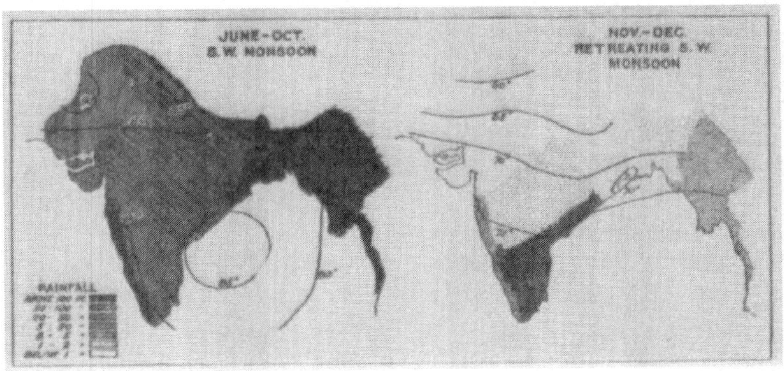


FIG. 106.

difference in temperature is reversed. The land speedily becomes hotter than the ocean, and the falling pressure of the atmosphere above it induces strong moisture-laden currents to set towards India from the seas south of the equator, where the pressure is rising under the influence of their winter's sun. Thus is originated the south-west monsoon, which usually reaches the west coast of India about the end of May, and is fairly established through the Northern Provinces by the end of June. Its action on the interior of the country is modified by the resistance that it encounters on its course, and this resistance is chiefly found in mountain altitudes, which arrest the currents, and lead directly to the condensation of the wind-borne vapour and the precipitation of rain.

As the monsoon currents sweep up from the south-west towards India, it is clearly the configuration of the western coast that will in the first instance influence the amount of local rainfall in the interior, for any cause which tends to cool the condensed vapours will precipitate the rain. If we look at a map of Western India we shall see that from Karachi to the Narbada River, north of which the Vindhya chain extends its terminal spurs towards the sea, there is no obstruction to the north-eastward sweep of the monsoon offered by elevated land or mountains. Along the valley of the Indus, and across the hot sands of Rajputana and Sind, the rain-bearing currents pass onward with no cooling medium to arrest their progress and precipitate the moisture with which they are charged, until they reach the Punjab and United Provinces, and finally burst against the outer Himalayan ranges in a watery deluge. The hills of Baluchistan stand almost on the edge of the area influenced by the monsoon, which loses much of its force in the northern part of the Arabian Sea, and is hardly perceptible on the coasts of Western Makrán. Karachi and lower Sind, with the skirts of the Baluch mountains, feel its influence, but the rainfall generally in Sind and Rajputana is small compared to that in the sub-Himalayan regions. On the southern spurs of the mountains between Kashmir and Nepal the average monsoon rainfall is about 80 inches.

South of the Narbada the line of the Western Gháts, which represents the western edge of the elevated plateau of Central India, faces the ocean at a distance of some 40 or 50 miles from the coast. Here the monsoon currents are compelled to rise into the cooler atmospheric strata in order to pass the barrier of hills, with the result that they lose the greater part of their moisture before they reach the Central Provinces or Madras. Thus the rainfall on the Gháts averages 120 inches, whilst a few miles only beyond the highest ranges of the Gháts it may fall to 20 or 30 inches.

But the most remarkable effect is produced at the head of the Bay of Bengal. Here the gathering masses of watery vapour are driven over the surface of the heated sea for hundreds of miles without check, till they break on the southern edge of the Khasia hills in Eastern Bengal. At this point the rainfall is extraordinary, 50 or 60 *feet* being a not unusual register at Cherra Punji on the edge of the plateau. At Shillong (which is about 40 miles beyond the edge) the rainfall becomes normal. It is interesting to note that with this terrific rainfall the climate of Cherra Punji is not unendurable. All the surface soil is washed away from the rocky substrata, and a scanty vegetation is maintained with difficulty, but the rain descends in liquid sheets for a certain number of hours only, and during the interludes the atmosphere is more free from mist and damp than is the case at many hill-stations with one-tenth of its rainfall, and double its surcharged environment of clouds.

The Central and Eastern Provinces of India are but very partially benefited by the south-west monsoon. The storage of moisture drawn from the sea is exhausted before it reaches them. They consequently retain a good deal of their surface heat after the north-eastern seas of the Bay of Bengal have cooled, and when the monsoon currents from the south-west diminish in force (which usually happens about the middle of September) they become diverted and reversed. A north-east monsoon sets in from the opposite direction, which, although it acts over a much more restricted area, fulfils a compensatory function of watering and fertilising for the southern portions of the peninsula. Thus Madras and the districts immediately north of it are subject to two monsoons yearly, the second only lasting for two months or thereabouts, and terminating usually in November.

Ceylon, of course, receives the benefit of both monsoons, and as the highest altitudes and main watersheds of that island are situated about its centre, it enjoys two distinct climates, one portion of it on the south-west falling under the full influence of the south-west rains, whilst the north-eastern section remains comparatively dry; and *vice versâ* when the currents of vapour set in the opposite direction. In the southern parts of Ceylon it appears to rain incessantly for eight months in the year from June to January.

As might be expected, the monsoon winds exercise a direct influence on the surface currents of the ocean surrounding India, these currents generally following the direction of the wind, and varying in intensity with the strength of the monsoon. The tidal action is regular under ordinary conditions of wind and weather. A very comprehensive system of tidal observations has been initiated by Government, and tidal stations have been established at important points all round the coast. The results of a scientific analysis of these investigations as a whole will be most interesting when completed.

Cyclonic disturbances in the Bay of Bengal cause tidal waves which are most disastrous in their effects on the low-lying delta of the Ganges and Brahmaputra rivers, and cause periodically enormous destruction of life and property. Mercifully they are rare.

The effects of the periodic and regular action of the south-west monsoon on the western outlines of the coast are very marked at certain points, where the sea encroachment can be readily measured. The temple of Dwarka, for instance, on the coast-line between Karachi and Bombay, is now perilously near the sea. Already some outlying portions of it have disappeared, and it is said that these can be seen at low water. The temple not long ago stood far inland. Farther north we have a somewhat difficult and unsatisfactory means of comparison between the shape of the coast outline in modern days and that which existed several centuries before the Christian era, between the mouth of the Indus and the Persian Gulf. The Greek galleys of Nearkhos (Alexander's admiral of the fleet) necessarily followed the coast-line when making their slow way from India to Persia, because they were more or less dependent on the land forces for their supplies; and the details of the voyage are given in his ancient log from day to day. It is almost impossible to restore an exact outline of the coast of these long-ago centuries, but enough can be gathered to show that great changes have taken place. Islands have certainly disappeared, and harbours or ports have as certainly been filled up. The Indus delta has advanced seawards to such an extent as to leave the ancient ports of mediæval days 30 to 40 miles inland. Old channels forming navigable "mouths" have disappeared even in historic times, and new ones have opened out, the great river itself having shifted 50 or 60 miles westward from its original course, which once terminated in the Rann of Kach. Within quite modern days the coast immediately contiguous to Karachi has shallowed from the results of dredging the Karachi channel, whilst monsoon influences are apparent in the gradual increase of sand encroachment. Northward of Cape Monze, in the north-east bend of the Arabian Sea (marked by Sonmiani Bay), the land has here and there gained on the sea, the classical harbour of Morontobara being now but an inland depression, and the fishing village of Sonmiani, which once stood on the edge of the bay, is already separated from the sea at low water by a mile or more of mud flats.

The sea has swallowed up many an island which must have once existed near the coast, and distributed the débris along the foreshore. A small island off the coast at Gwattar Bay was in the course of a single year (1890) split into two, and 6 fathoms of water were found in the channel that parted the divisions. Probably that island has now disappeared altogether. Many a bay on the Makrán coast north of the Arabian Sea has silted up into sandy scrub-covered flats during the last twenty-five centuries; the general impression formed by a comparison with ancient records being that, on the whole, the land has gained on the sea. Possibly the set or drift of the south-west monsoon may have some connection with the formation of the "bar," which is a prevailing feature of the entrance to nearly all the harbours and bays of the coast of Makrán or of India. The existence of this obstacle to free navigation renders some otherwise good harbours, with deep soundings and wide accommodation unapproachable on the Makrán coast, and is a subject of periodic difficulty, even in such ports as Karachi and Bombay. The narrow channel of the former is only kept clear by constant dredging; and the entrance of large steamers to Bombay is only effected under favourable tidal conditions.

On both east and west coasts the estuaries of great rivers lead to a shallowing of the sea approach for many miles from land, the rivers themselves failing to cut out a submarine channel which would render navigation easy. The Indus on the west is only navigated (like the Godavari on the east) by shallow flat-bottomed steamers of the very lightest draught; and off Coconada, which marks the mouth of the Godavari, it is hardly possible for ships of any size to anchor within sight of land. On all coasts alike there is an unceasing surf, rendering the process of landing difficult and occasionally dangerous. This is, of course, very much modified in the harbours and indentations of the coast.

It is impossible to touch the subject of India's coastline without reference to those "backwaters" which add so much to the magnificence of the Ghát scenery of Western India. Here the sea runs in narrow inlets, which are shaped in long reaches more or less parallel to the coastline, and extend in long arms of smooth water, sheltered and bordered by steep hills covered with dense vegetation, reaching from the water's edge up to their mist-crowned heights. More than one great artist besides Turner has sought inspiration from the scenery of the Western Gháts and seas. They are as remarkable for the peculiarity of their formation as for their unique beauty.

The effect of the monsoon rains in restoring the vigour of sun-dried nature, its influence on all the varied conditions of animal and vegetable life, is infinitely more marked by the strong contrasts presented before and after its appearance, than it would be under the influences of more temperate phases of climate.

The effect of the unclouded rays of early summer sun on the heated plains of Northern India is a recurrent experience to all whose work lies in them, and once experienced is not easily forgotten. The early hours of morning are the only hours when existence is pleasurable; the fitful coolness induced by a fall of 10 degrees or so in the register of the thermometer is speedily dissipated as the white-faced sun, seen through a veil of dust, moves upward into the brassy sky—a sky from which all vestige of atmospheric blue seems to have been washed out by heat. Then doors and windows are closed, and as much of the coolness of the morning as possible is trapped inside the house to last for another hour or so, whilst the sun-baking process continues outside. Birds, with their beaks open and gasping, seek shelter in such shade as they may find; cattle gather under the trees, some species of which, providentially, retain much of their freshness and give the needed shelter both to birds and beasts; the field labourer, who has done the little that is possible amidst his hard-baked plots in the dark hours of early morning, retires into the recesses of his mud-brick shanty, and all the outside world drops into a sweltering doze till the sun gradually sinks and disappears again.

The monotony of the long wearisome day is varied by speculations about the wind. Will it be strong enough and will it be hot enough to carry a draught through the soaking screen of "kuskus" grass which is set up on edge at the doors or windows in order to distribute a life-sustaining current of coolness through the house? The hot wind usually sets in about 10 A.M., and lasts till 4 P.M., and on its regularity depends a good deal of the comfort of European mankind. No artificial invention successfully takes its place as a powerful agent in evaporating moisture and inducing a cool current of air thereby. With it the temperature of a well-managed house may be reduced to 80° F. or thereabouts. Without it the thermometer in the shade of the bungalow and in the shadow of the garden trees will register much the same, *i.e.* anything between 90° and 110° according to the locality. The punkah does not of course affect the air temperature. It merely affects the temperature of the skin by the process of evaporation under a gentle current of moving air.

As the hot weather proceeds the first sign of the approaching regeneration of dead nature is usually the recurrence of sand or dust storms. Unpleasant as these rushes of dust-laden air may be, they do undoubtedly cool the atmospheric furnace, whether accompanied by rain (as is frequently the case) or not. There is much that is impressive about the resistless advance of a dust-storm, but it is not often that the phenomenon can be watched to advantage. I once watched an apparently solid wall of whirling sand sweeping along the plains of the Deraját until it broke eventually against the foot of the mountain on which I stood above it. I noted with astonishment the extreme regularity of its movements. There was no hurrying and no scattering of its force. No column of troops could have advanced with such a level front, with such apparently resistless action, or with one-fifth its velocity. There was not a break in the flat wall of dull red sand which reached upward some 200 feet above the plain, presenting its red-brown front to the mountains, with purple wisps and streamers curling aloft like the banners of a Dervish army. So long as the plain was unbroken and its surface level, not an opening or an indentation could be marked, but as soon as it reached the slanting spurs of the lowest hills, rushes were made from flanks and centre. Small clouds of skirmishers streamed up the narrow gullies between the spurs, mounting high and falling backwards, as waves fall, ere they reached the summit of the hill. Soon the whole atmosphere thickened, and although no great amount of dust reached upwards to the 4000 feet of elevation on which I stood, a smart shower of rain put an end to further observations.

The first heavy rain that denotes the arrival of the expected monsoon fills the whole country with gladness. In an almost incredibly short space of time the brown hard surface of an uninteresting level of endless plain is changed into a sea of vegetation. Not only do the young crops spread in vivid green expanse against the grey background with startling rapidity, but ill-gotten weeds appear in every crevice of the broken wall and pasture-land, and in every unoccupied space of the cultivated garden. The gardener rejoices in a new birth of flowers, and resigns himself to philosophical contemplation of the weeds, and watches both grow together under the magic influence of the rains in rank abundance. Life becomes endurable once more; birds begin to chatter (they never sing under any circumstances in the plains of India), and the cultivator turns to the consideration of his annual rotation of crops.

Closely connected with the climatic changes that are so marked in India is the all-important matter of their influence on European health and life. It is not simply the heat of India, nor the uncongenial surroundings of native apathy and perversity, so foreign to the nature of the European trained in British schools; not the expatriation, nor the yearning for the arts and graces of a newer and more familiar form of civilisation—none of these things, nor all these combined, would prevent the colonisation of India by Englishmen were the great barrier caused by ill-health and failing vitality to be removed. The first question asked about any locality to which the vicissitudes of official life may despatch the servant of the Indian Government is—"Is it healthy?" As a matter of fact no part of India is altogether suitable for European existence. Neither plains nor hills, jungles nor deserts, are altogether free from that slow but most pernicious influence which is called "malaria"; but the geographical distribution of the worst forms of that pernicious poison (or of the particular species of mosquito which distributes it) is worth attention.

There are many forms of the malady known as Indian fever; and inasmuch as it claims more victims in a year in one single district in India than all other diseases put together (even including epidemics, as plague and cholera), and is probably the greatest barrier that exists to the development of European life in the country, it becomes a subject of paramount interest to all students of Indian physiography. The locality of its original development is limited by the physical conditions of altitude and latitude. Above a certain elevation (which may be roughly defined as about 7000 feet above sea) it apparently does not germinate, and it is not to be found in north latitudes, the limits of which are as yet undefined, but which are at any rate north of India. It is probably not far from the truth to say that every European who passes any continued period of his life in the plains or in the climate of the lower hills which border the higher ranges is more or less impregnated with malarial poison. Equability of temperature is the great safeguard against its development, and therefore districts contiguous to the sea are more exempt from fever than those farther inland. At the same time nothing seems to arouse the dormant energies of the malarial microbe more than sea air after a long inland residence and apparent freedom from its effects. A change from the moist, warm climates of Southern India on the coast to the dry and apparently invigorating atmosphere of such hills as those of Baluchistan will frequently accelerate the disease and decimate a regiment before it has had time to acclimatise. The origin of all malarial germs seems to lie beyond dispute in decaying matter subjected to the influence of heat, and the distributing agent seems as certainly to be a particular species of mosquito; but it has hardly yet been fully ascertained how far locality influences the varied action of the fever germ, or tends to the reproduction of the mosquito.

Throughout Northern India the unhealthy season is reckoned to follow immediately after the rains. It is then that the earth is saturated with moisture, whilst the sun's rays are yet strong upon it, and there is the first touch of the coolness of coming winter abroad in the air. The jungles of the Tarai at the foot of the Himalayas, as well as some of the low valleys amongst the mountains themselves, become rank with malaria. No European enters them, and only such natives as appear to have purchased a species of immunity from long acquaintance with the malarial demon.

But this bane of fever is by no means confined to the districts where vegetation is rank. It pervades the agricultural districts of the plains and the streets of great cities alike. It knows no distinctions of locality except in degree. It follows the course of irrigation, and appears with special virulence wherever the earth is freshly upturned in places which have long lain undisturbed. As the season wears on and the drying process is gradually completed, when the shorter days are cooler and the breath of the cold weather is distinctly felt, fever gradually diminishes. By December all the northern forests and valleys are comparatively safe, and the sportsman goes abroad with freedom until the end of the hot weather in June. During the first month or so of the rains, before the earth is saturated, there is comparatively little risk. Local irrigation and flooding have rendered many a station in the Punjab and along the frontier of the Derajat notorious for malaria, where once it was comparatively unknown. It is during the annual desiccation of the paddy fields, where rice has been cultivated in the Peshawur Valley, that the fever poison is especially active and of a peculiarly malignant character. It is not the humidity of the monsoon alone that is accountable for the widespread character of autumn unhealthiness in Northern India. The ordinary processes of cultivation by means of irrigation have a large share in the development of poisonous influences, and some of the severest of the periodic outbreaks occur in districts where there is comparatively little vegetation beyond the ordinary growth of crops.

Within the limits of tropical India the duration of the healthy season in jungle-covered districts greatly diminishes. This is no doubt due to the gradual prolongation of the rainy season, as the action of the north-east monsoon in succession to that of the south-west becomes more and more developed, whilst at the same time the sun's rays remain effective for mischief for a longer period. There are certain tracts in the Central Provinces bordering the Godavari River, and extending from that river to the neighbourhood of the east coast, of which it is difficult to affirm that they possess any healthy season at all. The more southern districts of the Central Provinces and much of Northern Madras is perhaps the most poisonous tract in all India. Not all the well-known precautions with which every traveller in the wilds of India is acquainted will avail against the thorough saturation of his system with malarial poison if he remains long in these jungles. The exclusion of night air, the lighting of bonfires to promote circulation of dry currents, sleeping inside mosquito curtains (which is undoubtedly a protection) and on a bed raised high above ground, constant recourse to quinine (most valuable safeguard of all), and care taken to avoid work in grass or forest reeking wet from dew either too early or too late—all these combined will not save the sportsman long, even at that season of the year which in northern jungle-covered districts is reckoned to be fairly healthy. It is probable that during the early period of the south-west rainfall, when the low-lying forest-covered flats of the Godavari basin are actually under water to a great extent, the best chance of comparative immunity from fever might be found, but it is a season which otherwise is not adapted either to sport or work. The failure of the scheme for opening up the Godavari to navigation from the north of the Central Provinces to the sea was due as much to the impossibility of maintaining a body of workmen under efficient European supervision in this poisonous country as to any inherent engineering difficulties presented by the cataracts or rapids. All that remains of that scheme now may be seen in a half-completed waterway blasted through the rocky river-bed at a point some hundred miles above the mouth of the river, and in the fragments of forgotten and fallen bungalows in which lived (and died) many of the European staff engaged in the scheme. But the extension of Indian railways has long ago discounted the necessity for river navigation in this part of India.

Farther south again, though the Madras jungles still retain their reputation for a special breed of malarial microbe which renders existence in them most precarious, the narrowing of the continent and the culmination of Eastern and Western Ghâts in the plateaux and peaks of the Nilgiris and other groups of hills largely reduces the fever-stricken area, and introduces the healthy influences of sea-breezes and high altitudes. This, with the equable temperature of the province, which enjoys a climate which is described as "eternally hot," no doubt tends to maintain the credit of the Madras province as the healthiest in India. Into a disquisition on the varieties of Indian malarial fevers this is no place to enter. It is enough to say that there are so many different types that it is difficult to grasp the idea of a common origin for them all. From a close approximation to cholera symptoms, through those of intermittent "ague and fever" to enteric, and even to the oriental form of influenza known as "dengue," we have probably nothing to thank except the malarial germ and the ubiquitous mosquito. The latter deserves the very closest attention from our medical biologists and investigators; for the whole question of European acclimatisation and the future of India as a British colony is very closely connected with his suppression.

"Bartholomew's Physical Atlas" is a mine of wealth for information of a general character on the phenomena of climate in India. Excellent charts are also published in Calcutta, and the Reports of the Meteorological Department are full of instruction. Personal experience in many parts of the continent and the border countries, combined with the results of personal observations of a scientific nature, have also assisted largely in the compilation of this chapter.

# INDEX